FRONT ROW: John DeBrosse, Pat Conroy, Jim Halpin, Tee Hooper.
BACK ROW: Doug Bridges, Greg Connor, Brian Kennedy, Dave Bornhorst,
Dan Mohr, Al Kroboth, Bob Cauthen, Bill Zinsky.

# MY LOSING SEASON

ALSO BY PAT CONROY

*The Boo*
*The Water Is Wide*
*The Great Santini*
*The Lords of Discipline*
*The Prince of Tides*
*Beach Music*

NAN A. TALESE

DOUBLEDAY

NEW YORK    LONDON

TORONTO    SYDNEY    AUCKLAND

# PAT CONROY

---

# MY LOSING
# SEASON

PUBLISHED BY NAN A. TALESE
AN IMPRINT OF DOUBLEDAY
a division of Random House, Inc.
1540 Broadway, New York, New York 10036

DOUBLEDAY is a trademark of Doubleday, a division of Random House, Inc.

Endpaper photograph: From the 1967 *Sphinx*, The Citadel's yearbook

Book design by Ellen Cipriano

Library of Congress Cataloging-in-Publication Data
Conroy, Pat.
My losing season / Pat Conroy.—1st ed.
p.   cm.
1. Conroy, Pat—Childhood and youth. 2. Basketball players—South
Carolina—Charleston. 3. Novelists, American—20th century—Biography.
4. Citadel, the Military College of South Carolina. 5. College sports—South
Carolina—Charleston. 6. Charleston (S.C.)—Biography. 7. Failure
(Psychology) I. Title.

PS3553.O5198 Z465 2002
796.323'63'092—dc21
[B]
2002066212

ISBN 0-385-48912-9

PRINTED IN THE UNITED STATES OF AMERICA

November 2002

First Edition

1   3   5   7   9   10   8   6   4   2

This book is dedicated to my teammates on the 1966–67 Citadel basketball team. It was an honor to take to the court with you guys.

Dan Mohr
Jim Halpin
John DeBrosse
Doug Bridges
Dave Bornhorst
Robert Cauthen
Bill Zycinsky
Alan Kroboth
Tee Hooper
Gregory Connor
Brian Kennedy

And their lovely wives and children who made me welcome in their homes: Maria, Alexis, and Michael Bornhorst; Sandra, Rob, Macon, and Buffy Cauthen; Eileen, James, and Michael Halpin; Cynthia, Micah, and Erin Kennedy; Tina, Doug, and Guy Bridges; Barbara, Gregory, Jeffrey, and Jeremy Connor; Cindy, Matthew, and Elizabeth Mohr; Pam, J.J., Scott, and Katie DeBrosse; Sherry, Travis, and Amy Hooper; Patty and George Kroboth.

And to my wife, Cassandra King, the light of my life.

# CONTENTS

# PROLOGUE

I WAS BORN TO BE A POINT GUARD, BUT NOT A VERY GOOD ONE.
There was a time in my life when I walked through the world
known to myself and others as an athlete. It was part of my own definition of who I was and certainly the part I most respected. When I was a
young man I was well built and agile and ready for the rough-and-
tumble of games, and athletics provided the single outlet for a repressed
and preternaturally shy boy to express himself in public. Games allowed
me to introduce myself to people who had never heard me speak out
loud, to earn their praise without uttering a single word. I lost myself in
the beauty of sport and made my family proud while passing through the
silent eye of the storm that was my childhood.

Football and baseball were always secondary sports to me, and I
played them to appease my father, and because they were seasonal in nature. I tried out for baseball teams when farmers were planting cotton,
and I was putting on a football helmet to run back punts when they were
harvesting it. But I was a basketball player, pure and simple, and the
majesty of that sweet sport defined and shaped my growing up. I cannot
explain what the sport of basketball meant to me, but I have missed it
more than anything else in my life since it issued me my walking papers
and released me to live out my life as a voyeur and a fan. I was never a
very good player, but the sport allowed me glimpses into the kind of
man I was capable of becoming. I exulted in the pure physicality of that
ceaseless, ever-moving sport, and when I found myself driving the lane
beneath the hot lights amid the pure electric boisterousness of crowds
humming and screaming as a backdrop to my passion, my chosen game,
this love of my life, I was the happiest boy who ever lived.

Where did all those games go, the ones I threw myself headlong into as a boy, a rawboned kid who fell in love with the smell and shape of a basketball, who longed for its smooth skin on the nerve endings of my fingers and hands, who lived for the sound of its unmistakable heartbeat, its staccato rhythms, as I bounced it along the pavement throughout the ten thousand days of my boyhood? The one skill I brought to the game was my ability to handle a basketball, and if you tried to intercept me, if you moved without stealth or cunning, I would go past you. Even now that is a promise; I would pass you in a flash the entire game with you trying to catch me. I could move down the court with a basketball and I could do it fast.

But the games are fading on me now where once they imprinted themselves, bright as decals, on the whitewashed fences of memory. Once, I could replay them all, almost move for move, from the moment the referee first lofted the ball between the two crouching centers until the losing team launched their desperate, last-second shot, the horn sounded, and the players shook hands and drifted toward locker rooms and the judgment of our coaches. Yet, a few of those lost games maintain their power to thrill me with their immediacy and import. They take me back to a time when my life was pure action and my days passed among slashing elbows vying for rebounds coming off a clear glass backboard. Every practice and game contained the possibility of bones being broken. From the time I was nine until the day I left college, my knees stayed scabbed and tender from my scrambling for loose balls.

Because I was shorter than most college players, I tried to rule those lower regions, and when the ball hit the floor, it was mine, and too bad for you if you got in my way. I liked to put the big men on the floor when they fought me for possession of the ball as it was bouncing or rolling along the court. I substituted hustle for talent and the sure knowledge that if I did not want it more than my opponent, he would defeat and humiliate me with those gifts that nature denied me. What I had was a powerful will and a fiery competitiveness and the burning desire to be a great player in the Southern Conference when there was not even the slightest chance I could be a memorable one. I found myself constantly downsizing my dreams as a basketball player as my career was trainwrecked by mediocrity. But make no mistake, I desired greatness for myself and longed to be the best point guard who ever played the game.

From my ninth to my twenty-first year, I lived with a basketball in my hand, driving my mother crazy by throwing up imaginary jump shots in every room in the house. For years, I would try to take three hundred jump shots a day to improve my weakness as an outside shooter. I never left the court in my life after practice without making my last shot. This was not a superstition; this was a discipline.

The lessons I learned while playing basketball for the Citadel Bulldogs from 1963 to 1967 have proven priceless to me as both a writer and a man. I have a sense of fair play and sportsmanship. My work ethic is credible and you can count on me in the clutch. When given an assignment, I carry it out to completion, my five senses lit up in concentration. I believe with all my heart that athletics is one of the finest preparations for most of the intricacies and darknesses a human life can throw at you. Athletics provide some of the richest fields of both metaphor and cliché to measure our lives against the intrusions and aggressions of other people. Basketball forced me to deal head-on with my inadequacies and terrors with no room or tolerance for evasion. Though it was a long process, I learned to honor myself for what I accomplished in a sport where I was overmatched and out of my league. I never once approached greatness, but toward the end of my career, I was always in the game.

Because I grew up a complete stranger to myself, I did not even seem to catch a glimpse of a determined young man who developed in secret during college. I do not recognize the intense stranger who stares back at me in photographs faded and frayed around the edges. My coaches, throughout my youth, all approved of me because my attitude was upbeat and fiery, my enthusiasm contagious, and I gave everything I had. I liked that part of me also but had no idea where it came from.

As a boy, I had constructed a shell for myself so impenetrable that I have been trying to write my way out of it for over thirty years, and even now I fear I have barely cracked its veneer. It is as rouged and polished and burnished as the specialized glass of telescopes, and it kept me hidden from the appraising eyes of the outside world long into manhood. But most of all it kept me hidden and safe from myself. No outsider I have ever met has struck me with the strangeness I encounter when I try to discover the deepest mysteries of the boy I once was. Several times in my life I have gone crazy, and I could not even begin to tell you why. The sadness collapses me from the inside out, and I have to follow the thing through until it finishes with me. It never happened to me when I was playing basketball because basketball was the only thing that granted me a complete and sublime congruence and oneness with the world. I found a joy, unrecapturable beyond the realm of speech or language, and I lost myself in the pure, dazzling majesty of my sweet, swift game.

After a Citadel baseball game at West Virginia where I hit a double, I came to a decision that would change my life. I was reading in the back of a station wagon that trailed two other cars full of sleeping baseball players, watching the moonlight snakehandle a mountain river. The moon felt different to me in the mountains as though my South traded it in for a different model when it reached the high country. Two songs came on the radio and I can hear them now as I write this. The river and the music and the moon came together in the mountains of West Virginia as the Mamas and the Papas sang "Monday, Monday." Sarah Vaughan followed, singing a song that began with the words "How gentle is the rain." I had never heard Sarah Vaughan sing before and rarely heard a voice that affected me like hers. Coming down that mountain, the radio playing songs perfect for that light-dazzled moment and the boys sleeping around me, I promised myself I would try to become a writer, though I did not know what one was or how they lived or how to go about being one. It was what my mother had always wanted me to become, but I never realized how powerful a mother's dream could be to a dutiful, even worshipful, son. I made a secret pact with myself, in the dark; the music and river had awakened something asleep and I felt the writer stirring inside me for the first time. Once I woke him, I was never able to put him back to sleep in the porches of consciousness. In terror at what I had promised, I looked at the moon out of the back window as I watched West Virginia slip from my life forever.

During that same baseball season, I got my chance to share that small-craft epiphany I had experienced in the mountains. After a long road trip playing the small colleges of Georgia, the team was returning to Charleston at night. Chal Port was driving and I was riding in the front seat, which was something of a rarity. "Conroy," he once asked me, "how come you got all the goddamn answers and no goddamn hits?"

Chal Port was the best coach I ever had, and his love of his boys poured out of him the way it always does with the best of the breed. On this night, Coach Port turned serious and asked us what we planned to do for a living after graduation. His roll call echoed through the car. John Warley would become the lawyer he is today in Richmond, Virginia. Holly Keller would take over his father's piano store in Orlando, Florida. Mike Steele would enter the Army and rise higher and faster than anyone in my class; today he is a three-star general commanding the armies of the Pacific in Hawaii.

"What are you going to do, Conroy?" Chal Port asked. "Overthrow the elected government of the United States and all our allies?"

"I'm going to be a writer, Coach," I said.

I still hear the laughter in that car.

"No. No. Come on, Conroy. You've got to think about making a living. What're you really going to do?"

"I'm going to write books," I said.

Again, the laughter settled in around me—on that flat Georgia road heading toward the Savannah River and the South Carolina line, I had suffered for my art for the first time, and red-faced, I joined in the mirth and hoopla at my own expense. It was my first moment of complete honesty at The Citadel, and it began my happiest year ever. As a senior private in Fourth Battalion in Romeo Company, I became untouchable and proud. The boys who had tormented me as a plebe had all left campus to play out their mediocre and mean-spirited lives. No longer did my blood boil when I passed some minor-league sadist on the way to the library. I grew relaxed as a cadet for the first time and almost fell to my knees in gratitude to my college for being the first place I had ever spent four uninterrupted years. Since my birth, I had moved twenty-three times, and The Citadel and the hauntingly beautiful city of Charleston had given me a sense of security and belongingness I had never known before. As an English major, my job and purpose in life was to read the greatest books ever written by the most fabulous and imaginative writers. I felt a sense of bedazzled guilt that I loved my courses and teachers so much and could not wait to get to my classes each morning.

It was the year I began to catch small glimpses of the man I was becoming, moments when all the disfigurements and odd bafflements of my hidden childhood began to reveal themselves in unfocused glances into my nature. In this last year I would play organized basketball I came into my own as a player, not because of my team's success, but because of its crushing disappointments and failures. The season turned out to be a disaster for all concerned, except for me. I played the best basketball I ever played in the last half of what all remember as a jinxed and unprovidential season.

When I left The Citadel, I did not keep up with a single teammate from my losing season. It is the winners who have reunions, who stay in touch and whose wives and children know each other and gather together on those numerous occasions when their husbands and fathers try to recapture the uncommon glory they once felt when they were young athletes. The losing teams of the world disband without fanfare or any sense of regret. The names and faces of our teammates nick us like razors and recall moments of failure, disillusionment, disgrace. Losing tears along the seam of your own image of yourself. It is a mark of shame that causes internal injury, but no visible damage. The stigmata of that long-ago season have hurt me; I had let my team and my school down by not being good enough. As a basketball player, I always felt like a fraud and that same feeling has followed me into the writing life.

Yet I wish to be clear. I have loved nothing on this earth as I did the sport of basketball. I loved to break up a full-court press as much as anyone who has ever lived and played the game, black or white, male or female, in the shades of Spanish moss, beneath the roiled heat and sunshine of Dixie. I would not sell my soul to be playing college ball somewhere in this country tonight, but I would give it long and serious consideration. It was only when I had to give up basketball that I began to attract the unfavorable attention of the rest of the world. Basketball provided a legitimate physical outlet for all the violence and rage and sadness I later brought to the writing table. The game kept me from facing the ruined boy who played basketball instead of killing his father. It was also the main language that allowed father and son to talk to each other. If not for sports, I do not think my father ever would have talked to me.

I WOULD NOT HAVE RETURNED TO this year of 1966 if I had not experienced one of those life-changing encounters on the road that rise up periodically to let us know that fate remains inexorable in its utter strangeness and its capacity for astonishment.

At a bookstore called Books & Co. in Dayton, Ohio, during my long tour for *Beach Music*, the first novel I had published in nine years, I

looked up after signing my last autograph and I saw a man looking uncomfortable among the new novels published that season. Though I had
not seen John DeBrosse in nearly thirty years, I recognized him immediately and felt that rush of pleasure one gets when encountering a part
of the past that seemed irretrievably lost. When we had played together
on the Citadel basketball team, John had always looked upon my love of
reading as a form of mental illness. It amazed him I read books for
pleasure and not because professors made me. I had once coveted and
admired John DeBrosse's game; I had the capacity to hero-worship all
the boys who could play basketball better than I could, and my house of
worship was large indeed. John DeBrosse was a player who started every
game on every team he had ever played on, and he could shoot a basketball as well as the good ones. He was as serious as calculus and played
basketball with the same devotion that monks often display at lauds or
matins.

I was nearing my fiftieth birthday when John DeBrosse emerged
from his own life in the fevers and agues of his own time in Ohio to find
me. I rose up from the signing table to approach him, and we embraced.

"Ever been in a bookstore before, DeBrosse?"

"Yeah, once, Conroy. I was lost," John said. "Hey—my wife and kids
don't think I know you. They think I made it all up. Could you come
over to my house to meet them?"

John drove me toward his house in his huge van, very Ohio to me.
We talked easily about guys we had known at The Citadel, but my information was fresher and far more up-to-date since Citadel men have
always bought far more of my books than any other single group, and I
had run into scores of them on the *Beach Music* tour. Then John's conversation moved back toward memory and basketball. He had spent his
whole life as a basketball coach, teacher, and principal in the Dayton
area near his hometown of Piqua, Ohio. An educator of that most solid
sort—the ones who make for consistency and excellence in our nation's
public schools—he embodied the Ohio virtues: his life was smooth and
cautious and his prose was boilerplate. Put a man like John DeBrosse on
guard duty, and he would issue a challenge to everything that went bump
in the night.

Listening to him talk made it clear to me that his true love was
coaching because his voice changed timbre when he told me about
teams he had coached to championship seasons. The same charged-up

intensity I used to observe in John's face during the fury of games I now saw behind the wheel of his van as he described the high and low points of his career. Then he looked at me and said, "I was a lot better than you, Conroy." It was a statement of fact in the world of athletics, not braggadocio. "You couldn't shoot."

The truth of this remark stung me, hurtful as a handful of wasps. "Other people noted that. I made very few All-American teams those years."

"But you got after it," John said. "You went all out."

"Thanks."

"I've always told my players and coaches that something used to happen between us every practice, Conroy. Do you remember?"

Something stirred, then struck a huge chord of memory, and I got that slight shiver that happens when I catch a glimpse of a part of my past that has slipped out of sight.

"When the guards would split up from the forwards and centers and we would go to the opposite court to do drills," John said.

"I remember. I loved that."

"It always happened when you and I went one-on-one together. You guarding me. Me guarding you. There was nothing like it."

"You liked it because you were so much better than me."

"No," he said. "We went after each other like no two other players on the team. Not a word was spoken. No trash talking. Just pure respect. The whole atmosphere in that gym changed. I brought out the best in you. You brought out the best in me. Man, it was something."

"You beat me a lot more than I beat you," I said, "if memory serves me correctly."

"Damn right I did," he said, laughing in the darkness as we drove down a charmless avenue that could have cut through any city in America. "But you gave it all you had, fought all the way. I think about that team we played on. That shitty season. If we'd just had a banger. Some tough guy on the boards. As it was, we had only one hard-nosed son-of-a-bitch on the team and we needed about three or four more really tough guys."

"Who was the hard-nosed guy?" I asked.

John DeBrosse looked at me strangely, then said, "It was you, Conroy. Who the hell else could it have been?"

I spent several pleasurable moments, basking in the sunshine of those sweet words and sitting in silence, the first minute in my life I was aware that John DeBrosse thought I was hard-nosed. He could not have made me happier if he had told me I wrote like Vladimir Nabokov.

"Thanks, Johnny. I didn't know I was hard-nosed."

"You always came to play, were always around the ball. If it hit the floor you'd be flying across the floor after it."

"Were you hard-nosed?" I asked.

"I was good," he laughed. "I didn't have to be."

We went over the roster of the entire team that had endured that sullen and unsuccessful season so long ago, sharing any information or rumors we had heard about our teammates. "Conroy, do you remember that last game of your career? Against the University of Richmond. The Southern Conference Tournament?"

The question surprised me. "I'll never forget it."

"Remember how it ended?"

"I sure do. But I'd never have brought it up."

At a stoplight, he turned to face me. His good, earnest American face filled with emotion rare for a man like John DeBrosse, and he said, "I think that game partially ruined my life."

"C'mon, Johnny. It was just a game. We lost in overtime. Richmond knew we were in the game."

"It was a lot more than that, Conroy. I lost that game for us. I blew the layup that would've sent us into the next round against West Virginia."

"You missed a shot," I said. "We all missed shots."

"Not as important as that one," he said.

"It didn't come at a great time," I agreed. "But it was almost thirty years ago, Johnny. No one even remembers it now."

"I remember it," he said fiercely. "I didn't miss layups, Conroy. I never missed a layup in my life."

Again we came to a stoplight and John turned to me again. He reached over and grabbed my wrist and squeezed it.

"Pat," he said, the first time all evening he had called me by my first name, "I want you to know something. It's important to me that you believe it. That game. That last shot. I didn't miss that shot on purpose. I swear to you, I'd never do anything like that."

"It never occurred to me or anyone else, Johnny. You weren't even capable of thinking such a thing."

"One person did," John said. "And one person said it."

"Who?" I asked.

"Our coach. Mel Thompson thought it."

"Ah," I said. "Mel Thompson. Now there's a story."

"Mel came up and stood behind me. Then he said—I swear he said it—'Hey, DeBrosse, I know you didn't miss that shot on purpose. I know you wouldn't do something like that, would you?' "

"You'd never miss a shot on purpose," I said. "No one could think that of you."

"That's not true," John said. "My own coach did."

AFTER MY ENCOUNTER ON THE ROAD with John DeBrosse, I spent the rest of the *Beach Music* tour with that senior year insinuating its unwelcome presence into my roiled, middle-aged life. It began to pulse with new, sudden urgency. By writing *The Lords of Discipline*, I thought I had picked the bones of that year clean and left them lying, immaculate and sterile, on the road behind me. I was mistaken.

So it was in the fall of 1995, my heartsick and downcast team began to rematerialize slowly from the wreckage of time. There seemed to be a gathering force creating some collaborative centrifugal pull on all of us. I could feel our failure and disfigurement summoning us when Dave Bornhorst and Greg Connor showed up with their families at the Chapter Two Bookstore in Charleston; then Jim Halpin and Bill Zinsky materialized in Philadelphia. We seemed like lost cards from a tarot deck, yet each time one of my teammates appeared, my joy in our reunion sprang out in a rapturous burst of light. Their presence and the attendance of their families moved me. It did not feel like sentimentality to me, though I have an infinite capacity for the maudlin and false note. No, it was like something else entirely, like a form of enlightenment or the beginning of a journey.

At the end of that tour, on October 26, 1995, I stood in the divorce court of the City of San Francisco as I ended my thirteen-year-old marriage to Lenore Fleischer in a ceremony that felt like part self-evisceration and part *auto-da-fé*. I had walked into a travesty of a marriage and had done it with my eyes wide open and with the frantic warnings of all my family and best friends begging me to run for my life from the woman I loved. Even my father had warned me that Lenore was a gold digger, saying that I was an easy southern mark who did not understand one thing about the slippery, counterfeiting strategies of a big-city woman on the make.

I thought that the beautiful, flippant Lenore was misunderstood. I had met the dark woman at last, the woman who let me in on the secret that the ferocity of tyrants could hide in the sweet flow of mother's milk, that the words "I love you" could contain all the bloodthirsty despair of the abattoir, all the hopelessness of the most isolated, frozen gulag, all the lurid sadness of death row. Love came to me with all its soft words poisoned, its sweetness contaminated. As a boy, I was beaten up by my father, and my mother, whom I adored, could not protect me from his fists. The way I loved became bruised and disfigured—which is my fault and not Lenore's, and I do not blame her for this. In her darkness, in all her convoluted, flawed humanity and the immensity of her pain, Lenore had my name written all over her. She was the agent of my great passion and my even greater ruin.

If Lenore had been a country, I would have married North Korea, this is how murderous, cut off, and isolated the marriage had begun to seem to me. We lived our lives together in such a mind-numbing overload of event and melodrama that by the early nineties I found myself used up and desperate. I ran screaming out of that marriage, feeling like my hair was on fire.

My books all become Rosetta stones, giving me clues to how my life is going. I began *Beach Music* with a line that seemed to come out of nowhere, a startling cautionary image of despair: a beautiful, dark-haired woman is leaping to her death from a bridge in Charleston, South Carolina. This image frightened me because I was writing with a view of the Golden Gate Bridge and that bridge had begun to summon me with its wordless enchantment, its promise of release that had attracted the legion of disconsolate souls who had made their last walk there. Sometimes it looked like a great poem to me, a sonnet of almost idolatrous devotion to architecture, a flow of wire and steel as beautiful as the Marin headlands or San Francisco itself. But when the bridge began to call to me, not as a work of art, but as an agent of deliverance and immolation, I knew it was time to retreat to my getaway home in South Carolina.

By the time I made the move in 1992, I had deciphered the meaning of the book's first sentence: the woman leaping from the bridge was my wife, Lenore, and my interior self was signaling that my marriage was much more than just on the rocks. The black leap of that anonymous woman was the smoke signal from the interior that my marriage was over.

Such was my state of mind when I returned home from San Francisco licking my wounds, exhausted by the life I had chosen to lead. The writing of *Beach Music* had felt like a blood-letting and I limped home to my writing desk, unable to sit still there for a single moment. My heart slowed down in the disordered ruins that had become my life. The divorce enclosed me in a shell of edgy despondency. I wanted January along the marshes to cure me, but my basketball team and The Citadel began intruding on my life again.

There had been an earlier prophetic incursion of Citadel basketball when I was foundering in the writing of *Beach Music*. Living alone on Fripp Island, I was in the middle of a most terrible breakdown where I could not shake the obsessional urge to end my life. I found myself shopping for pistols in pawn shops, studying the veins of wrists and throat, and learning how to get to the roof of the DeSoto Hilton in Savannah. Guilt and despair overwhelmed me and I could see no honorable way out of the mess I had made of my life. Finally I imagined a perfect suicide in which I rowed my johnboat out into the Atlantic at the precise moment of a spring tide's turning, tied an anchor around my waist before I cut my wrists and carotid artery, then slipped into the water and out of the hours I could no longer bear. I had decided on this course when another Citadel point guard came roaring out of time to save my life.

On October 2, 1993, I read that Dickie Jones, a flashy point guard for the "Blitz Kids," the best team in Citadel history, had put a bullet in his brain while seated on a park bench in Mount Pleasant, a suburb of Charleston. A daily communicant in the Roman Catholic Church and the mayor of Mount Pleasant, the gregarious and joyous Dickie Jones, a man who seemed to have everything going for him and no acquaintance with darkness or calamity, killed himself and changed the history of his family forever.

Dickie Jones had helped recruit me when I made my official visit to The Citadel. His personality was upbeat and big city, just like his game, and I laughed at everything he said. He was influential in my decision to attend The Citadel because he ran a team with such nerve and showiness. After Dickie's funeral, when I called his home to try to comfort his widow and his children, I talked to a friend of the family whose name I cannot recall.

"Did you ever see him play ball?" I said. "My God, he could play the game."

"I heard he was good," the man said.

"He helped recruit me to The Citadel," I said, and then, to my complete surprise, I burst into tears and could not control my sobbing.

"Dickie affected a lot of people," the man said, "the same way he's affecting you now."

"No. I didn't know Dickie very well," I said, strangling on the tears. "It's something else."

I had entered into another of the great drifts that my life seems to take at least once a decade. My depressions have taken on a quality of serene artistry. I find myself exploring caverns of my psyche where the stalactites are arsenic-tipped, the bats rabid, and blind pale creatures live in the lightless pools dreaming of fireflies and lanterns shivering with despair. I have a history of cracking up at least once during the writing of each of my last five books. It has not provided the greatest incentive to head for the writing table each morning, but it's the reality I've lived with. I came out of my free-fall when I heard shrieking in Dickie's devastated home. It was Dickie's children, far too stricken to speak to me. I know the dark things that all suicides know, but as terrifying as these things were, none had prepared me for the image of my children and my family approaching my open coffin with bitterness and love tearing through them in alternating currents. My imagination has always kept me alive and it did so as I mourned for Dickie Jones's family. Out of nowhere, he had given me a sign that I was still needed in the game. The weeping and screaming of Dickie's devastated children saved my life. Dickie Jones died without ever knowing the great impact he had on me.

I had remembered the boldness of Dickie Jones's game. He played the game like it should be played, but until his death I had never thought of the deeper stirrings that move beneath the facades of those people we select to be our heroes—I had never once considered the sadness of point guards.

• • •

THIS IS THE STORY OF a mediocre basketball team that is remembered by few, a team that spent a year perfecting the art of falling to pieces. I thought I would be a senior on one of the greatest basketball teams in Citadel history. I could not have been more wrong.

Sports books are always about winning because winning is far more pleasurable and exhilarating to read about than losing. Winning is wonderful in every aspect, but the darker music of loss resonates on deeper, richer planes. I think about all the games of that faraway year that played such a part in shaping me, and it is the losses that stand out because they still make their approach with all their capacities to wound intact. Winning makes you think you'll always get the girl, land the job, deposit the million-dollar check, win the promotion, and you grow accustomed to a life of answered prayers. Winning shapes the soul of bad movies and novels and lives. It is the subject of thousands of insufferably bad books and is often a sworn enemy of art.

Loss is a fiercer, more uncompromising teacher, coldhearted but clear-eyed in its understanding that life is more dilemma than game, and more trial than free pass. My acquaintance with loss has sustained me during the stormy passages of my life when the pink slips came through the door, when the checks bounced at the bank, when I told my small children I was leaving their mother, when the despair caught up with me, when the dreams of suicide began feeling like love songs of release. It sustained me when my mother lay dying of leukemia, when my sister heard the ruthless voices inside her, and when my brother Tom sailed out into the starry night in Columbia, South Carolina, sailed from a fourteen-story building and plunged screaming to his death, binding all of his family into his nightmare forever. Though I learned some things from the games we won that year, I learned much, much more from loss.

# PART I

# THE POINT GUARD TAKES TO THE COURT

# CHAPTER I

# BEFORE FIRST PRACTICE

It was on the morning of October 15, 1966, that the final season officially began. For a month and a half, my teammates and I had gathered in the field house to lift weights, do isometric exercises, and scrimmage with each other. Right off, I could tell our sophomores were special and were going to make our team faster, scrappier, and better than the year before. In the heat of September, there was a swiftness and feistiness to the flow of these pickup games that was missing in last year's club. My optimism about the coming season lifted perceptibly as I observed my team beat up on each other in the vagrancy of our uncoached and unmonitored scrimmages.

I could feel the adrenaline rush of excitement begin as I donned my cadet uniform in the dark, and it stayed with me as I marched to mess with R Company. I could barely concentrate on the professors' voices in my classes in Coward Hall as I faced the reality of the new season and stared at the clock with impatience. It was my fourth year at The Citadel and the fourth time October 15 had marked the beginning of basketball practice. Mel Thompson was famous for working his team hard on the first day and traditionally ran us so much that the first practice was topped off by one of us vomiting on the hardwood floor.

I made my way to the locker room early that afternoon because I wanted some time to myself to shoot around and think about what I wanted to accomplish this season. Four of my teammates were already dressed when I entered the dressing room door. The room carried the acrid fragrance of the past three seasons for me, an elixir of pure maleness with the stale smell of sweat predominant yet blended with the sharp, stinging unguents we spread on sore knees and shoulders, Right Guard deodorant spray, vats of foot powder to ward off athlete's foot, and deodorant cakes in the urinals. It was the powerful eau de cologne of the locker room. I realized that my life as a college athlete was coming to its inevitable end, but I did not know that you had to leave the fabulous odors of youth behind when you hurried out into open fields to begin life as an adult.

As I entered the room, I waved to Al Beiner, the equipment manager. He and his assistant Joe "Rat" Eubanks were making sure that the basketballs were all inflated properly. Carl Peterson, another assistant, had just returned with a cartful of freshly laundered towels, still warm to the touch.

"The Big Day," Al said. He was reserved and serious and considered the players juvenile and frivolous. Al's presence was priestlike, efficient.

"Senior year," Rat said. "It all comes together for the big guy this year, right, Pat?"

Joe Eubanks was the only man on campus who called me "the big guy." Five feet five inches tall, he was built with the frail bones of a tree sparrow. His size humiliated him but his solicitousness to the players made him beloved in the locker room. Joe hero-worshiped the players, a rarity at The Citadel. His wide-eyed appreciation of me reminded me of the looks my younger brothers gave me. My brothers thought I was the best basketball player in the world, and I did nothing to discourage this flagrant misconception.

When I began undressing, Carl brought over a clean practice uniform and a white box containing a pair of size 9½ Converse All Star basketball shoes. Carl wore gold stars for his brilliant academic work and moved quietly among the players, silent as a periwinkle.

As I sat down to open the new box of shoes, Joe Eubanks slipped up behind me and began massaging my neck.

"Still hurt, Pat?" Joe asked. "It's been two years now." My neck had been sore since Dick Martini knocked me unconscious in a practice game.

Behind me Carl rumbled by with another load for the laundry room. Stepping out of the equipment office, Al warned us not to take our shoes out unless we signed for them. Joe brought a box of tape to Coach Billy

Bostick, the mustachioed seventy-year-old trainer who taped Doug Bridges's ankles as Danny Mohr waited his turn.

Jim Halpin sat to my right, struggling to put on the grotesque knee brace which supported his ruined leg.

"Still happy about your choice of colleges, Jim?" I asked.

"This fucking place sucks," Jimmy answered as I knew he would. For four years, all conversation between Jim and me began with this withering mantra.

"Tell me what you really think, Jimmy, don't hold back," I said.

"Conroy, Halpin says the same damn thing every day, year after year," Danny said, sitting at the last locker, both his ankles taped.

"Thanks for pointing that out, Root," Bob Cauthen said.

"Fuck you, Zipper," Danny said, not even looking at Bob. Danny we called "Root" because he was not much of a leaper for a big man and stayed "rooted" on the ground beneath the basket. Bob was called "Zipper" by Danny because he was long and skinny. He was given that name by a heckler from Georgia Southern, and it stuck.

"Don't you love the fellowship on this team?" I said. "Can't you feel the brotherhood? The coming together of a group of guys who can never be broken or defeated?"

"Conroy," said John DeBrosse, unbuttoning his uniform shirt as he approached his locker. "Speak so us poor peasants can understand you. I got to carry a dictionary around to understand what your sorry ass is saying."

"Thank you, Lord, for directing my path toward The Citadel," I said. "I love this place, Lord. I truly love this place. I've found myself a home."

"This fucking place sucks," Jimmy muttered to himself.

"You're onto something, Halpin," Dave "Barney" Bornhorst, a wide-bodied forward from Ohio, said. "Keep working on the details."

Danny said, "I had scholarships to Davidson, NC State, Wake Forest. Do I go to any of those great places? Oh, no. I come to El Cid so I can spend my life with Muleface."

I looked to the door, watching for the sudden appearance of our coach. "Be careful, Danny."

Joe Eubanks came through the locker room. "Twenty minutes to get dressed and on the floor."

"Eat me, Rat," Bob said.

"Don't irritate me, Cauthen," Joe said, putting his tiny fist against Bob's chin.

"Make me laugh, Rat," Bob said.

"Leave Rat alone, Zipper," Danny called down from his locker.

Bob stuck up a middle finger at Danny and said, "Eat a big hairy one, Root."

"What a team," Jimmy Halpin said, shaking his head sadly. "This fucking place sucks."

The new assistant coach, Ed Thompson, came into the locker room and walked down the straight line of lockers, squeezing our shoulders or slapping our butts, whispering words of encouragement. A sweet-faced, soft-spoken man, he looked like an aging Boy Scout as he imparted his own enthusiasm about the beginning of the new season.

"Let's get ready to go, boys. Let's win it all this year. This is the year for us. Can you feel it, boys? Tell me now. Let's get on out there."

After he spoke to each of us, he retreated from the locker room like an ambassador for a third-world nation intimidated by the hauteur of the Court of St. James's. "Little Mel," as we called him, was intimidated by us still and did not feel comfortable interacting with us quite yet.

"Why'd Little Mel take this job?" Danny asked the room.

"He just lucked out," Bridges said.

"What a sinking ship," Bob said.

"Hey, none of that, Cauthen," DeBrosse said. "We're going to have a great team this year. None of this negative shit. Leave that in the barracks."

"Who are you, the fucking Gipper?" Bob answered.

Danny Mohr finished lacing his shoes and said, "I like Little Mel. What in the hell did he see in Muleface?"

"He just wanted to coach All-Americans like you, Mohr," Cauthen said.

"Eat me, Zipper," Danny said, again shooting Bob the finger.

"Can't you feel the team jelling?" I said. "Feel the camaraderie. Feel the never-say-die spirit. Nothing'll ever get between this band of brothers."

DeBrosse said, "Get the dictionary. Conroy's moving his lips again."

Rat appeared suddenly at the door and said, "Muleface left his office. Hurry up. He's on his way."

There was a headlong scramble of all of us as we raced for the door that opened to the floor. The sophomores had not spoken a word. It was their first day on the varsity team and they were nervous and mistrustful.

"This fucking place sucks," Halpin said, then moved out toward the sounds of boys shooting around, limping in his knee brace.

# CHAPTER 2

# FIRST PRACTICE

THERE WAS A TENSION IN THE GYM AMONG THE PLAYERS WHEN THE first practice was about to begin. We were more serious as we took jump shots, awaiting the appearance of the coaching staff at exactly 1600 hours. DeBrosse hit eight jump shots in a row from the top of the key as I admired the perfection of his form and the articulation of his follow-through. The net coughed as the ball swished through again and again. It was the loveliest sound in a shooter's world. Bridges and Zinsky both practiced long-range jumpers from the corners. Everyone had his favorite spots to get to when shooting around before practice. The managers were feeding all of us retrieved balls as I caught sight of our two coaches, both named Thompson, skirting the bleachers on the way toward the court. Mel was talking quietly to his new assistant, and we wondered aloud if "Little Mel" had any idea what he had gotten himself into. Mohr believed that Mel Thompson was as charming in hiring new assistants as he was when he recruited us.

Coach Mel Thompson blew his whistle, shouted "Two lines," and without fanfare or commentary, our season began. He flipped me the ball and proffered me the honor of making the first layup in the first practice of my final year. A surge of enthusiasm rippled through the team as the line moved smoothly, expertly. One thing a college basketball player could do without thinking or breaking a sweat was to move effortlessly through a layup line. Style was important, and everyone brought his best moves into play during the warmup. The big guys dunked it as we little guys did reverse layups on the other side of the glass. You worked on being cool, disinterested, unflappable. You knew that this period was the last time during the season that the team would not be exhausted. Getting out of bed tomorrow morning would require the forbearance and strength of roommates.

A whistle blew again and Mel shouted, "Figure eights," and we broke up into three lines of four men in a line. I passed the ball to Tee Hooper, the sophomore guard on my left, and ran behind him as Tee threw to Bridges and cut behind him, who threw it to me, cutting behind me as I passed it to Tee, who put it in for a layup. Not once did the ball touch the ground. Coach Thompson also turned it into a disciplinary drill where we ran the figure eights until we were close to dropping. The guys with bad hands—always the big guys—had trouble sometimes handling the long passes and their awkwardness infuriated Mel.

"Catch the goddamn ball," he yelled at Brian Kennedy, a willowy sophomore. "Protect it. It's not a loaf of bread."

"Gee, it's not?" Cauthen whispered. "Why didn't someone tell me?"

"You got something to say, Cauthen?" Coach Thompson barked.

"No, sir," Bob said, lowering his head. Our coach required gestures of submission.

"You still ain't worth a shit, Conroy," DeBrosse teased me, slapping my butt as he ran by me.

"You're shorter than you were last year," I whispered, coming up behind him in the figure eight line.

"I'm a half inch taller than you, duck butt."

In truth, John and I were both very small basketball players, and that's why we were guards. John was prickly and defensive about his height while I was not; I was prickly and defensive about my shooting ability or lack thereof. All athletes disguised the secret shame of their shortcomings. John spent a great deal of time stretching his neck, lifting up, trying to convince himself he was taller than I was. When I was listed as five foot eleven in the program, DeBrosse went wild and said, "Honor violation, Conroy. HV. HV. Turn yourself in."

"I didn't say I was that tall," I said. "Our coach has always pretended I was. It makes him feel better."

"Why?" Johnny said. "You still can't shoot worth a shit."

In the middle of the figure eight drill, I got to study the sophomores up close for the first time. Their speed and athleticism impressed me, but it was their closeness as a class that was most unique. Their freshman team put together a remarkable record. With each game they improved at all positions. They were the first freshman team I had witnessed who did not seem completely undone by the plebe system. By the end of that first year, they had cohered into something very special. I thought they would make The Citadel a team to be feared in the Southern Conference. Even in the layup line and the figure eight drill, they hung together, a team not yet incorporated into our team. Incautious and reckless, they hurled themselves around the court and brought an enthusiasm to this first practice that made me feel a great affection for each of them. So much of our team's destiny rode on their shoulders. So much would be required of them, and no one knew how their egos would withstand the changeable nature of our tempestuous coach.

Years later I read a copy of a program from that year which spelled out this team's prospects in the words of Mel Thompson himself. Though it was still a cautionary tale with loopholes and escape clauses, I read between the lines that our coach was as optimistic about this coming year as I was.

PROSPECTS FOR THE SEASON by Coach Mel Thompson.
The 1966–67 season will again find the Bulldogs in a year of rebuilding. First, on a long list of musts, we must find a replacement for Wig Baumann, the team's leading scorer and floor leader. Our success will depend on finding a replacement for Baumann and the ability of our younger players to find their maturity in the early going.

Senior Pat Conroy and Junior John DeBrosse appear to have a shot at floor leading the Cadets. DeBrosse appeared in all 23 games last season as a guard. He scored 248 points averaging just over 10 points per game. Conroy appeared in 16 games scoring 74 points for an average of just over 4 points per game. Both boys are excellent ball handlers. Conroy excels in passing and dribbling. DeBrosse is a fine shot. He hit on 49 percent of his shots last year.

Our thin blue line will definitely be improved this year with a better overall depth than we have experienced for the past couple of years. Team speed also will be improved with the addition of this year's group of sophomores.

Dan Mohr, Doug Bridges, and John DeBrosse all started last season and should, with gained experience, be much improved. Mohr will be our tallest man at 6'7". He is an excellent offensive pivot man and is rated as one of the best pivot men in the Southern

Conference. Second in scoring last year with 314 points for an average of just over 15 points per game, Mohr was our top rebounder with 156 points in 20 games. Bridges was our third leading scorer, averaging 12.6 points. The year's experience should make Doug one of our most consistent players.

Bob Cauthen saw considerable action as a sophomore. He has displayed hustle and heart. The year's experience should improve Bob's overall performance and we expect him to have a good year.

One of our weak points again is the need for height. We don't have the big man and we will be hurting under the backboards. Rebounding definitely will be a problem.

Five of the twelve men of the Varsity this season will be sophomores. This group is led by the top three men in scoring on last year's freshman team—Bill Zinsky, Al Kroboth, and Tee Hooper. The ability of these boys to adjust to Varsity competition will be a key factor in our success this season.

We veterans knew something the sophomores would learn quickly. Each player would have to submit himself to trial by Mel Thompson, a season-long initiation in which our coach would search for the soft spots and breaking points of his newest players, then would go to work on them with a cruel finesse. By doing this, Mel thought he was making his players tougher and more resilient when the games came down to the wire. I had seen some kids crack under the weight of Mel's fiercest attention, which was no perversity on Mel's part, but simply an outgrowth of his philosophy as a coach. Coach Thompson could break a boy in a day or over a season or over a career. It was a gift that he brought to the art of coaching.

The whistle blew again and the rigid structure of our practice sessions locked into place as Mel shouted, "Two-on-two drill. Conroy and Halpin. You guard Hooper and DeBrosse."

Jim Halpin and I glanced at each other. We put on our game faces on October 15 and would wear them until the final horn was sounded at the tournament.

The two-on-two drill was an excellent teaching method combining both defensive and offensive skills in the open court. It utilized the entire floor and the two players on defense tried to stop the two offensive players from bringing it up the floor. It was also a much easier drill for the guards than it was for the big men. Sometimes, their awkwardness or slowness afoot would be highlighted by any drill that found them scrambling over the entire area of the court. This would often be enough to draw the wrath of Mel on one of the big guys.

"Move it, goddamn it. Move it, Mohr," he shouted. "What're you trying to do? If you don't move it any better than that, you sure as hell aren't going to be ready for Auburn."

"Pick it up, Pat. Pick it up," Ed Thompson said, the first time we heard the new assistant speak in practice.

The whistle blew again. We were sweating now and the sweat felt good on the skin. October was still hot in the Lowcountry, and the tide was going out in the Ashley River, fifty yards away from the field house where we practiced. Because Mel's practices were set in concrete, Johnny and I began moving toward the south end of the court before the command was given: "Guards at the other end of the court with Coach Thompson. Forwards and centers over here with me for rebounding," yelled Mel.

"I'm going to eat your jock this year, Conroy," DeBrosse said.

"They got any interesting boys in Ohio, DeBrosse? Or are they all like you?"

"You're faster with words, Conroy. But watch who sticks it in the net."

"I'll be all over your short squat self."

We communicated in secret using the skills of ventriloquists. I enjoyed John DeBrosse's cockiness and brashness on the court. It pleased me that he taunted me openly and tried to get me to retaliate. DeBrosse grabbed the ball from Little Mel as the guards lined up for one-on-one drills.

"Get out there, Conroy," DeBrosse said. "I'll teach you some new tricks."

I got down in my defensive stance and pushed off of DeBrosse's shoulders hard. He took a step forward and I retreated exactly that amount. When he rocked back to his original position, I moved up on him again. John was a jump shooter, a great one, but he hated to drive to the basket. He knew it and he knew I knew it. Ours was a cat-and-mouse game and we were like shadow selves with each other. He faked right, then went left, which was unusual for John, but I was on him close. I tried to flick the ball away from his left hand, but he turned his body and regained control of the ball with his right hand. Johnny then began backing me into the lane as though we were two centers fighting for position in the paint. Once we began playing, no words were spoken between us, ever.

Suddenly, Johnny whirled for the jump shot and I left my feet a fraction of a second late. The ball swished through the net.

"Good hustle, both of you," Little Mel said.

I trotted to the back of the line and watched as John took his defensive position against Tee Hooper, the sophomore guard. I had kept a sharp eye on Tee Hooper since his arrival as a freshman. His natural position was small forward, and he was a slashing, hell-for-leather kind of player who gave it everything he had every time he hit the court. His improvement from the first game to his last as a plebe had dazzled me. His game was still rough around the edges, but he was six feet five inches tall, had the best and fastest first step on the team, and was one of those rawboned, skinny kids who always found a way to score. To me, he carried an air of greatness about him, but I personally hoped that greatness would flower sometime after my graduation. Tee Hooper was a real threat to take my position and send me to the end of the bench for my whole senior year.

As DeBrosse waited for Tee's first move, I noticed how much taller Tee was than the rest of the guards. Yet he was quick as we were and his first step to the basket was a lunge move that swept him past John and into the lane where Tee went high and laid the ball high off the backboard.

"Jesus Christ," DeBrosse said as he joined me in the back of the line. "Did you see that, Conroy?"

"Worst defense I ever saw," I whispered.

"See how well you guard him," DeBrosse said.

When it was my turn to guard Tee, I played off him, giving him the outside shot because I noticed that Tee, like me, wanted to put the ball on the floor and whip by for the layup. I offered him the jump shot because I knew that Tee did not yet fully trust his shot. But he was game and fast, and he practically enveloped me and Johnny when he guarded us.

I put my hands on my waist as I watched Jimmy Halpin covering the freshman guard Jerry Hirsch. My hands. The subject was painful to me. I had the smallest hands I'd ever seen on a man. I was reading a book by

Bob Cousy on what made him so great, and he shocked me by revealing that one of the absolute requirements for a point guard was large hands. I could not palm a basketball; I was forced to use both hands for balance and control. There was no way for me to do a one-handed layup, but I had perfected the art of pretending to do one. With great care and some legerdemain, I kept all attention away from this liability.

I regarded Tee Hooper's great, spidery hands with envy as I listened to the big men battling each other under the board at the far basket. I was in trouble; this gifted, athletic boy had it in his power to steal my last season away from me.

On the opposite end of the court, in the land of the big man, a war was going on. The rebounding drills seemed like full-contact karate drills. There were often fights and scuffles under the boards. Mel liked it when the forwards and centers lost their tempers with each other. They pounded on each other with unrestrained fury for twenty minutes each day, and their tempers remained rent and frayed for the rest of the afternoon. Mel was excited by violence among the rebounders, cheering when the big guys made each other bleed.

The sophomore sensation, Bill Zinsky, was more than holding his own. He cut around Danny Mohr and stole a rebound from him. Mel launched into a stream of invective and profanity.

"Goddamn it, Mohr—don't you have any guts? Don't you have any fucking pride? You're four inches taller than Zinsky—he should never get a rebound from you. Not one. Block him out, Mohr! Jesus Christ! Is there anybody with any guts in there? Don't give me that look, Mohr! Give me some goddamn rebounds."

Dan Mohr's face carried hurt and aftershock that his teammates still remember. If Mel's volcanic temper had met its foil, it lay in Danny's proud but deeply humiliated face.

"You got something to say for yourself, Mohr?" Mel asked.

"I'm trying, Coach," Dan said. "I swear I'm trying."

"Shut the fuck up, Mohr. You're nothing but a can of corn. Now block out your goddamn man. Keep him off the board. Like this."

At least once a week, Mel demonstrated to the big men how to keep their man off the boards. Very few in the history of college basketball could rebound as well as Mel Thompson, and it was thrilling to watch him block Dan Mohr. Mel stretched his body out, crouched low, and his wingspan seemed gigantic. He felt around behind Danny then clasped him with his two great flared-out hands, then backed Danny out and away from the boards with his backside. He moved his feet fast in tiny, almost dainty steps, but when the ball came off the board he pounced on it with a hunger that all the great ones have.

"See," he growled. "That's how you do it. It takes heart, guts, courage to get the job done. You got the guts, Mohr?"

"Yes, sir," Danny shouted.

"Bullshit, Mohr. You ain't got shit."

The whistle blew and we lined up for a half hour of defensive drills. We walked through our defensive assignments, moved through all three zone defenses. The drills Mel used for defense were boilerplate and common among almost every basketball team. But Mel had always seemed uncomfortable coaching it, and this part of practice he wanted to get through quickly. His theory about defense was this: I give you a man and you stop the son-of-a-bitch. Don't expect any help from your teammates because they've got their own man to worry about.

That was Mel's inflexible philosophy, the one he played out in college and the one he lived by as a coach. He was inarticulate when it came to explaining how a defense was supposed to work. He screamed a lot, but there was little teaching going on. Then the whistle blew again and we readied ourselves for the scrimmage game that took place toward the end of every practice.

"Here's the first team I want," Mel said. "Mohr, Bridges, Zinsky, DeBrosse," and he paused and looked at me and Tee Hooper. "And Conroy."

Rat threw me the blue jersey of the starting team, and my heart danced. My prayers to the gods of basketball ricocheted off the steel beams of the Armory. For the first time in my varsity career I had been chosen as a starter by a coach. The second team turned their shirts inside out and wore the green jerseys of shame. But with pride, the second team called themselves the Green Weenies.

Danny Mohr jumped center against sophomore Al Kroboth, and Al won the tap. My final year began in earnest. The Green Weenies played like their very salvation was at stake. I led a fast break at full speed down the court and heard Johnny DeBrosse filling the lane on my right, Bill Zinsky on my left. I turned my head toward Johnny, picked up the ball, made a motion to feed it to him, then flipped it to my left, right into the hands of Zinsky, who laid it in off the board.

"Quit hot-dogging it, Conroy," Mel growled at me. I tossed the pass to Zinsky while looking at DeBrosse, but that was why it worked. I knew it even if my coach did not.

The first fifteen minutes of our first scrimmage of the season, the Green Weenies played like five All-Americans. The old pattern was reconfiguring, with Mel riding the sophomore Zinsky with irritation bordering on obsession. Nothing Zinsky did pleased our impatient and caustic coach. Zinsky began to look tentative and unsure of himself. I slapped him on the behind and whispered, "Don't let him get to you, Zeke." As a senior, my job was to protect the sophomores from melting under our coach's crossfire of criticism. I called it the "Mel Test."

But when the test suddenly came to me, out of nowhere, I wasn't prepared for it. Seeing Johnny trapped by Halpin and Hooper near the baseline, I sprinted down to help DeBrosse out. He lobbed the ball to me, and I took two dribbles to the right, then went up for a jump shot. My shot went in, but a whistle blew. Mel said, glowering at me, "Conroy, what do you think you're doing?"

"Shooting, Coach."

"Shooting? That's exactly what you're not supposed to do, Conroy. You can't shoot. Everyone knows that. I bet even you know that. Trade jerseys with Hooper."

I turned my jersey inside out and rejoined the second string, my native tribe. I huddled the guys together and I said, "Okay, Weenies. I'm back where I belong. Let's kick their asses and make Mel go wild."

The Green Weenies broke from the huddle with a mission. For the rest of the afternoon, we trounced the first string. It was clear to me from the first practice that I would play second-string guard for my entire senior year. I fought against despair. But I was a team player and was devoted to my sport and knew my responsibilities. I would make the first team better and make John DeBrosse and Tee Hooper better than they were supposed to be, by trying to stop me. Dressed in the color green, I made that vow.

We had practiced for one week when a camera crew arrived to report a piece on the upcoming season. I was one of the players Coach Thompson asked to appear on camera with him. We were dressed in our game uniforms, and Coach Thompson put his arm on my shoulders and said, "Pat Conroy is the finest dribbler and passer on this team. If Pat scores one or two points a game and runs the team well, we can't ask any more from him this year."

I walked back to the locker room in a state of shock. I undressed slowly, letting his words cut into me, like shards of glass. For weeks, his remark, that I could score only one point a game, ate at me. It haunted and followed me all over campus until I started to believe it. Its power was corrosive and subterranean.

I tried to hide it from my teammates and I tried to be funny in the locker room.

After the third practice, I walked toward the steaming shower room with my tall, beautifully built teammates. We were now in the middle of Mel's system, and we would be exhausted until the middle of March. But we were young and high-spirited and resilient. And we were all so hopeful about this season.

"Hey, Root," I said to Danny Mohr.

"Fuck you, Conroy," he said.

"Mohr, you're nothing but a can of corn."

And my team, my wonderful team, we laughed, I swear we laughed together. We could do that at the beginning of that dreadful season. I swear we could.

CHAPTER     3

# AUBURN

As I stare at The Citadel's schedule for the 1966–67 varsity basketball team, I mourn for the quicksilvery racehorse passage of time. Its swiftness has caught me with the same ineffable start that comes to every man and woman who lives long enough. It remains as the single great surprise of any life.

In the locker room, I got dressed for the game that would be the first game of the last year I would play organized basketball with real uniforms and real crowds and coaches who received paychecks because of their knowledge of the game. The tension in the locker room was almost electrical, special—like the atmosphere might be on Mercury, able to sustain only certain rare forms of organisms. Outside, the crowd was beginning to form and the parking lots were filling up with the makes of automobiles I now see only in period movies. The voices of strangers streaming down the sidewalk outside our locker room came to us through the cinderblock wall, barely audible, unformed, but brimming with excitement. What a good thing it is to go to games. What strange joy is felt as you leave the flatness of your daily life, the fatigue of routine, and the killing sameness of jobs to move among thousands toward a brightly lit field house at night. They passed by us in the darkness, their expectations risen by our first game with Auburn University, hope cresting that our team would prove memorable, and if we were lucky, legendary.

Auburn. It sounded so Big Time to a boy like me. "Good luck against Auburn, Pat," my mother had said on the phone, and just hearing her invoke the great name made me feel the weight of my own self-worth. I thought the entire universe would be watching me and my teammates take on the War Eagles that day in 1966. Auburn was in the Southeastern Conference, one of the proudest and showiest in the country, and recruited big-name athletes for a big-time program. I loved it whenever little Citadel invoked the myth and story of Goliath and scheduled us to play the great schools. Whenever people ask me about the teams I played against in college, I always say, "Florida State, Auburn, West Virginia, Virginia Tech, and Clemson." Never do I reply with "Erskine, Wofford, Newberry, and Presbyterian," who were the patsies and sacrificial lambs of our schedule.

In the big games The Citadel's corps always showed up in force, and that day there were nearly eighteen hundred of them on hand to offer their lionesque, full-throated allegiance to their team as we took the court. No one could rock a gymnasium like the Corps of Cadets in full ecstatic cry. When the Corps unleashed itself during the passionate fury of games, the energy was both intemperate and unforgettable to visiting teams. For us, it was like having an extra man under the boards, a sullen, mean-spirited one that could be worth six to eight points in a closely fought game.

In the locker room we heard the thunder of our violent tribe, and we felt the butterflies hatched in our stomachs. Danny Mohr sat at the first locker, the farthest away from the entrance; Jimmy Halpin sat next to me painfully putting on his knee brace; I laced up my Converse All Stars next to Mohr and regarded my image in the full-length mirror across the room.

Coach Thompson arranged us according to a strict class system: the juniors came next with DeBrosse sitting next to Halpin, followed by Bridges, Bornhorst, and Cauthen. Everyone on the team knew to keep Bob Cauthen and Doug Bridges separated. There was always a dangerous chemistry produced when those two scraped against one another.

Then came our dazzling collection of sophomores: Bill Zinsky, whose game was finished and mature; Tee Hooper, the tall slashing guard who had beaten me out for a starting position; Al Kroboth, the relentless rebounder; Greg Connor, the ex–football player whose intensity was a burning thing; and Brian Kennedy, irrepressible, clumsy, a little too loud for a sophomore.

I made my way up and down the line of dressing teammates, trying to relax the sophomores. I remembered the terror I felt before and during my first varsity game two years earlier when The Citadel had played

West Virginia in Morgantown. "Last year the upperclassmen tortured you and tried to run you out of school," I said. "This year they'll treat you like gods."

"Like they treat you, right, Conroy?" Cauthen asked.

"It's my third straight year as I stride this campus like a god," I replied. "I consider myself a Zeus-like figure."

"More like a leprechaun," Bob added.

"That was a racist reference to my Irish heritage and my diminutive size," I told the sophomores. "But know this—Bob fears my rapier wit."

"Say what, Conroy?" Bob asked.

"And my vast vocabulary," I said, returning to my locker.

"Hey, Conroy," Danny Mohr said as I pulled on my warmups.

Rat warned us of our coach's arrival. "Fifteen minutes, guys."

"Who's gonna be captain this year?" Danny asked me. "Muleface say anything to you?"

"Not a word," I said. "Maybe he'll make you, me, and Jimmy tri-captains, since we're the only survivors of our fabulous freshman team."

"God, we'd've been great if we could've stayed together," Jimmy said.

"He wouldn't make just you captain? Would he, Conroy? You're just a fucking Green Weenie."

"Don't worry about my feelings, Root," I said, and Jimmy Halpin almost fell off the bench laughing.

"We don't know what he's going to do," I said. "But he's got these three charismatic, Patton-like leaders to choose from."

Bob Cauthen, who made a habit of teasing me before practice and games, yelled from the middle of the locker room, "Hey, Conroy, how are you and the other homos getting along down in the English department? I hear the English profs are one hundred percent faggots."

"I lost my Maidenform bra, Bob. Could you help me find it?"

"At least I know how to take one off. Unlike you, Conroy."

"Get ready for the game, Cauthen," DeBrosse said.

"Eat me, DeBrosse," Bob said. "Anyone who thinks we can actually beat Auburn is full of shit."

Doug Bridges laughed as though he had just been told the funniest joke in the world, and Halpin joined him, then Bridges shouted, "Hey, Conroy. Our *team*, man. You can feel it coming together, can't you?"

Bob, wilted a bit in the glare of the sophomores, said, "If we were worth a shit, we wouldn't be playing at The Citadel."

"Hey, sophomores," I shouted. "It's the positive attitude in this locker room that'll lead us from victory to victory to victory this year."

My remark brought a strange, troubled laughter from the sophomores. Always, in the time I played for Mel Thompson, there was this unsettled, lunatic disjointedness to the atmosphere. In the locker room, you felt everything except what it was like to be part of a team. Year after year, the sophomores were cast adrift in the cynical laughter in an atmosphere that should have been joyous.

I tried once again to help them relax. "Best sophomore class in the history of this school," I said to them, then leaned down to Bill Zinsky. "This school isn't gonna believe this good a basketball player got through the plebe system."

"Quit the rah-rah shit, Conroy," Cauthen said. "That bullshit don't work. Especially not here."

Then Coach Thompson entered the locker room, wearing his game face, a midwestern scowl that looked like cloud covering, and moving with that loping shambling walk that had become a trademark to us, his face exuded no light, just various textures of darkness. Everything Mel did was studied and habitual, and he allowed no accidents or hazards to disrupt the afternoons and evenings of his life.

Al Beiner worked in the equipment room getting the balls ready for the warmup drills as Rat Eubanks put fresh towels in our lockers. Rat went behind me and massaged my neck with a towel still warm from the dryer. I put my hand behind my head and squeezed his thin wrist. Before every game during the year, this was our secret, unnoticed ritual.

Coach Thompson walked by us silently. He smoked his cigarette with deliberate slowness, then went into the shower room to urinate.

I offered a prayer to the God I was afraid of losing: "O Lord, I ask that something good come to me from this basketball season. My career, so far, has been an embarrassment to me. All I ask is for something good to come to me."

Coach Thompson returned from washing his hands, threw his cigarette on the cement floor, and crushed it beneath his polished, tasseled black loafers. Our coach was a fastidious man and a sharp dresser. Other teams might outplay the Citadel basketball team, but none of the other coaches in the Southern Conference could outdress Mel Thompson.

"Conroy," he said, "you'll be captain for tonight's game." This declaration caught me and my teammates by complete surprise. If he had asked me to put on a wedding dress to play the game it would not have astonished me more since second-stringers rarely had bestowed on them the mantle of captaincy. One minute before we took the floor against the strongest team on our schedule, Coach Thompson surprised us by humiliating our highest scorer and top rebounder from last season, Danny Mohr, and giving over the leadership role to me, who had demonstrated very little of it. We said the Lord's Prayer and then gathered in the center of the room, placing our hands over the hands of our fiery-eyed coach. His dark eyes smoldered with a malefic competitiveness as he screamed, "The SEC. The SEC. Let's see if we can play with the big boys."

Al Beiner flipped me a basketball as we lined up to enter the field house for the warmup drills. I handed the ball to Danny, but he gave it back to me and murmured, "You heard what the man said. You're the fucking captain."

Though Danny would not look at me, his hurt passed through the heart of my entire team. But then Rat threw open the door, and I led the way as my team burst out into the light and the sounds of "Dixie" (played better by the Citadel band than by any band in the world). The Corps rose and roared its praise, its validation of our oneness, our uniqueness—as we took the first steps into the mysteries of time and the reality of the season that would tear us in all the soft places of our young manhoods before it was over.

But I led my team to the center of the court, then broke for the basket and laid the ball in off the glass, taking care that I made the first layup of the new season that had turned suddenly real.

One of the referees came up behind me as I was shooting jumpers from the top of the key and said, "Captain Conroy, would you join us at center court?" It was one of the sweetest sentences in the English language ever directed at me, but I saw a wounded grimace cross Danny Mohr's face as I ran to meet with the Auburn men. Though I remember shaking hands with the Auburn captain, Bobby Buisson, and noticed that he and I shared the same number, 22, I held on to little of that momentous occasion because I kept saying to myself, "I'm the captain of the Citadel basketball team and we're about to play Auburn University." Since Coach Thompson had told me every day of my life at The Citadel that I did not have enough talent to play college basketball, that doctrine had assumed a form of catechism, and became one of my most deeply held beliefs. I had never dreamed that I would be in this place and time, under these lights, and with almost three thousand people watching me represent my school and my team.

The referees went over the rules with Bobby Buisson and me, but their voices blurred when I heard a cry of "Conroy, Conroy, Conroy" go up in the raucous cadet section, and I could see my roommates, Bo Marks and Mike Devito, leading the Romeo Company knobs in chanting my name. Bobby and I shook hands and wished each other good luck and I went back to join my teammates.

Unknown to me, I had just shaken hands with the best point guard I would ever play against. My wife Sandra's favorite saying is, "When the pupil is ready, a teacher appears." Bobby Buisson had appeared in my life at the perfect moment.

Because I was a senior, Mel Thompson started me at guard with John DeBrosse. Danny Mohr would jump center against the Auburn center, the aptly named Ronnie Quick, who was two inches shorter than Danny. It struck Doug Bridges as an oddity that The Citadel had a taller center than Auburn University. Doug himself and Bill Zinsky were both taller than the Auburn forwards, Wallace Tinker, who was six three, and Tom Perry, who was an undersized six two.

Danny Mohr crouched at center court against Ronnie Quick and the ref threw up the ball. As a portent of what lay ahead, Auburn took that tip and flew down the court at breakneck speed, establishing a race-horse pace they would keep up for a solid forty minutes.

I picked up Bobby Buisson, who carried himself on the court with a brashness and a gambler's instinct that delighted me. His greatness shone in the first moments when we stopped their fast break and he dribbled back out to the top of the key to set up their offense. I was Citadel bred and Citadel trained and I knew a natural-born leader when I saw one. The great engines of the Auburn offense started and ended with this radiant and handsome young man. Bobby threw a beautiful pass to the small forward, Tinker, who taught Doug Bridges that he was not the only pure shooter on the floor.

After Auburn scored, DeBrosse took the ball out of bounds and tossed it to me. John did not like bringing it up if he didn't have to. He would simply entrust the ball to me to bring it past their guards.

I ran the ball upcourt, but on the way past the bench I heard Mel yelling at me, "Don't shoot, Conroy. Don't shoot it."

As I crossed midcourt, Buisson was waiting for me as though I were a pizza he had ordered by phone. He played me too close and he felt like wrapping paper when I went by him. Even with the noise of the crowd, I heard my coach screaming, "Don't shoot." I threw the ball to Doug on the right side of the court and I ran my route into the corner, bringing Bobby with me. Mohr set a pick for Bill Zinsky on the other side of the court.

"Swing it," Coach Thompson yelled.

Doug threw it to DeBrosse at the top of the key who swung the ball to Zinsky on the left side of the lane, then John took his man into the far left corner. Mohr picked for Bridges on the other side of the court as I moved to the top of the key, Buisson covering me like a silk glove. I had to fake a backdoor move toward the basket to open up the passing lane between me and Zinsky when I saw Mohr break toward me as I shuffled him a pass. Danny dribbled Ronnie Quick deep into the lane, then spun and shot his lovely jumper down low. Mohr actually was taller than the Auburn center, but when Danny extended his long willowy arms, he played like he was six nine or better. For a big man, Danny had the softest, supplest hands, and his shots passed through the cords as if they were trying to nest there.

Auburn played a fast-paced game but Bobby Buisson controlled the tempo and action of everything the War Eagles did. His bursts toward the basket were rabbit-swift and I started to give him some room. In the first five minutes, Bobby had proven that he could drive the lane better than I could, an accolade I did not hand out often, and always grudgingly. So I played off of him, giving him some daylight to maneuver, and hoping he would take the opportunity for jump shots. He radiated with all the dangers of the penetrator, the kind that loves to kill defenses by attacking the dead center of their engines.

"Get in his face, Conroy!" Coach Thompson yelled over the noise of the crowd, but I had all I could handle with this kid. I was a Southern Conference guard trying to hold my own with a Southeastern Conference guard, and the difference was glaringly apparent. Bobby took in the whole floor in a glance, and he got the ball to the player who was open with crisp, split-second passes that landed in his teammates' hands soft as biscuits, and at that exact moment they were ready to shoot.

Bill Zinsky scored his first college goal on a short jumper he took after grabbing a long rebound. Thirty seconds later Bridges hit a long jump shot, pulling up while trailing on a fast break, his body already glistening with sweat from the frantic pace.

"Slow it down," Mel Thompson commanded. As he shouted this, Bobby Buisson swarmed all over me, his arms snake-striking all around me, trying to flick the ball away, but Bobby was operating too close, and I passed him in a flash. We raced for the basket, he closing the gap slowly with every step we took, as Auburn's center, Quick, slipped off of Danny Mohr to intercept my drive. I do not remember if Bobby fouled me or Quick or if it was Tom Perry, but whoever fouled me did it hard and made sure I did not score on the play.

I stood on the free throw line, made a sign of the cross because it irritated the Protestant boys I played against, and threw up my underhanded free throw and scored my first point of the season. When I made the next free throw, the buzzer sounded and Tee Hooper came in to replace me at guard. My role as The Citadel's starting point guard had lasted five full minutes, and we were tied 10–10 with Auburn University. The Green Weenies all stood and cheered as I took my place at the end of the bench, trying to hide my shame over having been pulled from the game so early. "I told you not to shoot, Conroy," Coach Thompson said.

I simply did not think I could endure one more season of riding the bench and watching a game that I loved more than anything in the world pass me by. My mediocrity at the game of basketball festered in me, tumored my normally buoyant spirit, tortured me into a kind of resigned submission as I considered the humiliation of spending my last season as a reserve guard. But I was not the kind of boy who would allow himself to fret or mope—that had not been my training. My teammates required my loyalty and enthusiastic championing of their play. And for the night of December 2, 1966, I was their captain, their leader on and off the floor, and I knew the power and necessity of being a team player.

So I fought the colossal disappointment of being replaced by a far more talented sophomore and got on with the business of cheering the Blue Team to victory. As Green Weenies, we never got to play much because in Mel Thompson's theories of coaching, you put your best athletes on the floor and let them win your basketball games with their superior skills. My coach did not believe in resting his best players because he never once asked to rest in his career as a center for North Carolina State. Fatigue was a form of moral cowardice to Mel, and all of his players understood that.

When Tee took my place, Bobby Buisson started to guard John DeBrosse, and the taller of the Auburn guards, Alex Howell, took on the rangy Hooper. Only when I returned to the bench did I realize how small Auburn's forwards were.

"Hell, we're bigger than those guys," I said.

"You ain't bigger than anybody, duck butt," Bob Cauthen said.

With six minutes left in the half, Danny Mohr, who was in the middle of playing a terrific game, hit three straight turnaround jump shots to pull The Citadel within three points. Taking a pass from Bridges, Tee left his man in the dust and flew through the entire Auburn team to make a beautiful, twisting layup against the glass. His layup narrowed Auburn's lead to one. Then Auburn got serious, and Bobby Buisson spent the rest of the night teaching me the great secrets of playing point guard. Watching him was like seeing Manolete demonstrate the proper use of the muleta to a Spanish boy maddened by the desire to face the great bulls in his own "suit of lights." In Bobby Buisson, I had found what I had been looking for my whole life.

In the realms of college basketball, the entire concept of the point guard was a new and developing one. I had heard the phrase used in my first summer at Camp Wahoo, but the necessity of having a guard who directed the offense and distributed the ball to the big men and the shooting guard (also a new concept) was gradually spreading around the theorists and innovators who created new wrinkles in offensive patterns and strategies. I could see that the five men on my team now on the court were, by far, the five best athletes The Citadel could field on any given night. Mohr, at center; Bridges and Zinsky at forward; DeBrosse and Hooper at guard—any one of these men was fully capable of scoring twenty points in any given game. Though it would take me four or five games to realize this, my team had one great, transparent flaw in its makeup: it lacked a point guard, a Bobby Buisson. Though John DeBrosse looked like a point guard, he was deficient when it came to possessing the proper temperament of the position. John was a shooter, pure and simple.

All five players on the court for my team were either scorers or shooters. There was not a passer among them. Bobby Buisson would begin to cut our hearts out in the second half. His utter joy in getting the ball to his hustling teammates was a besotted, almost maniacal thing. He was guarding DeBrosse so closely that Johnny was having difficulty establishing his game. Buisson was quicker, faster, and stronger than either me or DeBrosse—Auburn led by seven at the half, 50–43.

In the second half, with me and the rest of the Green Weenies in agonized witness, my Citadel team fell apart. The unraveling began with the opening tip-off. Our defense, never strong, simply collapsed under the full fury of the Auburn fast break. Auburn seemed to score on every possession. My team looked exhausted, spent, and beaten down by forces they did not seem to understand. After ten minutes, Auburn led 81–59. What had been a close and fiercely fought game turned quickly into a rout. It got so bad that Coach Thompson put me back in. Playing a desperate catch-up game, I drove the lane and scored my first 2-pointer of the season. Immediately Tee Hooper came back into the game.

"I told you not to shoot, Conroy," Mel Thompson shouted as I headed for the bench.

"Sorry, Coach," I said, noting that I had made the shot in question.

"That's your problem, Conroy," he said. "You're always sorry."

My team did not congeal as a team for the rest of the evening. Each time one of us made a move with the ball, it seemed individual, selfish, and unrelated to the other four players on the court, while Auburn was assassin-like in its delicious execution of its offense. They were a much better basketball team and much better coached, playing with brio, freshness, and unquenchable zeal.

I studied Buisson, dissecting his game and trying to steal as much as I could from him and graft his talents onto my own. First, I saw how much Buisson wanted to be there for his teammates, the joyfulness he took in delivering a pass to an open player and the gratitude they felt toward him for his childlike magnanimity. I basked in the bracing aura of his indomitable confidence. He flashed like a buccaneer across both ends of the court, brash, swashbuckling, all the elixirs of being fully alive and in control sparking off him as his team finished the joy of taking my team to the cleaners. The final score was an unbelievable 105–83.

But ah! There were bright spots for the Bulldogs. As the *News and*

*Courier* sports editor Evan Bussey would write the next morning, "Danny Mohr, The Citadel pivot man, again proved to be old Mr. Dependable in the scoring column. The 6-6 senior scored 20 points and at one stretch in the first half was about the only one holding the Citadel Bulldogs in the game. Sophomore Bill Zinsky got 16 points in his first varsity game and proved to be the best the Cadets had on the boards. He had nine rebounds.

"Doug Bridges had 15 points, DeBrosse 8, and Tee Hooper in a most impressive debut had 11."

I followed the rest of Bobby Buisson's career closely. He proved to be as good as I thought. His nickname was "Bweets," and Adolph Rupp was quoted as saying that Buisson was "one of the finest defensive players we've ever seen."

I agree.

Bobby Buisson. Wherever you are. I was an eyewitness to your mastery, the tender wizardry you brought to my home gym. I dedicated the rest of my year remaking myself in your image. It was an honor to take the court against you. I was no match for you and for that I apologize. But I took some things from your game that would hold me in good stead.

After showering, I walked in darkness behind the barracks on Plebe Walk, trying to control my shame. A second-stringer and a senior, I said, torturing myself. My season was already slipping away, and it had just started. In agony I made my way across the length of the campus alone, doomed to be a spectator while my life as an athlete went flashing past me on the fly.

Shame, I felt, the purest shame.

# PART 2

# THE MAKING OF A POINT GUARD

CHAPTER 4

# FIRST SHOT

L ET ME TAKE YOU TO THE SPOT.
In the city of Orlando, Florida, near the foul line of an outdoor court, Billy Sullivan took a pass from Gregory Rubichaud then threw it to me. "Let the new kid shoot it," he said.

I took my first shot ever at that basket in Orlando in my tenth year on earth and felt the course of my whole life change. I felt a bolt of pure wonder and joy—I had found a place I could take my terrified childhood to hide. Though I missed that first shot, I moved in fast to retrieve it and laid it in off the backboard.

"Nice shot, kid," Gregory said.

"Where you from?" Billy asked.

"Nowhere," I answered. Both boys laughed and I'd made my first friends in Orlando. They also had changed my world and place in it forever. From that first day, a basketball court provided me with a sense of home in whatever town I entered. I became a fixture on that St. James playground after school and would wait patiently until the older boys would invite me into a game or until they gave up and went home. Basketball, like a good book, gave me a place to be alone without the lacerating wounds of loneliness as an accompaniment.

I mark the year in Orlando as the happiest of my childhood. It is no accident that my father was away, spending that year on an aircraft carrier in the Mediterranean. It was a year spent fishing in a city dimpled with abundant lakes, or smelling the spiced air of my Uncle Russ's ferneries, climbing the trees of his pond-fed orchards to peel grapefruits, big as my head, with a pocket knife. Aunt Helen and Uncle Russ had a houseful of boys so an open door visitation of cousins spilled in and out of our house and theirs. We lived in a rodent-infested place on Livingston Street (with a baseball bat, I killed two rats perched on my brother Jim's crib), barely a mile from my cousins' house on North Hyer Street. It was the year I fell in love with the girl next door, Barbara Ellis, caught my first bass, became a patrol boy, and finished third in the county fifth-grade spelling bee by reversing the position of the inner *s* and *t* in the word "taste." That word still taunts me whenever I hear it. Each day, in season, I would go out and harvest an avocado lying under a tree, bringing the best one back to my mother as she sat on the front porch reading the *Orlando Sentinel*. With my pocketknife I would carve glistening, pale green crescents of the fruit and hand them to her. Mom would salt and pepper each slice, anoint them with the juice of lemons grown in the same yard, and moan with pleasure when she popped each morsel in her mouth. My mother was thirty-one that year, a knockout, and often men would wolf-whistle at her. Mom would wink at me as though she and I were conspirators who knew things the uninitiated could never know.

In November I made the fifth-grade basketball team, and in our first game the sixth grade stomped us and teased us so mercilessly that one of my teammates wept. A week later in a rematch on the same outdoor court, we lost by eight, clearly outclassed by the older boys. But in our third and final game, something happened to my little band of fifth graders that contained all the elements and seeds which go into the creation of magic in sport. There was a strange coming together when Gregory Rubichaud, the largest of the fifth graders, took me by the shoulders, stared into my eyes, and said, "We can beat these guys, Pat. You, me, and Billy Sullivan. We can beat 'em." I felt something change deep inside me.

In a hard-fought game, the fifth grade of St. James School beat the haughty sixth graders by one point. I scored the layup that won the game and felt the glorious rush of teammates trying to hug me all at once, the first taste of the ecstasy of victory, of prevailing over a better opponent.

After the game, I sprinted the mile to Livingston Street, the length of that tree-lined street, to that house, to the arms of that pretty woman who loved avocados. Bursting through the back door, I ran straight up to her, breathless and heaving, and said, "Mom! Mom! We beat the sixth grade. We really did. No one thought we could, Mom, no one! I was the high scorer. The high scorer. You've got to write Dad."

Before she could respond, I burst into tears of joy and threw myself into her arms.

My parents wrote to each other every day. That night when my younger brothers and sisters had been put to bed, I oversaw the writing of Mom's letter to Dad. I made sure that she emphasized the underdog role of my small-boned fifth-grade team and yes, the sixth-grade boys had been like a race of mean-spirited, taunting giants to me. With great care, I told Mom where I had scored each one of my points including the first foul shot I ever made. "Nine points, Mom. No one on either team scored that many. I was the high scorer."

"You've told me that a hundred times, Pat," my mother said. "That's the first thing I wrote to your father."

"Won't Dad love it, Mom? He'll just love it."

If my father loved it, he never acknowledged it in any of his many letters to my mother. He never mentioned that game until I drove him to the spot on the playground of St. James School, in 1997, and told him how we defeated the sixth-grade team. Basketball allowed me to revere my father without him knowing what I was up to. I took up basketball as a form of homage and mimicry, and like him, I grew up court-savvy and predatory and ready to rumble in any game that came my way. Though I tried to incorporate my father's big-city, Chicago-coarsened game into my own, I grew up in a South where basketball was still in a stage of infancy. I would hear his voice raised in mockery and vitupera-tion with every step I took. Dad was happy to step into the role of "the sixth grader" no matter where I went or how far I took the game I had once watched him play so uncommonly well. His greatness as a ballplayer was thrown in my face each time I achieved some new mile-stone as a player.

When my father returned from his tour of duty overseas he had a new assignment and my mother had to extract me from Orlando like a tooth. The year had been a fatherless idyll and I begged Mom to let me stay in the city with Aunt Helen and Uncle Russ and my beloved four cousins, the Harper boys. On his first day back, my father slapped my brother Mike in the face for the first time. Mike was four years old and did not realize that Dad was establishing his authority over a house that had gone soft in his absence. After he wept, Mike approached my father and said to him, "I want you to go back to the seas. I don't like you." In two sentences my brother had summoned up the courage to say out loud what I had always suppressed, and I waited for Dad to kill my brother or beat him into unconsciousness. My father surprised me by laughing as Mike shook with a four-year-old's helpless fury. I knew Mike's look and I shared his anger. My father looked like the strongest man in the world to me. When I asked Dad to come with me to the playground at St. James to shoot around before dinner, he appraised me, saying, "You come to me when you can give me a game. Then I'll kick the shit out of you."

My father had played on the Parker High School team that won the city championship in Chicago in 1938. He is still considered, by some, to be the best basketball player to attend St. Ambrose College in Davenport, Iowa, and his name hangs in its Athletic Hall of Fame. His college friend Ray Ambrose told me often that "when your father came to this part of the Midwest, everyone shot with two hands. When he left, everyone shot with one hand. Your old man brought the one-handed shot to Iowa." In a practice game against DePaul Dad outscored a young sophomore by the name of George Mikan, the first great big man in the game. George Mikan was named the best basketball player in the first fifty years of the twentieth century. The incomparable Michael Jordan took the honors over the next fifty years. My father had outscored the best basketball player of his time. "I caught Mikan young, before he became George Mikan," was all my father would say about it.

With my father's great gifts, he could've taught me everything about basketball I'd need to know, beginning that education in the schoolyard of St. James. Instead, he taught me nothing, and I went to The Citadel not knowing what a pivot was or how to block out on a rebound or how to set a pick to free a teammate for a shot or how to play defense. A beautiful shooter, a fierce rebounder, and a legendary defender, my father chose not to pass these ineffable skills on to any of his five sons. We grew up overshadowed by his legend and that legend did not lift a finger to help us toward any patch of light our own small achievements might have granted us. The Conroy boys learned their game in the streets. The Conroy girls grew up unnoticed and unpraised. Their brothers envied them.

My father pulled the '55 Chevy station wagon out of the driveway at 945 North Hyer Street as Uncle Russ and Aunt Helen stood with the four Harper boys waving a tearful goodbye to their five cousins and their favorite aunt and uncle. It was the first trip to a new assignment that we started in broad daylight. Normally, we left at midnight when the roads would be empty and we could "make good time," according to my father. He drove straight through to Arlington, Virginia, where he began a new job at the Pentagon as his family built a new life on Culpepper Street in Arlington. The Culpepper Street years were stormy ones between my parents—the only calm years they ever had was when Dad was called overseas. My mother and I had grown exceptionally close in the year he'd been gone, and now when Dad beat me it seemed like a punishment meted out for being liked too much by his wife.

But the basketball was wonderful in Virginia, with outdoor courts everywhere. Culpepper dead-ended onto the grounds of Wakefield High School, and in the first summer I shot around with a bunch of high school kids, one of whom was the son of a coach. The Wakefield gym was the first time I had ever played the game on a wooden floor or dribbled a regulation leather basketball. When the gym was closed I'd settle for an outdoor court by Claremont Elementary School. By myself, I would shoot all day, happy as a boy could be.

For three straight years, I attended Blessed Sacrament School in Alexandria and played in the church leagues from sixth through eighth grade. I did well in those leagues and was the star in my last year. Neither of my parents attended one of my games. My mother was overwhelmed with small children; my brother Tim was born in the hospital in Bethesda in December of 1957; and I was grateful my father was too overworked by his job at the Pentagon to be at my games.

It was during my Arlington years that I discovered the vast difference between the way black kids played the game of basketball and the way white kids did. The black kids would drift onto the courts near Blessed Sacrament and I would walk over to "Green Valley," the black neighborhood near Claremont where I'd be the only white kid in sight. From the beginning, I took to everything about basketball as it was played in the ghettos. It was high-speed, rough-around-the-edges, tough-talking, hand-checking, kick-ass basketball, the way the game was supposed to be played. It was hard for me to get into a game in Green Valley because I was white and because I was little. But sometimes I'd luck out and they'd need my body to complete a team. I'd get the ball to the best shooters on my team and do it quickly and often. Very early on, I learned that all shooters—black or white—value guys like me who get them the ball. I mimicked the showmanship and style of the fifty or so black kids I played against for the next three years. I loved their heart and their aggression and the fierceness of their bantering and back talk. They called me "white boy," "cracker boy," and "white fuck," as in: "Shit, we'll take the little white fuck."

The guy that called me "white fuck" was a grown man, unemployed and sad-faced, who played with the boys and young men of Green Valley because he had nothing to do and because he had a glorious jump shot, high and hanging and architecturally perfect. I fed him the ball every chance I got. When a new kid came to the court, he elbowed me, an eighth grader, in the back of the head and I went somersaulting out of bounds, sliding across concrete. The new kid walked toward me with his fists clenched and I prepared myself as well as I could for the beating. Then someone grabbed him from behind, a muscled arm around the kid's neck. "The rule, new boy. Don't fuck with the white fuck. That boy gets me the ball."

AFTER MY GRADUATION FROM Blessed Sacrament, the gypsy caravan that disguised itself as my family started up in earnest as though to punish us for our three years on Culpepper, the longest amount of time I'd ever spent on a single street (even though we had lived in two separate houses). After years of going to night school, my father had applied for the Operation Bootstrap program which sent officers whose college studies had been interrupted by the outbreak of the Second World War back to school to earn their diplomas. From far-flung sources, my father collected all the credits he'd earned at St. Ambrose and beyond and found a college that would allow him to graduate after taking a single year off from the Marine Corps.

Leaving again at night as was his habit, my father took us to the road once more, driving us down country roads through Virginia until he pulled into the driveway of the smallest house the Conroy family would ever live in, on Kees Road in Belmont, North Carolina. My father would spend the year as an undergraduate senior at Belmont Abbey College. I had only known my father in his mythological, unconquerable ideal of the Marine Corps fighter pilot so I had a difficult time making the adjustment to him as a college student who had trouble making C's. Among my brothers and sisters, we now conduct polls to discover which were Dad's worst and most violent years as a father. Belmont always ranks high on the list. It was the year my restless father had too much time on his hands.

My sister Carol became expert at excavating my father's graded essays which he went to great length to bury under his huge stack of intimidating college textbooks. Once she found an early essay from his American literature class and announced to the family: "Hey, everybody! Dad got a C– on his English paper. What a dope." I got to Carol before Dad did and sent her hightailing it to her room.

On the first day of school I walked into the comely entranceway of Sacred Heart Academy, a junior college for women with a boarding high school for girls. Several years before, the Sisters of Mercy had begun taking day students, including thirty boys from the local communities. Sacred Heart did not have enough boys to field a football or baseball team and barely enough to make up a basketball team to compete in the Catholic League of North Carolina. I followed a flow of students and found myself in the student lounge when the song "Poison Ivy" boomed out from the record player and smooth, good-looking Bud Wofford walked up to pretty Louise Howard and asked her to dance. The school was so intimate that I knew almost everyone by the end of the first week, and they knew me. I'd never seen such pretty girls, and walking down the hall of Sacred Heart was the happiest thing a ninth-grade boy could do. It was the year I would reach puberty and the last year I'd entertain my Catholic-boy fantasies of becoming a priest. The Catholic Church could fill up its seminaries if it forbade God from making women look as fabulous as they do. Even the nuns were pretty at Sacred Heart as well as being the kindest women wearing habits and rosary beads who ever taught me.

I tried out for the varsity basketball team in October and surprised even my father when Coach Ted Crunkleton chose me as his tenth player. In this school of thirty boys, the sisters of Sacred Heart had found seven neighborhood kids who could really play the game. No one was great, but all played with determination and all hustled every moment on the court. I was five feet three inches tall when I arrived at Sacred Heart and I would be five ten when the season ended in February. It was the year I grew into the body I would carry into adulthood, and my game improved at a faster rate than it ever had because I was playing against juniors and seniors every day. My teammates never teased or hazed me because of my size or age; rather, they took me in and cherished me and helped me get better in my chosen game.

The point guard was the matchlessly named Johnny Brasch who was cocksure and arrogant the way the good ones are supposed to be. He took care of the ball and directed traffic and got the ball to the guy with the hot hand. The other guard was Bud Wofford, the boy I had watched dancing on the first day of school, whose game had a touch of elegance and who possessed the best jump shot on the team. No one on the team was over six feet two inches tall; Sam Carr, Ted Frazier, and Buddy Martin made up the front line. Nicky Vlaservich was the sixth man and he and Buddy served as the team co-captains.

Though Coach Crunkleton knew very little about the game of basketball, he knew a lot about bringing a team together. He let us in on the fact that he found it a pleasure to coach us, and thought we might surprise some teams that year. In the first game of the season against Cherryville High School in their gym, we beat them so soundly that even I got into the game with a couple of minutes to play. Wofford passed me the ball at the top of the key and I threw up the first jump shot of my high school career. It swished through the net and Wofford cuffed me on the back of the head in celebration as we ran down the court.

Though the Sacred Heart Ramblers started out fast that year, we entered a phase of ennui and uninspired play in the winter months. We were 13–8 entering the Knights of Columbus Tournament in Charlotte that would bring some of the best Catholic schools in the South together, including the habitual powers Bishop England of Charleston and Benedictine of Richmond.

Coach Crunkleton prepared us for this tournament in the oddest, most unconventional way imaginable. At some time toward the end of the season, he became convinced that our team was not in shape, so he spent the week before the tournament running us up and down the country roads around Belmont. We never touched a basketball once and looked more like a cross-country team as Ted Crunkleton would call out of the window of his car, "Meet me at Belmont Abbey." Then he would scratch out of his parking spot and drive to the college to wait for us. When the team ran up to his car at the Abbey, our coach would yell out, "Meet me in Mount Holly."

"Mount Holly!" the team would scream, and our coach would

scratch off toward the small town three miles to the west. We bitched and cussed and grumbled for the next three miles. By the fifth day, Crunkleton had us doing ten miles of roadwork every afternoon and none of us touched a basketball during that crucial week leading up to the tournament. Only God's name was taken in vain more often than Crunkleton's as we jogged along country roads without a sign of life except the encroachment of impenetrable forest that crowded them.

"This isn't basketball," Bud Wofford said. "It's track and field."

"God, I could use a cigarette," Johnny Brasch said, causing the whole team to laugh.

Sam Carr said, "Let's go up to Charlotte Catholic and challenge them to a footrace."

Vlaservich and Martin led us down the back roads, upbeat and enthusiastic, and taught me how the captains of teams should act when the bellyaching got too loud. Always, Coach Crunkleton would drive to a spot several miles ahead and park his car on the shoulder of the roadway. When we would reach his parked car he'd be smoking a cigarette and would allow us to rest for five minutes. Then he'd say, "You know where that old stone quarry is? Run past that quarry and I'll meet you at the Old Gastonia Road."

With great symphonic moaning, the ten of us would start the four-mile run as Crunkleton's car disappeared in the distance. I heard every joke Johnny Brasch carried in his vast repertoire that week and I listened to tales of the greatness of Bishop England and their six-foot-eight center, Tommy Lavelle, and the classiness of the undefeatable Cavaliers of Benedictine of Richmond who had won the Knights of Columbus tournament for two straight years. To my freshman ears the names "Bishop England" and "Benedictine of Richmond" sounded much like the words "Troy" and "Sparta" would sound to an Athenian child in ancient Greece. The Sacred Heart Ramblers ran in good order the four miles past the stone quarry and toward Ted Crunkleton's car that sat on a slight rise beside a farmhouse on the Old Gastonia Road. Though none of us knew it on that final run on Friday, we were about to surprise our school, our coach, our league, and ourselves.

In a dangerous ride through snow, we arrived at Charlotte Catholic just in time to get dressed for our game with Asheville Catholic. Though we had beaten Asheville Catholic twice during the regular season, both games had been closely contested, and their point guard, Jerry Vincent, was one of the best players in the league. I received a shock to my system when Coach announced that I would start the game in place of Buddy Martin, who had hurt his hand over the weekend and was in a cast. It embarrassed me to be starting when both of our co-captains, whom I hero-worshiped, were sitting on the bench watching me. Yet it was Martin and Vlaservich who slapped my fanny hardest when we gathered for the final pep talk by the bench.

"We've got a great team here," Coach Crunkleton said. "I've known that all year long. Let's prove it to ourselves and everyone else."

When we walked out on the court and I shook hands with Jerry Vincent, it surprised me that I was taller than he was. When Johnny Brasch came over to encourage me, I saw that I was an inch taller than Johnny. Our center, Sam Carr, controlled the tap and Ted Frazier made a jump shot for our first basket. Vincent answered with a jump shot from the top of the key. Despite their two losses to us, Asheville Catholic had come to play. Jerry Vincent played a smart swift game and his teammates lifted up with him to play their finest basketball of the season. I drifted through the first quarter, surprised to be there, feeling inadequate to fill the shoes of our co-captain Bud Martin. Then Carr took down a rebound, hit Wofford on the wing, who threw me a half-court pass after I slipped behind my man and took off downcourt. Bud's pass was perfect and I took it over my shoulder, dribbled once, and laid the ball in. Running back downcourt, I passed our bench and both Martin and Vlaservich popped me on the fanny as I ran past them.

In the second, third, and fourth quarters of the game against Asheville Catholic, something happened that had never occurred to me before in sport. I lost all sense of myself in the great tidal movements of the game itself, in the thrusts and retreats, the surges and falling back of teams rapturously engaged in a sublime submission to their game. I began taking long shots on the wing, half jump shots–half set shots, and I arched them high in the air and they came down without much backspin. The shots were without artfulness or beauty or much hope behind them. So high did I arch them, that they hung in the air for a long segment of time, then fell like fruit from the sky. They swished through the basket with the sound of torn fabric. I hit three in a row toward the end of the second quarter. In the fourth quarter I hit another three and my game had shifted into a high plane where it had never gone before.

It took two overtimes to defeat the gallant team from Asheville

Catholic. Frazier and Carr, our two big rebounders, pulled the game out for us in final overtimes. Ted Frazier and I had both scored fourteen points and were high scorers. I looked up in time to see my father entering the gym with a busload of Rambler boosters he had driven to the game. My father had gotten lost in the snow and had found himself pulling his bus up to the campus of Queens College instead of Charlotte Catholic High School. He did not see me score a single point but my joy was so great I wanted to freeze-frame that moment of time and suspend myself in the honeycomb amber of that sublime moment.

The next afternoon, before a packed house, the Sacred Heart Ramblers took on the Cougars of Charlotte Catholic, the big-city team that had beaten us twice during the regular season, and we beat them by four points. After showering and dressing, my team sat together and watched the other semifinal game where the two most powerful Catholic schools in our part of the Southeast were about to take to the floor against each other. Bishop England of Charleston lined up against Benedictine of Richmond, which had a powerhouse athletic program that chose its athletes from five hundred Virginia boys. But it was only minutes into the game when we knew that Benedictine of Richmond was going to overrun Bishop England with its superior depth and firepower and speed. Bishop England went down by a score of 64–41, and I knew we did not belong on the same floor with mighty Benedictine of Richmond.

The next morning, the hallways of Sacred Heart shimmered with an excitement that was almost chemical in nature. Even the college nuns and coeds had caught fire with the improbable story of the thirty-boy high school competing against the largest Catholic school in the South, a high school power that looked all but unstoppable.

As I dressed for the game, I could feel the sudden paralysis come over me that terror brings to an inexperienced athlete's body. I'd experienced butterflies before, but nothing like this. I felt like vomiting all during the warmup period. The Benedictine Cadets looked every inch like the Boston Celtics warming up. They appeared to be three inches taller than us and carried themselves with an arrogant grace that let you know that playing us was a kind of insider's joke to them. They laughed and cut up on the sidelines. We were as serious as a quadratic equation, but I was the only one on our team who seemed afraid.

My first prayer to God that day was to thank him for healing Buddy

Martin's right hand. My knees were shaking on the bench as I watched Sam Carr jump center against their big man. It took about five minutes of a game played with extraordinary intensity for Benedictine to know they were in a game and at least another minute to realize they were in the fight of their lives. One minute Wofford would have the hot hand and the next Carr would distinguish himself, or the pure hustle of Martin would carry the day or the heart of Sam Carr or the tenacity of Nicky Vlaservich. Together, they blended so effortlessly that if a team stopped one player cold they lit a fire beneath another on another part of the court. But on this night, Benedictine had more than it could handle from the chain-smoking, tough-talking little point guard, Johnny Brasch.

Though not a great jump shooter, Brasch lit it up with long-range jumpers all night long to the ecstatic cheering of the entire community of Sacred Heart who filled the gym to capacity. Every nun from the convent had come over with my father in the school bus and their cheering section looked like a lost colony of emperor penguins.

When we went ahead by eleven points, Benedictine went into a blanketing full-court zone press. I knew we were in trouble the moment they moved their players all over the court. Their guards Meyer and Berry started stealing the ball frequently from our guards. They began cutting into our lead and I saw Coach Crunkleton giving me the eye. But with a minute and a half left, Bud Wofford fouled out of the game and I heard the coach call my name. After I reported to the scorer's table, I ran out to the court and took my position up against Jimmy Meyer.

By then, Johnny Brasch had taken over the game. He had assumed for himself all dribbling and scoring duties and let everyone else on the team know that he could do it, that he could pull us through and win the game for us. He came up to me, put his arm around me, and said, "Take the ball out of bounds, Pat. Get it to me. Then head up the court. If I get in trouble, come back to help me. Got it?"

I did what Johnny Brasch asked me to do. I got him the ball because I did not want it and lacked the courage to take the ball upcourt. My fear disgusted me but it consumed me. Brasch fought the whole Benedictine team and held them off all by himself. He broke the full-court press, with the help of no one. Once Meyer and Berry surrounded me when I received a pass and took it away from me with dispiriting ease and scored an open layup. I took it out of bounds and fed it into Brasch, who took the ball downcourt with everyone on the Benedictine team trying to stop him. He was heroic and magnificent and I fell to my knees and kissed the floor when the final buzzer sounded and we had prevailed 53–52 in the greatest upset in high school basketball in North Carolina that season. We carried Johnny Brasch off the floor, delirious with joy.

After my father had dropped off the nuns and students at Sacred Heart, he drove home in the bus with me standing up front beside him. His great dark interior disturbed the silence between us, and I knew better than to chatter when he had gone inward and his mood had darkened.

"You were afraid today, weren't you?" Dad said.

"Yes, sir, a little bit," I said.

"I could tell you were chickenshit and didn't want to go into the game," he said.

"I didn't want to lose it for us, Dad."

I did not see the slap coming, but its long looping arc caught me squarely on the mouth and I would have fallen into the well of the bus if I had not caught myself on one of the poles.

"Never be chickenshit on a basketball court again," Dad said. "That's an order, pal."

"Yes, sir." On the short ride home I promised to turn myself into a player who is reliant and impudent and highfalutin—I swore I'd be a guy my team could depend on, someone who could calm their fears and strike terror into the hearts of the enemy. From that day forward whenever I saw an opposing team go into a full-court press, I would call for the basketball and tell my teammates to get downcourt. By an effort of will and memory, I would turn myself into a Johnny Brasch.


WHEN MY FATHER RECEIVED his orders to report to the Marine Corps Advanced Amphibious Warfare Course at Quantico, Virginia, I broke down in front of my mother and raced into the woods behind our house where I wept for an hour. I loved everything about Sacred Heart Academy and was inconsolable at the thought of leaving such a blithe, sun-shot hermitage for the unknown. Though I had moved throughout my childhood, I'd never done it as a high school student and no community had ever enfolded me into its sweet, sufficient embrace the way Sacred Heart had done. My mother found me by following my dog,

Chippie, through the woods. Chippie licked the tears from my face and my mother sat down beside me and waited for me to compose myself.

"America needs a fighter pilot," my mother said. "It's this family's job to provide them with one."

"You tell me that every time we move," I said.

"It's true every time," she said.

"I could live with Bobby McDonnell's parents. Or Paul Ford's. Or Hal Van Pelt's. Bill Thomas's mother seems to really like me. I could ask her, Mom," I said.

"We're your family. You belong with us," my mother said. "You'll be gone soon enough anyway."

"Where will I go to school? Where will we live?"

"We'll be going back to the D.C. area," she said. "You'll go to some Catholic high school. We don't know which one yet."

"Great. I'll walk into a totally new school. I won't know a living soul. They won't know me. Finally, I'll make a few friends, then Dad'll get orders again and gee, guess what? I'm at another new school and I don't know anybody."

"I bet this is our last move before you go off to college," Mom said. "Let's be upbeat about this thing. I'll bet Dad gets a big Pentagon job after this and you'll be at the same school for three straight years."

"What choice do I have, Mom?" I asked, rising to my feet.

"None, Pat. But you know that. You're the son of a Marine. You grew up in the corps. You're going to suck it up. Make the best of it."

When we left Belmont at night, I was in mourning for the three years I would not spend at Sacred Heart. All moves had caused great sadness in me; I felt like I was being kidnapped out of my own life. I would never be fourteen again. Nor would I ever be a champion again.

My father drove toward Washington, D.C., and my appointment with the Jesuits and Gonzaga High School.

# CHAPTER 5

# GONZAGA HIGH SCHOOL

T HROUGHOUT MY NUN-SPOOKED, CATHOLIC SCHOOL LIFE, I HAD
heard and digested the urban legend of the Jesuits, the rottweilers
of a Catholic boy's education. The order had a reputation for intellectual ferocity and suffering fools lightly or not at all. They were a warrior
caste of the intellect, famous for the rigor of both their training and their
teaching. Founded by St. Ignatius Loyola as militant advocates of the
Pope, the Jesuits have always prided themselves on their fierce reputation as cunning foot soldiers of the far-ranging, free-thinking Catholic
mind. Astuteness, acumen, and razor-sharp perceptions were virtues in
the high precincts of the Jesuit world.

So began my one year I spent learning the desperate melancholy of
the commuters baby-stepping their way into the big cities. That was the
year I knew the sadness of inbound traffic when I saw Shirley Highway
slowing into gridlock each morning at 5:30, when the Marine who lived
across the street from us would find me waiting in his car each morning.
He'd turn on the *Eddie Gallagher Show* and we'd listen to the news and
good music for the fifteen congested miles it'd take us to drive to the
Naval Annex. The ride took exactly two hours, at which time the good
major would deposit me on the sidewalk in front of the Annex. I would
catch a bus to Twelfth and Penn, then transfer to another one that would
take me to the corner of North Capitol and I Street. My days among
Jesuits, like Gaul, were divided into three parts: three hours to get there,
three hours to get back, and three hours of the homework the Jesuits
proudly crowed that they saddled their students with each night. Soon I
found myself trapped in days that had too much of everything except time.

My memories of Sacred Heart Academy shine in a pearly light;

Gonzaga suggests far harsher tones. A dark sensuality and a celebration of the masculine virtues as tribal rites inhabited each corner and room of that beleaguered, ghetto-encircled school. Everything was tough about Gonzaga, including its neighbors. The Jesuits possessed a genius at making learning itself seem like a martial art. Before I met the Jesuits, I'd never encountered another group who thought that intellect and arrogance were treasures beyond price and necessities in waging wars against blasphemers, heretics, and the many faces of Protestantism itself. At Gonzaga I always felt as if I should be wearing a coat of armor instead of a coat and tie. The school taught Latin as though it was sorry it was not Greek, and Greek as though it was sorry it was not Mesopotamian. The paint was so drab that each classroom looked like it could have served as a holding cell for Galileo. The hallways stank with boy sweat and boy fear and candlewax with a light touch of incense leaking out of the church, and old Jesuits shuffling along in cassocks both shiny under the armpits and late to the dry cleaners. The whole school smelled like eau de Catholic boy, cheap pipe tobacco, and stiff drinks on the rocks. Gonzaga was the kind of place you'd not even think about loving until you'd left it for a couple of years.

I took one crown jewel from my Jesuit immersion at Gonzaga High School. When the scholarly, charismatic Joseph Monte walked into 2A that first day, he radiated an owl-like authority and a passion for literature I'd never come across in a classroom. The way he talked about fiction must have been similar to the post-Pentecostal apostles spreading the word of God. He brought his love of books and words and fine writing to us every day of that year, and he thunderstruck me with the mesmerizing power of his teaching. He came into my life as a rose window onto the world of literature. He opened me up to the pleasures of Greek tragedy, Shakespeare, Faulkner, and dozens of others. The first book I read for Mr. Monte for extra credit was *History of the Peloponnesian War* by Thucydides, the second was *David Copperfield*, and the third was *The Sun Also Rises* by Hemingway. Each time you finished a book you would have to find Mr. Monte to discuss the intricacies of that book with him. He gave off the aura of having read every book worth reading since Gutenberg invented the printing press.

"Read the great books, gentlemen," Mr. Monte said one day. "Just the great ones. Ignore the others. There's not enough time."

"How will we know the great ones?" Chris Warner asked behind me.

Mr. Monte shot Mr. Warner a look that was part bemusement and part contempt. "Ask me, Mr. Warner. Show a modicum of intelligence in these things."

In November, Mr. Monte suggested I read *The Sound and the Fury*. I took the book home and began reading it with enormous anticipation because I could sense Mr. Monte's reverence when he spoke about the pleasures of Faulkner, and he considered this his masterpiece. When I read the first ninety-two pages, I fretted, then despaired because it felt like I was reading the book underwater or weightless in outer space. I was not sure I understood a single line or had the slightest clue about where the book was tending or drifting. Shaken, I reread the same ninety-two pages that begin with the sentence of the curling flower spaces and ends with Benjy in Caddy's arms. The second reading left me even more panic-stricken and perplexed.

When I approached Mr. Monte in the cafeteria, I told him I was not yet smart enough to read Faulkner, that I had not understood a single syllable of the first part. Mr. Monte took off his glasses, cleaned them with a handkerchief, smiled, then said, "Mr. Conroy, how familiar are you with the works of Shakespeare?"

"I read *Twelfth Night* last year," I answered. "I read *Julius Caesar* in your class."

"Do you know where Mr. Faulkner's title came from, Mr. Conroy?"

"No, sir. I have no idea."

"Sometimes literature is direct and straightforward," Mr. Monte said. "Sometimes it makes you work and expand your mind. Mr. Faulkner has given you a clue in the title. Go to Act 5, Scene 4 of *Macbeth*. There you will find the key to your dilemma, if, Mr. Conroy, you're the student I think you are."

I rushed to the library and walked straight to the Shakespeare section and removed a copy of *Macbeth* from the shelf. Sitting down in one of the straight-backed wooden chairs I turned quickly to Act 5, Scene 4, where I read the words of Malcolm spoken to Monteith. Although I was lost in a play I had seldom heard of, the words of these unknown and fictional men rang true to me and I found them easy to understand. Then I came to the entrance of the sexton announcing to Macbeth that his queen was dead. When I read the words I did not know that the queen was his wife or that Lady Macbeth was an immemorial fictional creation. I did not know I was nearing the end of one of the great tragedies ever conceived. But I found the answer to Mr. Monte's question in Macbeth's heartbreaking response to the news of Lady Macbeth's death. Word for word, I wrote that speech down in the spiral notebook Mr. Monte made us keep in his class. As I copied the last line of that speech, I felt like one of those forty-niners who pan for gold in rushing western streams for years, until they reach the summary and defining moment of their gambled-out lives and lift a pan from the ungenerous stream brimming with a king's ransom of gold. I thought about the first section of *The Sound and the Fury* and I thought about Macbeth's speech when he hears the news of his queen's death. I put them together. I unlocked the mystery.

The next day I approached Mr. Monte again. His great reserve made it difficult to draw close to him, but I thought I carried the goods he wanted delivered.

"Do you have something for me, Mr. Conroy?" he asked.

"I think I do, Mr. Monte." I opened my notebook.

"Do not waste a moment of my time, sir," he said, his eyes twinkling. "If you have something, show it now. Out, out with it, Mr. Conroy. Why did I choose that phrase?"

"Macbeth says, 'Out, out, brief candle,' when he hears about the queen's death."

"What does he mean by that, Mr. Conroy?"

"How short life is, sir," I said.

"What does that tell you about Mr. Faulkner's book?"

"Nothing, sir. It's later in the speech. When Macbeth says, 'It is a tale told by an idiot, full of sound and fury, signifying nothing.' That's why I was confused, Mr. Monte. I was reading a tale told by the idiot, Benjy. It was surfaces and shadows and what Benjy thought he was seeing. Faulkner was writing through Benjy's eyes . . . through an idiot's eyes."

Mr. Monte opened his grade book, which he carried with him everywhere, and he entered a notation beside my name. "A+, double credit, Mr. Conroy. This is a good moment in the life of your mind. It's a good moment in my life as a teacher. We should both cherish it."

Goose bumps marched the length and breadth of my body and the back of my neck tingled as I knew for the first time that learning itself could carry the sting of divine inextinguishable pleasure. Joseph Monte could make the intellect look like the most lustrous and forbidden city of all. After my single year with Monte, I wanted to be curious and smart and unappeasable until I got a sentence to mean exactly what I ordered it to mean. Whenever I wrote an essay in that spiral notebook that he checked once a week, I tried to show off for Mr. Monte, distinguish myself from my classmates in a unique way. I took off on one boilerplate English assignment and wrote what I now realize was my first short story. When I turned the story in, I spent an uncomfortable weekend thinking that Mr. Monte would consider me pretentious or worse for not following the assignment literally. When he passed out the notebooks the following Monday, I turned to the story, breathless, and saw this notation: "More of this, Mr. Conroy. A+, double credit. For imagination."

Monte rubbed my face in his theory of great teaching. It was oxygen, water, and fire to me. I could not get enough of it; I could not get enough of him. Before I left his class, he passed out a list of great books that he'd compiled. "I've put down one hundred novels it would behoove you to read before you go to college. The scoundrels and ne'er-do-wells among you will toss it in the trash before you leave today. But for those of you with a faint pilot light flickering in the stove, it might offer you a path to enlightenment."

Before I left for college, I had marked all one hundred of those Monte-championed books off my list. Joseph Monte hit me like an ice storm, and I still think that great teacher was sent into my life by God who saw the directionless, blemished slide my life was taking in my disfigured household. The great teachers fill you up with hope and shower you with a thousand reasons to embrace all aspects of life. I wanted to follow Mr. Monte around for the rest of my life, learning everything he wished to share or impart, but I didn't know how to ask. All I knew was, I was not the same boy who walked into Gonzaga that previous fall.

In November I had gone out for the junior varsity basketball team, drawing down the wrath of my father who wanted me to try out for the varsity. I explained to him that only one sophomore had been invited to try out for the varsity and only because he had excelled on the freshman team the year before. Coach Mike DeSarno cut the JV team down to sixteen and I breathed a sigh of pure gratitude when I saw my name on the list. There was no scene I dreaded more than that imaginary one where I'd have to return to my house to inform my father I'd been cut from a team.

By making that JV, I began the hardest and least manageable part of my Gonzaga experience. The freshman basketball team started their practice at four in the afternoon, followed by the varsity at five, then followed by my JV team at six. When practice ended at seven, I walked to Union Station to take a train into Alexandria where my father would meet me every evening at eight o'clock for a twenty-minute ride to our house in Annandale.

Before practice I would often go to the National Gallery of Art to do homework on one of the benches in one of the garden rooms. Admission was free and soon the guards grew accustomed to my presence as I did my Latin and algebra and biology homework amidst the palms and the sound of falling water. If I finished my homework early or just grew bored, I could wander through the galleries, studying the paintings and trying to memorize the names of the artists who painted them. So often did I come to their gallery during basketball season that year, that whenever I return as a grown man, it has the feel of a homecoming to me.

It was not a successful year for me as a basketball player, nor was it a total bust either. The squad I played on was a very good one, and all sixteen of us could play the game at a fairly high level. It was the most evenly matched team I was ever a part of, but we could not seem to find our identity. My coach, the itchy, unreadable Mike DeSarno, was a man more comfortable with football than basketball. He carried himself with great authority, was careful in his grooming and dress, and ran a quick and efficient practice. When Coach DeSarno shot the basketball, he displayed exceptional style and form, his mechanics were flawless, but the ball almost never went into the basket.

The team was explosive and erratic. DeSarno told us all year long that we had the makings of a great team. He could never make up his mind about a starting lineup, and we had a dizzying series of changes over the year. I started a third of the games, but DeSarno would always taunt me with the fact that I was a military brat who could disappear overnight.

"Conroy, what does Gonzaga get out of it? I mean, I could be playing a kid who'll be here for four years instead of one. I'm making you a better basketball player for another school that neither of us even knows about. Argue with me. Tell me where I'm wrong."

"My parents think I'll be here three years, Coach," I said.

"Can you promise me that?" Coach DeSarno said. "Can you put it on paper?"

"No, sir. We might go to war or something."

"Then I can't start you. Do you understand? I'm hurting the school down the road. You can understand that?"

"Yes, sir," I said, trying to disguise my misery.

DeSarno was generous in allowing his overstocked team adequate playing time, and he ran us in and out of games. We ended up wearing down those understaffed teams who depended on the stamina of a starting five. Our talent was evenly distributed and we played well together even though we lost our big games by shockingly close scores. We lost to DeMatha, on its way to becoming a national power in high school basketball, by two points, and to our archrival, St. John's, by a single point.

After our loss to DeMatha, Coach DeSarno singled me out in a team meeting after the game and said, "I'd like to apologize personally to Pat Conroy for taking him out of the game after the first quarter. He was playing a hell of a game. But I kept thinking of next year, Pat, and we don't know whether you'll be back or not. The old story." I had scored eight points in the first quarter of the game when DeSarno replaced me with Buzzy Vail. His doubts about my availability were prophetic.

The following month I was in my room catching up on the voluminous homework that was the scourge of every Gonzaga boy's existence when my mother knocked on the door.

"Could we have a talk, Pat?" She was carrying my infant brother, Tom, who'd been born in October.

I read her face and said, "No, Mom. Not again. I can't move again. I won't do it. You can't make me."

"The good news is that we're going to Cherry Point," my mother said. "You've always loved Cherry Point."

IN THE BEGINNING OF MAY, my father came into the city for the annual father-son banquet and the awarding of letters to Gonzaga's athletes. Gonzaga had become my home and I wanted my father to see for himself how easy I was navigating its hallways and shortcuts. I gave him a brief tour of my domain, even taking him down to the grotesque basketball court, a converted swimming pool, that was, by far, the worst gymnasium I ever saw. I walked him up to 2A, a room I had fallen in love with, and introduced him to all the teachers he had heard me talk about during the year.

My father's mood was withdrawn and saturnine that night, and he resented my perpetual sunniness. We ate dinner among the other fathers and sons without Dad directing a single word to me or to any of the fathers. He brought a closed shop to that banquet and I put a quietus on my own ebullience when I saw his blue eyes go arctic.

After the banquet, the crowd moved toward the school's compact auditorium where the athletes were seated in the fifteen front rows with our fathers seated behind us. The Jesuits possessed a gift for both order and organization, and each athlete had been given a number which told us where we'd be seated during the ceremony. I found a piece of paper with the number 63 taped to the back of the chair that corresponded to the number I carried in my hand. I sat down between Chris Warner and my basketball teammate Tim McCarthy.

When Father McHale, the headmaster, finished his opening remarks, Father Coleman walked up to the front row and barked, "First row of athletes, please rise." The first row, led by the now-famous William Bennett, walked up to the side steps of the stage, then walked across the stage one by one as Father McHale called their names and presented them with their letters.

Finally, the line of boys sitting directly in front of me were ordered to stand and they responded. A Gonzaga boy sitting to my right, next to Warner, deftly took one of the taped numbers from the seat in front of him and attached it to the bottom of the sports coat of the unwary sophomore who stood with his back to us. Gonzaga boys were famous for their tireless pranks on one another, and this seemed innocent enough. Chris and Tim and I laughed when we saw the poor kid walking toward the stage trailing his seat number behind him.

The evening had turned so tedious that no one expected the guffaws and explosive laughter that broke through the audience when this kid walked across the stage with a white tail fluttering around his buttocks. All the Jesuits' love of control collapsed when the absurd little practical joke caught the audience by surprise. The young man shot the audience a Chaplinesque look of bewilderment, the laughter increasing when Father McHale said something about his unauthorized tail piece. The boy looked behind him and saw nothing and kept spinning around until Father McHale ripped it off and dangled it before the embarrassed boy's eyes. Father McHale then barked at us to settle down, and the rest of the awards ceremony moved with swiftness. I received my two junior varsity letters for football and basketball and felt great pride as I examined them after returning to my seat.

When Father McHale offered final congratulations and dismissed us, I joined the slow procession of boys who drifted down the center aisle to join our fathers in the back of the theater. Moving slowly with the other student athletes up the carpeted rise toward the milling fathers, I was talking to a boy on my left when I received a stunning backhand across my right jaw that sent me crashing to the floor. The blow was delivered with such force that I did not know if I was going to be able to rise, but a furor had taken hold of the men above me. There was shouting and pushing and obscenities. Slowly, I rose off my knees and stood up on unsteady legs, disoriented, humiliated, and confused by where the blow had come from and why. "Are you okay, Pat?" a father asked me, and I smiled and nodded my head, knowing for the first time that any Gonzaga father knew my name. The second backhand caught me on the left jaw, harder than the first, and I went down to the floor again. Then a free-for-all began.

I looked up from the floor and saw my father being tossed around like a Raggedy Ann doll. Gonzaga was a tough, ethnic, inner-city school and many of our fathers were blue-collar, working-class men—big Irishmen, Poles, and Italians—who were making their hard way in America. They had no idea who my father was and did not care. They saw a stranger knock a Gonzaga boy to his knees and came roaring to my defense. Someone punched my father in the back of the head; if I'd known who that man was I'd have sent him brownies every Valentine's Day. I struggled to my feet, grabbed my father's arm, and led him through that angry mob of men, getting him safely to the parking lot and into his car.

It was in this car and on this night that my father took me apart. He gave me a beating like none other I would receive in my childhood. "It was you who taped that number on that kid's ass!" he yelled.

"No, it wasn't, Dad. It was another kid. I swear I didn't do it." His fist landed so hard on my forehead that I thought the back of my head would go through the passenger-side window. Again, he punched my face and I covered up as he began raining blows all over my body. He beat me until he grew tired of it. "You shouldn't have laughed," he said. Then he started the car and drove home to Annandale, and I never came out of my rolled-up crouch until he sent my mother out to the car to get me. She had to peel my arms and hands away from my head. I was hysterical when I heard her voice, and Mom screamed when she saw my face. She refused to let me go to school for the next few days and would not let me show myself to my brothers and sisters. I ate in my room and caught up with my homework and wondered if a son ever hated a father as much as I hated mine.

Ten days before graduation, Father Anthony McHale summoned me to his office. I had come to know McHale only slightly, but he recognized me in the hallway and sometimes he would stop me to quiz me about my progress in Latin or algebra. He had a great sense of justice and duty, but lacked that leavening one of humor. When I entered his office, he was studying my file. He looked up at me and said, "You've made your mark here at Gonzaga, Mr. Conroy. I didn't think you'd survive first semester. You're well thought of by your fellow students. Your coaches and teachers speak well of you. Mr. Monte speaks highly of you. We have decided to award you a full scholarship for the next two years. We understand your parents are moving out of the area. We'll arrange for your room and board."

That night, I heard my parents arguing. Later I heard a tap on my door, then my mother tiptoed into my room. She said, "Your father ripped up the scholarship, Pat. He said Gonzaga or no one else is going to steal his kid from him. He loves you too much to let you go."

"No, Mom," I said coldly and in despair. "He hates me too much to let me go. He hates it when good things happen to me."

"Your father wants the very best for you, Pat. He always has and he always will."

After the moving van left in June and headed down the highway toward our new quarters at the Cherry Point Marine Corps Air Station, my mother locked up the empty house and walked toward the station wagon, laden down with excess baggage and seven kids. Halfway to the car, a phone rang in the empty house, and my mother ran back to answer it. She returned to the car and said to my father, "It's for you, Don. Headquarters Marine's calling."

The children grew restless in the fifteen minutes Dad spoke to the unseen Marine who was in the process of changing all of our lives. When he returned to the car, Dad started up the engine and began backing out of the driveway.

"What did he want, Don?" my mother asked.

"My orders have been changed," he said as Carol and I both groaned aloud. "Shut up, you two," he demanded.

"Where are we going to be living next year?" my mother asked in a calm, measured voice.

"Beaufort, South Carolina," he said.

"I've never heard of Beaufort, South Carolina," Carol groaned.

"It's where Parris Island is," Dad said. "They built an air station there a couple of years ago."

"Do they have a high school there?" I asked.

"Have no idea, pal," Dad said as he moved the car out toward Shirley Highway and headed south, away from Gonzaga High School forever.

# CHAPTER 6

# BEAUFORT HIGH

A CONVERSATION OCCURRED WITH MY MOTHER SOMEWHERE ON THE road between Cherry Point and the Beaufort Air Station. The family had left my father behind to clear up some paperwork connected with his change of orders. My mother knew I was close to despair and was doing everything in her power to make the transition into Beaufort easier. That I seemed inconsolable only made her more determined to ease the pain of the transfer.

"Mark my words," Mom said, "this move'll be the best thing that ever happened to you. Didn't you love Gonzaga?"

"Yes, ma'am."

"Didn't you love Sacred Heart?"

"Yes, ma'am."

"You'll love Beaufort most of all," she said with great authority.

"I won't know one single kid when I walk into Beaufort High School," I said.

"Here's what I'd do, if I were you, son," she said. "I'd go up to every kid there and say, 'Hey there. My name's Pat Conroy and I'm new here. How about showing me some of the ropes?'"

"I'm a teenager, Mom," I said. "I'd feel like an idiot doing that."

"You'd be taking the bull by the horns. You'd be mastering your own fate."

"I'd be making sure I didn't have a friend in the world," I answered.

She thought about it, then said, "I'm trying to help you come up with a plan."

"I could've stayed at Gonzaga. That was my plan."

"Now you need a new one. One you can live with."

"Mom, do you know I didn't talk to a single girl last year? I've never danced or held hands with a girl, much less kissed one."

"Plenty of time for all that," my mother said. "Here's my advice. Go into Beaufort and tell yourself: This is my home. We'll be here for two years. Make this town your own. I know how much you've missed having a home. Make Beaufort your home. You deserve one and need one."

The family station wagon, laden with Conroy children and one black dog named Chippie, crossed the Combahee River into Beaufort County and a new life. When we crossed the Whale Branch Bridge, I pointed to the green fringes along the river and asked, "What's that stuff, Mom? The green stuff?"

"That's called marsh," she said. "The Great Salt Marsh."

"It's pretty."

"That's my boy," she said. "That's putting a happy face on things."


THE SUMMER FELT MUCH LIKE being buried alive as the temperatures outside our Capehart house, 138 Laurel Bay Boulevard in base housing, climbed to a hundred degrees around noon. It seemed like a pickling process, a salting down that made my skin feel like beef jerky after I mowed the grass or even took the garbage out in the late evening. All summer, I did not meet another teenager, and even worse, the one basketball court at the air station was closed for repairs. Even my game was stolen from me that first summer in Beaufort.

In August, I was preparing to try out for the football team at Beaufort High School after my father had first reconciled himself to the fact that I'd never graduate from a Catholic high school. One of my father's brothers, the diminutive Uncle Willie, came to visit us, and my duty was to entertain Willie by taking him golfing or fishing. Uncle Willie was a terrible golfer, and no low-country fish was endangered when he cast his bait into the water, either.

At dinner that night, my seven-year-old brother, Jimbo, asked permission then raced outside to play before dark. The rest of the family continued eating while Uncle Willie told my father about every hole of golf he and I'd played. Willie was not a gifted weatherman of my father's stormy moods so my uncle had no idea that his voice was grating on my father's nerves like a noisemaker. As Willie got to the only par he shot all day, at the twelfth hole, there was a knock on the window outside the dining area. It was my brother Jimbo, climbing the tree outside, waving happily to his still-seated family. The younger brothers and sisters laughed and waved back until my father barked, "Knock it off. You're gonna get hurt, Jimbo."

Jim climbed higher. Then, hanging by his legs from a branch on the tree, he knocked at the window with an impish grin, happy showing off for his family—until the branch broke and Jim disappeared from sight, landing on his head. All of us froze when we heard his screams, and he came running into the house with his nose and lips bleeding, rushing into my mother's arms. Desperately, my mother tried to quiet my hurt brother, but her frantic efforts at damage control were fruitless. My father called out in a voice of cold rage, "Get over here, Jimbo. I knew that was going to happen."

Jim's crying grew louder and more frightened as he approached my father, for good reason. Everyone in the room, with the possible exception of Uncle Willie, knew what was coming next. My sister Carol and I had recently written a play satirizing the Conroy family dynamics. Carol had rechristened us the Bon-Bonroy family, and in one scene, she had a bawling infant being slapped around by Colonel Bon-Bonroy for the treasonous act of crying within the earshot of an American officer.

"Stop your boo-hooing," Dad ordered, then slapped Jim hard across his still bleeding face. Where before Jim wept because he was hurt, now he screamed out of the shock and terror of my father's assault. My mother began screaming at my father and I kept my eyes fixed on my plate as an old pandemonium began gathering its strange magnetic powers, its unpredictable dance around my family.

Carol, who sat on my father's left, had turned her back on him, her face inches from mine, when I saw her red-faced and grimacing trying to contain her laughter. She was straining so hard to cut off a guffaw that she looked comical and grotesque at the same time. We both knew she was dead meat if Dad caught her laughing at him while he waged his war on one of his kids.

It was not Carol who laughed.

It was me, and it came bellowing out from deep within, from an uncharted and forbidden place. The belly laugh caught everyone in the room by surprise, especially me, since the act seemed suicidal and lunatic. In horror I saw my father staring at me with his furious blue eyes. I watched him lift his full iced-tea glass and hurl it at me with the same motion a major-league pitcher employs when he delivers a pitch high and tight to a cleanup batter. He was less than five feet away when he threw the glass. I still do not know if it shattered against my left brow bone or when it hit the table.

I put both hands over my eyes, blood pouring through the fingers of my left hand, and I heard my mother's voice. "Nice going, Don. You've blinded him."

In the chaos that followed I remember nothing except my mother screaming at my uncle. "That's it, Willie, skulk out of here and pretend you didn't see what happened!"

The next memory I can pull out of that lost night is the sound of my mother's voice composed, even serene, as she drove me to the naval hospital emergency room. I was holding a bloody dishrag over my gashed eyebrow.

"Okay, Pat, here's the story, what we tell the doctor. We're going to run through the details a couple of times to make sure we have them down. You know that exposed water spigot that sticks out of the ground between our yard and Colonel Penn's?"

"Yes, ma'am," I said.

"Well, the whole family was playing a spirited game of touch football. Just like the Kennedys. In fact, I'd mention the Kennedys. It gives the story believability. So we're involved in this game and your father breaks away from Uncle Willie and Mike, and you're the only one who can prevent your dad from scoring. So you leap to put a tag on him, forgetting the water spigot. That thing's such a hazard anyway. I've called base housing about it twice already. You slid into that water spigot and cut your eyebrow. Okay, let's go over it. What game was the family playing?"

"A touch football game," I said, my voice mocking. "A spirited one."

"Get rid of that tone, young man," my mother said. "This is serious business."

"Why don't I tell him that my father hit me with a tea glass after my little brother fell out of a tree?"

"Don't play cute with me, young man," she said. "If your father ever got picked up by the MPs for hitting his wife or child, that would mean the end of his career. We wouldn't have a roof over our heads or a pot to pee in. We'd be out on the streets without a penny. You could forget about college, kiddo. Everything depends on us protecting the flanks of our Marine. He may not be perfect, but he's all we got. This doesn't come under the category of lying. Tonight you're going to save your family's life, your one job. Can I trust you, Pat? Otherwise, I'm going to turn this car around and you can bleed to death for all I care. If you don't care about me, you could at least think about the futures of your brothers and sisters. Their lives and futures depend on how well you tell your story tonight."

When the doctor asked me how I hurt myself when he was stopping the flow of blood, I told him about the touch football game, about my family's deep devotion to the Kennedy family, about my Uncle Willie's slowness afoot, my father's fabled athletic prowess and his breakaway run. I told the doctor about my lunge at the imaginary goal line and my being spun at breakneck speed into the spigot. I told the story without a hitch or a quiver or attracting a single cross interrogation. My mother added that everyone in the family, including her, had bruises and skinned knees from those rowdy games every night.

The doctor suggested we not play any more games as a family for a while, unaware that he was in the middle of one of them as he stitched my eyebrow back together. Long before I ever wrote my first line of fiction, I had years of practice in making up the stories of my life.


BECAUSE OF THE GASH ALONG MY EYEBROW, I couldn't go out for the Beaufort High School football team when it began practice in the middle of August. I entered Beaufort High with two butterfly bandages holding my brow in place, making me an object of curiosity as I walked the hallways in the first days of school. I had my English class in my first period, and I stood by my seat waiting for the teacher to give the class permission to be seated. My Catholic education had brainwashed me to such an extent that I had never sat down in any classroom without saying a prayer, then having a nun or priest grant permission for me to sit. The room was noisy and chaotic when my teacher, J. Eugene Norris, entered and noticed me standing my lonely vigil beside my desk. He eyed me peculiarly, put his books down, then walked down the aisle toward me. "Sit yourself down, boy. Have you gone crazy or something?" He pushed me lightly and I took my seat as the first delicious moments of the anarchy of public education settled into my consciousness. At this school, I could take my seat whenever I saw fit.

In the first week of school, Mr. Norris played Ravel's *Bolero* during class then ordered us to write an essay on whatever the music brought to mind. I wrote about a gypsy encampment outside of Seville which is massacred in the middle of the night by either the Loyalist forces or some of Franco's men. I'd just read Hemingway's *For Whom the Bell Tolls* and was deeply embedded in my Hemingway period when I tried to make all my sentences true and good. My essay was a derivative mess, but it was different from any others written in my class, and after he read and graded it, Mr. Norris approached me and said in his exaggerated and heavily accented up-country patois: "You're something, boy. You ain't nothin'. You got some things to say, don't you?"

I went out for the Beaufort High School varsity basketball team in the middle of October. My father bet me a dollar I wouldn't make the team, and I prayed that he was wrong. When I was dressing for the first practice, my heart fluttered when I heard the news that last year's basketball team had won only three games, losing fifteen. I'd not picked up a basketball since my final game on the Gonzaga JV team, and I felt hamstrung and rusted out and lead-footed as I went through the layup line for Coach Jerry Swing on the first day of practice. He barked sharply at us that first session, but it was out of custom and not predilection. I always liked coaches who yelled because they thought it was expected as part of the natural order of things. In the companionship of boys, Coach Swing had a gruff but good-natured style without a trace of the bully. Fifty boys went out for the team. After a week, I held my breath as I walked up to the typed column of names listing the twelve who had survived the final cut. All week long I'd rehearsed what I could say to my father if I didn't make the team. I had considered running away or feigning a serious injury or dropping off the team to concentrate on my studies. My play at practice had seemed uninspired and second-rate. I couldn't summon up a portion of razzle-dazzle or pizzazz if my life depended on it, and I, for one, thought it did. I missed my name the first time down the list and thought I'd faint. On the second run-through I found it listed alphabetically after Ray Burgess. I felt relief but not a scintilla of joy.

That night on the long ride to Laurel Bay my father asked in the great silence that lay between us: "You got cut, right?"

"No, sir. I made the team."

"Bet a dollar you don't make first string," he said. "You'll ride the pine, just like at Gonzaga."

I looked over at him, terrified, and thought about betting a hundred dollars that I'd start, but kept my mouth shut. I'd let my game do the talking.

Something happened to me in our first game against Ridgeland High School that had never happened previously. It was on the court in front of the largest crowd I'd ever played before when a thought struck me with an immense, impersonal force. Though I couldn't see myself that night, I could see a change in the faces of the Ridgeland players as they tried to stop me, and I could see a transformation in my teammates' eyes as the game progressed. I could hear the humming of the crowd whenever I took off on a fast break or dribbled the ball into the paint. I had come into my own without my knowledge. The dreaming I had laid out for myself as a ten-year-old boy ignited into flame on the court as I took my longed-for place as a player to watch. Cries of "Go, Conroy" rattled through the gym all night, and I bloomed with pride as I heard the Ridgeland boys asking my teammates, "Who's this guy? Where'd he come from?" My teammates had no idea where I came from, because none of them had asked.

Toward the end of the game, I took a pass on the wing from Randy Randel at center, and brought it to the middle of the court where the two Ridgeland guards lined up to stop me. When I reached the top of the key I went behind my back when the first guy tried to steal it, then flew by the second guy and scored on a reverse layup on the left side of the basket. It brought the crowd to its feet. It brought my mother, brothers, and sisters to their feet, but not my father. My mother blew me a kiss and I blew one back at her, but disguised it as though I were wiping perspiration from my face.

Then I heard it for the first time from one of the Ridgeland guards, and it would become a common theme among my opponents for the next two years. "Hey, number thirteen. You play just like a nigger. You know that?"

"Sure do," I answered, swollen with pride.

I scored twenty-eight points in my first game as the point guard of Beaufort High School, more points than I had ever scored in a basketball game. I was so accustomed to walking down a school corridor with no one knowing my name that I received a shock the next morning when the entire school seemed to be calling out my name. Scores of kids called, "Good game," as I passed them in the hallways, yet I didn't know a one of them. That day, Bruce Harper, a basketball teammate and the vice president of the Student Council, asked me to spend the night with him that weekend; I had not seen the inside of a Gonzaga boy's home. That season I would go on to score twenty-five points against St. Andrews and Garrett high schools out of Charleston, and thirty-one against Conway after a defeat the previous night against a Myrtle Beach team that would go on to win the state championship. My game had finally caught up with what my imagination told me it should be, and I averaged eighteen points a game that dream-born junior year. Basketball had put my name on the lips of every student at Beaufort High School, and the following May, my classmates elected me the president of the senior class. My mother broke down and wept when I told her. My father judged my class with more severity when he said, "Talk about a lack of leadership, pal. That class of yours must be pathetic."

IN THE SUMMER BETWEEN my junior and senior years, Bill Dufford, my principal, gave me a key to the Beaufort High School gymnasium and a job as a groundskeeper for the summer. Because of some incurable wound my father suffered during the Depression, the Colonel instituted an ironclad rule that none of his seven children could take a paying job. Mr. Dufford was delighted that I'd move tons of dirt from one end of campus to another while refusing to take a single dime. I thought the physical work would be good for me as an athlete, and I spent the summer in the blazing heat, resodding and planting grass on every bald patch that disfigured the vast greensward of my pretty campus. Mr. Dufford also let me practice basketball in the gym the last three hours of the day before he made me close up at six. But I practiced hard, pushing myself to absolute limits. Every day, I set up long lines of folding chairs that stretched from one end of the gym to the other, and I dribbled right-handed, left-handed, weaving between them at full speed, sprinting as hard as I could go. My ambitions exceeded my talent but I didn't know that then, so I drove myself to the point of collapse. I worked on going to my left all summer, and during one of those hours

I'd only dribble with my left hand and only throw up left-handed hook shots off the drive. I invented dribbling and passing drills for myself, playing imaginary games from start to finish in my head. Those games, populated by a whole nation of made-up players, were my first attempts at composing short stories, and all games ended the same way, with me in a heroic, winner-take-all, last-second shot on a drive down the lane with my invisible enemies closing the lane down around me.

In the first days of my senior year, I caught the mumps and never fully recovered from the five weeks of classes I missed. When I got back to Algebra II and trigonometry, my natural weaknesses in math overwhelmed me, and the figures on the blackboard looked like Sanskrit and chicken scratch to me, lost in a funhouse of ghastly numbers. Though I developed a crush on my French teacher, Nancy Rogers, I never attained the sangfroid it required to stand up in class and order a meal in French with the comely Miss Rogers. I struggled in economics and physics, a course my father insisted I take after he made me drop a typing course.

When basketball season dawned, the students and teachers of Beaufort High School looked at me through different eyes. The school expected a lot of my team and it expected the world of me. Unlike the previous year, when I came on in the tailwinds of my father's orders, I'd take no one by surprise either in my school or in my league. On the first day of practice, Coach Jerry Swing named Robert Padgett and me as the team's co-captains and told us all that he knew this was the best basketball team in Beaufort High School history. Swing trimmed the team down to twelve men who could all play ball. If my team had a single weakness, it was a noticeable lack of height. In the team photograph taken by Ned Brown that year, it looks as though we are all the same height—though we ranged from five ten to six one. We were quick and game and an easy team for a coach or a school to like. A buzz of high expectancy hung over the breezeway as I held my breath for the opening night. Half the school wished me luck as they passed me in the hallways. Julie Zachowski, the senior class vice president, gave me a garter she had sewed to wear beneath my sock for luck. So much was riding on the success of this basketball season that the worst case of the butterflies in my career had almost bent me double in physics class that morning. Butterflies are what fear masquerades as in the cocoon of an athlete's stomach.

As I lay down in my top bunk, resting for the game, my father came into the room to talk about the coming season. He kept his voice low so my mother wouldn't hear him.

"Hey, jocko. Want to hear my prediction about you and your team?" Dad said.

"Yes, sir."

"One game below five hundred," he said. "I don't think you'll win half your games. You've got no height. No big guys to get you the ball under the boards. This league's going to be gunning for you this year, son. I don't think you do well under the spotlight. You scored over eighteen a game last year. The other teams make adjustments and I say you score less than ten a game this year."

"Thanks, Dad."

"I bet not a single college scout comes to watch you play," he said. "I think my baby boy's going to wilt under all the pressure."

"I hope not."

"You're a loser, son. Your mother can't see it, but I'm a Chicago boy and I know a pussy when I see one."

My father's laughter rang down the hallway as he walked toward the kitchen.

AGAINST ST. PAUL IN THE OPENING GAME, before what seemed like the largest opening-night crowd in history, I faced my first double-team and realized that the St. Paul coach was gambling that if he could stop me, his team could defeat the Tidal Wave. But the two guards assigned to me had never double-teamed anyone for a whole game, and they found it harder to do than it looked on a blackboard. I kept busting through a seam up the middle and heading for the basket. During the game I kept hearing a voice through the noise of the crowd shouting, "Get Conroy, put Pat Conroy on the deck," and recognized it as the voice of my father. A Marine brat by the name of Billy Swetnam had entered Beaufort High School and joined me in the back court. He could play the game and had a nice short-range jump shot that made teams regret double-teaming me. Our big men controlled the boards, Chris Edwards and Robert Padgett with finesse, and Benny Michael with the brute strength he brought intact from his fullback position on the football team. We defeated St. Paul 49–34. I scored a workmanlike nineteen points and knew that I was in for a far different season from the honeymoon of my junior year when I was one of the league leaders in scoring. But my team and I sustained each other and fought for each other and we were 3–0 going into our annual road trip to play Myrtle Beach and Conway.

In Conway, the gym was packed with a rowdy, enthusiastic crowd as we loped out of the locker room for warmups. Their coach, Tom Eady, walked over and shook my hand as I moved to the back of the layup line.

"Go easy on us, Pat," he said. "You killed us last year." Last year I had scored thirty-one points against Conway, by far the best game I'd ever played.

Coach Eady, an elegant and handsome man who had a gift for the right gesture, had come to find me in the locker room to congratulate me. He was an excellent coach and that night proved it by stopping me cold. Coach Eady introduced me and my teammates to a defense called the box and one.

An aggressive guard named Harold Branton was the one, and his only job that night was to bird-dog me all over the court. If I got around him, his four teammates were to move out as one in a disciplined zone to stop me until Harold recovered and got back into position. Conway encouraged my teammates to shoot often as Branton followed me around the court with the persistence of halitosis. I could not shake the kid and our offense had no way to get him off me. We never solved the problem of the box and one that night and lost to the Conway Tigers 52–39. I stunk up the floor, disgraced my school, only scoring eleven points by intercepting errant passes and taking the ball downcourt for layups.

We lost three of the next four games; the league teams had figured out a foolproof way to contain me on offense. I grew accustomed to seeing two men inch out to intercept me when I brought the ball upcourt. My team grew worried and diffident around me. I could see in their eyes that I was failing to hold up my part of the unspoken covenant, lifting this team to victory. I scored seventeen in a two-point loss to Garrett, fifteen in a 49–41 victory over Berkeley, and fourteen in a 51–42 loss to St. Paul. My play was flat and undistinguished, and much worse, it was cowardly.

My father recognized the cowardice, not me. In the disappearance of my game, I had submitted to a strange lassitude that fell somewhere between surrender and vagueness. I was lost somewhere in the fogs of myself and didn't know how to recover. When my father picked me up to take me home to Laurel Bay, he asked how the St. Paul game went.

"We lost, Dad," I said.

"How many did you score?"

"Fourteen."

He backhanded me into the passenger-side window. His slap had caught me relaxed, and my nose started bleeding profusely. If the blood had not flowed, the beating would have continued. Because I was an expert in translating the fury of my father's eyes, I knew that the first backhand was a warmup for a long night spent warding off his blows. I unzipped my bag and pressed my nose into my uniform shirt. I could always tell my mother that I'd been elbowed under the boards by St. Paul's center.

"You don't get it, do you, mama's boy? This is a kick-ass world that doesn't have time to wait around for pussies like you to wake up and read the fucking headlines. You're not as good a ballplayer as you were last year, pal. Understand that? These teams have your number. They're eating your jock. Because you've got a pussy between your legs instead of a dick, it's working on you. I'd've gone through this league like shit through a goose. Their teeth'd be lying all over the floor like Chiclets. I'd shuck teeth from their heads and make them believe it was corn. You listening to me, pal? Ah, you're not crying, are you? Sweet little Pat. Mama's little baby loves shortenin', shortenin', mama's little baby loves shortenin' bread. Itty-bitty baby feel bad? Daddy's so sorry. You haven't received one letter from one college about playing ball next year. Not one. No one's scouted you because word's getting out that you're a quitter and a loser. You won't be going to college next year, son."

There was nothing my father could not teach me about the architecture of despair. I knew all its shapes and its blueprints, the shadows of all its columns and archways. My father could send me reeling down its hallways and screaming into its bat-spliced attics with a curl of his thin-lipped mouth. He brought madness home every time he entered the many houses of my overlong childhood. His cruelty baffled me, shamed me, and I promised myself I would never be anything like him.

I came back the next game against Walterboro with nineteen points, and our team won 69–41. My father was in the stands and I waved to him for the first time all season, enraging him. Against Georgetown I scored twenty-two of my team's forty-four points as we won by eight points. Against Berkeley I scored twenty-one of forty-nine points, and I had found my way back to myself and my game again. In the middle of the Berkeley game with my friend Bruce Harper shooting two free throws, I walked over to where my father and family were seated among the hometown crowd and waved. I waited for the look of rage to cross my father's face—and it was quick in coming. "Hey, showboat," he yelled at me, "let's get serious about the game."

In my secret self, the one my father didn't know about, I said in silence, "Fuck you, Dad." I smiled and waved again, but this time only to my father. At the end of the third quarter we were tied up with Berkeley 30–30. In the fourth quarter I scored twelve points and we won the game going away. On the drive home, my father critiqued every aspect of my game, slashing the air with his index finger to emphasize his points as he listed my shortcomings, his voice a soundtrack in the garden I was tending in the high-country of self that was lush and fatherless.

IT WAS THAT SEASON, IN 1963, when I first met Mel Thompson, who came to Beaufort High School to do a scouting report on me in a game against Chicora High School. When Coach Thompson took his seat in the top row of the visitors' section I had no way of knowing that my fate, inexorable and cat-footed, had come riding into town. The Citadel's coach sat in silence and judged me as a player he might recruit for his team. Later, he told me he had been looking for a ball handler. I could have told him, if that was the order of the day, he had come to the right place.

I was in the middle of the best week of basketball I would ever play, if the number of points scored is the measurement of achievement. On the previous Tuesday night in a small-town gymnasium, heated by a woodstove, I scored forty-three points against Ridgeland High in a game we won in the final minute. Every shot I made seemed to float magically through the basket. I felt possessed, enraptured, flush with gladness, and I did not think there was a boy in the whole world who could stop me.

While we were riding home that night, my father, still in his Marine uniform, bawled me out for thirty miles for playing lousy defense. I am certain my father was right because I'd not even begun to understand defense. I was accustomed to my father's screaming after games but it couldn't dull my pleasure at having scored forty-three points in a closely fought contest whose outcome was in doubt almost to the final whistle.

It was the box score of the Ridgeland game that brought Mel Thompson into my life. What Coach Thompson would see during our next game against Chicora was not a true reflection of my ability. He watched a far better basketball player than I was on a daily basis, for again I found myself on fire against this team that was favored to beat us. I roared around that gym, magnetized, bewitched, and again, all but unstoppable. I ran the court as though my blood had turned to quicksilver. This night would prove the only time in my career that two such games occurred back-to-back, during the same week. I lay awake that week in sheer amazement at what my own body had done.

The largest crowd in the history of Beaufort High School showed up for the Chicora game and the pep band put everyone into a state of near frenzy as my team burst out of the locker room high on Coach Jerry Swing's emotional pregame speech. In this one glorious night, I lifted right out of myself and turned into the kind of basketball player who could change the way a town felt about itself. The score was close all game, and Chicora was coached brilliantly by Ray Graves, once a star forward at The Citadel.

Every Chicora boy who played that night fouled me in my reckless drives through the lane. I was in the middle of a senior year when I would average twenty-two points a game, leading my team to a 13–3 record. When that final buzzer sounded, I always felt like Cinderella as the clock tolled the midnight hour and I'd find myself transformed back into the painfully shy boy I was, not a star who'd just scored thirty-six points that helped beat a superior team. In the locker room, I sat beside my open locker as my teammates pounded my back, not wanting to get dressed because I wanted to hang on to the sweetness of this one night. I had scored seventy-nine points in two games, something I never thought would happen.

Coach Swing brought the tall, dark-eyed man into the locker room to meet me. I watched as Mel Thompson made his way through a locker room full of ecstatic boys. My fate approached me with a great, loping walk.

"Pat, you remember that Citadel game I took you to last year?"

asked Coach Swing. "Well, this is The Citadel's head coach, Mel Thompson."

"Hello, sir," I said. "I saw your team play George Washington in D.C. two years ago. I loved how Dickie Jones played."

"You reminded me of Dickie Jones," Mel Thompson said.

"Thank you, sir."

"I told him all about you, Pat," Coach Swing said. "They don't make them any better, Coach."

"You'll be hearing from me, Pat," Coach Thompson said. "Good game." He smiled as he left me.

I played under Mel Thompson for the next four years, and he never again said "good game" to me. Nor did he smile at me again. Ever.


IN MARCH, COACH MEL THOMPSON of The Citadel wrote me a letter inviting me to visit the college the first weekend in May. He did not mention the word "scholarship" but my parents thought that such an invitation implied a promise of financial aid. When I returned home from baseball practice each day, I'd ask my mother if there was any mail for me from a college, but there never was. Years later, my mother would admit that there had been letters of interest from Furman, Presbyterian, Wofford, and Erskine, but she and my father had thrown them in the trash because they were Protestant colleges.

In April I was called out of Millen Ellis's English class by a messenger from the principal's office. I walked into Mr. Dufford's office, and he introduced me to a tall friendly man by the name of Dwayne Morrison. His name was vaguely familiar, then Bill Dufford said, "Coach Morrison is Chuck Noll's assistant up at the University of South Carolina, Pat. He wants to talk to you about playing for Carolina."

Stunned by this unexpected news, I stared at Coach Morrison with my jaw loosened and my mouth agape as I hunted for the proper words.

"How'd you like to play for Carolina, Pat?" Coach Morrison asked me.

"More than anything in the world, Coach."

"We hear you got the attitude, the heart, the will—everything but the jump shot, kid."

"Pat'll work," Mr. Dufford said quickly. "He spent the whole summer in the gym. He's got the best work ethic of any kid we've had here."

"That's what we like to hear."

Coach Morrison took me by the elbow and led me into the office next to Mr. Dufford's. His personality and enthusiasm dazzled me; he was the kind of coach I'd dreamed of having since I was a kid. He made me feel like I was the best basketball player he had ever talked to, and he made me believe in every single aspect of Chuck Noll's program. He talked about "redshirting" me for a year, putting me on a weight-training program, sending me to summer basketball programs for extra seasoning, and teaching me all the tricks of the trade that a point guard would need to know in the highly competitive Atlantic Coast Conference at the time South Carolina still held membership in it. He asked me if I would accept a scholarship from Carolina if one was offered, and I said yes sir. Coach Morrison asked me if I would give my heart and soul to make Coach Noll's program take its place as one of America's best, and I said yes sir. He inflated my ego to the breaking point, seeming to know everything about my skills and deficiencies as a ballplayer. When he talked about his university, he made it sound like some grand easement into paradise. When he asked me if I thought I could play against the Tar Heels of Chapel Hill and the Wolfpack of NC State, I told him I'd dreamed of playing those teams since I was a child. What I learned in that half hour was that Coach Morrison was a wizard in the art of recruiting. He could've talked me into walking across burning embers or a live minefield. When he left me that day he said, "We're going to try to make this work, Pat. I can see you in a Gamecock uniform. We've got a couple of other kids we're going to look at. But I can practically guarantee you, you're the kind of guy we're looking for. A good point guard's worth his weight in gold these days. He's the quarterback, the brains of the team, the guy who gets it done. It's you we want, Pat. You. Got it, buddy?"

"Yes, sir," I said.

In my great naïveté, or innocence, or stupidity, I thought that the scholarship to South Carolina was a sure thing, and I made the mistake of telling my mother that USC was giving me a free ride when I got home from school that afternoon. To be perfectly accurate, I think most probably I confided to my mother that Coach Morrison had offered me a full scholarship but not to tell anyone until it was official. My mother danced around the kitchen when she heard the news, and in her ebullience, I felt the first shivers and pangs of confusion about the reality of the scholarship. I warned her not to tell Dad a thing until I received confirmation from Coach Morrison, but she told him the moment he arrived home from the base. My father walked up to me and put out his hand to shake mine.

"A scholarship to the University of South Carolina," Dad said. "That's the best college basketball conference in the country, son. I was wrong about everything I said about you and your game."

"Ask him how the crow tastes, son," my mother laughed.

"It's not official yet, Dad," I said.

"The guy offered you a scholarship, didn't he?" my father asked.

"He practically did, Dad. He sounded like he really wanted me, that the team really needed a guy like me."

"Well, sounds like a done deal to me," my father said as he walked to the phone, where I heard him telling several of his brothers they'd better start making reservations for the ACC tournament next year if they wanted to see his son help defeat the North Carolina Tar Heels.

In less than a month, I was the laughingstock of my father and his family. I never heard from Dwayne Morrison or received a single letter from the South Carolina athletic office. My father ended up calling Coach Morrison who regretfully told him that they had completed their recruiting for the next season, but he felt sure I would land a scholarship with a good program. "That's a great kid you've got there, Colonel. He'll go places."

But my father's report to me had a sterner edge as he said, "Bottom line, pal. You're not only a loser, you're a liar. The coach said he never offered you a scholarship."

My father possessed a small genius for scab-flicking, for zeroing in on that tenderest spot of the psyche where healing was most difficult, exposing the rawness of the wound again and again. His cold blue eyes would twinkle with malice for long weeks after my imaginary scholarship to Carolina was exposed as fraudulent. He'd say, "The lawn looks like it needs mowing, ACC." Or, "How 'bout opening me a beer, ACC," or, "When's your next baseball game, ACC?" "Looks like ACC could use a haircut."

To survive the long march of my father, I taught myself to be stoical and unreadable. I disguised my face even from myself. In April I quit asking about the mail and hadn't a clue about where I was going to be the following year. Then Dad got orders to Offutt Air Force Base in

Omaha, Nebraska, and my despair was bottomless. Only when Dad received these orders did I realize the depth of my attachment to Beaufort. The next day, I opened a letter informing me that I'd been selected as one of the players to represent the South in the annual North-South All-Star game in Columbia that July. I ran around the house screaming with joy, a renewal of hope that I'd have one more chance to impress the college scouts who had missed me on the first go-round.

"Write them back today," my mother said. "Tell them you can't play."

"What do you mean, I can't play? I wouldn't miss it for the world."

"We'll be in Nebraska then," she said.

"I'll be in Columbia, South Carolina, then," I said. "It might be my last chance to win a scholarship. Mom, I'll walk from Nebraska to South Carolina if I have to."

Dressed in my shorts and T-shirt and basketball shoes, I ran out of the house and jogged toward the Broad River and the path into the forest that began when base housing made its last encroachment. The sun had oiled the calm river with a last forfeiture of gold as it slid behind the banked clouds in the west. I passed the tabby ruins of an abandoned fort and came to a small beachhead hidden by the bonneted roots of fallen water oaks where I retreated when I wanted to think. Five porpoises hunted schools of baitfish, causing a silvery panic along the sandflats. The sun caught the velvety green backs of the porpoises in sudden trapezoids of fire. I danced for myself and gave myself up to a rapture of what seemed like pure joy. I began screaming at the porpoises and the sun and the river, something I had wanted to give voice to since I got the letter, something I was dying for my mother to say to me, but she had not understood what the true measure of the letter was, or what it could have meant to me. But, by God, I knew what the letter meant as soon as I read it, and I shouted at the top of my voice words I needed to hear said, screaming aloud: "I'm All-State! I'm an All-State basketball player from South Carolina. Did you hear me? I'm All-State and no one can take that away from me. I'm an All-State selection. I'm All-State!"

When my father got home that night, I positioned myself in the living room as he read the day's mail with maddening slowness. He read four or five letters before he got to the one naming me to the All-State team. I watched him as he read it over twice, and Mom came out of the kitchen to measure his reaction.

"What do you think about our boy, Don?" my mother asked. "Not bad, huh?"

My father folded the letter up carefully and replaced it in its envelope, then said as he put the mail on the coffee table in front of him, "Mister ACC."

MY MOTHER TOOK GREAT STOCK IN the significance of my official visit to The Citadel in the middle of May. For a week, she put me through a short course on the courtesies and mannerisms I should display when being escorted through the campus. Since I was almost oily with politeness anyway, I suffered no lack of confidence that I would revert to the etiquette of a Cro-Magnon simply because I was out of my mother's sight and control. But she had become desperate that there be some kind of satisfactory resolution to the dilemma surrounding my college education. I think my whole family, myself included, had suffered some incalculable wound when no college had stepped forth clamoring for my services on their basketball team. Somehow I had let my family down.

When my mother dropped me off in front of the Armory at two o'clock the following Friday afternoon, she told me, "I think The Citadel's your only chance for college, Pat. I really do."

I stepped out of the car and into a fierce recruiting war in which I played no part. A splendid guard from Lima, Ohio, named Bill Taflinger had come to The Citadel accompanied by his working-class family, and I soon learned that a number of midwestern schools were interested in signing Bill to a grant-in-aid. Coach Mel Thompson met both Bill and me in his office and told us what he had planned for us over the weekend. Our guide around campus was to be the captain of next year's team, Mike West. Mel was charming and solicitous. He handled Mr. and Mrs. Taflinger's questions about the rigors of the military lifestyle at The Citadel with alacrity. "We keep our boys away from the military as much as we can, Mr. Taflinger. They're over there and we're over here. Two different worlds with two different purposes and never the twain shall meet. It gets a little dicey during plebe week, but that's like fraternity rush, then it's over. Bill'll do just fine here. I've seen him play and this is one tough kid. These military guys won't make a dent on him. C'mon, let's go see a parade."

Before the parade started, Mike West joined our group with an easygoing charisma that made leadership an instinct with him. I liked him from the moment I met him and had already fallen in love with his game in the four Citadel home games I'd witnessed in the past year. The whole campus seemed both drawn to and mesmerized by him.

At that same parade as the companies marched out from all four barracks to the beat of the drummers, Mike West suddenly sprinted through the crowd to embrace a young man I knew I'd seen before. Mike brought the man back with him and introduced Bill and me. "This is Dickie Jones, one of the best athletes to attend The Citadel. He was captain of the basketball team my sophomore year."

"I hear you've been named captain next year, Mike," Dickie said. "Congratulations. Maybe one of you'll be captain your senior year at The Citadel."

"Mr. Jones, I saw you play George Washington up in D.C. You were terrific, sir," I said.

"You saw me play up there?" Dickie said. "I'd do anything to be playing college ball. You boys enjoy every bit of it. You won't believe how fast it all goes."

Bill and I drifted back to watch the parade as Mike continued to talk to Dickie. I wanted to ask Dickie Jones what he had majored in at The Citadel, and I walked up behind the two men and waited for them to finish their conversation before I interrupted them. I heard Mike telling Dickie, "Thompson's hot to trot to sign Taflinger. Conroy's just along for the ride."

I took a few steps backward then rejoined Taflinger and watched the rest of the parade, hurt beyond all telling. But the parade gave me time to compose myself and gather my thoughts as the companies passed in review in perfect order. I finally admitted to myself that my chances of going to college the following year were growing dimmer by the hour. It was the middle of May and I hadn't applied or been accepted for a calendar year that was to begin again in three months. I tried to imagine myself as an ex–basketball player and couldn't conjure the image, just as I could not reconcile myself to missing out on college. My accidental overhearing of Mike West's insider information helped me prepare for the inevitable scene when Coach Thompson informed me that he couldn't offer me an athletic scholarship. I tried to think of alternatives, but there were none. I had come to the end of the line and had come up short and had thirty-six hours to prepare myself for Coach Thompson's farewell address to my basketball career. I think I would've gone to pieces in his office if I hadn't gotten Mike's bulletin as an early-warning system. My optimism could often be a form of neediness that did not always serve me well. For no reason whatever, I had assumed that Coach Thompson was going to offer me a scholarship and had already planned an acceptance speech in which I told him that I was honored to be selected and would make him proud of his decision and would never let The Citadel down under any circumstances—those unspoken words dried up.

On Sunday morning, the Taflinger family and I waited outside of Mel Thompson's office together. They had taken me to breakfast, invited me to visit them in Lima, Ohio, and told me I could stay with them for the whole summer if I so desired. They were a large-hearted midwestern family written in bold capital letters, and they smiled broadly when Coach Thompson called them in for a "little powwow." Alone, I sat in the hallway on a bench in the otherwise deserted building. I was trying to find the proper words to tell my father that I had failed to land a scholarship from The Citadel. It would make for a difficult ride back to Beaufort, but I hunted for the right way to say that I had let my family down in the most humiliating way.

I heard a roar go up from the Taflinger family and knew that Bill must have signed his grant-in-aid. Soon, the whole Taflinger family boiled out of Coach Thompson's office, Bill wearing a broad grin. Mr. Taflinger said, "Bill just inked his name. A full four-year ride. Isn't that great news, Pat?"

"The best," I said. "Congratulations, Bill."

Bill surprised me by taking me by the shoulders and saying, "I want you on my team, Pat. Let's make The Citadel great."

"I'd love to play on the same team as you."

"Let's load up, kids," Mr. Taflinger said. "We've got a long ride back to Ohio."

"But it'll be a happy ride," Mrs. Taflinger said. "Go see Coach Thompson, Pat. He's in there waiting for you."

"You'll take the scholarship if he offers you one," Bill asked, "won't you?"

"I've got a couple of other offers I'm looking at, Bill," I said, the lie embarrassing me the moment it passed my lips.

"Sign here," Bill said. "That's an order, smackhead."

His family and I both laughed as I went into Mel Thompson's orderly office.

"Good morning, Coach," I said as he motioned for me to sit down on a chair in front of his desk.

"Good morning, Pat," he said. "Did Mike West show you a good time?"

"A great time, Coach. What a great guy he is."

"I agree. Did Bill tell you he just signed on for a scholarship?"

"Yes, sir, he did."

"That was our last one, Pat. I don't have any more scholarships to give. We've had our best recruiting class ever and we got boys to sign up we didn't think we had a prayer of getting," Coach Thompson said. "We got us some real blue-chippers."

"That's great, Coach," I said.

"But it leaves you with the short end of the stick, Pat," he said. "We wanted you since we first saw you. If I had you, I wouldn't worry about a full-court press for the rest of my life. But I just ran out of scholarships. If you come to The Citadel as a walk-on, we'll take care of you. We'd like to have you."

"I'd love to come here, Coach," I said. "I'll have to talk it over with my parents."

"In my opinion, Pat, the boys we signed have skills that make them much better basketball players than you are at this point." Coach Thompson said it with tenderness and kindness. "But you could find a place on this team. We liked your heart."

"Thank you, Coach," I said. "I'll let you know what my folks decide."

I stood up and shook his hand, then walked out of the gym and saw my father waiting in our car. I was hoping for some time to compose myself before facing him, but he was there waiting for me. Entering the car, I tried to make conversation. "Isn't this campus pretty, Dad? You should've seen the parade on Friday. These guys march as well as Marines do, I swear they do. I was introduced to General Mark Clark by the captain of next year's basketball team and . . ."

"Cut the yappin'," my father said. "Did you get the scholarship or not?"

"Coach Thompson wants me to come out for the team as a walk-on next year. He said he liked my heart, Dad."

"Hey, jocko, I didn't ask for the directions to China and back. Did you get a scholarship or not? Negative or affirmative?"

"No, sir," I said. "I didn't get a scholarship."

The slap caught me with my mouth wide open and staring out the front window, another humiliation in a lifetime in which my father brought nothing but an accumulation of both public and private embarrassment. My full-blown hatred of him bloomed as my mouth filled up with blood. We did not exchange a single word or glance on the seventy-mile run back to Beaufort.

When we entered the house, my mother was waiting to hear the good news, but read the signs when I tore past her and retreated into my bedroom, but not before hearing Dad tell her, "Your sweet boy dropped the ball again, Peg. He didn't get zip. Nada. You need to look for a home ec scholarship for the kid. No one wants him to play ball for them in this loser state. No one."

Two weeks later on June 4, 1963, I graduated from Beaufort High School, a school that had taken me in and cherished me and loved me at the end of a shameful boyhood. The town of Beaufort was the first place I'd ever come to that had the authentic feel of a homeplace to me. Leaving Beaufort was a killing, irrevocable act to me, yet my father's car was packed for the move to Omaha when I walked across the stage that night. At the ceremony, I received the senior class Sportsmanship Award that my father immediately dubbed "The Pussy Award," and claimed he would have shoved it back into Bill Dufford's face if he'd tried to give the medal to him. I received my diploma and had not yet applied to a single college. My brilliant class had more scholarships than any graduating class in the history of Beaufort High, ranging from Princeton to Stanford.

When the ceremony ended I took off my graduation gown and burst into tears as I said goodbye to Gene Norris and Bill Dufford and Millen Ellis and Grace Foster Dennis and Dutchin Hardin and Marty Moseley and all the other wonderful teachers who'd made me happy in their classrooms. My father had commanded that I skip all the graduation parties, that it was more important that we hit the road and make good time on the trip to his family's home in Chicago. My brothers Mike and Jim and my sisters, Carol and Kathy, waited for me in the car with my father. Mom and the two babies were flying to Chicago the next day.

"Say goodbye to this loser burg, kids," my father said. "We ain't never coming back to this place."

Wanna bet? I said to myself as my father pulled away in darkness.

"You're the navigator, pal," he said to me. "Any mistakes, you face a court-martial."

"There won't be any mistakes, sir," I said, opening the map. Twenty-four hours later, pausing for pit stops and gas, my father pulled our station wagon to the front of his brother Willie's house in Chicago, where we stayed for a week. Then we went to Uncle Jim's remote cabin on the Illinois side of the Mississippi River across from Clinton, Iowa, where Uncle Jim was the Catholic chaplain of Mercy Hospital. My mother and her seven children spent two of the most miserable and isolated months of our lives in that ill-equipped cabin as Dad went on to Offutt Air Force Base to begin his new job. I fumed all summer about my future and could not get my mother to talk to me about college because she had no news to report on that front. "Your father's working on college," was all she'd say.

In July, I took a long train ride to Columbia, South Carolina, to participate in the North-South All-Star game. The game was good for me and taught me lessons in humility that the realm of sport can always teach its athletes. I discovered I was not the best basketball player in South Carolina as I had thought, I was the fifteenth or sixteenth best. I played on the same team as Don Whitehead and John Bloom and Hyman Rubin, all superb players. I played against the gifted Jim Sutherland and Mike Muth and Bob Cauthen for the North team. It was during that game that I noticed the apartheid nature of athletics in South Carolina sports and wondered aloud where the black All-Star game was being played.

I was out of shape and disillusioned and played the game without distinction except for three driving layups I made in the second half. But after the game, a well-built, handsome man wearing a Citadel polo shirt came up and introduced himself as Hank Witt, an assistant football coach at The Citadel.

"Pat, great game, son. You're just what the doctor ordered. Mel Thompson apologized for not being here. But he wanted me to welcome you to The Citadel."

"What do you mean, Coach?" I asked.

"Your father enrolled you at The Citadel yesterday, Pat," he said. "You're going to be a Bulldog. You're part of the Citadel family now, son."

I was going to college. Thanks to my academic scholarships, I was going to be a "college" basketball player, and I thought I was headed for the big-time.

# CHAPTER 7

# PLEBE YEAR

I ENTERED THE CITADEL AS A WALK-ON, A PLAYER WHO MAKES THE team without the benefit of scholarship. My first year, Mel hadn't offered me a scholarship because, as he told my father, "I signed two guards a lot better than Pat," and he was telling the truth. "Walk-on"—this still remains the proudest word I can apply to myself. Walk-on—there are resolve and backbone in that noun.

My parents never considered the possibility of accompanying me to my first day at The Citadel. Instead, they found the cheapest mode of transportation to get me from Omaha to Charleston during plebe week in August. My mother, a bargain shopper of heroic proportions, found a southern version of the slow boat to China and, weeping hard, put me on a train in Omaha that made its ponderous way through the American Midwest, stopping everywhere to take on freight and passengers. For two and a half days I slept sitting up, eating a box of saltines and the banana sandwiches my mother had packed for the trip.

That journey through the heartland was my first great adventure. Aloneness itself seemed like a prize possession to the oldest of seven children, and I drew in the rolling beauty of the American landscape as it sped past the train window. I spoon-fed myself with lush, fabulous images of my country spinning by me in ever-changing light and shadow. On my own for the first time in my life, the exhilaration I felt lent an air of bright enchantment to the passenger compartment. I was on my way to play college basketball, and I didn't think that life could get any better.

But it did. Somewhere in Ohio a young black woman came into my car and sat in a seat across from me. Like me, she was going to college in the South, so we began to talk with an ease I didn't often achieve with other young women. Her personality enchanted me, her outspokenness charmed me and caught me by surprise as we talked about politics and books and the state of the world. Whenever the train stopped she and I would go out to the platform and listen on her radio to reports of the March on Washington that was taking place at the same moment we were moving toward Cincinnati. I had long grown accustomed to being silent around girls, but I marveled as this uncommonly pretty girl dragged things out of me that I did not even know were there. Right away, she told me since she'd never met a southern white boy, there were a lot of questions she had for me. She shared the fried chicken her grandmother had made and I tried to foist one of my mother's banana sandwiches off on her. Together, we listened to the great Martin Luther King speech and fell silent afterwards. I told her I'd met Dr. King at Penn Center in Beaufort, South Carolina, when my English teacher took me to a community sing at Penn Center on St. Helena Island. My brother Jim would later say that we were lucky to be raised in the South by two people who didn't have a racist bone in their bodies. That day, I tried to tell this loveliest of women the same thing, but youth had engineered barriers that cut me off from thoughts that surged around me in that inland sea where hormones raged. My words kept tripping over her loveliness.

We stayed together on a six-hour layover in Cincinnati; I've always loved the city of Cincinnati because she was at my side as we wandered through the rough-and-tumble district around the central city train station. On the same night that we heard Martin Luther King talk about the sons and daughters of slaves holding hands with the sons and daughters of slave owners, this kind and brilliant and gorgeous woman took my hand in the darkness. I fell asleep wondering how you tell a girl like this you were in love with her.

When I woke the next morning, she had departed my life forever. In the middle of the night, when we crossed some invisible borderline of the harsh and ruthless South where I was raised, the conductor had led her away. The train had entered that zone where the racial codes were honored to the letter of the law. She was moved by the loutish white conductor to the string of "colored" cars at the rear of the train. He confronted me with the old nastiness and told me he knew what I was after. I tried to find her, but my way was blocked by another conductor who had all the panache of a moonlighting Klansman. He informed me that I'd be arrested at the next town and put off the train if I "set one foot in the colored section." My shyness had prevented me from asking her name. Maddened, I patrolled the platforms whenever we reached a city in Virginia or the Carolinas, walking obsessively past the cars carrying hundreds of black passengers, praying to spot her pretty face looking out the window, trying to find me.

Now, as I remember her, she must've been shaken by her first encounter with that evil and embittering South that I'd first tasted in my mother's milk. I hope my South did not harm her after that. With her vitality, ebullience, and a delight in her own prettiness, she could pollinate a room with an infectious sense of joy. She'd accomplished something no girl had done to that point; she had made me feel handsome, prized, fascinating. I lost her to Jim Crow, the bastard who had made my childhood South part inferno, part embarrassment, and all shame. She was the third girl who had ever held my hand.

SIXTY HOURS AFTER I LEFT MY FAMILY in Omaha, I stepped off the train in Charleston and found myself in the merciless embrace of The Citadel's plebe system. When I first walked on campus, the plebe system held no fear because Mel Thompson had promised that athletes were protected from its cruelties and excesses. But the train was late and I arrived in Charleston five hours after Coach Thompson had asked us to meet him at the field house the day before the other cadets reported. On campus, I became disoriented when the guard at Lesesne Gate, the entrance to The Citadel, began screaming at me. After making a phone call, he ordered me over to Second Battalion where a group of his friends were waiting for me.

Since I was the only freshman in the barracks, ten or twenty sophomores got to practice their black arts on me. More and more cadets heard the noise and soon joined the pleasantries. It was the first time the pack would go after me, but it would not be the last. The screaming became louder as it began to grow dark. I did pushups until I dropped, ran the stairs until I dropped, held out a rifle until I almost dropped it (a crime beyond forgiveness in the world of a plebe). Then, suddenly, I was thrown out of the battalion and told to run for my life. I ran the mile to Highway 17 where I hitchhiked the seventy miles to Beaufort. A Marine corporal dropped me at The Shack, the place where teenagers gathered in the town I had left three months earlier, as innocent an American boy who has ever breathed southern air.

Someone greeted me as I walked along the line of cars with trays on their window and the smell of hamburgers and french fries in the air. I approached the car of my chemistry teacher, Walt Gnann, and two of my favorite English teachers, Gene Norris and Millen Ellis. Gene was the most important and necessary teacher of my life and one of the best friends I've ever had.

"What are you doing here, scalawag?" Gene said. "You're supposed to be at The Citadel."

"I didn't like it."

"Didn't like what?" Gene said. "It hasn't even started yet."

"If it hasn't started, I hate to see what it's like when it does."

"I wouldn't go there on a bet," Millen said.

"I ain't talking to this boy," Gene said, getting out of the car. "I don't care if you quit, boy, but at least give the place a chance."

Walt Gnann motioned for me to get into his car. "Come on over to my place, Pat. We'll see how you feel about it in the morning."

I spent the night in my chemistry teacher's house. I was a terrible chemistry student but that night, Walt and Millen folded kindness over me like a shawl. The next morning, Gene had arranged a ride back to The Citadel with Ray Williams, a Beaufort boy who was a senior and a cadet officer. Ray dropped me off in front of Second Battalion where I walked through the gates to begin the seminal year of my young manhood.

I SUFFERED GRIEVOUSLY UNDER THE SPELL and sway of the plebe system. It left me terrified, brutalized, altered, and introduced me to a coward that lay deep inside of me. I was afraid the moment the plebe system began until it ended. I displayed no courage because I found none to offer. To me, it was mind-numbing, savage, unrelenting, and base. It broke me a thousand times and then a thousand more, then expertly glued me back together and sent me out to be broken again. After my eighteen-year trial by father, the last thing I needed was a long exposure to the most vaunted plebe system in the country. They called the first week "Hell Week," and Dante Alighieri could not have coined a more accurate nomenclature.

Because I had failed to connect with the freshman basketball team the night before the plebes reported, the athletic department assigned a senior named Bud Aston, a member of the Fourth Battalion Staff, to deliver me to my team. It was Mr. Aston who taught me to salute, the proper way to do a right, left, and about-face, and how to march in step. He marched me across the parade ground to Mark Clark Hall and straight into the barbershop where Mr. Rampey sheared my scalp like a Highland sheep. I didn't recognize the boy who stared back with his raw, gleaming skull.

As he took me to be measured for uniforms and to collect the paraphernalia for the next four years as a Citadel cadet, Bud Aston gave me advice I'd need to survive. After I'd been screamed at by two sophomores who measured me for shirts, Mr. Aston whispered, "Remember this, Mr. Conroy. I was exactly where you are three years ago. It's terrifying. It's supposed to be. Most of you won't be able to stand it. But the best of you will. Don't take it seriously. Laugh at it. Those two sophomores who just racked you? They were knobs last year, just like you. Do what they say. Be enthusiastic about it. The year'll pass quickly."

During the two days he spent with me, Mr. Aston passed on hundreds of tips for surviving the acid probation of the plebe system. Because I had missed the hour-long instruction in rifle manual, Mr. Aston taught me to handle my M-1 with dispatch and expertise. When I failed to snap the rifle into my left hand properly at his command, "Left shoulder arms," he corrected me with great economy.

The barracks was a vessel of pure noise, the constant screaming of the upperclassmen unnerving, but Mr. Aston constantly reassured me. "Don't let the noise bother you. That's all it is, noise. Hell Night's tonight. That's when you'll find out what you're made of. They'll teach you how to brace in the corner alcove room of R Company. Big R is the most military of all the companies in the Corps. They take this shit seriously. Go along with them. Anyone who fights the system gets run out. Remember that, Mr. Conroy. I'll check on you tonight. Good luck."

Hell Night still burns through the scaffolding of both my fate and my history like a pillar of flame. Even my eighteen fearful years spent quaking beneath my father's frightful gaze did little to prepare me for this lunatic attack on the souls of boys. It was a night that my own soul felt like an acre of Omaha Beach on D-day. I was still recovering from the trauma of it a year later. Those were the last years of General Mark Clark's tenure at The Citadel, and he'd vowed that the school would have the toughest plebe system in the world. I personally attest that he succeeded admirably.

When I wrote the section called "The Taming" in *The Lords of Discipline* I said everything I wanted to say about The Citadel's plebe system. It surprised me when older graduates of the school read my account and thought I'd made it up to harm my college. Over a period of time, the system had evolved into the extreme form of mob violence my classmates and I experienced. Because so many American soldiers had broken under torture and duress during the Korean War, The Citadel's system was to be so horrific that Citadel men could be counted on, no matter how inhumane the conditions or cunning the abuse. Citadel men were expected to provide an unshakable bulwark against the rise of Communism in the Western Hemisphere. I have yet to meet the Communist who has treated me as abominably as the cadre of R Company did my plebe year.

My roommate and I had barely spoken to each other when we finally shook hands on the day of Hell Night. His name was Bob Patterson, and he was from Longmeadow, Massachusetts. I knew immediately that Bob, nice looking and soft-spoken, would survive this test by fire. "This place sucks, doesn't it?" were the first words he spoke to me. I couldn't have agreed more.

"Let's show the fucks. Let's you and me make it," Bob said, and I could see he meant it. By accident The Citadel had hooked me up with the right guy.

It was nightfall when they stood me in the first squad of the first platoon of R Company in the utter silence of a blacked-out barracks. The cadre had withdrawn into the shadows of the stairwell and had left us alone, bracing for the first time, our chins racked in uncomfortably against our throats. Dressed in bathrobes, field caps, and flip-flops, the plebes prepared themselves for the onslaught.

A harmonica played a haunting, aching version of "Home, Sweet Home" as the guards made an elaborate ceremony of slamming and locking the metal gates with keys as long as a man's hands. I'd grown so accustomed to their screaming and profanity that the silence felt malignant in the tropical, tide-scented air. Mosquitoes siphoned blood out of the back of my knees, my ears, my forearms. The speechless fear of boys scented the air like the charged ions after a thunderstorm. For me, standing in the darkness waiting for Hell Night to break over me felt like a fitting exclamation to a childhood I'd hated from the time of first consciousness. Two hundred forty plebes awaited their fate and destiny with me in Fourth Battalion. Eighty-three of them would survive until graduation.

The regimental commander, William Sansom, spoke into the intercom in a clear, loud voice. "Gentlemen, the plebe system for the class of 1967 is now in effect."

The lights flooded on, and the four cadres of N, O, R, and T companies roared into sudden life and poured like liquid flame through the shocked, overwhelmed ranks of plebes. In the sheer force of their assault, they blew us out like candles, one by one. The barracks turned into containers of overripe noise and chaos. Someone screamed in my right ear, "Right face, smackhead." But at the same time, the scream came into my left ear, "About face, maggot." A face materialized in front of me, feral and out of control. "Left face, douche bag! You better do what I order you to do, wad-waste."

Paralysis set in quickly. The uproar was so cataclysmic that I just held on in the first ten minutes until I adjusted to the pure maelstrom. The cadre overwhelmed us and seemed thousand-voiced and ubiquitous as they cut wide swaths through us. When I executed a left-face, I was a foot away from the terrified face of a chinless boy who could not stop trembling. When I did an about-face, I was inches away from an overweight boy who had begun to cry. The trembling and the tears attracted swarms of upperclassmen who sensed the fragility of both boys, frothing with pleasure when the boys came apart. I never saw either boy after that night, and they made up part of the lost wreckage of my torn-apart class.

I was grateful when ordered to do twenty-five pushups because that generally meant the cadre man was going on down the line to scream at someone else. "One sir, two sir, three sir, four sir," I'd shout. When I leapt back up, bracing again, someone else would appear and the games would begin anew. The cadre wanted you to memorize their names and do it quickly. I screamed those names back in a plague of words, discordant as a broken hive of killer bees—those debased names cut through the air around my ears. Before the night was over, I knew the cadets who were just doing their jobs and the ones I'd learn to fear. The Citadel was a crucible of authentic leadership, and to a much lesser degree, a hothouse where sadists perfected their grim arts. Nothing has surprised me so much or lingered in memory so long as Hell Night, and, until I endured it, I'd never understood what an overfearful, shakable boy I was. I still wear that night as wound and rite of passage, and the hour where I watched my boyhood die in tears. What I couldn't stand was not my own suffering, which was bad enough, but the suffering of the nameless plebes around me, the acne-scarred, the oversensitive, the nervous nellies, and the mama's boys forced into The Citadel by undermining fathers. It wasn't pretty but it was effective. I saw boys lining up at the gates of Stevens Barracks trembling, desperate to remove themselves from this sanctioned madness. Eight freshmen left R Company that night. Seven more would not survive Hell Week. I would have joined them cheerfully had I not feared my father far more than the wrath of the cadre.

Toward the end of that night, a cadet first lieutenant came to me from the side and said, "Relax your knees, Mr. Conroy. That's it. Your classmates are fainting because they've locked their knees. It's almost over. You're doing well. You've survived Hell Night. I think you're going to make it."

It was Bud Aston, his voice brotherly and humane. "Sir, yes, sir," I said, almost blind in my own sweat.

Bud Aston moved out of sight and out of my life as a cadet. When the bugle sounded a merciful end to Hell Night, I heard the shouts of "Get to your rooms, dumbheads. Move, smacks." I took one step and fell to my knees. With most of my fellow plebes, I crawled to my room. An upperclassman mounted me and rode me like a pony all the way to my doorway. I remembered his high-pitched laughter as he slapped me on the ass to make me go faster.

In the room, I was on my hands and knees gasping for breath when Bob Patterson crawled in beside me. We spent a long minute gasping, then Bob reached over and touched my shoulder. "You okay, Pat?"

"I don't know, Bob. How 'bout you?"

"Jesus Christ. Can you believe that shit?"

"I might have made a slight error in my choice of colleges," I said.

When Bob spoke to me with such great tenderness and when we laughed together in that darkened room, the brotherhood had begun its deft, healing work. When they began screaming for us to get to the shower room, Bob and I helped each other rise to our feet. I was terrified to go out on the galleries to face them again, and I paused at the door. Bob pushed me and whispered, "Let's show the fucks," and we headed out toward them.

In the bathroom, the screaming was nightmarish as they ran us into a hot shower, had us soap ourselves down, then sent us back to our rooms before we could wash the soap off. Bob and I stood by our sink and washed off as well as we could. Because I'd done so many pushups, I couldn't climb into the top bunk until Bob let me step on his back. I lay awake long enough to hear him breathing easily in his sleep, but before I fell into a troubled, exhausted sleep, I swore to myself, "I'll never raise my voice to a plebe." And I never did, not once, during my four-year test at The Citadel.

The following Sunday, which marked the official end of Hell Week, the rest of the Corps returned to join up with the cadre that had trained us in the art of becoming cadets. After mess that night and the evening ritual of the sweat party, my roommate and I were summoned into the alcove room of the four senior privates who had moved in next door. Bob and I came in bracing and fearful, expecting the worse.

The four seniors were as relaxed as the cadre were bubonic. They laughed good-naturedly when they saw us bracing and red-faced.

"At ease, dumbheads," one of them said. Since no one had given that command to us before, Bob and I had no idea what to do, so we remained locked into our braces.

"It means relax, boys," a red-haired senior said. "We come in peace. You've nothing to fear from us."

"Do you believe in slavery, dumbheads?" the first guy said, apple-cheeked, his eyes glittering with humor. "Pop off."

"Sir no sir," Bob and I said.

"You've been assigned to us," Jim Plunkett said. "I personally don't believe in slavery, but it exists here at The Citadel. Right, guys?"

"It's terrible," Dave Keyser said. "I'm a man of God, dumbheads. I'll be entering the seminary next year with slavery on my conscience."

"I'm going to like having slaves," Mr. Hough said.

"You'll clean our room every morning, smacks. You'll make our beds, clean our sinks, sweep our floors. This room will be shipshape before you leave for class. You'll shine our shoes, clean our brass—just normal practices common to slaves everywhere. Do you understand, dumb squats?" Plunkett said.

"Sir yes sir!"

"Except for me," he continued. "I'm an exceptional case. I'm famous for running shit on the system here. I'm a special kind of senior private, right guys?"

"A pig," LaBianco said.

"A disgrace to The Citadel," Hough added.

"He sets a new low for senior privates," Keyser agreed.

"I'm a slob. A legend among my classmates. I'm allergic to shoe polish. Brasso makes me gag. You shine for these guys. You let me decay at my own speed."

Then Gary LaBianco said, "Gentlemen, you help us and we'll help you get through this fucking shithole. You lucked out, boys. We're very nice guys."

"Sweethearts," Keyser agreed.

"We don't rack ass. We don't buck for rank. And we're not military dicks," Hough said.

"Wait a minute," LaBianco said. "Are you boys bucking for rank?"

Bob Patterson surprised me by saying, "Yes, sir. I'm bucking for rank."

"What about you, Conroy?" Keyser asked.

"No, sir. I want to be like you guys, sir," I said, sealing my identity in R Company for all time.

"Yep, we got us some good slaves," Jimbo Plunkett said. "One's a dick. One's a human being."

And, in time, good slaves did Bob Patterson and I become. First we had to learn how to sweep a floor that would satisfy the antiseptic fanaticism of a surly corporal, and clean a sink where bacteria feared to grow. We had to master the mystery of spit-shined shoes and polished brass. Bob and I learned the Citadel way of folding underwear and socks in clean white sheets of paper. We became the sworn enemies of lint and dust and disorder of all kinds. It took us a month to master the domestic arts of being a plebe, but by the end of the year, I could get a job as a manservant in a Henry James novel.

The mess hall was central to the plebes' worse nightmare during my time at The Citadel. It was at the dining table that cruelty found its proving ground among the cadre. The six weeks I spent with R

Company at mess before the basketball season began were desperate. I learned many ways to break a man during my time as a plebe, but none were as effective as starvation. For thirty minutes the cadre could harass us up close as we sat braced and rigid on the outer six inches of our chairs. We learned to fill their water and milk glasses as soon as we sat down. They tested us on our proficiency at plebe knowledge. I still know all the company commanders from that year, and their names make up a fearful litany of Satan's lieutenants that I bring as cargo with me.

The Monday after Hell Week was the first time I caught up with my fellow freshmen basketball players. All six of them were in the same state of shock when I met them. We looked like survivors of a death march, and our glazed eyes gave the locker room a hushed, funereal aura. Coach Paul Brandenberg, the freshman coach, introduced me to my team-mates.

"Hey, Pat. We lost you in the crowd somehow. It's taken a week of red tape to get you over to the gym. What happened to your train?"

"It was five hours late, Coach," I said.

"How'd you do the first week?"

"Never had so much fun, Coach," I said, and heard Bill Taflinger laugh.

"Told you he was funny," Bill said, coming over to shake hands with me.

Coach Brandenberg said, "This is Danny Mohr, Pat. One of the best players out of North Carolina last year. He's from Wilmington, a southern boy like you."

"I used to live at Camp Lejeune and Cherry Point, Danny," I said.

"Another southern boy, Donnie Biggs of Macon," Coach Brandenberg said.

"I was born in Atlanta," I said to the six-six forward who was built as well as any boy I've ever seen. Donnie was so depressed that he could barely look up to greet me.

"You guys are the first three boys we've ever recruited from the South in this basketball program," the coach said.

"Lucky us, huh, Donnie?" I said to the big man from Macon.

When we dressed and went out to the main court to shoot around, I noticed right away that I was the smallest man on the team by four inches. As I watched the five scholarship boys making jump shots from around the perimeter, I felt the first attack of panic set in. These guys were not just better basketball players than I was, I was not good enough to be a manager in their league. When we played a three-on-three half-court game later that afternoon, the difference became even more apparent to me. Jim Halpin, who I learned led the Catholic League of Philadelphia in scoring his senior year, was a six-foot-two-inch guard who covered me like a film of sweat on defense and had the quickest, most accurate jump shot I'd ever seen. Taflinger, the other guard, at six three kept posting me up down low, using his height and long arms to score at will.

That Friday before practice I sought out Paul Brandenberg and told him, "Coach, I'm not good enough to play on this team."

"Who says so?"

"I do, Coach. I've never seen guys this good. Taflinger scores on me every time he gets the ball. Halpin takes the ball away from me every time I dribble."

"No one's ever taught you how to play defense, Pat," he said. "We'll teach you that. That move Halpin has—he flicks the ball away by going behind you when you dribble. That's a big-city move. You only see it in the Northeast. Especially in Philly. We're going to have to break Jim of that habit. The refs down here have never seen it. They'll call a foul on him every time."

"Jimmy hasn't fouled me yet," I said. "I can't figure out what he's doing. I dribble by him, he ducks behind me and flicks the ball out of bounds."

"Try this," Coach Brandenberg said. "The second you go by Halpin, do a crossover dribble. Just change hands."

That afternoon with Jim Halpin guarding me again, I took my coach's advice and switched hands on the dribble the instant I flashed by him. He kept slapping the hand where the ball had been and I was sailing through the lane for a layup. In the far corner of the gym I watched Coach Brandenberg observing the game in secret, since it was against NCAA rules for coaches to oversee practices until October 15. Smoking a cigarette, he pointed at me and nodded his head in approval. Good coaching is good teaching and nothing else. I saw him walk behind the bleachers to his office.

That Sunday I went over to Mark Clark Hall to place a collect call to my family in Omaha. I flooded with emotion when I heard the phone ring in another strange house I barely knew. Though I'd tried to hide my disappointment, it had hurt my feelings that I was the only freshman I saw on the day the plebes reported who arrived without his parents. I heard the operator say, "Collect call from a Mr. Pat Conroy. Will you accept charges?"

I exploded with rage when my mother said, "No. Sorry, operator, but we don't know any Pat Conroy."

Slamming the phone down, I immediately made another collect call and when the operator spoke I said, "Accept the damn phone call, Mom."

With great reluctance she did. "Don't make this a habit, young man. You know this family isn't made of money. How's your first couple of weeks in college going? You having a ball?"

I began weeping and couldn't stop. I'd suffered a mild breakdown of spirit and character as I lost a grip on all the words I'd planned to say to my mother. For thirty seconds I sobbed until I could gain control. "Mom, you sent me to a torture chamber," I gasped out finally.

"Well, it'll be good for you. It'll make a man out of you."

"It'll make a man like Dad out of me," I snapped back.

"Just how bad is it?" Mom asked. "Give me an example."

"It's worse than Dad—that's how bad it is. I'd much rather be living with Dad than going to this school."

After a long pause, my mother said, "Oh, my God."

Then my father took the phone, and I heard his despised, mocking voice. "It sounds like my little baby boy's having some boo-hoo time with Mommy. If baby boy wants to do some whining he can talk to Daddy-poo."

"I don't like The Citadel, Dad," I said, controlling the quaver in my voice. "I'm thinking about coming home."

I heard my father's laughter, then the hardening of his voice as he asked, "Where's home, son? You no longer have a home." He hung up before I could talk to my brothers or sisters.

In Colonel John Doyle's English class, I was one of forty plebes who sat in exhaustion as he told us what he expected of us in English 101. Colonel Doyle was fastidious and cultivated. He twinkled when he spoke to us in an elegant accent from the midlands of Virginia. He passed out a piece of paper and asked us to list every novel we'd read in high school. Taking the assignment seriously, I was listing my fortieth novel when I became aware of a strange murmuring. I looked up to see my classmates staring at me with hostility. For ten minutes, I'd been the only cadet in the class still adding to his list, and they didn't appreciate my show-offy gesture at all. I put my pencil down quickly, and Colonel Doyle asked that we pass up the papers.

At the next class Colonel Doyle asked us to write an essay on any topic to give him some idea about our skills in the use of the English language. "Take your time. Write carefully about a subject that has meaning for you."

Before I began, I studied Colonel Doyle's face, which registered a kindly sensibility as opposed to the cult of masculinity I was facing each day in the barracks. His voice sounded like silk polishing ivory as he warned us to watch for the dangle of participles and the gentlemanly agreement of verbs. He had a face and a manner I trusted, and I began to write. Colonel John Doyle never forgot the inflammatory essay I wrote for him in that heat-dazed English class in 1963.

I described every single thing I could remember about Hell Week, leaving nothing out. I gave Colonel Doyle a cook's tour of The Citadel seen through a knob's eyes when the details were still fresh and pulsing. Taking him through sweat parties in the shower rooms, I told him of doing so many pushups I couldn't even reach up to remove a field cap from my head. I wrote of being marched in a platoon of knobs down to the marsh's edge where the gnats and mosquitoes feasted on us, and we weren't allowed to move a muscle to drive them away. I bore witness to the starvation that took place every day at mess and the indefensible cruelty the cadre displayed to ugly boys or pimpled ones or the skinny and fat boys whose faces burned with shame at the ferocity of the abuse. The barracks were a place where young boys' souls went to die, and I questioned how a man of his disposition and kindness could take such an active part in such inhumanity. At the end of my essay I had an anonymous plebe walk out onto the middle of the quad at 0300 hours and excrete solemnly in the moonlight air as a revolutionary act to express his utter contempt for The Citadel's out-of-control plebe system. I signed my name with a flourish, and after the papers were handed forward I considered the possibility that I'd just performed a reckless, even suicidal act. My college career hung in the balance of my instincts concerning John Doyle's character.

At the beginning of the next class, he handed out the marked and corrected essays, and the room filled with the murmurous discontent of plebes. Doyle was notorious for his rigorous standards and tough grading, and he had flunked four-fifths of the class for their initial performance on the art of the essay. To my infinite relief, he had awarded me an A, but made an appointment for me in his office at 1400 hours the next Friday. "You seem to be having some problems adjusting to the plebe system, Mr. Conroy," he wrote with an economy of both phrasing and emotion that would become familiar to me.

On Friday afternoon, I sat beside Colonel Doyle's desk as he studied the list of the novels I'd itemized for him at the beginning of his class.

"You are widely read, Mr. Conroy," he said.

"My mother's read everything," I said. "She passed that on to my sister and me."

"You listed more novels than all the rest of your class. Are you unhappy here?"

"I hate this place," I said.

"This essay you wrote . . . you were testing me, weren't you, Mr. Conroy?"

"I'm not sure what you mean, sir."

"You knew I could have you thrown out of college if I turned this paper over to the commandant," Colonel Doyle said.

"Yes, sir, I think I knew that."

"I gave you an A instead," he said. "I hope I passed your test."

"With flying colors, sir," I said.

"I'm sorry you're having such a difficult time at The Citadel," he said. "But I'd like you to know the young men who graduate from this college are the finest men I've ever met. A Citadel man is quite the work of art. Your time will be well spent here."

"If I stay that long, sir."

"You'll stay," he said.

"How do you know, sir?"

"Your essay," Colonel Doyle said. "The plebe system can't touch the spirit of that boy."

OUR COACHES HADN'T THE FOGGIEST NOTIONS of what we were going through in the barracks when we left them at the Armory each night. Nor could they have done a single thing about it had they known. My teammates were as tough and strong as any boys in America yet every one of them had trouble surviving the fury of that system. It was not the physical rigor that came near to breaking us, it was the psychological harassment that was a part of those murderous days under the Charleston sun. I stayed at the point of mental breakdown for the entire nine months. I found I was an oversensitive, touchy boy trapped in a milieu where sensitivity won no merit badges and touchiness itself was a capital crime. Very early, I learned that the cadre admired a good attitude, so I tried to bring a boundless enthusiasm to whatever indignity they required. When my first sergeant asked me to do fifty pushups, I dropped to the ground and began pumping them out as though he had flung me a fistful of hundred-dollar bills. It was the boys who flashed anger or irritation that attracted the malignant attention of the upperclassmen hungry for rank. "Racking ass" was an art form among the cadre, and the best among them could break a weak boy in an hour or less. The cadre tried to dismantle me and succeeded every night, but I didn't reveal that coming-apart to them. I disguised myself as a tough guy, a jock, and time seemed to crawl on its hands and knees. I prayed that the year pass quickly and it slowed to a snail's pace. I begged my mother to let me leave. I planned a hundred versions of my escape. In darkness I told Bob Patterson that the end was nearing for me and that he needed to think about getting another roommate.

"We're not like that, Conroy," my quiet roommate would say.

"Like what, Patter-knob," I said, using the nickname the seniors next door had given him.

"We're not quitters. Just the way we were raised."

"I want to be a quitter," I said.

"Then quit," Bob said. "You talk about it every night."

"You know what would really help me get through this year?"

"What?"

"I need you to develop a much better personality. You're a quiet guy, Bob, and I hate quiet guys. I like guys with fabulous personalities, chatterboxes, guys with diarrhea of the mouth. Open up to me. Tell great jokes."

"Fuck you, Conroy. Go to sleep," Patter-knob would say, half asleep. His solidness got me through that year, the good-natured competence he brought to the smallest tasks as well as his refusal to take cruelty seriously.

My only glimpse of normal life in the barracks came each morning when I cleaned the room of my four senior privates next door. I made their beds, swept their floors, folded their laundry, straightened their personal items in the four presses, cleaned their sink, and took out their trash. I became efficient and grew to enjoy the easy camaraderie of the four privates who seemed uncorrupted by the lust for rank displayed by most of the cadre.

My freshman basketball team was a superb collection of athletes and we played superbly together. We lost a single game to Clemson that we should've won running away, but we ran most of the other teams out of the gym. Don Biggs was a force of nature under the boards; he was aggressive and well-coached and I loved the way he and Mohr always looked for the cutoff man on the wing when they pulled a rebound off the boards. Craig Fisher and Taflinger were terrific forwards and Jim Halpin was the best shooting guard I'd ever seen. Our team averaged over ninety points a game and developed such a good reputation in the Corps that we started to draw crowds for the freshman games, a rarity.

Coach Brandenberg was laconic and soft-spoken, and devotion to him came easily. His joy in the company of boys spilled out of him, and we would've torn the gym down and salted the earth for him had he ordered us to do so. We hungered for his praise, which he was generous with. We ran the floor for him as though our uniforms were on fire. We embarrassed teams because we wanted our coach to look so marvelously gifted. We fast-broke teams from one end of South Carolina to another, making our college proud in the process.

But the plebe system reached hard into the ranks of my freshman team. When Don Biggs scored twenty-five points against Clemson, he was met by a half-dozen of his cadre when he returned to the barracks. They gave him his own special sweat party so he wouldn't be in any danger of getting a swelled head. It happened to Taflinger and Fisher after the Davidson game, and Halpin and Mohr after the Furman game. Halpin had scored thirty-two points against Furman and I'd never seen a human being bring that hot a hand to a basketball court. I spent the night feeding Halpin as we ran the pick-and-roll. Coming off me in a flash, Halpin'd be up in the air with a snakelike quickness impossible to defend against, making sixteen out of eighteen jump shots. A Company gave Halpin his own individualized sweat party when he returned to the barracks. The cadre made sure they sullied a freshman athlete's night when he brought glory to the playing fields of The Citadel.

Because I was the only basketball player in Romeo Company, I had a contingent waiting for me after every game that year. They'd halt me under the stairwell and make me run the stairs or do pushups until I dropped. I had scored twenty-four points against the Davidson freshmen, and it enraged the cadre that my name was mentioned in the morning paper.

"You missed three sweat parties, douche bag," my squad sergeant said. "Hit it for fifty, dumbhead."

"You feel bad about shitting on your classmates, abortion?" someone shouted above me as I pumped out my pushups.

"Sir yes sir!" I shouted.

"They had PT, a parade, SMI, and you were out gallivanting about with the other jocks eating ice-cream sundaes. Isn't that right, Conroy? Pop off."

"Sir no sir," I said, rising to my feet and bracing in front of them for the inevitable, "Give me another fifty, Conroy."

"You think you're better than your classmates, don't you, wadwaste? Pop off."

"Sir no sir."

"You think you're special and valuable while your poor classmates are over here putting out for the Corps while you're taking naps and jacking off over at the Armory, right, smackhead?"

"Sir no sir."

"You think you're hot shit when you get your name in the paper, don't you, douche bag?"

"Sir no sir," I said, then all of us heard Jim Plunkett's voice.

"Conroy, get to my room," Plunkett ordered. "Clean it up or I'll rack your ass till daybreak."

"We're not finished with him yet, Jimbo," a conciliatory squad sergeant said.

"Yeah you are," Plunkett said, wading through them. He hit me hard on the chest with a closed fist. "Get your ass in my room, dumbhead. Scrub the floor with a toothbrush."

The other three seniors were at their desks, studying hard, when I entered the alcove room and grabbed a broom. I heard some juniors arguing with Plunkett and learned as I listened that the highest-ranked juniors in the Corps lacked the power to overrule the will of the lowest senior private. At The Citadel, the class system was paramount. It was a gallant, if foolhardy, underclassman who dared write up a senior for any infraction at all. Plunkett ran them off with a tirade of well-chosen profanity.

"Mr. Plunkett has a problem, Mr. Conroy," Mr. Keyser told me. "He's closing in on a hundred demerits. They kick a senior out of school when he breaks the century mark."

"It's no sweat," Plunkett insisted.

I went to Plunkett's bed where his scrofulous shoes were displayed, picked up three pairs, and took them over to my room to shine them. My roommate and I spent the entire evening study period polishing up Jimbo Plunkett's scruffy and unsanitized senior private lifestyle. We cleaned every piece of brass in his press and arranged them like crown jewels. When we finished the job as taps was playing, Plunkett's corner of the Citadel world looked like it was inhabited by an anal-retentive plebe. He had accumulated eighty-six demerits and Bob and I pledged to do everything we could to keep our senior in school. We could rescue Mr. Plunkett from his own worst instincts.


HERE IS THE FIRST POEM I HAD PUBLISHED at The Citadel. Its title was "To Tom Wolf." It bothered me greatly that my editors had misspelled Wolfe and shortened his name to Tom. But I was a plebe and my editors were not particularly open to criticisms by freshmen.

> *O sleep now, Tom, your pen is quelled.*
> *You have a grave to show it.*
> *But I have heard an eagle say*
> *"These mountains need a poet."*

I, of course, had never encountered an eagle who said any such thing, or anything at all. The poem wandered on for three more queasy stanzas until it mercifully ended on a bright, triumphant note of half-baked and completely unearned ecstasy. Not a single member of the Citadel community ever commented on my feverish ode to Thomas Wolfe. It was a stone dropped into torpid waters and made not a single ripple. But my second poem, a bit of doggerel I tossed off one night after a sweat party, gave me my first taste of fame as an author, and I learned the invaluable lesson that fame could be a killing thing, something I am not sure that my literary hero Thomas Wolfe ever learned. For several days, I became the most famous poet in the history of The Citadel when I published these four lines:

> *The dreams of youth are pleasant dreams,*
> *Of women, vintage, and the sea.*
> *Last night I dreamt I was a dog*
> *Who found an upperclassman tree.*

Upperclassmen from all four battalions were kind enough to visit me to discuss my poetry in depth. Not a single one asked me a question about Thomas Wolfe, but all expressed curiosity at my desire to urinate on them. They encouraged my passion for poetry by making me do pushups until I dropped into a pool of my own vomit. My squad sergeant and I engaged in a brief, illuminating discussion of my theory of poetics. A man of few words, he made the eloquent gesture of urinating on my back while I was doing pushups for him. I was barely eighteen, and I had already suffered for my art.

That single poem changed my whole life at The Citadel, the way I was regarded by my classmates and the Corps as a whole. Before its publication, I'd blended in the lower phylum of the Corps of Cadets with the flawless instinct of a chameleon. Playing basketball was the singular mark of my distinction. The poem made me seem much more cocky and daring and risk-taking than I actually was. My classmates in Romeo Company thought I'd taken momentary leave of my senses and that I was to be more pitied than scorned. I didn't regret writing the poem, but had serious reservations about the wisdom of publishing it.

My roommate chuckled every time he read it and said, "You really ran some shit on those guys, Pat. I heard one of them say you're the gauldiest knob in the Corps."

As a knob, you longed for disengagement and invisibility . . . a "gauldy" knob, with its implication of the renegade and outlaw, was the lowest form of life in the Corps. The Corps prided itself as a hive of conformity for the inspection of outsiders, but allowed its individual members broad access to both strangeness and eccentricities once the barracks gates were shut. The writing of poetry was one of the oddest activities a cadet could indulge in, but for a knob to write a poem so openly disrespectful of the upper classes and to do it for the fall issue of a magazine published at Homecoming was unprecedented.

I awaited the worst and the worst finally came. The cadre came for me and for me alone. When they wanted to run a freshman out, they set the pack loose on him. No one knows how he will stand up to the pack when it comes at him in its full fury. I broke easily.

The cadre pulled me into the shower room and eight of them went after me. All eight screamed out conflicting orders at the same time, and when I chose one order to execute, the other seven were all over me, punching me in the chest, in the back, and soon the chaos of pure noise overwhelmed me. One shouted for me to name all the company commanders in the Corps, while another shouted at me to recite the cadet prayer, while another demanded that I recite the guard orders. Even when I was doing pushups, cadre members were down on the floor with me screaming in both ears. In less than ten minutes, the unraveling started and once it did I lost control of everything. When I tried to answer a question, I couldn't find my voice and heard one of them shout triumphantly, "He's cracking! He's cracking!"

They increased the volume of their voices until it seemed that this bedlam of noise and hate was worldwide and my brain was afire and lost and making no connections. Tears streamed down my face, the first sob burst from my chest, and I wept on my knees before them, prostrate, defenseless, as they swarmed all over me, coming in for the kill.

"Gutless fuck. Little baby boy. Cry, little girl. Cry, little girl. Ah, we hurt baby's feelings. Tell us you're quitting, Conroy. Let us know you're quitting, Conroy. We'll walk you to the gate. We'll shake your pussy hands goodbye. Little girl can go home to Mommy. Mommy makes it all nice."

If I could've spoken, I'd have quit school at that moment; there was nothing I wouldn't have done to end this degradation. But I'd lost all powers of speech and could only sob with my face against the tiles as the storm of their shouting passed over and through me. There was nothing left to save when I heard a disturbance at the door. My seniors had come for me, my four wonderful senior privates, the boys without rank that I'd come to revere came running into that shower room when my roommate told them where I was. Plunkett swung at one of my tormentors and Hough and LaBianco and Keyser pulled me to my feet. Amidst great shouting and cursing they moved me swiftly through the crowd of cadre who pressed forward to have a go at me again. They'd lost me at the very moment I cried uncle, and they knew it. My senior privates had stormed in for the rescue and I'd love them the rest of my life for it.

"You chickenshit fucks keep away from Conroy," Plunkett warned them at the entrance to my room. "I'll kick the living hell out of anyone who tries to bother him tonight."

My roommate put me right to bed with great solicitude. I still couldn't control my sobbing and wept through the rest of the evening study period. Periodically, Bob would rise from his desk, come over and squeeze my shoulders and adjust the covers. Gentle and encouraging, the four seniors came over to see how I was doing.

Plunkett said, "It can't get worse than this. You survived the worst of it, kid. Remember, they can't kill you. They went to the limit of what they can do. They're not allowed to kill you."

LaBianco said, "They'll go for you again tomorrow, Conroy. Get yourself ready for them. Prepare yourself."

"You'll stand it better next time," Keyser said. "Pray tonight. Ask for God's help. I'll be praying and as you know, next year I'll be a man of God."

Mr. Hough said, "Pull it together, Conroy. We can't afford to lose a slave as good as you. We trained you too well."

Later I would find a piece I had composed in Colonel Goodheart's history class trying to find a way to honor the heroism of my four seniors:

> *Plunkett and Keyser, LaBianco and Hough*
> *Men of substance and incredible stuff*
> *I could live forever and not thank them enough*
> *Plunkett and Keyser, LaBianco and Hough.*

But on the night of my meltdown, at my lowest moment as a brother and ruined plebe, the armors of the brotherhood began to form their secret shells around me, to enfold me into the house where the regiment whispers its softest words to its initiates. The seniors checked up on me all during evening study period. My classmates from R Company sneaked down to my room to offer words of encouragement and solidarity, and to ask me to stay. Robbie Miller came and so did Dennis Webb and Robbie Schear. Mike Devito and Bo Marks came, then John Worrell and Carroll Pinner, Hobie Messervey, Wade Williford, and Charlie Claghorn all came. The boys who'd suffered with me since Hell Night looked in on me, spoke gently to me, comforted me, and tried to ease my suffering, though I couldn't stop myself from weeping. My classmates came and left me a gift in their wake—they sealed forever my desire to be one of them. What I hated most about The Citadel had occurred in that shower room, but what I honored most about it happened in my room when a solid line of head-shaven boys made their way to my bedside to lay the hands of brotherhood upon me. In the plebe system I endured and loathed, I could also feel the weight and shape and great bonding taking place in the darkness. That night my classmates showed they cared for me and they brought the assets of this fire-tested solidarity all night—there is little on earth so fierce and inarticulate and life-changing as the love of boys for other boys. Every plebe who came to my room that night did so illegally, but they came in secret to make one last effort to pull me back into the brotherhood. By the time study period ended at 2230 hours, I'd stopped crying. I washed my face and looked at myself in the mirror. I stared at my image and tried to kill off anything that remained soft in that boy's face.

I walked over to the next room and thanked my seniors for coming to get me. I told them I'd have quit if I could've uttered a word.

"We didn't give a shit about you personally, Conroy," Plunkett said. "We just didn't want to have to train another dumbhead."

"You're a smackhead to us, Conroy," Keyser said. "The scum of the earth."

"You mean nothing to us personally," LaBianco said.

"Nothing," Hough agreed.

"All of you are lying, sirs," I said. "Thank you again. I'll never forget it, sirs."

"They'll make another run for you tomorrow, smackhead," LaBianco warned.

"Be ready for them, Pat," Plunkett said, the first time an upperclassman had called me by my first name. It was the sound of the brotherhood again, recruiting me back into the house of the regiment.

"I'm ready for them now, sir," I said. I'd gotten my voice back, and the Red Army couldn't have run me out of school after surviving that one hellish night.

THEY CAME AT ME ALL THE NEXT DAY. News of my breakdown circulated through R Company and the cadre made a run at me after breakfast, another at noon formation, and a group took me alone to the shower room after evening mess. Where the night before I broke quickly, I found myself steely and resolute the following night. I chose one order to obey and obeyed it swiftly, no matter how many conflicting commands were shouted. The plebe knowledge that had forsaken me came back in a ceaseless tide, and I answered every question, doing it in the required military manner. Again, their assault was brutal, but I was game for it. There were ten cadets in the shower room with me on the second night, and I got to be friends with some of them the next year. They were good guys whom I enjoyed getting to know, though I'd never agree with their way of breaking plebes or their method of showing belief in "The System." Two of the cadets in that shower room were loathsome, spiderous boys whom I'd not urinate on today to put out a brushfire along the hairline of their cheap toupees. It was not that they were overzealous in their molding of plebes, it was the maniacal pleasure, carnal in nature, that they brought to the task of ungoverned sadism. My heart skipped with joy the following year when I discovered that their own classmates reviled them as much as I and my brother plebes, and had turned them into outcasts in the barracks.

In the middle of the sweat party, Jimbo Plunkett opened the door and watched me pumping out fifty pushups on the shower room floor. His presence made the cadre nervous after the confrontation the night before.

"You doing all right, dumbhead?" Mr. Plunkett asked me. "Pop off."

"Sir yes sir," I shouted.

"You need me, smack?" he asked.

"Sir no sir."

Plunkett surveyed the room then said, "Assholes," as he left. It was the last night the R Company cadre ever tried to run me out of The Citadel. I had learned how to hide the smell of my fear. Never once did I lose that fear, but I discovered how to mask its shameful scent.

· · ·

BEFORE MY FRESHMAN TEAM FACED EAST CAROLINA, my teammate Don Biggs asked me to step outside the field house after practice
one February night. Don possessed an angelic face on the body of a
bruiser. He could mix it up under the boards as well as any player I'd
ever seen. He was averaging seventeen points and pulling down fifteen
rebounds a game when we walked out beneath the winter stars. Don and
I had become extremely close since we returned from Christmas break.

"Pat, I haven't told any of the other guys yet," Don said. "But my father's driving over from Macon to pick me up tomorrow."

"You're leaving us, Donnie?" I asked, my voice downcast. "We've
been through so much together."

"This place isn't for me, Pat. I'm a big friendly southern boy, that's
all I am. I can't stand this screaming. I'm unhappy here, Pat. I've been
unhappy since the first day, and so have you."

"I certainly have, Donnie," I said. "I've made no secret of that."

"My parents said to bring you with me, Pat. You can stay at our
house in Macon. We can get jobs, apply to a new school next year."

"Sounds like heaven, Donnie," I said. "But I can't go with you."

"Why? You hate this place like poison."

"If I leave, my father'll beat the hell out of my mother. Then he'll
take it out on my brothers and sisters," I said.

"I'm so sorry. That's just awful. But you're always welcome to my
house in Macon. You'd love my mom and dad. They're the sweetest
people."

"I know their son. I know how sweet they are," I said.

The plebe system would claim over half of that magnificent freshman team. Craig Fisher, Bill Taflinger, and Dan Coope would follow
Biggs out of Lesesne Gate and play out their destinies in other states and
other schools. From our original team, Dan Mohr, Jim Halpin, and I
were the only survivors who limped our way into our sophomore year.
All of us had suffered grievously under the iron reign of the cadres. I'd
miss the companionship of Don Biggs for the rest of my life. My freshman team was stunned the next day when they heard news of his departure.

In February, I was quick-timing my way out of the barracks when I
spotted the R Company tactical officer conducting an unannounced
room inspection on the third division of N Company. I halted on the
gallery, did an abrupt about-face, and hurried to my seniors' room in the

alcove. Sleeping soundly in his bunk was Jim Plunkett. Since I was studiously aware that he was eight demerits short of being expelled from school I shook him awake. Or tried to.

"Mr. Plunkett, Captain Rose is in the barracks! He's inspecting the barracks, and it's five demerits if he catches you in bed. Get out, sir. He's on his way here."

Mr. Plunkett pushed me away and said, "I'm a senior private, dumbhead. He'll find thirty of us in the rack this morning."

"Yes, sir. But you've got too many demerits, sir. I've got to get you up and dressed," I said, pulling a disoriented Plunkett to his feet. He took a halfhearted swing at me, but I ducked it and left the room as he was putting his pants on.

"I'm going to rack your ass tonight, dumbhead," he shouted at me.

"Just being a good slave, sir," I said, hitting the gallery and racing to class, where I was burned for being late by my chemistry teacher, Colonel Durkee.

Jim Plunkett carried himself with a slouching, devil-may-care style that I found both charismatic and dangerous. He was the only cadet I ever met who could angle his hat in a way that said "fuck you" to the world. Though he was contemptuous of cadets who bucked for rank, all the top-ranked cadets in the Corps seemed smitten by him. He was a natural-born leader who was up to no good, and he knew all the places where trouble hung its hat. My roommate thought that Plunkett was a terrible influence on me, and he was right. There was not a knob in the company who feared the approach of Jim Plunkett or any of my other senior privates, and that was the kind of cadet I wanted to ripen into if I remained a part of the Corps.

During exam time, Plunkett had gotten in the habit of taking amphetamines or "black beauties" to help him stay up all night to study for his exams in electrical engineering. At the end of February, he began a five-day binge that caused him to be seriously disoriented. I'd helped get him out of bed on the first day of this regimen, but Plunkett kept taking them to get through a stretch of exams early in his final semester. He'd study all night, then sleep through most of the day. His waking moments were zombielike and disorderly.

Bob and I were studying when we heard our seniors yell out, "Room Ten-hup," next door. The officer in charge, Captain D. C. Hilbert, was conducting a surprise room inspection, and he caught my seniors completely off guard. Keyser, LaBianco, and Hough were all standing at strict attention by their desks when Captain Hilbert approached the sleeping Plunkett's rack. On the fifth day, Jim had been sleeping most of the day. Keyser tried to wake Plunkett up, but Plunkett hit him. Captain Hilbert was not amused. Plunkett smiled deeply in his sleep, turned over, and resumed his drug-induced nap. When Hilbert made his report, he didn't burn Plunkett for sleeping during evening study period, but burned him for "assaulting another cadet." When that punishment came out, Jim Plunkett went to General Mark Clark's office to receive his expulsion papers, even though Dave Keyser pleaded with the commandant that he didn't consider himself assaulted, and he was the alleged victim.

"You're a cadet," Keyser was told. "You aren't capable of deciding whether you were assaulted or not."

When Patterson and I returned to our room after lunch, there was a commotion in the alcove room next door. The battalion commander, Bob Fletcher, walked out of the room as we came in, followed by the R Company commander, Chuck Klotzberger. They both looked grim and troubled. As senior officers, they seemed bronzed to perfection, metallic in their untouchableness. It was impossible to imagine that our own classmates would one day wear the same stripes and chevrons as these peerless leaders of the Corps.

"Get in here, dumbheads," Keyser said at the door. "There's trouble in paradise."

When Bob and I entered the room the atmosphere was tense and funereal. Mr. Plunkett sat on his bed with his head in his hands and it looked like he'd been weeping. LaBianco and Hough looked shellshocked and Keyser puzzled. None of them could think of a word to say to the grieving Plunkett.

"Sir, what happened, sir?" Patterson asked.

"They threw Plunkett out of school for excess demerits," LaBianco said, running his fingers through his red hair.

Plunkett looked up at us in despair. "Four kings and two slaves. We made a good team, didn't we, guys?"

"Sir yes sir," Bob and I said, both shaken. Plunkett had centered our world for us, translated The Citadel's madness and let us in on its passwords and secret handshakes.

Plunkett rose and walked over to me and stuck out his hand, saying,

"I'm not going to be here for the recognition ceremony, dumbheads. So I'm doing it right now. Pat, my name is Jim Plunkett. I'd like to welcome you to the Corps of Cadets."

We shook hands, and I said, "Thanks for everything, Jim."

Outside Lieutenant Colonel Nugent Courvoisie, whom the cadets had nicknamed "The Boo," was waiting for him on the quadrangle, and Jim Plunkett walked out the gate and all of our lives. I had lost my first antihero to something as small-time as demerits.


DURING GRADUATION WEEK, the editors at the *News and Courier* chose an article I'd written for the school newspaper, *The Brigadier,* as the best-written feature article of the year and presented me with a check for fifty dollars, the most money I'd ever held in my hand at one time. I was going to use that money to hitchhike to colleges around South Carolina to arrange a tryout with their basketball programs. I'd targeted small schools like Newberry and Erskine, Presbyterian and Wofford because the academic scholarships that paid for my first year were not renewable, and my parents had not told me if they'd pay for my sophomore year or not. Then I received a summons to appear in Mel Thompson's office the day before graduation.

When I entered his office Mel was talking with my freshman coach, Paul Brandenberg, a man I had come to adore. Coach Thompson was brusque and no-nonsense as he said, "Pat, you did everything we asked of you this year. We were pleased with your progress and we want to of-fer you a basketball scholarship."

"We offered you a full ride, Pat," Coach Brandenberg said. "But your father made a change himself."

"He crossed out the clause where you'd receive laundry money," Coach Thompson explained. "We thought it odd, but the folks in the athletic office were delighted."

"Your dad thought the extra money would just get you in trouble, Pat," Brandenberg said.

"Trouble?" I said. "In this place?"

After I signed my grant-in-aid and left the field house, Paul Brandenberg caught up with me from behind. "Pat, we didn't think you were going to make it through the plebe system. We really didn't."

"I didn't do well, Coach," I said.

"No one has ever been affected by the plebe system like you were. No one," he said. "We haven't heard you talk since Christmas. Not a word. You didn't have a bad attitude or anything. You just seemed so sad."

"Do you coaches know what goes on in the barracks?" I asked.

Coach Brandenberg took a drag on his cigarette before answering. "Mel and I make it our business not to know."

"Let me give you a hint, Coach," I said. "I just played on the best freshman team in Citadel history. Over half of that team has already left. That's what goes on in the barracks."

I walked away with my scholarship in my hands, but my teammates would call me a walk-on for the rest of my life. I walked back toward the only college education I was going to get.

# CHAPTER 8

# CAMP WAHOO

IWAS AT THE END OF MY SOPHOMORE YEAR WHEN THE LETTER ARRIVED from Bill McCann, the coach at the University of Virginia, telling me that I had a job as a basketball counselor at Camp Wahoo. He welcomed me to the staff. My father had come out of the Depression scarred by the deprivation his family had suffered and vowed that his children would not be forced to work as hard as he did during those troubled years. My youth was spent on the playing fields of the South and I rarely had a dime to my name. I do not remember how much Camp Wahoo paid, but I felt like a rich man for the first time in my life when I drove off the mountain after the last session had ended.

This was the summer I dedicated to improving my game and becoming the kind of player other teams feared. During the previous year, I began to understand how far behind I was compared to both my teammates and my opponents. My coaching in high school had been shaky and haphazard at best. I didn't have a single clue about anything I did on the court. I'd learned everything by imitating players better than me. Coach Brandenberg surprised me by stopping a freshman practice and telling the team that I had the best reverse dribble he'd ever seen, even in the pros. I didn't have the foggiest notion what he was talking about.

When he demonstrated what he wanted me to show the team I said, "So that's what you call it."

For all practical purposes I was illiterate about the fundamentals of my game and had drifted through high school oblivious to the most basic concepts of the sport. Never a natural athlete, I was getting along on mettle and a kind of implacable staunchness. I was a "feisty little shit," according to Coach Brandenberg, who had placed the call to Bill McCann to get me the job at Camp Wahoo.

In the spring, my father surprised me by buying me my first car. My mother had told him of my deep unhappiness at The Citadel, so my father answered my discontent with a 1959 gray Chevrolet that he bought for seven hundred dollars at Harpers Motors in Beaufort. The sum seemed princely then.

"He's rewarding you for getting a scholarship last year," my mother said.

"I don't know how to drive, Mom. He never let me get my driver's license."

My mother said, "He didn't want you to turn into a hood or a juvenile delinquent."

"We live in the South, not Chicago. I've never seen a hood," I said. "I've never met a juvenile delinquent."

"Whatever," she said. "But your father's theory worked. You've turned out to be a very nice young man."

"It's not because I couldn't drive."

"That's *your* theory," my mother said, maddeningly.


THE CAR WAS UNGAINLY, HOMELY, unprepossessing, and I've never loved another car so much in my life. In the first month, I drove it as though moving a truck full of dynamite through a minefield and with the earnest incompetence that only neophyte drivers know. Slowly, I began to savor the thrilling taste that freedom of the road grants to Americans as our birthright. There is nothing like the automobile to make you fall in love with the laden profligate majesty of the American landscape. My father had denied me deliverance from the hard eye of patriarchy that a license confers; I fell in love with driving the moment I sat behind the steering wheel of my commonplace car that my mother christened "The Muskrat."

So the Muskrat and I roamed the back roads from Orlando, Florida, to the foothills of Virginia. Even then, lost in the secret future of my life, I'd seized upon the romantic conceit fed to me by Thomas Wolfe that an author must gorge himself on ten thousand images to select the magical one that can define a piece of the world in a way one has never considered before. I drove down strange roads for the sheer pleasure of going the wrong way. Stopping the car, I'd slip into rushing mountain rivers in the Blue Ridge Mountains because they were so beautiful and I was so free. For four days I wandered the South free as a red-tailed hawk, daydreaming about the novels I'd write when I finally had something to say. On the Blue Ridge Parkway, I hiked to a waterfall and discovered a shelf of rock behind the falls where I sat and stared at the hills through rainbows of falling water. Since I'd never seen the world through a waterfall before, I promised myself to honor this moment, its sacredness, its surprising and unconditional completeness. I'd have to live deeply in moments like this, surrender myself absolutely to the duties imagination requires from a writer to make a reader cry out in rapture at the beauty of a lived-in world. Lost in the joy of my first road trip, I suddenly realized I was driving around the mountains of North Carolina on the very day I was due to report to work.

Looking at a map, I saw no good way or straight path to take me into the outskirts of Charlottesville, Virginia. The route I chose could not have been slower, even if I had burrowed a tunnel, molelike, from the Blue Ridge to the midlands of Virginia. Because I was raised under the aegis of the Marine Corps and spent my college years at a military college, I prided myself on punctuality and disliked people who made a habit of being late. They are time thieves who consider their time more important than yours.

Driving along a gravel road in a high hill country without benefit of road signs or human habitation, I began to panic. Though I didn't know it, I was coming into Miller School from the back way. As a new driver I felt a gathering sense of dread as I pushed up a gravel road that seemed embarrassed to be there. The sun was setting to my left when I started down the other side of the mountain and saw lights off to the right coming from a large red-brick building a quarter of a mile away. My spirits soared as I turned down a long winding driveway leading up to a series of handsome buildings. When I pulled up to the front steps of what appeared to be an administration building, I saw a large group of women and children gathered on the stairs.

They looked up as I pulled up and leaned my head out of the window. "Excuse me, please. Do any of y'all know if this is Miller School?"

They looked as though I had asked the question in Chinese. One of the women said, "No. This isn't Miller School. What gave you that idea?"

"This has got to be Miller School," I insisted, checking my map with a flashlight. "Have y'all ever heard of Miller School?"

"No. Miller School. Never heard tell of it."

"Did you say Miller School, son?" an attractive woman asked me. "Never heard of no place like that. You sure that's the name?"

"Camp Wahoo," I said. "I've been hired to be a counselor at Camp Wahoo, which is run by some great basketball coaches. Bill McCann. Bones McKinney, Weenie Miller, or Gene Corrigan. Do you know Camp Wahoo? Have you heard of any of those coaches?"

"Nope. Never heard of Camp Wahoo. Never heard of any of those gentlemen," another woman said. "Any of you kids ever heard of Wahoo?"

"No, ma'am," the children answered in what was now total darkness.

Despairing, I laid my head against the steering wheel and said, "Oh my God, I'm a dead man. Late for my first job and I'll never find this place tonight."

In the gathering darkness, the wives and children of Bill McCann, Bones McKinney, Weenie Miller, and Gene Corrigan erupted into laughter on the front steps of Miller School, Virginia.

My first job had begun.


AS I THINK BACK TO THE GREAT LUCK that brought me to Camp Wahoo, gratitude washes over me in a sweet aura of memory. I know of no one connected with Wahoo who does not grow sappy and nostalgic when describing the experience. For two straight summers, I luxuriated in my passion for basketball, lived in the center of the game through the sunburned clinics where I assisted famous coaches and players teaching the fundamentals to young boys as eager as beagle puppies. As much as the enraptured boys who flocked around the coaches and players like moons orbiting Saturn, I listened to men like the incomparable Jerry West explain the rudiments of ball handling and shooting and defense. My face lit up with the same transformational pleasure as any boy in that camp when Jerry West shook my hand. When I fouled him in a coun-selors game, I went to bed that night with a voice ringing in my head, "I fouled Jerry West. I fouled Jerry West. I fouled Jerry West." He carried himself with a kingly, benign dignity and treated the boys around him with gentleness and good humor. Jerry West is the reason I would like to take a baseball bat to the swollen heads of the ex-major-league ballplayers who charge kids money for their signatures at baseball-card shows, refusing even to acknowledge the child who approaches him in the tenderest posture of hero worship. Every boy who approached Jerry West was met with a gentlemanly kindness, a genuine engagement, and unfeigned courtesy. Even meeting my literary heroes—Gore Vidal, James Dickey, William Styron, Eudora Welty, Reynolds Price, Joyce Carol Oates, and others—pales in comparison to that day at Camp Wahoo when I met Jerry West, one of the ten greatest basketball players of all time, and fouled him during a counselors game. If you are one of those who think that great athletes shouldn't have to be role models for the young boys and girls, I offer you this: I have tried to treat everyone I meet as Jerry West treated those bedazzled boys who approached him as he walked the grounds of Miller School. He taught me much about basketball, but he taught me much more about class and the responsibilities of fame.

The campers arrived on Sunday with their parents, and twenty fifteen-year-old boys were assigned to my dormitory room that first summer at Wahoo. I took to the role of counselor, my experience as the oldest brother of seven children providing an ease in the camp environment enjoyed by few others. I was easy in the company of young boys, especially the sassy, rebellious ones sent by parents who needed a vacation away from their mouthy sons. Camp Wahoo's genius lay in the fact that it kept even the crossest, most bellyaching kid exhausted and out of breath. Wahoo taught you everything about basketball, all in a breakneck-paced week that was relentless in its intensity.

An odd, unsettling event took place on my very first workday when I was walking with other counselors and campers toward the ballhandling station at court number five. I was moving past the main steps of the administration building when a voice called out: "Conroy!"

I turned around and was shocked to see Mel Thompson, my coach at The Citadel, smoking a cigarette on the steps. He seemed as surprised to see me.

"What the hell you doing here, Conroy?" he asked.

"I needed to work on my game, Coach."

"That's the truth. Who told you about Camp Wahoo?"

"Coach Brandenberg got me the job."

He eyed me obliquely. "He did, huh?" Coach Thompson always looked at you from odd angles, as though there was a tree or a bush blocking his view. "Why didn't you tell me about it?"

"I didn't know you'd ever heard of Camp Wahoo, Coach."

"Okay." He finished his cigarette. "Get out of here, Conroy."

In the two summers I worked at Camp Wahoo, that was the last time Mel Thompson spoke to me, even to say hello. Our every encounter was an entanglement, a thorny unraveling of fate, and one that always left a bad taste in my mouth. His failure to acknowledge me left me feeling sullied and insulted, especially when he seemed to relate so well with the other counselors, the boys from rival colleges. Often when Coach McCann blew the whistle that signaled the end of each Wahoo hour, I'd see Mel grin with pleasure as the campers changed stations, the playful, easy banter of sportsmen caught up in moments of leisure. At other times, I would see Coach Thompson's car packed with other coaches and counselors driving into town for a hamburger and a movie. I witnessed his laughter but always from a distance, and when he smiled, his face was transformed, making it softer, almost handsome. Those two summers in Virginia, I studied my coach in secret as he passed me by without a sign of recognition. To his eyes I was invisible, made of glass or air, and yet I had long held the suspicion that Mel Thompson liked me. It was only because I was his player, his property, that I was anathema to him, untouchable.

In sports there are no natural athletic gifts that cannot be improved and shaped by the power of discipline. The coaches at Wahoo had dedicated their lives to the teaching of the game of basketball; their instruction was clear and distinct, their zeal bracing and sustaining. Much of what I learned about teaching I owe to those generous men. Coach Bones McKinney used me as an example during a rebounding clinic and had me block the great center Lenny Chappell off the boards. Lenny was the best big man ever to come out of Wake Forest until the arrival of Tim Duncan.

"Even a little pip-squeak like Conroy can take a rebound from a giant like Lenny. It takes guts and heart. You got the guts, Conroy?"

"Yes, sir," I screamed, my butt level with Lenny Chappell's knees. I tried to back Lenny out farther into the lane, but he felt like a parked Chevy truck.

Bones threw two rebounds off the backboard and I got the first two, drawing the cheers of the campers.

On Bones's next shot, Lenny Chappell put his huge hand on my shoulder and vaulted up toward the rim and dunked the ball through the basket while driving me to the floor.

"Guts, Conroy, you got," Lenny Chappell said, bowing to the applause of the campers. "But no damn heart." I basked in the glow of his jesting voice for the rest of the day because an NBA player had said my name out loud for the first time in my life.

In the morning with the sun rising up from the Virginia tidelands, I couldn't wait to take to the court. My days at Camp Wahoo passed in a dreamy blur of pivots, stutter steps, crossover dribbles, and outlet passes. The language of my chosen sport flowed out of me in psalms of pure melody and praise. Though overwhelmed by my lack of knowledge and being outclassed by the other counselors, I was taking something into the pores of my skin that seemed like the very essence of sport. That first summer, when I competed against players the caliber of Hot Rod Hundley, Rod Thorn, Lenny Chappell, Jerry West, John Wetzel, and Art Heyman, my game improved. I was a baitfish struggling upstream with the silvery, leaping wild salmon, but I was swimming in the same river and happy as a sunbeam to be there.

It took me hours of lonely practice to incorporate new moves into my arsenal of attack. I tried to memorize every single trick or feint or backdoor move that each coach drilled into us, but only by breaking a move down into its component parts, only by practicing it over and over again during thousands of precise repetitions could I incorporate it into my own flawed game. In sport the mind serves as the acolyte and apprentice of the body. Nothing interferes with the flow of the game more than the athlete who obsesses about his every move on the court. You move, you react, you recover, you drive, and the thinking is seamless and invisible in the secret codes of your game.

My second summer—the summer after a dreadful 1965–66 season—I'd returned to Wahoo with an unshakable sense of mission. My time on the bench during my dismal junior year had frustrated me greatly, and the modest dreams I'd entertained as a player were quickly slipping away.

So I used that summer as a springboard to remake myself as a basketball player. I needed to improve my jump shot and learn how to run a basketball team and play smothering defense on the opposing guard. After Camp Wahoo was finished I signed up to be a counselor at Vic Bubas's basketball camp at Duke as well as the one at Dartmouth College run by Doggie Julian and a young Rollie Massimino. My summer was dedicated to my sport and my sport alone. I had one year left as a basketball player and I desperately desired to salvage something of value from it. The world of sports lacks compassion; its judgments are pitiless. I was mediocre, a benchwarmer, a loser—and I could absorb all that—but I wanted to be on the court with games on the line. I had never played a college varsity game from start to finish. But determination—a need to see how far desire alone could take me—burned like pure ore in my psyche. If the call came, I would be ready.

THAT SECOND BLISSFUL SUMMER AT WAHOO, I hung on every word spoken by the coaches and pros who conducted clinics as though they were bringing me newly discovered gospels which would point me the way toward my salvation as an athlete. Again I was placed in the ball-handling clinic, with Coach Gary McPherson of VMI, who at twenty-seven was the youngest head coach for Division I. But Gary also taught defense and shooting. Our station is where the point guards came to learn the intricacies of their positions, and I memorized every word Gary spoke. After practice each day, Coach McPherson, with a generosity that moves me to this day, stayed late to work with me on my shooting. I had confessed to him that no one had ever taught me the proper way to execute a jump shot.

"Square your shoulders, Pat. Pick a spot just over the rim. Bring the ball up over your head. Keep the movement fluid. The great shooters do the same thing every time. The shot is part of who they are. Concentrate. The hands are always in the same position on the ball. Be comfortable. Stay loose. Now release. Snap the wrist. The index finger points the exact spot you want the ball to go. The wrist bends toward the basket. Your hand looks like a duck head as the wrist snaps it forward. Every time you shoot, you think it's going in. Develop a shooter's mentality. Practice your ass off." Like a mantra, I repeated those words until I was left with the shot itself. I wanted the jump shot to be the center of my game. In the coming season, if the opposing guard anticipated me driving the lane and dropped off, I wanted to pull up and stick in a jumper. I wanted to hurt that sucker and make him come out to play me so when he came out to cover the jumper, I could drive past him, in the lane, tenacious and loose in the country of the big man, my native land. I had it all planned.

DURING THAT SECOND SUMMER OF fiercely contested night games with the campers filling the stands, the counselors split up into evenly matched teams and went to war against each other. I have never enjoyed the game of basketball as much as I did in those post-twilight games in the Virginia hills, nor have I ever played it so well or against players any better.

I was a bottom feeder among the counselors, one of the journeyman players—fact, not modesty. Because I passed the ball during those run-and-gun games, I often played on the team selected to highlight the visiting pro. The star that summer was Art Heyman, Duke's fast-talking, gum-chewing first-team All-American who won the basketball Player of the Year award his senior year, beating out such greats as Walt Hazzard and Bill Bradley. When Art entered the room the barometric reading rose, and his outrageous big-city ways became the focus of every eye. His arrival at Camp Wahoo is still the stuff of legend. I remember him driving his convertible beneath the porte cochere with a blonde looking like the embodiment of original sin seated next to him. Often I'd read the word "floozie" in certain kinds of novels but had never encountered one in the flesh. The car, the floozie, and the All-American were all part of a package deal: Art Heyman was to teach us all a new sensibility that was then making its presence known in basketball circles across America. With no apologies, Art's game was urban black, big-city, kiss my ass and hold the mayo, in your face, wiseass Jewish, no-holds-barred and a hot dog at Nathan's after the game. He seemed to delight in and feed off the hatred of those southern boys who filled up the ranks of the counselors—boys out of VPI, Hampden-Sydney, Wake Forest, and Richmond—much more at ease with the aw-shucks, pass-the-biscuits-ma'am variety of heroism embodied in Jerry West and Rod Thorn. Art Heyman would stride among us as antihero heart of darkness, the harbinger of all that terrified us about the chain-netted boroughs of New

York. His West Side Story stormed down to do battle with our Wahoo Walton Family. Heyman came up to me before the jump ball and whispered, "It's show time, peanut. Get me the ball."

I knew what my job was and for forty whirlwind minutes I threw passes to the best college basketball player of 1965. Everyone on my team knew the unwritten rules and that we simply provided filler on the court, bodies to clog up lanes and grab rebounds. Our real job was to let everyone in the gym marvel at the extraordinary gifts of Art Heyman.

Our opponents seethed with a loathing of Art that he seemed to take for granted. John Wetzel, the dazzling forward from Virginia Tech who would later play for the Los Angles Lakers and serve as head coach of the Phoenix Suns, was first to guard Heyman, and he did it with a rabid intensity. He covered Heyman in the first half like a sheen of sweat. UVA's Chip Conner drew the assignment the second half. The loathing for the All-American was palpable all over the court, and Heyman, who seemed to enjoy it, ran his mouth the entire game. Art was the first trash talker I'd ever met, and there's nothing white southern boys hate more than a trash talker. But take it from me, Art Heyman could back it up.

That night the court shimmered with competitive zeal, like sheet lightning shooting through the overheated gym. I brought the ball up-court, fast, but I was guarded by Virginia Tech's Spider Lockhart, a six-five jumping jack with long arms who was always a threat to steal the ball. But my dribbling—always the best part of my game—got me around him. The moment I was free I'd look for Heyman, who'd be engaged in a wrestling match with John Wetzel on the left-hand side of the court. Wetzel fought hard to front Heyman, but Heyman used his body brilliantly and always got himself in a perfect position. Then with a call of "Right here, peanut," he'd motion with his huge hand where he wanted the ball. And I would fire Art Heyman the ball, right there.

At that moment, Spider and I would retreat to the other side of the court and become spectators in a gymful of transported boys as Wetzel and Heyman battled for control of the boards. For acolytes in the game of basketball, watching two athletes as gifted as Heyman and Wetzel was like being in church.

I learned that night that I looked like an All-American point guard when I was flipping the ball to Heyman because he was a great player. Though Wetzel and Chip Conner were excellent defenders, the great offensive player will always have the advantage over the defender for the simple reason that it is easier to go forward than backward. Heyman could score, almost at will, even though all five opposing players dropped back to block his move to the basket. But the cocky Heyman would pivot, then throw up a pump fake, then again, then another with Wetzel not taking the bait. Then Heyman's whole body would seem to rise up toward the rim, and Wetzel would leap high in the air for the block. But Heyman had faked again, this time pure artistry and cheap trick combined.

One play stands out in my mind. Heyman stole a pass intended for Wetzel and raced downcourt with a breakaway move that did not quite spring him free. Both Chip Conner and Wetzel ran with him, step for step, bird-dogging his every move, matching his cuts and hard, headlong charge. Both men were faster and better leapers than Art. I'd broken right behind Heyman and found myself filling the center lane, trailing the play ten feet behind.

At the top of the key, Heyman lifted up with a slight change of pace, then drove hard for the rim, rising upward with Conner and Wetzel matching his every move with countermoves of their own. To me, a breathless foot soldier of the lowest rank, the three men were kingly in their skills, lords of a highborn dance. I didn't even see the moment when Art Heyman at the top of his leap flipped the ball back to me. Running full speed, I caught the pass belt-high, as soft as an exchange of feathers between children. As the three players crashed to the floor in a pile of tangled limbs, I laid the ball into the hoop without a soul around me. It was the most beautiful and precisely delivered pass I had ever seen. Art Heyman, who was rumored to have thrown about four or five passes in his whole career, had just taught me a lesson about passing I'd never forget. His intuition and uncanny court sense had informed him that I was coming up behind him. It was not something he thought about or planned for, but he made that pass with the instincts that genius grants to very few.

As I watched Heyman make his way downcourt, I studied his immersion and ease in himself and the game. I saw that he understood his indisputable place in the game, his right to be on center stage with the game centrifugal to his every move. Because he was fearless and gifted, Heyman could surrender himself to his game fully. He could risk everything, because he had taken possession of his time on the court and had perfect faith in his skills and instincts. The important thing was to be alive in the moment, open to every possibility and configuration, and make that moment yours only, again and again. You cannot risk what does not belong to you, so I took that pass from that man and tried to apply its lessons to my life. I needed to open myself to all the possibilities around me, to hold nothing back, to live in the moment at hand with my art and my game on the line.

Since every athlete learns by theft and mimicry, I stole that pass from Art Heyman. His pass did not even register in his consciousness, it was simply show business, part of the razzmatazz and the glitter of big-city hoops that he brought to the game. But I used that pass four times my senior year, and it worked every time.

My second task that summer at Camp Wahoo was to learn how to play tough, no-nonsense defense. Until college, no one had instructed me in the art of defending a man on offense. The coaches of Camp Wahoo were both passionate and eloquent about its importance. I attended every clinic on defense I could. Tom Carmody, who coached at Bethel Park High outside of Pittsburgh, was highly respected for his knowledge of defense. What defense required, Coach Carmody said, was hustle and desire and sacrifice. It took courage and commitment and the heart of a Siberian tiger. Hearing nothing to keep me from being a member of the club, I burned that summer with a desire to help my team win games by refusing to let my man score even a single point. This had never happened to me, and was revolutionary in the advancement of my game. For me, defense was the boring grunt work of the sport, while offense was a race to the dessert line. At Wahoo that last summer, I vowed to become a defensive specialist.

I lived for those night games. All I wanted to do was make beautiful passes to my teammates and to shut out the man I was guarding. I stayed low and in my man's face the whole game. I shadowed him every inch of the court. Defense became something I dreamed about at night. I stopped Spider Lockhart on a Tuesday, and Hugh Corliss of LaGrange College on a Wednesday, and the gifted Paul Long on Thursday.

On Friday night, I faced off with Johnny Moates of the University of Richmond whom I had guarded on occasion in the Southern Conference for the past two years. The games that summer were an offensive show put on for the enjoyment of the campers, a factor that worked in my favor. None of the pros or the counselors put much effort on the defensive end, except in those rare encounters with the big cats like Heyman and Wetzel. My sudden dedication to defense struck some of the players as weird. Johnny Moates did not like it worth a damn.

I picked Moates up full court my last night at my beloved Camp Wahoo, and I stuck to him like a wood tick the entire night. No one set a screen for Johnny the whole game. No one helped him to get open or to get me off of him. Johnny's frustration turned to anger. He was a great scorer and the great scorers need shots the way otters need streams. They fall apart when denied the basketball. The game was an agony for Johnny Moates, and he began to push me away from him when I got too close.

"Just play ball, Conroy. This is bullshit," he yelled, then pushed me off him again.

The more he pushed the closer I stuck. If he put a hand up high to receive a pass, I raised a hand up to intercept it. I was not a step away from him the entire game, and Johnny Moates did not score. When the final whistle sounded I was the happiest son-of-a-bitch in the state of Virginia.

Only two people would remember my defensive play that summer: Mel Thompson and Johnny Moates.

Five of my Citadel teammates were at Wahoo that summer. Mel never spoke a word to any of us. None of my Citadel teammates knew if Coach Thompson watched the counselors games or not. He never sat where we could see him. After the Friday game I went out into the darkness and looked over at the buildings of Miller School, watching the campers and counselors drift slowly toward the dormitories. Young boys called my name and reached out to touch me as they flowed past me.

Just then, someone slapped my fanny, disrupting my reverie. A large, dark shape moved past me on the left—Mel Thompson, my college coach, smoking, that slap his wordless praise, my reward and trophy, and his acknowledgment of the hard work I'd put in that summer.

I left the mountains of Camp Wahoo thinking I had learned to play great defense. The following season, Johnny Moates would teach me otherwise.

# CHAPTER 9

# RETURN FOR SENIOR YEAR

I T IS TIME ITSELF I AM TRYING TO RETRIEVE.
I long to pin it down in the surreal hyacinth-light of both memory and dream that now have faded where once they were three-dimensional and rich. I want to write down how I felt and thought as I made my way around The Citadel during my last time as a basketball player and my first that I thought of myself, with a sense of dread and unworthiness, as a writer. It was the year I woke up to the dream of my own life.

As I walked across the parade ground during the first week, I began the long, terrifying process of turning myself into the southern writer my mother had told me I would be since I was five years old. Always, she emphasized the word "southern" and told me I must never turn my back on her region of the rough-born South. During my three-year test at The Citadel, I had tried to transform myself, to drink in the landscape and tell exactly what it was to submit to the discipline of the Corps of Cadets. Since I had observed all those rites of submission, I could feel The Citadel's story forming on my tongue, and all the language of outrage and brotherhood cleaving to the roof of my mouth.

For the first time since becoming a cadet, I felt myself accepting the school for what it was. I no longer blamed The Citadel for not being the Harvard or Duke that my parents could not have afforded for me had I been smart enough to get into them. I experienced a rush of happiness each time I woke to bugles, as well as gratitude and belonging when taps played over the barracks at night. Next to the chapel across the parade ground, a whole library of books awaited my astonished inspection. I had promised myself to complete a single poem every day for Colonel John Doyle's poetry writing seminar in addition to improving the short stories I was writing for *The Shako*, the campus literary magazine. I would use the year to learn how to think and see the world as a writer. For the first time, I knew the repleteness that comes from filling up with words. Language became a honeycomb brightening the eaves of my brain.

But I was a college basketball player, too. From day to day, I was caught up with the rhythms of my game. Basketball provided the nearest approach I've ever made to the realms of ecstasy. The sport consumed the best part of my dreaming self, and I found myself in reverie after reverie moving swiftly in the flow and anarchy of games. My whole philosophy of life was caught up with what I believed were the responsibilities of a point guard—the importance of outhustling your opponent, watching for the unexpected, moving teammates to their proper spots on the floor, barking orders and calling the plays, exhorting and inspiring your team, and never quitting until the buzzer has sounded.

ON THE LAST DAY OF PLEBE WEEK, I received a note from an orderly of the guard to report to Coach Mel Thompson's office at 1500 hours. Being summoned to Coach Thompson's office was never good news, but I was a senior now, part of the senior leadership, and concluded that I would be spending much of my time in Mel's office discussing team attitude and personnel. I could not have been more wrong.

Before my last season as an athlete began, I sat outside his office conjuring a portrait of my fascinating, scowling, and unforthcoming coach, Mel Thompson. At the outset, I knew so little about him I found it bewildering. For three years, six months of the year, I saw him for three hours every day. He did not know either of my parents' names after those three years nor anything about my personal life. He had no interest in getting to know the individual members of his team, and required of us only that we fear, respect, and obey him. The terror we felt for him was real. His powers of ridicule were considerable, and his bitterly cutting dismissals of his players could feel like acid thrown in your face.

Something smoldered inside Mel Thompson. He was the type of man you would cut open and expect to see lava flow instead of blood. There was nothing soft about my coach. I studied him up close and came to know him only as mask and stone wall, as sphinx and empty vessel and hidden passageway. I watched for clues that would elucidate his character, but the graffiti that cut into the granite wall of him were written in a language not even he could speak. Mel Thompson is the insoluble enigma and the Rosetta stone of this book.

What I did know about Mel Thompson was that as a six-foot-three-inch player for North Carolina State, he was one of the best rebounders of the early fifties. For three years, he started for the Wolfpack in the best basketball conference in the country, coached by the legendary Everett Case who along with Adolph Rupp introduced big-time college basketball to the South. Everett Case referred to his player Mel Thompson as the "most competitive player I ever coached." Case was famous for treating his players like dogs, yet a distinguished fraternity of coaches came out of his program, including Vic Bubas at Duke; Norman Sloan at The Citadel, Florida, and North Carolina State; and Les Robinson, Eddie Biedenbach, and a long list of others. Old man Case may have been hard-nosed and ornery, but something about his toughness made his team want to play for him. He made his teams feared in the ACC, and his boys went after you with everything they had. Everett Case exemplified a certain philosophy of coaching whereby a team of young players could be molded into greatness by the use of fear and intimidation. Case dismissed out of hand the softer ways of the lesser breed of coaches. Mel Thompson adored Coach Case and brought that philosophy to his job at The Citadel.

Mel was the assistant coach under Norman Sloan at The Citadel when Sloan directed the "Blitz Kids," the best bunch of Citadel basketball players in the college's history. When Sloan departed for Florida in 1960, Mel took over the head coaching position, a year after he had taken over as The Citadel's freshman basketball coach. Mel led those same Blitz Kids to a 17–8 season, a remarkable achievement for a first-year head coach. But that was followed by an 8–15 season and a disastrous 1962–63 year in which his team went 3–20. Coach Thompson righted himself in the next two years and fielded two winning teams in a row. The 1964 team finished 11–10 and the team I played backup guard on as a sophomore went 13–11. It is a rarity that a modern Citadel basketball squad put a winning team on the floor for two consecutive years. Since 1940, only Norman Sloan ever won for three consecutive years, and Les Robinson cobbled together consecutive winning seasons in 1979 and 1980. Winning basketball games in a military college is as perilous a way to earn a living as exists in American coaching.

Mel Thompson appeared at the door and barked out my name. "Conroy, get in here." No "how was your summer" or pleasant handshakes or idle chatter to break the ice after a long separation. "You know why I called you down here, Pat?" he said. He had not called me "Pat" since he tried to recruit me in high school.

"No, sir, I don't." I was actually shaken by his friendliness.

"I'm thinking about making you captain of the team," he said. "What do you think about that?"

It was a lifelong dream of mine to captain our team, but that is not what I said to Coach Thompson. "What about Danny Mohr? Or Jim Halpin? It might hurt their feelings."

"Feelings, Conroy? I don't give a shit about feelings. I care about winning. I've always been a winner, and losing kills something inside me. Danny Mohr's not a leader. Halpin's got a gimp knee. I was depending on you for leadership. But the hell with it. You've always wanted to coach this goddamn team. Get the fuck out of my office."

I got up to leave, until he held out his hand to stop me. "Except for your ball handling and passing, you're barely college material. You're just mediocre, and that's the truth of the matter."

"The truth of the matter" burned through me like fire as I walked back through the shadow of the field house. As a boy, words had stung and lacerated me far too much, and I'd tried to learn to defuse their power when launched as weapons. "You're just mediocre" would echo in my head every minute of the season that had not even begun. My mediocrity stung me, which is why I'd worked so hard in the summer for my last year as a basketball player.

On Hell Night, I drifted from R Company over to Tango Company where three freshmen basketball players were having the worst night of their lives. In the chaos of the plebe system's first great disruption, I went to introduce myself to the three most highly prized recruits of the class of 1970. I watched as three cadremen worked over Jerry Hirsch and was standing in front of him when he rose after completing twenty-five pushups.

"Good evening, Mr. Hirsch," I said.

"Good evening, sir," he screamed.

"How you liking college?"

"Sir, I love it, sir," he screamed.

"I'm a basketball player, Mr. Hirsch. A senior. My name's Pat Conroy, and I'm going to get you through this year. I was standing in this same spot three years ago. Think of it as a game. A joke. Some of the guys screaming at you tonight will be the best friends you'll ever have. Bend your knees. That's it. You're doing good. If I can help you, let me know. But you're going to make it. I hear you've got a great jump shot."

Young Mr. Hirsch surprised me by saying, "Sir, one of the best, sir." I knew that Jerry Hirsch was going to make it just fine. I had the same encounter with Willie Taylor and a mountain of a boy named Bob Carver, who looked both bewildered and terrified. "Mr. Conroy, sir, permission to make a statement, sir."

"Please feel free," I said.

"Sir, Coach Thompson said I wouldn't have to go through any of this, sir. He promised to keep me out of it, sir."

I looked around at the cadre moving through the knobs in the stormy loosening of havoc in their ranks. "Mel doesn't seem to be doing a very good job, Mr. Carver."

"Sir, he promised me," Carver said with greater urgency.

"He lied, Mr. Carver. But he's consistent. He lied to every one of us, to every basketball player on this campus. But you'll get through it and I'll buy you a beer in June."

On Friday at the end of plebe week, I went for afternoon tea at Colonel John Doyle's house on campus overlooking the Ashley River. Once a month Colonel Doyle and his wife, Clarice, invited me to their quarters for an afternoon tea as formal as an English garden. It was as a plebe, in the Doyles' living room, when I first discovered that not all tea came in bags and that it could be served without ice.

I was about to knock on the Doyles' door when a booming voice rang out, "Halt, bubba!"

The Boo's voice, always startling, had the same effect on me that a lion's roar had on a herd of wildebeest. I froze and awaited his approach as the smell of his Thompson cigar announced his arrival. I could feel the heat of the cigar as it drew close to my ear, and the Boo shrouded my head in a plume of smoke.

"Stop that, Nugent," I heard Mrs. Courvoisie say to her husband. "Leave Mr. Conroy alone."

"Bolshevik," the colonel said, "I thought I sent you out of here to mess up Clemson. You are not Citadel material, don't you understand that yet?"

Because of my role in placing a coded but obscene poem in *The Shako* the previous spring, the Boo had recommended that President Hugh P. Harris kick me out of the Corps of Cadets.

"If General Mark Clark were still president, you'd been long gone, bubba. Harris is new, still feeling his way around. He thinks of you cadets as human beings. He doesn't know you for the lowlife bums and scoundrels I know. You better not fart through cotton this year, bubba, or I'll crucify you without nails. Got that?"

"Nugent, we're late," Mrs. Courvoisie said.

"One mistake, bubba," the Boo said. "Just one and you're history. You ever walked tours?"

"No, sir," I said.

"Well, if I don't get you here," he said, "look for me in hell. I'll be waiting for your Bolshevik ass."

"Great to see you, Colonel," I said as he walked back to his car. "My summer was great, sir. Thanks for asking."

The Boo was laughing as he got into his car and I knocked on Colonel Doyle's door.

Colonel Doyle met me at his back door and warmly shook my hand and thanked me for the letters I'd written him during the summer. He was dressed in an ascot and a smoking jacket; I'd never seen a man dressed like him except in period movies. Clarice Doyle was wearing a dress, stockings, high heels, and pearls. I never saw this cultured couple let down their hair when I visited them. Entering their house always felt like stepping back a hundred years or more.

"Do you think Mr. Conroy will take to Darjeeling, John?" Clarice asked.

Colonel Doyle answered, "I think we can assume Mr. Conroy is the adventurous type."

I cherished my time with John and Clarice Doyle at The Citadel, yet always felt clubfooted and inappropriate when I was sitting with them, the three of us talking like characters out of an unpublishable British short story written by a librarian with a stutter and a drinking problem. The conversation always seemed surreal and disconnected from all reality.

"John, have you lined Mr. Conroy up with some delicious courses for the new semester?" Clarice asked her husband. It made me happy to see how much she loved him.

Colonel Doyle beamed at her. "I think I may have come up with some tasty morsels, dear. Perhaps, even one or two bonbons."

"Bonbons," I said, having no idea what anyone was talking about, but wanting to be part of their close-knit yet inexplicit alliance. Always, I felt like the Doyles were telling jokes but letting me guess the punch lines.

"You will be in my modern novel class," Colonel Doyle said.

"Now there's a bonbon," Clarice said.

"You seemed enamored with Colonel Bowman last year, so I put you in his abnormal psychology class. I trust you will study the subject, Mr. Conroy, and try your best not to become abnormal yourself. We'll have none of that."

"Oh, John," Clarice said, holding her stomach as she laughed.

"But wait—I have solved the problem of your senior essay, Mr. Conroy."

"Wonderful," I said. The senior essay was the crowning glory of four years at The Citadel, but I'd been particularly uninspired in choosing a subject. I'd turned the job over to Colonel Doyle who would both oversee and grade the project as my academic advisor.

"I'd like you to compare the novels of William Faulkner of Oxford, Mississippi, with the novels of Sinclair Lewis of Sauk Centre, Minnesota. Both from small-town America, both recipients of the Nobel Prize for literature."

"Nobel. That's very big," Clarice said.

Colonel Doyle nodded. "You will find that Mr. Lewis is not quite up to snuff when it comes to the Lion of Rowan Oak."

"A year spent among Nobelists, Mr. Conroy," said Clarice. "A judicious way to spend one's senior year."

"I suggest you start with *Light in August*," Colonel Doyle said to me. After tea, he led me upstairs to his small, book-lined office where he'd written his books and essays. John Doyle was an expert on Robert Frost and a signed copy of his book *The Poetry of Robert Frost* sits on my desk today. I sat facing him as he opened a folder that contained the poems I'd written over the summer. In a clear, accented voice, he read each poem aloud to me, reading them with complete openness as though they all were not hopelessly amateurish and flawed. To John Doyle writing was a religious act, the teaching of it a work of holy orders. His voice lent beauty and gravitas to poems that lacked both. I couldn't breathe as I listened to my own words read back to me with uncommon gentleness. Each time I came to this room to have Colonel Doyle take my writing with a seriousness it didn't deserve, I'd fill up with gratitude for him again and again. Though we were nothing alike, we shared a passion for the English language that bound us like brothers from the first time we met until the last time we spoke on the phone, the week before he died.

"Now this is the hard part for all writers, Mr. Conroy, but it is necessary. You must learn to think of yourself as a writer."

"I'm not good enough yet, Colonel Doyle," I said.

"No, you're not. But you're getting better. You're doing the hard work. But you must tell yourself that you're a writer. A work in progress, but a writer. Can you tell me that?"

"Not yet, Colonel. I can't make a sentence sound like I want it to. It won't say what I want it to say."

"That will come. Do you think that Hemingway knew he was a writer when he was twenty years old? No, he did not. Or Fitzgerald, or Wolfe. This is a difficult concept to grasp. Hemingway didn't know he was Ernest Hemingway when he was a young man. Faulkner didn't know he was William Faulkner. But they had to take the first step. They had to call themselves writers. That is the first revolutionary act a writer has to make. It takes courage. But it's necessary, Mr. Conroy. This is your last season as a basketball player, isn't it?"

"Yes, sir," I said. "I stink at that, too."

"You say that about yourself as a writer. You say that about yourself as a basketball player. Mr. Conroy, may I give you some advice? You are far too young to know this, but your life is precious and your time is short. You are blind to yourself, Mr. Conroy. You're too hard on yourself. For reasons I don't understand, you are deeply unhappy, and it pains me. Know this. I think you could be special if you only thought there was anything special about yourself. Someone has taught you to hate yourself. I hope I haven't crossed some line, Mr. Conroy. I value our friendship very much."

"You should've been a coach, Colonel," I said. "That's the greatest pep talk I ever heard."

When I left Colonel Doyle's quarters, I drifted past the obstacle course, walked the length of the practice baseball field lush with freshly mown grass, and walked along the marsh until I came to the Citadel marina. This was the spot I'd discovered my freshman year where I could come to think and to separate myself from the life of the Corps. I climbed a ladder of the Citadel yacht, the *Southwind*, and sat on a deck chair and looked out toward the Ashley River. The tide was coming in, and the sun was lowering in the west. I thought about Colonel Doyle and my good fortune that he found me in my first despairing days at The Citadel and offered his hand in friendship. From the day I met him, Colonel Doyle carried an unshakable faith that I'd one day write novels for a living, which seemed as unlikely to me as my ripening into a good point guard. I linked my destiny as a writer to that of myself as a basketball player because both seemed to represent realms of achievement that would always be denied me.

I sent out a silent prayer above the Ashley River. I asked God to let good things happen to me this last basketball season, a season I could look back on without shame. It seemed like a modest, ungreedy prayer. I asked that I complete a short story I was working on, and that I be granted a sign that I was supposed to write novels for a living.

Standing in the bow of the *Southwind*, I looked back toward The Citadel, a college that was now part of my history and my fate. I promised myself something of great importance to me. "I'll remember everything," I said. "I won't forget a single thing."


BASKETBALL PRACTICE WOULD BEGIN on October 15, 1966.

# CHAPTER 10

# CLEMSON

WHEN I THINK OF THE WORD "SNAKEPIT," THE IMAGE OF THE claustrophobic, hostility-steeped field house where Clemson University played their basketball games springs to mind. For a visiting team, a game at Clemson was as hallucinatory and disquieting an encounter as a basketball player could experience. It was close to miraculous for even the great teams of the ACC like North Carolina to come into the harrowing environment of the Clemson gym and return home with a victory.

In my sophomore year, I played on a very good Citadel team that beat the University of West Virginia in Morgantown, breaking the longest home winning streak in American college basketball. It was as good as the game of basketball could get. The Corps of Cadets listened to the game in Charleston on radio and in celebration threw every garbage can in the barracks off the four divisions and onto the cement quadrangle. The team would go 8–2, defeating a wonderful Virginia Tech team, before the particular malaise set in that seems to undermine the long seasons of almost all the basketball programs at military colleges. That 1964–65 team finished 13–11, the only winning varsity team I would play for at The Citadel.

As a sophomore, my spirit was puppylike and unbridled because, as Dick Martini liked to say, "Mel hasn't had a chance to break your spirit yet. It won't take long."

In the fall of my sophomore year, it was Dick, our Italian center and captain from Passaic, New Jersey, sitting beside me on the bus taking us to our game, who first told me of the pitfalls and dangers of playing at the Clemson Tigers' gym.

"I got something to say to you, weasel," Martini said in a conspiratorial whisper. "You just listen to Uncle Dick and don't say a word until I'm finished or I'll crush your little guard ass like a roach. Now, you're a rookie and have never played at Clemson in your putrid life. This ain't like no other normal game, rookie. Clemson's only got these big, mean, stupid redneck boys like yourself, only these boys are farm boys with no teeth. They grew up fucking sheep and who knows what else. These boys are so backward they major in agriculture and shit like that. Agriculture! Plow 101. Milk a Fucking Cow 202. Turn On a Tractor 303. Clemson guys are the meanest, dumbest, fightingest sons-of-bitches in the whole world."

"It'll be that much more fun to beat them," I said.

Dick put a large hand over my mouth. "Don't talk like that, midget. That's exactly the kind of talk I don't want to hear coming out of your stupid southern mouth."

"Dick, we beat West Virginia in Morgantown," I protested. "We can beat Clemson up there."

"Midget, midget," Dick said sadly. "You don't understand. If we beat their team, the Clemson boys will storm the court and tear us apart with their bare hands. They'll kill us. We just got to hope they don't fuck us before they kill us. But when you get in the game, don't do nothing stupid like trying to win. Got me, smackhead?"

Looking into Dick Martini's eyes, I saw to my astonishment that he was terrified. The largest, most powerful Italian man I had ever met had a grave, unappeasable terror of my mother's southern people.

"Agriculture," he kept saying. "They go to college to major in farming," said the tenth leading rebounder in Citadel history who once pulled twenty-two rebounds from the boards in a game against Richmond. "That'd be like me going to college to major in pepperoni."

I never knew what to make of Dick Martini's metaphor about farming and pepperoni, but later that night, I knew everything I ever wanted to know about the heartburn and melancholy of playing basketball in Clemson's satanic gym. When our uniformed team walked in carrying our bags, we passed in review of four thousand rabid Clemson loyalists. The freshman game was under way and we had to make our way single file to the locker room. The crowd was so close to the out-of-bounds line that the football team had to move their feet to let us pass. Of course, they refused and a couple of them actually tried to trip us. So, my whole team walked on the open court as the crowd began a thunderous, mocking chant: "Hup, four, hup, four, hup, two, three, four." Captain Martini led us into the field house, staring straight ahead, as though he was following an invisible prison warden to his own execution.

Clemson murdered us that night of my sophomore year, 90–75, but the game was not nearly that close. I got in the game late in the second half and tried to lead the effort to catch up. When Wig Baumann told me to take the ball out of bounds, I received my first lessons in the manual of courtesies and virtues of Clemson's fans. I had to jump among the raucous fans who churned along the sideline. Two of them pinched my butt hard and two more put cigarettes out on the back of my legs. I went flying toward a referee and shouted that someone had burned and pinched me, but I could not even hear my own voice above the crowd. The referee simply shrugged his shoulders, and I could see he carried some of the same terror of the Clemson crowd as Martini did. Five cigarette burns branded my legs before that game was over, and Clemson fans had depilated a third of the hair from the back of my legs.

In the final minute, I was racing after a ball going out of bounds when I dove for it near Clemson's basket and slid along the floor and into the football team. Clemson guys dove out of the way and my wet jersey slalomed me along the slippery floor. I disappeared through a hole beneath the bleachers and the Clemson football team made me fight through their legs to get back onto the court. The crowd at Clemson was not just hostile; they were lunatic in their advocacy of the Tigers.

On December 3, 1966, my team walked into the Clemson visiting team locker room, a testament to the disdain the Tigers felt for their opponents. The sheer dinginess of the room was nearly heroic. The whole building had the feel of a place designed by a testy little man who had flunked all his engineering courses and hated basketball players with a passion. But we could hear the stands filling up above us.

Our trainer, Coach Billy Bostick, was taping ankles when Doug Bridges opened his bag and discovered he had forgotten to pack his uniform shirt. Forgetting one's shoes or uniform was a high crime in Mel's list of commandments.

"Mel's gonna kill me, Barney," Doug said to Dave Bornhorst.

"Yeah, but it won't take long," Barney said.

"Bridges forgot his jersey," Bob Cauthen said to the whole room. "What an idiot."

Bridges said, "Watch your mouth, Cauthen."

"Take Conroy's," Danny Mohr said, on the taping table. "He sure as hell won't need it."

Cauthen said, "Bridges would forget his dick if it wasn't attached."

When he received the bad news, Al Beiner, our head manager, went looking for Mel, then returned, saying, "Coach wants to see you. Right now."

Mel glowered as Doug approached, which did nothing to assuage the younger man's terror. The relationship between the two of them was surly and vinegary in the best of times.

"Bridges," Mel said scowling, "you never, ever forget the tools of the trade. Got it? You'll owe me some laps for this one."

"Sorry, Coach," Doug said, lowering his eyes.

Coach Ed "Little Mel" Thompson entered the locker room with a most unpleasant task. "Dave," he said to Bornhorst, "Coach says you have to give up your shirt to Doug."

"Sure, Coach," Dave said with such brio and generosity that he turned a painful moment into a lesson in the subtle, but difficult, art of teamwork. In his clumsiness and self-deprecation, Dave's deficiencies as an athlete faded into nothingness when placed beside the essence of his character.

The two Coach Thompsons entered the dark locker room. "De-Brosse, you'll be the captain tonight."

Mel's announcement cuts me deeply even thirty years later, and still wounds Dan Mohr. I felt like Mel had slapped me in the face in front of my teammates. I am sure it made John DeBrosse as uncomfortable as it made me and Danny. To appoint a junior the captain of a team when two seniors were sitting in the same room is as huge and personal an affront as a coach could deliver, especially in the strictly hierarchal world of The Citadel. Though I thought it was a serious mistake not to name Danny and me co-captains for the Auburn game, I had wrongly assumed the captaincy was my booby prize for riding the bench.

It was the second straight game that Mel Thompson had gone out of his way to insult Danny Mohr, his highest returning scorer from our previous year. I do not remember a single word of Coach Thompson's pregame pep talk on that long-ago Saturday night, but I remember my darkly burning face and my eyes on the floor as Mel went over the defensive assignments and the scouting reports on the Clemson players. Because this was my final season and I'd played these boys before, I did not need to listen to any in-depth assessment of the Clemson team. Beating them was a snap. All you had to do was stop Randy Mahaffey and Jim Sutherland. Stop those two magnificent athletes and the rest was mop-up time for the Green Weenies. Theories of how to do so flowed easily from Mel's lips; executing them, however, was a far more complicated matter.

So far, I have spoken with awe and nostalgia about my terrific freshman team. Our only loss that season came at the hands of the Clemson freshmen where we found that we could not handle the powerful six-foot-six Mahaffey under the boards, or the formidable six-foot-five Sutherland at shooting guard on the outside. They were aggressive, banked with all the necessary competitive fires, and were uncannily graceful.

Jim Sutherland served as president of the student body at Clemson, made straight A's in his premed courses, and had averaged over fifteen points a game in the ACC his junior year. I hoped I would get the chance to play tonight because I wanted to tell my children I had once guarded Jim Sutherland.

"Conroy," Dan Mohr said as we waited our turn to do layups, "can you believe he named DeBrosse to be captain? What the hell's he doing?"

"He's the boss, Root," I said.

"It ain't right," Dan said. "It just ain't right." Then, looking down at the Clemson team, "Goddamn, Mahaffey's a big son-of-a-bitch."

In Randy Mahaffey, the third Mahaffey brother to attend Clemson on a basketball scholarship, all the grace and speed of impalas and lions combined nicely with the strength of water buffalo. He was long-limbed and long-strided and was a natural meat-eater under the boards. When I was a sophomore I tried to block him off the baskets for a rebound and he sent me reeling out of bounds with the barest movement of his hip.

As we gathered together by our bench and placed our hands in a circle before the first tip, Mel issued our final instructions. The Tiger Pep Band, sitting directly behind the visiting team's bench, repeatedly and maddeningly kept playing "Tiger Rag," Clemson's famous, repetitive fight song.

The referee approached the crouched centers, formal as candelabras in their stillness, and lofted the ball upwards as Mohr and Mahaffey sprang toward the lights. The game began in ugliness and unsettledness. From my seat on the bench, I watched Clemson forward Randy Ayers foul Mohr hard when he went to put the ball on the floor. Danny made the free throw and we led 1–0. Then Randy Mahaffey slashed and dazzled for the next ten minutes with radiant backup play by Jim Sutherland.

The Clemson offense was fluid and smooth and worked efficiently to get the right man open—often Mahaffey, who would post Mohr up then back him into the paint with elegance and precision. Mohr was overmatched physically; Mahaffey was fast, explosive, and intimidatingly strong. His sheer physical presence overtook the game almost as soon as it began. It helped both Mahaffey and Clemson that in Mel Thompson's defensive scheme, we were not allowed to help our teammates out unless a complete breakdown occurred.

The pace of the game was brutal from the start, and the mood quickly turned malevolent as the big guys roughhoused on the boards. As peasantry from The Citadel, we were not supposed to mix it up with the lordly squires of the ACC. Mahaffey's face bristled with resentment if Danny even attempted to block his movement to the board. ACC refs could be as fair as those rabid Nazi judges who screamed obscenities at the men accused in the attempted assassination of Hitler. Early in the game, it became readily apparent that all close calls would go to Clemson.

If Mohr was having trouble with Mahaffey, sophomore Tee Hooper was in the process of learning profound lessons from a seasoned Jim Sutherland. As always, Sutherland was far quicker than it seemed he should have been. Not quite as quick as Tee, Jim used his edge of sixty games of varsity experience to great advantage. Jim would pump fake on a jump shot, then lean into the leaping Tee, and Tee was in foul trouble early.

Five minutes into the game, a moment of exceptional beauty took place when Danny Mohr brought down a fought-for rebound with Mahaffey on his back, then he pivoted and found DeBrosse in place on the wing. He threw to DeBrosse, who hit Tee with a dead-on pass as Tee assumed the point, and the fast break developed with textbook perfection.

Zinsky and Bridges filled the outside lanes, then broke for the basket at the exact same time. Tee hit Zinsky with a superb pass on the left side of the basket and Bill laid it in, even though he was fouled. Zinsky hit the free throw and the ideal execution of the play gave my team a sudden infusion of energy.

But the rebounding grew more militant and hostile. So brutal was the play under the basket that it made me happy to be a guard on the bench. Whenever any contact or collision occurred under the boards, the referee almost always called the foul on one of the Citadel big men, drawing a huge roar of approval from the crowd. If you do not think that contempt of home crowds does not file down the rough edges of a referee's psyche, then you know little of the game of basketball.

It was a shooter's night for John DeBrosse, and his form was immaculate every time he went up and his hand flicked the ball toward the basket and his wrist bent and held there until the ball split the net. He looked lit up from the inside. I watched all this from the bench, with two trombone slides whizzing past my ears, playing the ugliest fight song in the country. That is one of the most important of the point guard's duties: knowing which of your teammates carries the hot hand in the game of the moment. Being hot as a shooter is an exalted state that has a brief and fragile life span and the point guard must be able to mark his teammates when struck by this unpredictable and transient condition. For shooters like DeBrosse and Mohr, it is what they live for. But we point guards learn to discern it in the eyes of our teammates and get them the ball when the fever reaches full pitch.

Mel's halftime talk was blistering. He complained about our many turnovers, when we had thrown the ball away or had it stolen from us. Mel's speech, although contemptuous and sneering, never approached the volcanic heights which he was fully capable of scaling. To some of us, he even seemed content that we were only ten points behind them at the half. The big guys' uniforms were soaked with sweat. I had not even broken a sweat during the warmups. An undamp uniform is only one of the humiliations of sitting on the bench. A dry basketball player is a loser and a benchwarmer and that is how I viewed myself when we trotted out to begin the second half.

Tee had his hands full trying to stop Sutherland, who was always strangely wonderful even on his worst night. "Try to make him go to his left, Tee," I advised. "He's good going to his left, but not great."

Tee nodded but I was not sure he heard me above the roar of that unruly crowd—that, and the accursed trombones that awaited the poor Green Weenies on the bench.

"Let's beat up the fucking band," Cauthen suggested as we sat down to watch the tip-off.

Both teams spent the next half snarling at each other and grappling fiercely under the baskets. Among the Citadel players, John DeBrosse was in the middle of the best college game he would ever play. He performed with an aristocratic elegance on this night, delighting me with the perfect fluidity of his shot. So hot was DeBrosse that he later told me he expected to see smoke coming off his fingers. He made thirteen jump shots over the much taller Clemson guard, and he carried himself on the court like a man possessed.

Barney leaned over and yelled over the sickening din of the trombones, "Beaver shot. Eleven o'clock. Another one. Two o'clock."

Bornhorst handled the shame of sitting on the bench by becoming an aficionado of spotting the panties of coeds with casually parted legs. The piety of my young Catholic and southern manhood was so extreme at the time that I never once looked into the stands for that secret and harmless thrill that gave us Green Weenies our only pleasure as we sat and watched our lives pass by without us.

With fourteen minutes left to play, Tee fouled out. As I entered the game to replace Tee, I saw a look of unadulterated suffering cross his face. The game had wounded this high-strung competitor.

"You get Sutherland," DeBrosse said to me as Sutherland shot his foul shot.

"Thanks a ton," I said. "I want Ayoob."

"Not a chance. Get me the ball, smackhead. I'm hotter than shit."

"Think the kid didn't notice?"

The game got nastier for both teams and I thought both Zinsky and Bridges were going to start swinging at the men guarding them. John and I posed a slight matchup problem for Clemson. Though Jim was seven inches taller than I was, and Ayoob five inches taller than John, we were both much quicker than they were. I started setting picks on Ayoob that DeBrosse would use to perfection, coming off me like we were part of the same body. I would flip him the ball and John would dribble once, then leave his feet, the mechanics of his flawless jump shot textbook, and the ball would arch high over Sutherland's outstretched hand, then split the net with the sound of razored cotton.

When Sutherland saw I was guarding him, he looked at me like I was an hors d'oeuvre. He called for the ball as he was supposed to when he found himself guarded by a midget, which is what I felt like as he began to back me toward the basket. I tried to use my quickness to flick the ball from him, but he was Jim Sutherland, and I was me, imprisoned in a body that had little business on a college basketball court. He faked right, then spun in a tight, sweet move to his left and went up for a jump shot. Far below him, I grabbed his shooting arm, deciding that he would earn his points on the free throw line, which he promptly did.

"We're losing by a million. Where's our big man?" I asked De-Brosse.

"Over there," DeBrosse answered, pointing to Mohr on the bench.

Mel had taken Danny out with more than thirteen minutes to go and never put him back in the game. This was unfathomable to me. I started seeing various members of the Green Weenies reporting in at the scorers' table as DeBrosse and I went into high gear and began fast-breaking every time we got the ball, playing sloppy, catch-up basketball.

But the fast break was my native land, the country where I felt most at home in my chosen, lovely game. Fleet of foot, I loved pushing a basketball up the court as much as I have loved anything in this life. That night Zinsky and Kroboth were like racehorses on the wings, and I could always depend on them filling the lanes. I hit them whenever they were open.

The Green Weenie Brian Kennedy got in for his first minute of playing time in his varsity career, joined by Greg Connor. Looking for his first college rebound, Brian was matched against the peerless Randy Mahaffey. Brian flung himself at the ball, but Randy got to it first and ripped it out of Brian's grasp. Randy caught Brian's jaw with an unconcealed elbow and one of the referees called a foul on Brian. Then Brian surprised the entire gym, and especially Mel Thompson, by throwing a punch that, had it landed, would have taken Mahaffey's head off.

Two whistles blew and Brian was called for a technical foul ten seconds into his varsity career. Mel sent Bob Cauthen into the game to replace the fired-up Kennedy.

I went over to Brian and said, "Hey, Brian. Pick a fight with someone who ain't built like Samson."

"You see what he did to me," Brian snapped.

"Don't take it personal. He does it to everyone."

With 6:12 left in the game, Coach Bobby Roberts took mercy on our Citadel souls and sent in his second team. The two second teams ("Hey, they got Weenies, too," Cauthen said) ran up and down the court, the scrubs flinging up shots anytime we touched the ball. Mere sloppiness transformed itself into the shameful bedlam that emerges when discipline leaves the gym in the wake of a rout. Never have I seen more turnovers in a single game. "Hold that Tiger" never stopped playing and the crowd never stopped roaring. The only good thing about that awful game is that I could not hear Mel screaming at me not to shoot every time I touched the ball.

With a single minute left, Mel sent Dave Bornhorst into the game for Doug Bridges. Only when Barney removed his warmup jersey did the fans realize he had surrendered his shirt to Doug. Shirtless, Barney ran onto the floor before a disbelieving Clemson crowd. Doug, exhausted and spent by the night-long catfight under the boards, peeled off Barney's shirt and handed it to his teammate at midcourt. When Barney put on that sweat-soaked shirt in full view of four thousand people, the gymnasium rang out with a disgusted cry of "Oooooh." With that one strategic coaching move, Mel managed to humiliate both Bornhorst and Bridges, but both men howled with laughter at the memory years later.

The *News and Piedmont* headline the next day was "Tigers Romp Past the Bulldogs 102–85," while the *News and Courier* said more tersely that "Tigers Claw Bulldogs." Clawed and beaten up, my team certainly felt, and it was becoming clear to everyone that our defense could not stop anyone. Mel told the *News and Courier*'s reporter, Jimmy Powers, "To put it in simple language, Saturday's game with Clemson was sloppy. It was a bad ball game all the way around. We didn't play well and I don't think Bobby Roberts was satisfied with his team's performance, either. I know neither one of us was pleased with the calls made by the officials. It was just sloppy from start to finish. We aren't playing defense in any sense of the word. We are just making too many mistakes both on offense and defense, but the defensive ones appear to be showing up stronger. It is real odd that we outscored Clemson by one field goal and outrebounded them by sixteen, but they shot twenty-seven more free throws than we did."

Coach Thompson uttered not a word describing the superlative play of John DeBrosse who had scored twenty-eight points, the best game yet of his distinguished career. Bill Zinsky followed with twelve, and Danny Mohr and Al Kroboth had eleven, and I had pitched in a messy, undistinguished ten points—only the third time in my varsity career I had scored in double figures. But not to have singled out DeBrosse at all seemed a mistake to me. When I read that article it was the first time I had ever made the connection that Mel lacked all gifts or talents required by the language of praise.

# CHAPTER 11

# GREEN WEENIES

B EFORE THE WOFFORD GAME, MEL HAD DANNY MOHR PAY HIM A VISIT in his office at the Armory. Like the rest of us, Mohr dreaded these infrequent encounters and, as he told me years later, cannot remember emerging from a single one of them feeling good about himself or his game. According to Dan, Mel Thompson never looked at him for four years with anything but hatred and contempt in his eyes. He entered the office and said, "Hey, Coach, how're you doing?"

Mel looked up and stared darkly at his center. "I don't know who I'm going to make captain this year. You and Conroy don't show me jackshit for leadership. My seniors are letting the team down."

"Seniors have always been the captains, Coach," Dan said.

"I've never seen that rule carved in stone, Mohr. You seen it carved in stone? Show it to me."

"Maybe the team could vote on it," Dan suggested.

"You think this is a goddamn democracy, Mohr? This isn't a democracy by any stretch of the imagination. This is a fucking dictatorship and you know who's in charge. Right?"

"I guess you are, Coach," Dan offered.

"You *guess*? You fucking *guess* I'm in charge? Is there any doubt in your mind, Mohr?"

"No, not any, Coach."

"That's good, Mohr. If you ever doubt I'm in charge, let me know and I'll run your ass into the ground. I don't know if you have the guts to be captain. You don't show me a smidgen of leadership out there on the court. I even saw you smile at our players on the bench when Clemson was kicking the shit out of us. Smiling."

"I was trying to give the guys some encouragement, Coach."

"That's not your job," Mel shouted.

"Coach, the guys get down. You don't know what we have to put up with in the barracks."

"What happens in the barracks is irrelevant to what happens on the court. You guys are on scholarship. You owe full allegiance to this program. We own your body and most of your soul. Full commitment, Mohr. Do I have it from you, Mohr? Will you put yourself on the line for me?"

"Yes sir, Coach," Danny said. "You can count on me, Coach."

"Bullshit, Mohr," Mel screamed. "Bullshit. You're nothing but a can of corn."

Later that same day while returning some paperwork to Mel's pretty secretary, I caught Mel and his assistant, Ed Thompson, in the middle of a drifting, desultory conversation about the team and its prospects against Wofford. Then the subject shifted to Tee Hooper and how well their experiment of putting him at the number two guard position was working out. Then Mel put a bolt of lightning through my life by saying, "I don't know if Conroy will get into another game this year. We need to develop some of these young kids."

I staggered out of the field house into the bright sunshine of that December day, feeling as if I had been hit by a car. I had trouble breathing and trouble walking, my head ablaze with Mel's despair-inducing words. Slowly, I walked in front of Murray Barracks and made my way back to the Fourth Battalion. From long experience, I knew that once Mel had made up his mind about a player there was no such thing as redemption or a second chance. Devastated, I returned to my room and tried to work on my senior essay comparing the works of William Faulkner and Sinclair Lewis. Neither *Light in August* nor *Arrowsmith* could touch the struck-down athlete in me who grieved for his lost season.

Before the game against the Wofford Terriers, Mel wrote the names of his starting lineup on the blackboard: Bridges, Zinsky, Mohr, DeBrosse, Hooper. As I read the names, I had to admit that those five were the best athletes on the team and gave The Citadel its best chance to win. I hated that it was so, but it was so. After going over the defensive assignments, Mel surprised his team again when he pointed to Danny and said, "Mohr, you're captain for tonight." This caused some minor discomfort for DeBrosse, who had played the best game of his career while serving as team captain against Clemson. Mel had managed to pull off a hat trick. There were now three of us sitting in the locker room who could go through life claiming to be captain of the Citadel basketball team. It all felt slipshod and ill-considered to me. This eccentric game of musical chairs with the team's captaincy added a touch of bewilderment and misdirection to a season shakily begun. This does not feel like a team, I remember thinking.

The door flew open and we entered into the sudden light with the band going wild and Dan Mohr leading us out on the court dribbling the ball and making the captain's honorary first layup. Wofford was one of the smaller colleges put on The Citadel's schedule to serve as baitfish for us, a team that provided us a breather after our games with the leviathans, Auburn and Clemson. Unfortunately, Wofford refused to play dead for us. Before 1,582 fans, the Terriers came out scrapping and clawing from the opening tip-off until the final buzzer. It marked the real coming-out party of our sensational sophomores and it was their play that dominated the game. Still, we were fouling everybody in sight and did not seem to be able to move without putting a Wofford kid on the foul line. The big guys were beating each other up so badly in practice that they did not seem to know how to stop when game time began. Both Bridges and Mohr had three fouls in the first half and had to be replaced by Kroboth and Cauthen to save them for second-half action. Going into halftime, Wofford led us 44–43.

I never got into the Wofford game and neither did any of the other Green Weenies except Bob Cauthen. "I rotted on the bench" is the most accurate phrase I can think of. I always felt a putrefaction setting in as I watched the games go by without my participation. Since I had overheard Mel's plans not to play me for the rest of the year, I had to surrender my dreams of that season to the sure knowledge that my position had been taken from me, fair and square, by a far superior athlete. Even though I would not play this year, I still had to shoulder responsibilities to my teammates. I could be a great Green Weenie and get the starters ready for the hard games coming up on our schedule. And I could cheer, yes, cheer my ass off for the good of my team. The Green Weenies were always the best cheerleading squad in the gym wherever we played. We possessed a genius for firing up and supporting our starters and no one was noisier or more zealous about it than we were. I cheered Tee loudly, then silently offered a prayer that he would break both legs. Horrified, I would right myself and scream my support for DeBrosse, then quietly pray that his pancreas might fall out onto the floor. This despicable pattern of applause and indefensible prayer got me through the second half of the Wofford game. It was disgraceful then and it shames me today that I did it.

When the game ended, I had not even broken a sweat and my uniform was so dry and clean it embarrassed me. Our five starters all had broken into double figures. Bridges had a quiet ten and Mohr had a businesslike fifteen. His man Willie Pegram was the game high scorer for Wofford with twenty-seven, and Mel would torture Dan about those twenty-seven points for most of the next practice. Our guard play was superb with DeBrosse scoring eighteen and Hooper with seventeen points.

Louis Chestnut, the executive sports editor of the *News and Courier,* quoted Mel Thompson in the paper the next day: "The turning point in the game was our defense in the second half. We have had trouble with our defense and we had to be made believers. I think we were made aware of it in the second half tonight."

I did not know what my coach meant by that when I first read those words thirty years ago, and they remain mystifying to me as I read them again today. I was in the middle of the lunatic process of trying to turn myself into a novelist in a college that turned out colonels, but I would spend a baffling, imbalanced year trying to figure out what Coach Thompson was trying to tell the world.

But one thing I knew for certain: I had heard him say I would not play, and I believed it with all my heart—a heart that after the Wofford game was a wreck.

So, I resumed my life as part of the audience of my last basketball season. Any joy in the game would have to come in practice, and I reclaimed my position as leader of the Green Weenies with as much panache as I could muster. Humiliated as I was by not playing in a game as a senior, I had long been drilled in the importance of subsuming my own ego for the good of my team. In fact, putting the team before self was the essence of being a good point guard. So I adjusted my ambitions for myself as an athlete and returned to my role as career second-stringer.

But still, day after day, practice after practice, the Green Weenies could whack and ambush and humiliate the Blue Team every time we took the court. There were reasons for this. First, we Green Weenies played the game with no pressure on us. In Mel Thompson's world, a second-stringer was a loser by definition and an afterthought at best. There was no way that any of us could excel at practice and work our way into the starting lineup. To Mel, we were invisible. I think I was the only one of the Green Weenies who knew how good our team was. We also got to run the offenses of our next opponent. From scouting reports, Ed "Little Mel" Thompson would take us to the far end of the court and instruct us on the intricacies of offenses that were beautifully conceived. It was a pleasure to run offenses that were inventive and full of the possibilities that came from misdirection and surprise. The defenses we ran were scrambling and complex, put together by brilliant, inventive coaches on the cutting edge of their sport.

At the same time, the Green Weenies knew, by heart, every single thing the Blue Team was going to do long before they did it. But the Blue Team never had a clue about what offense we were going to throw at them until we went into action. Mel's malefic glare was fixed on them like a jeweler's eye and no one seemed the slightest bit concerned over the Weenies' play. The first team was supposed to kick our butts every practice because they were, by far and in fact, the superior athletes. But sport is often strange and contradictory.

On the Green Weenies, I had my pick of Al Kroboth, Bob Cauthen, Greg Connor, Dave Bornhorst, Brian Kennedy, and the superb freshman center Bob Carver under the boards. Kroboth was the great surprise of the sophomore class and was getting more and more playing time because of his flawless attitude, his nose for the ball, and his unceasing hustle. He would ripen into one of the best rebounders in the history of Citadel basketball. Big Al could get me the ball anytime I called for it. Two flashy freshmen guards, Jerry Hirsch and Willie Taylor, gave us a formidable backcourt.

The much maligned Bob Cauthen was as much a presence beneath the boards as the soft-spoken Kroboth. Alone among my teammates of that year, I rated Cauthen as the best and most fierce rebounder on the team. I remembered with great clarity the Duquesne game in Pittsburgh the year before with Mohr and Bridges hurt when Mel, in desperation, inserted Cauthen into the lineup, and I watched Bob take on the entire Duquesne team. He scored nineteen points and pulled down sixteen rebounds in the greatest performance by a reserve I had seen in my career as a Citadel basketball player. He followed it up with an almost magical game against East Carolina when he scored twenty-one points and pulled down another slew of rebounds. Then Doug and Dan healed and Cauthen joined the rest of us Green Weenies on the bench, rarely to rise again. Though Bob's caustic wit and negativity irked my teammates, I always admired his courage under the basket. The Blue Team never understood the humiliation of warming the bench, but the Green Weenies taught them the humiliation of being soundly trounced.

"You're letting *these* guys kick your asses? The fucking Green Weenies? What in the hell are you going to do against George Washington or Davidson?"

Every day of that indecipherable, overlong year, the Green Weenies stomped the Blue Team and it still irritates them thirty years later.

When I saw Bill Zinsky at Doug Bridges's house in Columbia, South Carolina, recently, the memory was visibly painful to him. He said, "There was absolutely no pressure on the Green Weenies. We were a lot better than you guys and you knew it. We knew there was nothing any of us could do about that. It was Mel's great negativity that tore us down. He was a black hole. We played badly because he wanted us to play badly, wanted us to lose to a group of guys who couldn't hold our jocks. You guys were having a ball. You were having fun. We were having Mel. Do you understand that, Conroy? We were having Mel."

The following Saturday night at the Armory, we took on the visiting George Washington Colonials. In the locker room before the game, after posting the starting lineup and designating the defensive assignments, Mel shocked us again by naming me captain. I felt Dan freeze up beside me.

When DeBrosse had served as captain against Clemson, he scored the highest number of points in his career. When Mohr had gone to shake hands at center court with the Wofford captains, he had come away at the end of that game with our first victory of the season. Rat flipped me the ball as I took my place of honor to lead my team out onto the court when Dan whispered to me, "What's going on, Conroy? You didn't even take your warmups off against Wofford. It doesn't make any damn sense to me." Then the first strains of "Dixie" sounded as I ran out into the lights and noise of the crowd. I think the breaking of Dan Mohr began in earnest that night. It hurt him when the referee tapped me on the shoulder for the meeting of the captains at center court. When I shook hands with Joe Lalli, it shamed me to be there. He was fast, bold, and cocksure like a point guard was supposed to be, and a good two inches shorter than me or DeBrosse. He scooted around the court like a manic waterbug, making the bigger guards covering him look slow-footed and earthbound. His game smelled like the New York City school grounds to me. He hummed with pure energy as we listened to the refs explain the rules. I did not feel like the captain of my basketball team. I felt lost and haunted and ridiculous, an afterthought, a mistake. If I could not even get into the Wofford game, I certainly did not deserve to stand at center court facing the best point guard in our conference. Already, I avoided looking at either DeBrosse or Mohr when I returned to my teammates who were taking their first warmup shots.

Our sophomores were magnificent, especially in the first half. The game unveiled the rapidly developing game of Al Kroboth, whose long arms always seemed to appear above the rim at exactly the right moment. In addition, Bill Zinsky's presence was a lordly one on the court, his beautifully chiseled body glistening with sweat as he guarded Ed Rainey of the Colonials with a catlike fierceness. From past experiences, I knew that Rainey was a good ballplayer, but Zinsky was all over him from the tip-off until the moment Rainey fouled out trying to guard Zinsky.

Sitting on the bench praying for the death of Tee Hooper, I immediately filled up with shame again and began cheering for him all the harder. I cheered as I retreated to the country place I keep behind my eyes, the place I return to in times of danger and despair, the hermitage and refuge I kept secret to all but myself. I employed it as summer house, lecture hall, resort, and private lair. In the madness of my terrible boyhood, it was the den I fell back on when my father beat me with his fists, when the plebe system tore me apart in the soft places, when the screaming of the coaches grew too loud or hit too close to home. I was the only one with the key to this inn of interior peace that I had built on the other side of retinas and corneas and the soft tissues of my face. It is a manse of solitude and shade and refuge. It is the place I go to every day to write the books which explain who I am to myself.

In my years on the bench at The Citadel, I practiced the art of writing during every game and had not the vaguest notion that I was doing so. One part of my mind remained on the game, like an idling motor, and I followed the routes and fortunes of my teammates and cheered when appropriate or moaned with displeasure when disaster struck. But the other part, an embassy of a completely sovereign nation, would fling its doors open to the most authentic part of me. My eyes would light on a human face in the crowd, and I would invent stories about that face and that body until these complete strangers would brim over in an amazing and vital life. Sometimes I would hone in on the assistant commandant for cadets, Lieutenant Colonel Nugent Courvoisie, and his wife, Elizabeth, and begin their courtship in Europe when they met during the war in the snowy, perilous days that led up to the Battle of the Bulge. I had the Boo's artillery battery tearing up a road of advancing German tanks as American troops fell back in terrible disarray all the way back to the Ardennes forest. Mrs. Courvoisie had been a nurse during the war and was grievously wounded in Belgium, and I had her present at fearful amputations, her hand wiping the foreheads of doomed young soldiers whose intestines were slithering out of wounds too horrible to imagine. I had the Boo take the young nurse to a lunch in Brussels on leave and he ordered a very fine wine (I didn't know the name of a single wine then) and then a fabulous Belgian meal of whatever rich and gracious Belgians ate. I knew only of waffles, and that lacked romance to me. Then my eyes would travel higher and another nurse, pretty Sylvia Cox, would come into rapturous view. I had a crush on Sylvia for the four years I was a cadet, which put me into solid competition with the other two thousand Citadel cadets who flirted with her whenever they visited the infirmary. Once, I called to ask her for a date, but hung up the receiver as soon as she answered the phone and I heard her lovely voice. But under the false light of field houses, I would plot out in my mind the long serious courtship of the unknowing Miss Cox, my canoeing her down the Edisto River, taking her to plays at the Dock Street Theater, and reading her long poems I had composed in praise of her loveliness. Of course we would live in Paris in a small garret with a view of the Seine and the Eiffel Tower where I would begin to write the books that would change the course of world literature and bring the literati of the Western world to my modest doorway. Sylvia would find them there on their knees. We would eat only in Left Bank cafés, and I would wear a beret to cover my thinning hair. The guard at the Louvre would know us so well he would wink and wave us in without a ticket.

DeBrosse hit a jump shot coming off the dribble near the foul line.

The next time down the court John put another one in at almost the same spot. Thirty seconds later Kroboth broke through underneath with a twisting layup that their forward could not block. Walking down the rue Vaugirard, I would take Sylvia's hand and tell her the French words I loved the most: hyacinthe, époussetage, rosette, reconnaissances, peintre—I would try to think of other beautiful French words and wish I had studied harder in Colonel Smith's French class. In my retreat behind the eyes, I spoke a perfect colloquial French. Sylvia and I always had more money than we needed, and the flowers in the Luxembourg Gardens were always in full bloom as the cadets' hot hands cooled off in the beginning of the second half as the George Washington defense stepped up the pressure. DeBrosse was playing a terrific floor game and holding the slippery Joe Lalli at bay. Quicksilver fast, Lalli could make a defender look bad by driving by him hard, then pulling up for a quick jumper. I had found this out the hard way in a game the previous year.

A man rose out of a seat in a top row and I watched him make a signal of some kind to his wife. The wife looked beleaguered, worried, and at that moment I knew the man was the son of a one-eyed tobacco farmer near Mars Hill, North Carolina, and a woman who had only finished third grade and was famous in the mountain country for frying perch and handling snakes. The man sold flood insurance by day, but was a cross-dresser who secretly went to a nameless bar near the Merchant Seaman's Club that required your own key to gain entry. They had a bitter fight on the way to the game because the wife had confronted him sneaking into their house wearing her hose and brassiere and dress. He had gone to phone a client that a friend of his had a dog about to give birth to a litter of Boykin spaniels. The man in the flight jacket in the third row killed fourteen Cambodian villagers when one of his rockets strayed off course as he bombed targets along the Ho Chi Minh Trail, and that blond woman ran a numbers racket out of the backseat of her surgeon husband's Jaguar, and the redheaded man with the mole above his lip . . .

"Conroy!" Coach Thompson shouted. My warmup was already off when I reported to my coach.

"Get in for Mohr. You bring it up the court. Nobody else. Got it?"

"Yes, sir," I said, looking up at the clock, having no idea what the score was.

Bob Nugent, a six-foot-eight substitute, had entered the game when the center, Ed Rainey, had fouled out. Nugent scored two quick baskets to tie the score at 77 all, then the Colonials moved ahead on a free throw by Nugent.

When George Washington put on a full-court press, "Conroy" was the first word out of Mel Thompson's mouth, and it'd been that way since I arrived at The Citadel. I ran out on the court and got a cheer from the Corps because they liked to watch me dribble a basketball and I liked to dribble for them.

I took the inbound's pass from DeBrosse and waved for him to go downcourt. Then I faced the two George Washington guards moving toward me and one of them was the sneaky-quick Lalli. I picked on the other guard and, dribbling with my left hand, blew by the kid like his foot was nailed to the court.

"Don't shoot, Conroy," Mel yelled as I passed him on the run and threw the ball to a wide-open DeBrosse who found it a resting place in the net. The pesky Nugent hit a jump shot from the corner and again the race was on. John shuffled me a pass after he took it out then cleared the court for me again. I dribbled to my right and Lalli made a mongoose-quick move to slap the ball away, but I could bring a ball up-court and anticipated his move and went behind the back, leaving Lalli to the rear. I put a crossover dribble on the other guard and charged up the court pursued by a duet of Colonial guards. I charged toward the basket and saw Kroboth's man move out to challenge me, so I dished it to Mr. Kroboth who got to make the layup. Al was fouled by the weak-side forward in the process. Oh yes, and Mel Thompson shouted, "Conroy, don't shoot," when I surged past him.

At the time I played the game, dribbling the basketball was an art form and few players could do it as it was supposed to be done. The fingertips controlled the basketball entirely and the ball was kept low on the floor and you had to be good or lucky to steal it from a point guard who knew what he was doing. I knew what I was doing but the fan of today cannot appreciate the art of dribbling I am talking about. The great players of the later era—Magic Johnson, Larry Bird, John Stockton, Michael Jordan, Charles Barkley—palmed the basketball every time they handled it. The game has advanced or retreated in such a way that what these players call dribbling, our referees would have called turnovers.

Each time George Washington scored, I dribbled through their whole team for the rest of the night. Evan Bussey wrote the story for the *News and Courier*'s morning edition the next day: "It took a pair of free throws by little Pat Conroy of Beaufort and a last-second goal to seal the Bulldogs' second victory of the season."

We were 2–2 as we entered the shower room. Bridges came in last in his slow-loping gait and passed Dan Mohr as the center stood mutely in the shower. Unlike the other guys, there was no horsing around or small talk for Danny.

"Good game, Root," Doug said with sincerity and kindness.

Every member of the team remembers his reply. Dan stuck up the largest middle finger on the team and said, "Fuck you, Bouncy." Doug's nickname came because Cauthen thought Doug "bounced like a nigger" when he ran the court.

The whole team lapsed into shocked silence before we howled with helpless, senseless laughter. It became the signature moment of the entire lousy year.

# CHAPTER 12

# OLD DOMINION

M Y TEAM WAS 2–2, AND WE WERE ABOUT TO PLAY A TEAM FEW OF US had ever heard of before we read the schedule. Today, several of my teammates look upon this game as the central point when our team began to founder, but all agree that our game with the Old Dominion Monarchs, an unknown and uncelebrated team out of Norfolk, Virginia, set forces loose that would have melancholy consequences all year. Someone let us know that the Old Dominion coach, Sonny Allen, had practically begged Mel to get his little team from the Mason-Dixon Conference into our mighty Southern Conference. In the days leading up to the game Mel spoke of Old Dominion with withering contempt. Since he had starred on the high mountain passes of that Massif Central known as ACC basketball, he held not a smidgen of respect for coaches or players who labored for their schools in the unhonored, trash-fish leagues around the country. To Mel, my teammates and I were unspeakable losers because we played in the Southern Conference, but the very idea of lowering his standards to include such a new, unproven program on our schedule rankled him. To us, he made Old Dominion sound like we were playing a team composed of paraplegics and Lou Gehrig's disease sufferers.

This game marked a moment of history I was proud to be a part of because the two starting guards at Old Dominion were both black, and Bob Pritchett and Arthur Speakes would have the honor of integrating the Armory on the Citadel campus. Black kids were appearing more and more in the lineups of southern basketball, but none had made it to our home gymnasium until this night. And the appearance of Pritchett and Speakes brought me back to the days of Washington, D.C., and

Arlington, Virginia. I took it to the hoop the way those flashy black guards from Spingarn and Eastern high schools did on the outdoor courts around the city. "Let the little white kid play" were the happiest words I could hear on a Saturday morning when the pickup games would begin.

For reasons that still remain unclear to me, Mel named me as captain for the Old Dominion game, the first time this season anyone on the team had been captain in two consecutive games thus far. Even more mystifying and inexplicable to me, I was named captain for every single game for the rest of the season, but never knowing for sure that Mel would appoint me for the next game or not. The sound of my name began to hurt Danny Mohr, and there was nothing either one of us could do about it except endure it with grace.

Our coach was an extraordinarily superstitious man. He would not let me wear my high school number of 13 because he considered that number to be anathema. His life was stylized and ritualized to the point of parody, and the schemes of his life were all obsessive. Once you caught on to the major currents of his patterns of behavior, Mel would never surprise you. By my senior year, I could read Mel as clearly as a windsock on some matters.

"Old Dominion," Mel sneered as he began his pregame pep talk. "Old Dominion. We don't know much about this team, but how much do you need to know about Old Dominion of the Mason-Dixon Conference? Now here's what I want you to do. We've got these two black guards named Pritchett and Speakes. Now Tee and John, you don't play black kids like you do white kids. You play 'em tough. You get in their faces and rough them up. Black kids don't like to play rough-and-tumble kick-ass Citadel basketball. They like to play pretty and fancy-Dan like Conroy, but they sure don't like taking their licks. I don't know if black people have a place in this game or not [prophecy was not Mel Thompson's long suit] but I want these goddamn kids from Old Dominion—all of them, not just the black ones—to leave this field house tonight knowing they've been in a war. Now, get out there and show them what Southern Conference basketball is all about."

We roared out onto the court to the sound of "Dixie," and ten minutes later the first two black kids ever to play ball on the hardwood of the beautiful Armory shook hands with DeBrosse and Hooper. Let it be known that the two five-foot-eleven guards Bob Pritchett and Arthur

Speakes were that night kingly with their gifts and magical with their skills. The guys, as they say, lit it up, and we white boys looked as though our Converse All Stars had been glued to the floor. In the first five minutes of play, Speakes and Pritchett flew past Hooper and DeBrosse, humiliating both players.

"Get in their faces, Hooper. Get up in there tight, DeBrosse," Mel would scream, and both Hooper and DeBrosse would move in tight. The two black kids would cut through them like wind through a cornfield. Right in front of me, John moved in pressuring Speakes who drove by him so quickly that DeBrosse looked up in pure surprise and said in a startled, helpless way, "Fuck."

It was at that moment that it struck me that John DeBrosse and Tee Hooper had never played against any black kids. I ran down the bench to Mel's side and knelt beside him. He looked down at me as though I were a typhoid carrier.

"What the hell are you doing here, Conroy?" Mel said. "Have you gone nuts?"

"Coach, Tee and John've never guarded black kids. They need to back off them. Those kids are fast as hell."

"Get back to your seat on the bench. Did General Harris hire you as coach? Do I need to hand you my whistle? Ed, get rid of him."

Ed "Little Mel" Thompson, his sweetness almost a salve to Mel's gruffness, said, "Pat, go on back to your seat now. We'll discuss it at halftime."

"They're going to kill us, Coach," I said, returning to the last folding chair away from my coaches. And then it dawned on me that neither Mel nor Ed Thompson had played against black competition, either. It was painful to watch Tee and John running after the swift and agile Pritchett and Speakes. All night long, the Old Dominion guards drove the lane with boldness and flash. Speakes had a beautiful outside shot from long range. The box score claims that I hit a single basket, but I have no memory of being in that game because of what happened during halftime.

When we entered our overheated locker room at halftime, Old Dominion was beating us badly. The managers distributed Cokes to all of us. We knew we had five minutes to relax and gather our thoughts until Mel would enter and scream at us for the last five minutes of the break before we had to report back to the court for the second-half tip-off.

Brian Kennedy, frisky all year from lack of playing time, lightened the heavy atmosphere by announcing, "You know, it seems to me that black people might, just might, have a place in this game."

The team exploded in suppressed laughter—suppressed because laughter is the last thing Mel would have wanted to hear in our locker room. Then Dave Bornhorst compounded the damage by saying, "I'll tell you one damn thing, Old Dominion sure found out what Southern Conference basketball is all about." The team fell apart for a second time, the first authentic laughter we had shared the whole year. Guys kept repeating the lines.

"You think black people might have a place in this game? No way, man," said Connor.

"Old Dominion's gonna spread the word. Don't fuck with those boys in the Southern Conference," said Cauthen.

"Stay away from the Southern Conference if you know what's good for you," said Connor.

Most of the talk came from the bench-warming Green Weenies. Members of the first team laughed, but they were also exhausted and humiliated by the fast-paced ordeal of the first half. They knew they were due for a blistering verbal assault from our all but unhinged Coach Thompson. Rat came flying through the door to say, "Knock it off. Coach is coming and he looks pissed."

It seemed early for our routine-loving coach to arrive, but it occurred to us that the coach needed extra time for a good ass-chewing. All of us put on our game faces, faces that could not submit to defeat by a bunch of bush leaguers from the Mason-Dixon Conference. Our coach entered in the same manner he had before every game and during every halftime of the fifty-some games I had played as a Citadel Bulldog.

I was surprised—no, that is not a strong enough word—I was stunned to see my teammate Doug Bridges walking through the door smoking a cigarette. He looked preoccupied, overserious, and he walked with a long-strided, loping gait that looked familiar. The others began falling down laughing all around me. Mohr and DeBrosse were on the floor. I still had not quite gotten it, then it hit me: Bridges was doing the most extraordinary imitation of Mel Thompson imaginable. Not once did he break character. What he was doing seemed dangerous and forbidden and fabulous to all of us.

Like the rest of my teammates, I recognized every step of Bridges' brilliant send-up of our inflammatory coach as an exact mimic. Bridges smoked his cigarette exactly as Mel did his, taking preoccupied puffs and exhaling in long, heavy sighs indicating that he, poor Mel Thompson, should be doomed to coach such an unmanageable posse of slackers and whiners. When he reached the shower room, Doug turned to the right and we heard Bridges-Thompson pissing in the urinal. Again we fell apart. The sound of Mel Thompson pissing as we awaited a bawling out is a memory every member of this team carries to this day. Doug urinated casually, broodingly. He passed into sight for a brief second as he walked to the sink and when we heard Doug washing his hands, Brian Kennedy sank to his knees in laughter. We heard the water run as Doug cleaned his hands and the pure genius of his performance was in the perfect timing of each gesture—Doug washing his hands for the exact same length of time as Mel. I was howling and helpless with laughter when Bridges emerged from the shower room wiping his hands with the towel, slowly, smoking his cigarette, ignoring us tumbling down around him. When Doug neared the blackboard, he wiped it clean with his towel, then in a final brilliant act of mimicry, he drew the last puff from his cigarette, threw the butt on the floor, and extinguished it with his large right foot, grinding it compulsively until completely extinguished.

In all the years I played sports, I have never seen a team in less condition to be bawled out for poor play than this one. We had guys with tears streaming down their faces as some of the other guys said, "We've got to get it together . . . We've got to stop this."

Until this moment, no one on the basketball team knew that Doug Bridges possessed such a chameleon gift of mimicry. No one.

Then Rat appeared in the doorway. "Coach's coming. For real this time."

Some of the guys tried coughing to stifle their laughter. Others threw their warmup jerseys over their heads, some wheezed, but the sudden suppression of enormous laughter into the shamed silence of a team being beaten by an inferior foe left the atmosphere brittle and perilous. Of course, Mel had no idea of Doug's drop-dead imitation of him, but when I looked up and saw my coach enter the locker room exactly as Doug Bridges had, I knew I was going to have a difficult time. I was strangling on my own my laughter as strange noises that sounded like a possum being asphyxiated came from my throat. My mistake was to watch Mel do exactly what Doug had just done. Mel carried the towel draped and folded carefully over his left shoulder, and he smoked his cigarette with deep and brooding detachment. His slouching, forward-leaning amble had all been stolen perfectly by Bridges. When Mel made the turn and we heard him pissing in the urinal, the team broke one more time. The laughter was in every face, but subterranean and forbidden, and we had only seconds to right ourselves.

I was too near hysteria as Mel crossed over to the sink to wash his hands, but I was desperate to come up with a foolproof way to calm myself. Mel treated laughter like some capital crime. He was wiping his hands with the towel as he began his slow, deliberate promenade the length of the locker room, smoking his cigarette expertly as he moved in his oddly shuffling gait toward the blackboard. I made it through the cleaning of the board and I think I would have gotten through the whole thing cleanly except that I had not counted on the completeness of Doug Bridges' genius in his spooky parody of Coach's behavior. When Mel took the last puff of his cigarette and threw it on the floor, I was in control of myself. But when I saw Mel's huge, tasseled wing tip on his right foot solemnly crush that cigarette with exquisite thoroughness, I laughed as loudly and as completely and as idiotically and as hysterically as I ever have in my life.

Only me.

My outbreak was met by the stoical silence of my teammates. Coach Thompson looked at me as though I had told him that I had cooked and eaten the baby Jesus for breakfast that morning. But I kept laughing and the more I tried to hold it back, the more the high tide of hysteria poured out of me in guffaws and belly laughs and snorts. Snot oozed from my nose and tears rolled down my cheeks.

Then Mel exploded. "Conroy, you think it's funny? You think it's funny that fucking Old Dominion is kicking our asses to hell and back? Losing's funny to you? Losing eats my guts out and makes me want to puke. I'd rather die than to be a loser, Conroy. Die! Get the fuck out of this locker room. Get out, now. I won't have you on my damn team."

Laughing still, I staggered out of the locker room thinking I had just ruined my life.

When the team returned to the court, I went into the empty locker room, removed my uniform, and showered alone for the first time. The second half started and I could hear the sound of the basketball hitting the oak floor, one of the loveliest sounds to me. Devastated, I dressed and walked the long way back to the barracks by the baseball field and the obstacle course and behind the mess hall.

In memory, that walk looms colossal in importance. Now I knew the dismayed horror of being the agent in the destruction of my own life. I wondered if Mel would revoke my scholarship tomorrow. In the darkness I tried to form the words I would use to tell my mother that I had been kicked off my college basketball team. From bitter past knowledge, I knew my parents would not spend a dime on my college education. From even bitterer knowledge, I thought of my bullying, brow-beating father's reaction and thought that in his rage, The Great Santini might try to beat me to death. I imagined the fist fight I would have with the strongest Marine colonel I had ever met, and it surprised me that I was even thinking about fighting back. Then a sudden surge of pure fear shot through me as I realized the Vietnam War was raging in Southeast Asia and that I would be drafted the day I told the comptroller's office I could not pay the tuition for the final semester of my senior year. I could see the headline in *The Brigadier* on the day my death was announced in the mess hall: "Conroy killed by mortar fire because he laughed at Thompson."

The sheer absurdity of my situation overwhelmed and sickened me. I kept having imaginary conversations with my mother, who had not gone to college. My graduation day was as important for her as it was for me, and I imagined telling her what had happened, trying to make her understand what had taken place in the locker room.

On that long walk to the barracks, I knew in my bones Peg Conroy would never get it.

THE NEXT DAY IN THE TRAINING AREA WHERE the jocks gathered to be fed, Rat came up to me and said, "Coach Thompson wants to see you at 1500 hours, Pat."

"Been nice to know you, Conroy," Mohr said, from the opposite side of the table.

"You're history," Cauthen said.

"Hey, Bridges," I said to Doug. "How do I explain to Mel why I was laughing my ass off last night? I'm having trouble with this."

"Your ass is grass, and Mel's the lawn mower, bubba," DeBrosse said.

"It doesn't look good, Conroy," Bridges admitted. "I've never been more afraid as I was last night. I thought Mel was going to kill you. Did you see the look on his face? He wanted you dead. Dead, Conroy."

"I couldn't see the look on his face because I was laughing so hard," I said. "Bridges, I've sat by you at mess for a couple of years now, and practiced with you every day. Don't let this hurt your feelings, but you've not demonstrated the greatest wit or personality. When did your ass turn into fucking Jack Benny?"

"The guillotine, Conroy," Bob Cauthen said, drawing a bony finger along his throat.

"You gonna tell Mel what happened?" DeBrosse asked me.

"I can't do that. It sounds too nuts. Do you know that what happened to us last night never happened to another team?"

"Bouncy," DeBrosse said to Bridges, "you got nineteen last night. Hell of a game."

"Doug finally got to play among his own people," Cauthen said.

"Fuck you, Zipper," Bridges said, shooting a bird.

"Fuck *you*, Bouncy," Cauthen said right back.

And my team's happy journey across time continued on course.

At exactly 1500 hours I was in Mel Thompson's office, sitting on his couch, enduring his intimidating scowl. The air in the room felt tamped down. I had erred egregiously and I knew it. Whatever punishment, no matter how severe, I had earned it fair and square.

"Well?" Coach Thompson said.

"I can't explain what happened, Coach. It was so painful to be losing like that. So I tried to think of some joke I'd heard in the barracks, one that really tickled me."

"What's the joke, Conroy?" Mel asked.

This question caught me off guard. I am one of those men doomed to walk the world crippled by a dazzling inability to remember jokes. Jokers are not my favorite companions as I make my weary, tear-stained way through this world.

"You surprised me last night," Ed Thompson said from his desk in the corner. "You're one of our solid citizens."

"If we can't depend on you, Conroy," Mel said, "what're we supposed to do?"

"Let you down. Let the team down. Let my school down. I can't tell you how bad I feel about it."

"What's the joke, Conroy?" Mel asked. "The one you heard in the barracks?"

"I have two Italian roommates, sir. Bo Pig and Mike Swine."

"What's that got to do with the price of corn?"

"Sir, they're very sensitive about being Italian. So I collect jokes to tease them."

"This is going nowhere fast, Conroy," Mel said.

"I told them this joke the other night. There was a pig farm that was the stinkiest, smelliest place on earth. An Englishman decided to find out which race could stomach garbage and filth more than any other. So he sent an Englishman, an Irishman, and an Italian to live with the pigs."

"This better be good, Conroy," Mel muttered.

"You'll be on the floor, Coach," I said.

"After the first day, the Englishman came running out puking his guts out, saying he couldn't stay another minute. At the end of the second day, the Irishman came running out vomiting and smelling like shit. And, on the third day, the pigs came running out," I said.

Mel Thompson looked at me in soundless disbelief, but Ed Thompson chuckled from his chair in the corner of the room. Mel turned and glared at his young assistant, but I think Ed's chuckle saved me.

"That's the worst joke I've ever heard," Mel told me.

"It really isn't that good," I agreed.

"We're gonna forget about last night, Conroy. You've been a model citizen for this team since you got here. That was out of character. Don't let it happen again."

"Coach, that's a promise I give you my word on."

"Okay, get the hell out of here. Get ready for practice."

"I can't thank you enough, Coach."

Mel dismissed me with an angry gesture, and I left his office moving fast. But the writer who was secretly blooming inside me had noticed something in that office. I could smell my own fear as I entered Mel's office, and I know he smelled it, too. But for a single instant, I felt something new register on the screen where all the data and fragments of my four-year encounter with Mel Thompson were stored. The writer, not the basketball player, took note of it, a fast blip of insight and consciousness. Mel Thompson had not kicked me off the Citadel basketball team. Not because I didn't deserve it, but because he loved the boy I was and the player he had helped shape. He could not help it. The writer was busy sending news from the depths that day. As I walked slowly to the locker room I was shaken to the core by my urgent and material affection for my coach; no, I was overwhelmed by the profoundness of my own strange loyalty for Mel Thompson. In my life thus far there was nothing odd about this; love had always issued out of the places that hurt the most, and I feared few men as I feared Mel Thompson.

In the locker room, I packed for the trip to New Orleans, the road trip that would change my life and destiny as an athlete forever.

# PART 3

# THE POINT GUARD
# FINDS HIS VOICE

# CHAPTER 13

# NEW ORLEANS

O N THE FLIGHT TO NEW ORLEANS, I READ *A STREETCAR NAMED Desire*. I was kindling in the hands of Tennessee Williams. Because I was going to the mythical and flamboyant city for the first time, I wanted to read the play before I began prowling the back streets of the French Quarter searching for the chance encounters and rich images that would one day add salt and ambience to my future. All year long, I escaped into books the way a cat burglar would take to the woods at the first sign of trouble. My teammates thought my reading habits both odd and off-putting, another way of not inhabiting the world around me.

"Isn't the guy that wrote that book a faggot?" Bob Cauthen asked me with more curiosity than meanness.

"I don't know," I answered.

DeBrosse said, "Conroy, I love these road trips because I *don't* have to read."

Barney Bornhorst, sitting behind me, said in a low voice that only the players could hear, "New Orleans, boys. Naked women. Strip shows. Liquor flowing in the street. Barney's kind of town."

Our laughter was boyish and forbidden. Then I returned to the country of literature where Blanche DuBois and Stanley Kowalski were locked in a powerful dance of bizarre and tragic attraction. They seemed so much more alive and animated and dangerous than my poor teammates and I. The dialogue crackled across the page, laced with sweet malice in every scene. I finished the play almost at touchdown in the city of New Orleans.

As we waited for our luggage, I thought it sad that life had set me down among such dullards and laggards, and the poor colorless bastards on my basketball team. I needed to be hanging around people like Colonel Sartoris and Lady Brett Ashley and Amanda Wingfield instead of Bridges, Bornhorst, and Cauthen. It never occurred to me a single time in the year I am writing about that I was in the dead center of living out my own life, accruing the experiences and gathering the raw materials to form the only life I was ever going to have. As I saw it then, my life had not yet started. I had not escaped my parents' death grip on my imagination.

I had arrived in New Orleans to search for the literary haunts of Tennessee Williams and William Faulkner. I ended up leaving the city thinking I had encountered one of the best basketball teams I had ever played against in my life. We had not studied Loyola on film so none of us knew that we were facing one of the hottest teams in the nation. Loyola had already beaten Texas Christian and LSU when we came to town.

In the wake of my shock at again being named team captain, especially after my disgraceful behavior in the locker room during the Old Dominion game, everything about the Loyola game seemed surreal and otherworldly. The floor of the field house was raised, the first I had ever played on where you had to run up a flight of stairs to enter the game.

Mohr and Zinsky started out strong, The Citadel was leading 17–12 with 12:59 to play in the first half when the sky fell in for the Blue Team. For the next ten minutes, we could not seem to make a shot or pull down a rebound or stop the Wolfpack from scoring at will. First we looked hapless, then we looked hopeless, then we looked like we had no business even being on a court. Our starting team seemed drugged and lifeless. For the second game in a row, Hooper and DeBrosse were battling two much taller guards, both of whom turned all-world against our smaller guards. In fact, Ronnie Britsch and Charley Powell dominated this game more than even Pritchett and Speakes had for Old Dominion. Tee Hooper guarded Powell, a smooth, sweet-shooting black kid who was averaging twenty-two points per game. He was quick coming off the ball and got his shot off in a hurry. Again, poor Tee from Greenville, South Carolina, was getting far too many lessons on integration far too quickly for a southern white boy. DeBrosse had his hands full with Ronnie Britsch who was a flashy, cunning white guard.

I had never seen a Citadel basketball team get overwhelmed so quickly and so thoroughly. The game turned into a rout and then a comedy routine. Then it began to have the makings of a tragedy. When Mel called time-out and the Green Weenies swarmed around the first team, shouting encouragement to them, patting their rear ends, trying to jump-start them into life, they could barely respond. Even Mel's screaming took on a desperate cast that had rarely been there before. Our first team had simply vanished out of themselves. They were not only being beaten; they were getting killed in every phase of the game.

The atmosphere in the locker room at halftime felt like midnight at Gethsemane. I had never seen my teammates closer to despair. Tee held his face in his hands, humiliated beyond measure. The rocklike DeBrosse seemed lost and tentative. In agony, Mohr stared at the concrete floor, a towel draped over his head, hiding from his coach, his team, and perhaps most of all, himself.

But the one we were losing fastest was the one I thought untouchable to the raw malice of Mel Thompson, the sophomore Bill Zinsky. "Zeke?" I said to him. "You okay, son?"

Zeke nodded his head sadly, barely lifting his eyes to acknowledge me. Something seemed broken in a player I had thought would make first-team All-Conference in our league. If self-combustion was possible, Mel Thompson would have entered the locker room as a pillar of flame. There was a choler and rancor to his fury that night that none of us had seen before. His tantrum seemed more nervous breakdown than halftime talk. He seethed and screamed and snarled at us until he was left staring and sputtering and raging at a roomful of boys. "Does anybody in this room have any pride left? Do you have no guts, no balls, no manhood, no nothing? How can I appeal to gutless wonders? What the fuck am I to do? We got plays, don't we? Can we just run the goddamn things? Can somebody guard somebody out there? Is that too much to ask? Jesus Christ. Just guard somebody. Anybody. Jesus Christ. That's the most embarrassing play out of a team I've ever seen. They're kicking your asses to hell and back, and you don't seem to even fucking care," he screamed, throwing a folding chair across the room and into a bank of lockers. "Son-of-a-bitch! Son-of-a-bitch! Son-of-a-fucking-bitch, this beats anything I've ever seen. Mohr, can you get off the fucking line? Zinsky, can you show any sign of life? Bridges, quit giving me that Citadel stare. Wipe it off your fucking face. Bridges— All of you. Get it off your faces. I won't stand for it. We'll start over, by God. Jesus

Christ! What am I supposed to do with these goddamned guys, Ed? No guts, no balls, no points, no rebounds, and what do we have? Not zip. Not shit. Goddamn it!" He hurled another chair. "I might even play the Green Weenies. What quitters—what fucking losers."

Mel threw a towel that landed between me and Dave Bornhorst, then stormed out into the night like a Tennessee Williams character— Mel Thompson starring as Stanley Kowalski, misanthropic, brutish in his exit, in his manner, in his essence. Taking his own cue, Ed Thompson drifted out in Mel's wake, leaving us to marinate in the acids of our coach's wrath.

In the circle of hell where we now sat in agony, I watched my broken teammates trying to gather inward strength that could combat the awesome forces of Mel's negativity. Our coach could yell and rage and throw chairs and yell obscenities and make us run laps until we dropped and suicide drills until we vomited—but in the well of this existential moment among boys suffering from the ferocity of Mel's pitiless charge, I heard a voice scream out inside me, an actual voice—embryonic and unsure—cry out from within me in alarm: "Mel can destroy us and loathe us and demean everything about us, but he cannot and never will coach us. He cannot make us into a team. He cannot teach us to be the thing we need to be."

With this strange and disloyal insight in a gym in New Orleans, I think I was born to myself in the world. That night in New Orleans a voice was born inside me, and I had never heard it before in my entire life.

I looked upon my devastated teammates in the heartless, pitiless wreckage of their season which had barely begun, and they were too bereft for bitterness and too outcast for hope. My teammates had found themselves reduced to a state that was birthplace and hermitage and briar patch to me—a despair with no windows or exits, a futility that made hope vain and the future unthinkable.

This moment felt like home to me, and I knew why. My father never touched me unless he was hitting me or pounding my head against Sheetrock. If he was not beating me, I could enjoy the many pleasures of watching him beating my mother or my smaller brothers and sisters. I was trapped in a child's body, a boy's body, and could not protect my mother from the brute she had married.

In the bell-jar shyness of the young man I was, I began to speak to my team in the voice I had just found. It was the first time I had ever spoken to the group by myself and certainly the first time I had ever tried to exhort them with words or lift their spirits or even fire them up.

My voice was halting and amateurish as I began and I did not even stop when I heard Bob Cauthen say, as he had done the year before when Wig Baumann had called a team meeting, "That shit don't work, Conroy. That's high school shit."

I continued and I remember the talk because it was the first and last one I ever gave as a Citadel athlete. What I said is lost forever, but here is what I think I said: "When we were little boys, we played basketball because it was the most fun a boy can have. Then we noticed something. We were better at it than other boys. We loved it like no other boys. We played it until our mothers came out to shout that our dinners were getting cold. Guys, we need to make this game fun again. We play it because it brings us joy."

As we took to the court for the second half, I made a secret vow to myself that I would never listen to a single thing that Mel Thompson said to me again. I would obey him and honor him and follow him, but I would not let him touch the core of me again. He was my coach, but I was my master. Whenever I got in the game for the rest of the year, I would play it as I was born to play it, I would play it with reckless abandon. If Mel Thompson did not like it, he could choose not to play me. I felt a loosening, an opening up. I had done many things in my life but this marked the first time I had felt myself change. I was not the same young man when I returned to that court at the college of Loyola in the city of New Orleans.

Despite Mel's locker room hysteria, nothing that he did or said could reverse the pathetic play of my team in the second half. Watching the agony on my coach's face as he screamed at Mohr, Bridges, and Zinsky to do something, anything, was almost unbearable. When he called time-out, I saw the look of utter vacancy on the faces of all five starters as they endured another withering attack. The louder he screamed the worse our team played. Only Al Kroboth, substituting for the big men, played with any style or panache. Everything Big Al got he got from pure hustle on this night. The other players went through the motions as the Loyola Wolfpack poured it on the Bulldogs. At one point we were behind thirty-four points.

Now it was garbage time and Mel gave the word to Ed Thompson to put in the Green Weenies. The Weenies leapt up and sprinted out onto the court and relieved the beaten and exhausted starters as a Loyola player was shooting a pair of free throws. It was the first time the Green Weenies had played as a unit in a game this season. Going around to each one of my second-string teammates, I slapped them hard on the fanny and said with urgency and passion, "Get me the goddamn basketball, then catch my ass. Let's kick the living shit out of their Green Weenies."

And we did, by God, we did. I was electric that night, and I could feel the currents of myself humming in my bloodstream for the first time since my sophomore year, before Mel had tied my game to his own self-image. The flashy guard sputtered into life. I dribbled behind my back and through my legs the first time I touched the ball and headed down-court as fast as I could go. Mel hated my flashiness, but that was too bad; something had snapped in me. Kroboth, Kennedy, Cauthen, and Connor were all over the boards, bringing down rebound after rebound after rebound, then turning to find me on the wing. I was there every time, and they got me the ball swiftly the way they did every day at practice. Know this, world: my Green Weenies could rebound like a secret race of giants.

For ten minutes, we ran and ran. I would catch the ball on either wing, then put the ball on the floor, streak to the center line then fly the length of the court. I felt like an uncollared cheetah fleeing the raja's court. I burned with the combustible joy I took from leading a fast break, the lanes beside me and behind me filling up with unhappy, un-praised boys like myself, humiliated by our lack of talent, and invisible to our coach.

"Don't shoot, Conroy," I heard Mel scream, and I shot it from that very spot far out of my range. I threw behind the back passes to Kroboth and Bornhorst, drove the lane whenever I felt like it, took seven free throws and made all seven.

The Green Weenies went wild, encouraging each other, urging each other on, forcing each other to do even more. "Get me the goddamn ball, Weenies," I would scream and the Green Weenies got almost every one that came off the glass. We began whittling away at a twenty-seven-point deficit. "I want the ball, Weenies," and it came to me often and I took it to the hoop every time I could in the last ten minutes of that humiliating and wonderful game.

The Green Weenies were not humiliated; we were transcendent and unstoppable and grand. We played like we knew how to play basketball, and we played like young men who admired and trusted each other. We played like a team who beat the living daylights out of the first team every day and never received a single word of recognition or praise from our coach. We played our hearts out and worked our asses off because this was the only way we could tell each other how much we loved being Green Weenies. It was the only place you could go to on Mel Thompson's team and have any pride in your game at all. Wildly, we played that night because of our wordless, ineffable, and unstealable love of each other.

With two minutes left, Coach Ron Greene stuck two of his big men back in the game because his margin of victory had become a bit too narrow. But I was greedy now, a cocky, strutting pain-in-the-ass point guard. I wanted to bring those two magnificent guards back into the game to see if they could slow me down. We closed to within eight points. My team was fiery and intense. We lost by ten, 97–87.

The Green Weenies strutted off the court with our heads held high. I do not remember playing in the first half at all, although John Joby, in the Charleston paper's account of the game, says, "Just before intermission Pat Conroy made two driving layups for The Citadel to reduce the margin to 51–33." But the game does not come alive to me until the Green Weenies took the floor as warriors together, no first-stringers allowed. The Green Weenies scored fifty of our team's eighty-seven points, and most of them we scored together. We had proven to ourselves that we were the only members of our team who could play like one.

As Joby said: "For The Citadel, Al Kroboth, a reserve who picked up the scoring slack in the second half, was the leading point scorer with 16 points, followed by another sub, Pat Conroy, who had 15. Loyola's next foe will be nationally ranked Michigan State Tuesday night in the Field House. The Spartans are third in the UPI poll and eighth in the AP rating." Loyola would defeat Michigan State, the third-ranked team in the nation.

In the shower room after the game, the humiliation of our first team kept down any sense of jubilation the Green Weenies might have felt. Then Mel Thompson, who never came into the shower room after a game, ever, shocked us by announcing, "The Green Weenies are going to start at the Tampa Invitational."

Silence greeted this announcement. I was glad I was in the shower because I felt tears rush into my eyes. Mel Thompson had seen us at last.

AFTER THE TRAINER BILLY BOSTICK CONDUCTED the bed check, the whole team tumbled down the fire escape of the grand old hotel on Canal Street and headed for the bars and clubs of Bourbon Street. In my euphoria over the game and my surprise at the militancy and confidence of the voice that had risen out of me, I walked the backstreets of the Vieux Carré the way I thought a writer might. I tried to drink up every sight and image I passed. I stood before Antoine's and Brennan's and I breathed in the air that floated like clouds out of those restaurants, perfumed with garlic and the brine of oysters and the great brown pungency of sirloins. Someday, I promised myself, I would return to these restaurants and sit myself beneath the diamond-backed light of chandeliers and order all the meals I had read about in books but had never eaten. People would eat well and drink well in my books, I thought, and all my point guards would be flashy, by God, my point guards would be flashy as hell. Drifting alone in the city, I read every plaque on every house I passed. By accident, or perhaps by some unknown design, I found a house where Tennessee Williams had lived as a young playwright loose in the city and wondered if it was the house where Blanche and Stanley were born in his tortured and baroque imagination. Though I was looking for a house where the great Faulkner had lived, I could not find one, but I unknowingly passed the house where one of my mother's favorite writers, Frances Parkinson Keyes, was living. There was no plaque on the door for Miss Keyes, but there would be nineteen years later when Houghton Mifflin rented that same house for my publication party for *The Prince of Tides*.

ON SUNDAY MORNING, THE FIVE CATHOLICS on the team rose early for mass at St. Louis Cathedral. Conroy, DeBrosse, Bornhorst, Connor, and Kennedy—you can hear the shuffle of immigrants' feet from Ireland, Germany, and France in that muster of fresh American names. Our insistence on attending mass every Sunday baffled Mel, who often had to adjust our travel schedules to accommodate his Catholic boys. Generally, I think Mel approved of our fidelity to our beliefs and considered it one of the many forms that discipline could take. When I took Communion that morning, I thanked God for the game He had given me at Loyola. That year, my relationship with God was direct and personal and conversational in nature. I was losing Him and I wanted Him to help me. Though there was majesty in His silence, He had finally managed to send me a good game. I considered this a good sign.

All season long, I would look for signs of His imminence and concern in my daily affairs. I prayed hard and only gradually became aware that this fierce praying was a way of finding prologue and entrance into my own writing. This came to me as both astonishment and relief. When I thought God had abandoned me, I discovered that He had simply given me a different voice to praise the inexhaustible beauty of the made world.

Outside the church, Dave Bornhorst and I strolled beneath the feathery ironwork of balconies as gypsylike women tried to read our palms and sharp-featured men tried to lure us into card games and black children danced madly in tap shoes and put out their top hats for dimes. The whole city, by daylight, felt strange with injustice and fatigue. Barney and I both thought it was a mortal sin to have our fortunes told. Both of us were looking for Christmas presents for our mothers. Street artists and caricaturists were in full cry as we passed by them, raucous as crows.

Since we had little money, we stopped near an artist who did portraits for two bucks apiece. The others charged five or more. In the vanity of sons, we both thought that our mothers would love nothing more than pictures of their favorite boys. We studied the drawings of the strangers' faces he presented as examples of his work of portraiture. He seemed talented if literal. In my Citadel uniform, I endured my first sitting, thinking in some small insubstantial way I was contributing to the support of the arts. In less than five minutes, the artist, whose face did not accompany him in time's journey, handed me my portrait, then quickly began work on Dave's.

I did not recognize the face he handed to me. It was not simply a bad drawing, but a grotesque one. I looked evil around the eyes and mouth, stone-faced and idiotic as a gargoyle. The artist had found all the strangeness he could find in a human face and all the pain. The face grimaced and looked as if it should be wearing a crown of thorns. Barney's portrait was cartoonish and just as bad. New Orleans had hustled two more rubes from the mainland.

# CHAPTER 14

# TAMPA INVITATIONAL TOURNAMENT

W HEN I SAW THAT THE UNIVERSITY OF NORTH CAROLINA WAS ONE of the four teams at the Tampa Invitational, it was a moment brimming with deep pleasure. If luck was with us, The Citadel and North Carolina would meet in a game. They would cheerfully mop the floor with us, but I could tell my children and grandchildren that I once took to the court to do battle with the lordly Tar Heels.

Several of my teammates remember me saying, "Don't you feel sorry for Dean Smith, coach of the Tar Heels? Poor guy's got insomnia, hasn't gotten a decent night's sleep in months, trying to devise a defense to stop Conroy."

"You're so full of shit, Conroy," Mohr whispered across the aisle of the jet winging across the Gulf of Mexico to Tampa. "My God, it's getting worse."

"Root," I said, still exuberant after the Loyola game, "when I take my place as point guard with the Celtics, I want you to know that I won't forget the fart blossoms and losers who held my game back at The Citadel, the guys who failed to see my talent for what it really was."

"Why don't you and DeBrosse develop that damn talent by throwing me a pass every once in a while? You know, once or twice a season," Mohr shot back, bringing DeBrosse into the fray behind us.

"You ever thought about moving your sorry ass to get open, Root? Try to establish a passing lane every once in a while," John said.

"Passing lane? You wouldn't know a passing lane from a jockstrap, DeBrosse. Anyone ever see DeBrosse throw a pass?"

"Yeah," Cauthen said. "Once, with a girl."

Our coaches sat in the front of the plane and the players crowded together in the back. Seats were not assigned in those faraway times, but we thoughtlessly arranged ourselves according to our classes. The class system at The Citadel cut deeply and invisibly across our system-tested psyches. We aligned our stars with the boys who had witnessed both our suffering and our resolve. During our freshman year, Mohr and I had compared cigarette burns that two of the cadremen had left on his chin and my arms.

"Zits, Coach," Dan had explained to our beloved freshman coach, Paul Brandenberg.

"Floor burns, Coach," I said. "Got 'em diving for the ball."

That is why I always sat near Dan Mohr; it is why the class system at The Citadel remains the unbreakable, the unseverable bond. In the back of the plane, the five sophomores, wary and still unacclimatized, studied the customs and procedures of the juniors and the seniors. They were still early in their varsity careers and just six months away from the last indignities of their own plebe year.

"Hey, guys," I said, whispering as I walked toward their area in the back of the plane. "How do you like playing big-time college basketball?"

Again, the sophomores had to contain their snickering. Mel did not allow horseplay or any member of his team to look like he might be having a good time, especially after a defeat. Their buried, covert laughter made a forlorn sound, like the call of barn owls.

When we landed in Tampa, a bus drove us to the hotel. By the time we had unpacked our gear, the Corps of Cadets back in Charleston had called the final roster and been released for their Christmas furlough. My team rejoiced because that meant that we could also wear civilian clothes in Tampa with the single caveat that we dress in coat and tie since we were still representing The Citadel. Thus began an annual humiliation for me and Dan Mohr.

When we gathered in the hotel lobby to take the bus to the amphitheater, the team seemed transformed into normal earthlings. In fact, my teammates looked camouflaged, almost deceitful, in their civilian clothing. Bob Cauthen and Tee Hooper and Doug Bridges dressed in the most stylish clothing, wearing their slacks and sports coats with great flair. Their loafers gleamed with the brightness of fine leather. The rest of the guys wore basic, off-the-rack sports coats, the kind they would wear for church or special occasions back home.

On the other side of the lobby stood Dan Mohr, wearing the same sweater he wore last Christmas break in Pittsburgh before we played Duquesne. Hanging back, I wore the same sweater my mother had bought me for a dollar at a yard sale in Beaufort my senior year in high school. Dan and I both wore our cadet shoes in a glittering pool of Bass Weejuns. When Dan felt shame, he raised his chin higher and from my vantage point across the room, I could see his Adam's apple in perfect bas-relief.

"Nice sports coat, Conroy," DeBrosse said.

"I didn't know you were from the Alps, Conroy," Cauthen added, a remark that stung because I thought the sweater made me look like Heidi's brother.

When our impeccably dressed head coach entered the lobby, he looked his team over with the same note of approval. Mel knew his clothes and the sharpness of his attire was an integral part of his unreadable character. It did not unlock any mysteries about him, but it at least gave you a clue. I saw the exact moment when Mel spotted Mohr out of uniform for the third straight Christmas break.

"Mohr, did I stutter?" Mel said in disbelief. "I said sports coat and tie. Did you hear me say anything about sweaters? We're still representing The Citadel and we should do it with some class."

Then Mel spun around and saw me by a column near the center of the room. Some said I waved and lifted my eyebrows. Then Danny said, "Coach, I left it back in the barracks. I forgot to pack it with my uniforms."

"My two seniors. You guys are supposed to be setting the example," Mel said. "What's your excuse, Conroy? Look, even the sophomores managed to get it right."

"No excuse, Coach," I said. "I just screwed up."

"You making it a habit, Conroy?" Mel said.

"No, Coach, promising you I'm not."

"I've got to run you for two hours before the Christmas practice," Mel said. "You both understand that, don't you?"

"Yes, sir," we both answered since we had run two hours in our last two Christmas practices.

"Okay, get on the bus. We'll see what you got for Florida State."

Neither Danny Mohr nor I owned a sports coat or a pair of loafers, but we wouldn't tell each other that for thirty years.

Danny and I, three times inducted into the brotherhood of the sweater, rode together on the bus to face Florida State in the opening game of the Tampa Invitational. The whole aura of the tournament had the clean, good feel of the big time to me, and I was as impassioned about the games to be played as any I had encountered in my life. I had written a letter to my family, and I can remember my hand tingling with pleasure when I wrote the words, "If we manage to beat Florida State, we'll go up against the Tar Heels in the championship the next night." The North Carolina Tar Heels, the Cadillac of southern basketball, were warming up when my team entered the Curtis Hixon Convention Center.

"The AP poll came out today, Root," I said. "The Tar Heels are ranked number three in the nation. If we beat Florida State, we'll play them tomorrow night."

"Yeah, fat fucking chance," Root said.

"That's the spirit, Root. Never say die."

Before going into the locker room to suit up we watched the Tar Heels warm up. I studied two players and two players only. I had seen the ethereal and vastly gifted Bobby Lewis play for St. John's in Washington, D.C., when I had played on the junior varsity of Gonzaga High School. At Chapel Hill, Bobby had averaged thirty-six points a game in his freshman year, then twenty-seven points per game as a sophomore. He had extraordinary leaping ability and moved on the court with all the presence of a young king. Then my eyes moved to number 44, Larry Miller, who fired jump shots from the corner, a darker, more brooding court presence than the sunnier Lewis. They were the stars of this tournament; the true stars of basketball have all eyes in the building studying their every move because of the sheer magnetism of their great gifts. I turned to the invitational rosters and found the names of Bob Lewis and Larry Miller, then with my finger I went down the page and saw my own name printed along with the other Citadel Bulldogs. In one night I had tied my destiny to the lives of two legitimate All-Americans and it thrilled me to see my name listed on the same page as theirs.

When the game began, it took only a couple of times up and down the court for North Carolina to establish its superiority over the Columbia Lions. Columbia was missing their seven-foot-one pivot man,

Dave Newmark, because, as the Tampa newspaper said, "of the giant's toenail problems."

Miller and Lewis, together on a basketball court, blended like balsamic vinegar and the richest olive oil. Miller's darkness matched Lewis's lightness and speed on the court and their congruent talents made everyone around them better basketball players. Bill Bunting and Dick Arbor and Rusty Clark had to raise their own games to a higher level and that was part of Lewis's and Miller's genius—they wove their brilliance through the moves and passes of their teammates, wonderful basketball players all, but mortals like me.

So hello, Bobby Lewis, and hello, Larry Miller. I salute you from the secret place to which lost nights go. I tell you how splendid the two of you were that night and the next night and all through that long season. I have never forgotten the dark fire of Larry Miller or the breathtaking swiftness of Bobby Lewis and I did not deserve to be in the same building with them. It was with great reluctance that I followed my team into the locker room to suit up for the game against Florida State.

Mel's promise to start the Green Weenies proved an empty one. This felt like a great mistake to me that night and it strikes me the same today. Before I had mistrusted my coach's unimaginativeness, but I had never once doubted his word. Distrust poisoned the air around my team. That and the great sudden pain of the wonderful sophomore guard Tee Hooper. This night would mark the beginning of Tee's dismantling. He put his hands over his face and eyes in a gesture of cautionary despair.

I looked to the blackboard and received my greatest shock of a season that would contain many. My name was written in the starting lineup. Slyly, I tried to check my teammates for any sign that they recognized the wrongness of the moment. When Mel gave us his pregame talk, I could tell he had still not forgiven us the fiascos of Loyola and Old Dominion, nor did he believe we could beat Florida State. He inoculated us with a sense of hopelessness before we took the court. We could feel him losing faith in us as a team. In turn, we were not a team, we were much more like a lost archipelago, floating islands sharing straits and bays and rivers, but not linked together in any cohesive way. Tee's sudden and surprising demotion was an amputation. In my own estimate of my talent, I could not wear Tee Hooper's jock, and we all knew it.

The Green Weenie in me, the realest part of my image as an athlete, stirred and I said to myself, "Does this mean I have to play with the damned Blue Team?" as Mel named me team captain for another night.

When we took to the court for warmup, I made the first layup and Danny made the second, then we sized up the Seminoles on the other end of the court. They looked like a race of well-fed giants to me, long-limbed and stately. They carried themselves with the confidence of a team who knew The Citadel was not in their league.

"That team makes you look short, Root."

"How do you think it makes you look, midget?" Root shot back.

When I went to center court that night as the starting point guard, I felt a small sense of a shifting of my fate, though I could not tell you what it was. After shaking hands with their guard Jeff Hogan, I lined up for the tipoff with an anthem or mantra going through my mind: "I'm the starting point guard against Florida State." My Green Weenie identity had not allowed me to hope that a moment as distinguished as this would ever fall to me as a college athlete. Florida State won the tip and would win every tip on this less than brilliant night.

I spent the evening, self-conscious and tentative, trying to look like I belonged on the court. DeBrosse told me to guard Brian Murphy, a five-ten guard from Pompano Beach, and this was the first time I realized that John always picked the defensive assignments of the guards. Later, he would say to me, "Conroy, why do you think you always guarded the biggest guy they had or the highest scorer? I wanted to conserve some of my energy for offense, so I always gave you the guard with the most height or firepower. Think I wanted to look like shit on defense? Hell no. I wanted you to look like shit, baby. It was a great system. Conroy busting his ass all night on defense while DeBrosse got some much-needed rest."

If this was indeed the system, DeBrosse made a serious error of judgment in this Florida State game. Brian Murphy and I were evenly matched, his smallness and quickness mirroring my own, two Irish Catholic boys locked all night together in competition that was clean and fast moving. He was better than I was, but I stayed in there with him.

Because he had known him in Ohio, DeBrosse put himself on Jeff Hogan of Akron and I spent the entire game grateful that I was not guarding that classy, well-schooled guard who played an astonishing game with poor DeBrosse scrambling to keep up with him. Somewhere in the first half, I realized that Hogan was the lord of this December night. His game flowed with quiet brilliance and he was shooting the eyes out of the basket all night.

At a time-out, I whispered to DeBrosse, "Anybody tell you you're supposed to be guarding number ten, DeBrosse?"

"Goddamn, he's good," John said, in pure admiration.

Jeff Hogan scored twenty-five points, and we could not do a thing to shut him down. Under the boards the Seminoles killed us. They were simply too big and fast for us. Theirs was a big-time program; we were bottom feeders. Mohr and Bridges played as though they were sleep-walking and kept looking to the bench every time Mel yelled at them, which seemed to be every time downcourt. Their faces were glum with confusion and hurt and they never seemed to be able to place their hearts in the center of the fray. Their legs seemed gluey and unresponsive. Mohr scored six and Bridges four—and both of them were fully capable of scoring twenty a game. Kroboth and Zinsky both played hard and busted their humps under the basket. With his bird-of-prey face and his fiery intensity while rebounding, Al Kroboth was still my biggest surprise of the season. I felt no pressure as a point guard to get the ball to "Big Al" because his perpetual hustle kept him always near the center of action, and his points came from his fierce nose for the ball. He held his ground while rebounding against Florida State and he was beautiful to watch.

It was the first game in which I counted the shots my teammates took. It was a trick I had learned at a clinic for point guards at Camp Wahoo. Rod Thorn had talked about the importance of the point guard in distributing the ball evenly to his teammates, making sure that the shooters got their fair share of the allocated shots. "Shooters need to shoot. It's the nature of the beast," he had said. I had three shooters on my team: DeBrosse, Bridges, and Mohr. If I was going to be successful at the point, I had to involve my shooters in their game. So I began the silent count that would go on for the entire year: "Ten shots for Mohr, six for Bridges, eight for DeBrosse," I would say during the course of the game. "Get it to Doug."

We lost the game 83–67, and we never made a real run at the Seminoles. Their coach, Hugh Durham, ran a very disciplined team.

DeBrosse scored 18, Kroboth 14, Zinsky 13, and I had 12. John and I provided 28 points from the backcourt, which was nothing to be ashamed of against such a team. We moved like a matched set. I had earned DeBrosse's respect for the night, and it felt good. I had gotten through the game without humiliating myself or my team. I shook hands with all the Florida State players. Trotting off the court, I realized I had lost all chance to play the Tar Heels in this lifetime.

# CHAPTER 15

# COLUMBIA LIONS

THOUGH I HAD LOST MY ONLY POSSIBILITY TO TAKE THE COURT against the North Carolina Tar Heels, I was the one guy on the Citadel basketball team who fully understood what the Ivy League meant in our country's intellectual life. For that reason, I took the consolation game in Tampa against the Columbia Lions with seriousness and wanted to go through life crowing proudly, "Conroy, undefeated by the snot-nosed Ivy League." Because I also know about the culture of basketball as it was played on the courts of New York City, I knew that Columbia could pick and choose among thousands of high school boys who grew up playing the game the way it was meant to be played. Those New York boys could all take it to the hoop and they carried irregular, melting-pot names as they drove the cement lanes toward the chain nets of the great city. I studied Columbia's roster with the curiosity of the rube southerner unfamiliar with the dazzling, singing rhythm of the foreign names I would find in the New York telephone directory in later life. I shivered with pleasure as I got ready to play boys with real immigrant attachments in the rush of consonants to their names: Gamaramuller, Florial, Garsricus, and Walaszek. Basketball had always been a game for the poor kids of the big cities, the game where the boys of immigrant families could prove themselves while navigating their ways along the mean streets and fierce ghettos whether they were Jews, Irish, Poles, Lithuanians, or the soon-to-be-dominant black kids.

There was another thing I knew about the Columbia players that cut my pride deeply: I knew that their team was a lot smarter than my team and that only two or three of my teammates could have cut the mustard with SAT scores high enough to be accepted by Columbia, and

I certainly was not one of them. Because I was worried that my attendance at The Citadel would hurt my career as a novelist, I was keenly
aware of the other young men and women of my generation who shared
my ambition and were in the process of getting fabulous, life-changing
educations at the Ivy League schools that would open up deep, un-
bridgeable abysses between their preparation for the lives of writers and
mine. My jealousy of the whole Ivy League was the driving force that fu-
eled my secret descent into class war against the Lions before we took
to the court against them.

Our team came out cold and tentative. It was the first time I had
ever started two straight games, and I was as puzzled by it as Tee
Hooper. Because I had never been called on when I was not supposed to
break up a press at the end of a game, I still felt unwanted on the court,
a ghostly presence filling in for Hooper until Thompson could forgive
him for whatever crime poor Hooper had committed. Columbia's team
were all Yankee boys, and they knew how to play the game. In the first
half we played sluggishly, as though we were wearing wingtip shoes.
Nothing flowed, nothing seemed to come out of our offense. Mel
screamed and screamed, but I was shutting him out now and not listening to him. It seemed to me we were getting throttled again, but I tried
to keep myself loose and in the flow of things.

I give myself up to the anonymous reporter from the AP who wrote
about that game: "The Bulldogs were quick to get into foul trouble in
the first half, drawing seven in the first six minutes of the game. The
Lions, however, had trouble hitting the free throws when they had the
chance to break away early. With the Lions missing, the Bulldogs stayed
close, until with about ten minutes left to play in the half, the Lions
pulled away. Two field goals and a pair of free throws by Roger Walaszek
suddenly stretched a four-point lead into 10 points.

"DeBrosse countered with a field goal, but John Dema made good
on a three-point play and Walaszek got consecutive baskets while limit-
ing the cadets to one free throw. That gave the Ivy League their biggest
lead of the half—13 points at 35–22.

"With about three minutes left to play in the half, the Bulldogs came
alive. Bill Zinsky got three points, while DeBrosse got two field goals.
With three seconds in the half, Pat Conroy got inside for a shot that
closed the gap six points 39–33 at the half."

I do not remember one moment of this game just described, not even my heady arrival in the narrative account of the game with three seconds left. Its vanishing is complete and unrecoverable and I can add no credibility to this description of a game where I was both witness and participant. What I do remember was something that happened in the second half.

Back to the unnamed reporter: "The Bulldogs had stretched their lead to five (the boys had come back) on goals by Kroboth, Conroy, and Mohr before the Lions came back to tie the score 53–53. But Kroboth went to work again and got five points, while Mohr and Conroy added two each and the Bulldogs moved ahead by seven. Then lightning struck in the form of a Columbia press, and the Bulldogs' lead disappeared. The Lions put eight straight points up in the board before Mohr finally broke the streak with a pair of free throws. Hoffman put the Lions up by one with a long jumper, but Zinsky hit a free throw with 50 seconds to play to make it 65–65 and send the game into overtime."

It is the moment of the lightning strike that I recall with fierce clarity. All game long, the Lions had thrown at us a 1–3–1 half-court zone press that took some adjusting to since I had only seen full-court presses at the end of games. I loved breaking up full-court presses, but the half-court press presented the obvious physical problem of less space. The Columbia guards were taller and longer-limbed than John DeBrosse and me, and it took a while to figure out that if I broke by the guard, I was quick enough to break through the three-man alignment that would close in on me driving the lane with their center coming out to meet me, leaving Mohr open in the middle with Zinsky and Kroboth on the wings.

But in the last minutes of lightning, the Columbia Lions had made a wickedly effective adjustment on their half-court press. They brought the other guard out to meet me at the half-court line, forcing me to pass it to the wide-open John DeBrosse on my left wing. As soon as I threw to DeBrosse, the Lions swarmed him. I tried to run to DeBrosse, but Walaszek defended the passing lanes well, his long arms flailing as John kept looking for help from the big men who were having trouble of their own. It was only after four straight turnovers and eight straight points that I realized Columbia *wanted* me to throw it to DeBrosse and had adjusted their defense to make sure I did.

The next time down the court when I burst across the line, they tried to trap me in the corner, but we little guys who know how to dribble are hard to trap. I went through them again, getting quickly into the lane and forcing their center to decide whether to block my layup or stay back on Mohr. He came at me and I slipped the ball to Danny, who would have scored if a forward had not recovered and fouled him hard. The ball never went to DeBrosse again with that devastating press on. But the press was the place where I was born to be, and the Columbia Lions had run the best one I'd ever come up against.

I am looking at a clipping of this game played so long ago where my name is in the headlines for the first time in my college career: "CONROY GIVES CITADEL VICTORY."

The article continues, "Pat Conroy dropped in four free throws in the final minute of an overtime period here last night to give The Citadel a 74–71 victory over Columbia University in the consolation game of the Tampa Invitational Basketball Tournament.

"In the championship game, unbeaten North Carolina, ranked no. 3 in the nation, downed Florida State 81–54. It was the seventh straight victory for the Tar Heels." (I include this only because there is no other place that poor Conroy's name is associated one paragraph away from the Carolina Tar Heels.)

"Danny Mohr hit five points in overtime before fouling out. Then, with the Lions trailing by one point and a minute to play, Conroy hit both shots in a one-and-one situation to put the Bulldogs ahead.

"After a Columbia shot, Conroy was fouled again and hit two shots. The victory broke a three-game losing streak for the Bulldogs and sent them home for Christmas with a 3–5 record."

Hooper and Bridges looked poleaxed and dumbstruck after the game. When Rat handed out the stat sheet as we dressed, I was surprised that Tee had only scored a single shot and Bridges had failed to score. These were the two most superb athletes on our team.


MY BEST FRIEND AT BEAUFORT HIGH SCHOOL, Bruce Harper, had recently become engaged to the dazzling Melinda Lee Crowe of Tampa, and Melinda had invited me to a party after the game. I asked Melinda if I could bring along my team, and she said that would be wonderful because the party was thrown by some Converse girls home from the holidays. So my teammates gathered, handsome in their coats and ties, at a Tampa house, and I saw them dancing with pretty girls and mingling with other college students. I would listen to Bruce talk to Melinda and try to memorize the words that college boys said to their fiancées. I still turned mute when girls drew near me. The vastness of my shyness distressed me. Melinda's face was as pretty as those profiled beauties in the stillness of cameos. Bruce was handsome and elegant in his movements. I would be in their wedding the following summer in Tampa. I will always remain grateful for Melinda asking my team to that party. It was the only normal college life we experienced in the year I am writing about, the only party we attended as a team.

Al Kroboth sat down and played the piano with great skill, and I could not have been more surprised if he had made me a dress. My teammates, I thought, what lovely young men. We gathered around the piano and young women drifted toward us. It all felt so right and it would never happen again.

# CHRISTMAS BREAK

For a Citadel basketball player, the Christmas break was a disturbing, fragmented descent into nightmare. Mel Thompson will always rise up in Dickensian glory as my Ghost of Christmas Ruin. After The Citadel, I treated Christmas as though it were some fierce, gathering storm roaring up out of the Bahamas, the eye of the hurricane ineluctably headed for my front door, already named "Mel" by the National Weather Service. My basketball coach made Scrooge look like some prancing jim-dandy sentimentalist about Christmas. Few of my teammates can discuss Christmastime without wincing, without a searing memory of downfall and pain.

In the Tampa airport, the managers, Al Beiner ("Albino") and Rat, handed out our plane tickets home for the holidays. Mel huddled with us and warned, "Don't play around too much when you go home and don't eat too much of Mama's home cooking. Because you know that food might end up on the gym floor when I get you back on Christmas Day."

For reasons still unclear to me, Mel always made us come back Christmas Day for a vicious practice at four o'clock in the afternoon. All of Mel's practices were hard, but the Christmas Day practice became the stuff of legend. Dick Martini used to tell of a Christmastime lunch where Mel made sure his team ate their fill, then suddenly called for a surprise practice and told them to get to the gym and dress out immediately. Martini recalled that he had never seen so many boys puking at the same time when the practice ended.

I flew on Delta to the inevitable stop in Atlanta, where I made my annual Christmas phone call to Terry Leite, a girl I had gone to Beaufort

High School with, and who had come down for the Graduation Hop my freshman year. I, of course, had fallen for this beautiful, fascinating girl, and I think she had fallen for me a little bit. I wrote scores and scores of love letters to her when she attended St. Mary's College in South Bend, Indiana. Terry saved all these feverish, show-offy letters and recently let me use them to see a glimpse of the mysterious boy I was when I wore a Citadel uniform. Reading them made me understand perfectly well why Terry would choose to marry a Notre Dame man rather than me. But they were also the writings of a sweet boy trying to learn the mysteries of the way to a young woman's secret heart.

When Terry answered the phone that Christmas, she told me that she was going steady with a Notre Dame man in law school, and they were planning to become engaged the following summer. I congratulated her and told her I hoped that she would find great happiness in her life. She would not, and neither would I. I mention the annual Christmas phone call to Terry Leite because it represented the sum total of my sexual life over the course of three holiday seasons. I looked forward to those calls.

MY FATHER, RESPLENDENT IN HIS Marine Corps uniform, met me at Washington National Airport and drove me to Falls Church, Virginia, where I would spend Christmas in still another strange house. My family had moved in late summer and I had written letters to another address I had not seen. Dad was never friendly or bantering with me when I was in college. I kept my hatred of him in a tight hermitage—I was his Northern Ireland; he was my England. We rode for ten miles without saying a single word. I turned on the radio, found a station I liked, and he snapped it off.

Finally, he spoke. "Your team is shit."

"We're having a little trouble getting it together, Dad."

"You're shit. I saw the George Washington box score. You scored three big ones. I wouldn't even let 'em put my name in the box score if I only scored three."

"We won that game, Dad," I said. "By three points, I think," I added cautiously.

"You couldn't carry my jock. I ate guys like you alive for breakfast," he said, looking at me for a reaction. He got none.

As a small boy I remember my father taking over every basketball game he played in, an intimidating figure who taunted enemy crowds with angry gestures and fighting words. My mother once moved my sister Carol and me out of a crowd of sailors who were screaming obscenities at my father, who was jawing back to them with gusto. My father was the dirtiest basketball player I have ever seen. It pleased him every time he heard me say it.

In silence we drove another five miles before Dad said, at a light, "Florida State kicked the shit out of you."

"They sure did, Dad."

"You get in?"

"Yes, sir."

"Score any?"

"Twelve, Dad."

"Bullshit. Somebody on Florida State's team would've had to die during the game for you to get twelve."

"Got lucky, Dad," I said, staring straight ahead.

"You beat those Ivy League pussies, though," he said.

"Columbia University."

"Ivy League. There's pussy basketball at its best."

"Bradley's at Princeton, Dad. Can't forget that."

"You get in?"

"Yes, sir."

"Score any?"

"Twelve, sir."

My father looked at me to see if I was lying, then said, "Bullshit. They must have stunk up the floor."

"Got lucky, Dad."

"Hooper break a leg? He's the one who beat you out."

"He's been in a slump, Dad. Just a sophomore. He'll be back. He's great."

"He'll beat you out again. He'll sense that you're a loser."

Thus I received my annual Christmas pep talk from my father, who drove the rest of the way home in silence.

At home, my four younger brothers and two sisters engulfed me in a wave of sweetness that always felt cleansing and right. I hugged my mother, her eyes set with all the charm and hysteria and unhappiness that house could produce in its terrifying inadequacy. The family had picked up two tailless, feral cats named Wart and Halloween, who hid in the closets and under sofas, periodically lunging out to claw or bite a passing bare foot. The pets were perfect metaphors for the damage being passed out all around. I felt the familiar tension of this house where none of the children felt safe. None of them were; nor was the wife.

"Show Pat his room," Mom told my brother Mike, who was about ten years old then, and some of the kids giggled.

"You can't expect to have the best room, Pat. You're not part of the family now. You're in college," my mom said.

One of the great surprises I had when I went away to The Citadel was that I never had a room or a bed in my parents' house again. I followed Mike down the stairs to an unfinished basement where Mike had his bed. It was cheap and ugly and degrading to him.

"Oh, this is swell," I said.

"It gets better," my brother said. "Guess where you're sleeping?"

"I haven't a clue," I said, shaking my head, looking around the room for another bed.

"In here," Mike said, opening up his closet door. He reached up and grabbed two coat hangers and flung out both his hands in opposite directions. Then Mike pointed to a hole cut into the pasteboard large enough for a dog to get through. Mike low-crawled through the hole and I followed behind him. A shaft of light from a half window revealed a hidden, unfinished section of the basement. One of the tailless cats, Halloween, shrieked in the shadows, leapt at my foot, and bit me on the ankle. The cat then shot through the opening and raced under Mike's bed. In my hideaway there was an old skinny mattress on the floor that Mike had dragged in there only that morning. There were no lamps, no lightbulbs, no electricity, or no furniture of any kind. The mattress smelled like dirty sweat socks.

"Nice room, Mama," I said to my brother. "Nice fucking room." And my brother fell on top of the mattress giggling. I joined him in the stifled, softened laughter of children who grew up in dangerous houses. I was home for the holidays.

CHRISTMAS MORNING WAS THE ONLY TIME OF the year when you could be absolutely sure that my father would not slap you. My two baby brothers, Tim and Tom, wrestled me awake on the dank mattress at four

in the morning, begging me to get up and go upstairs, so they could begin unwrapping their presents. The house tingled with the buzz and excitement of young children, and my mother had already put the coffee
on at 4 A.M.

"Good morning, Pat," my father said, his voice full of goodwill.
Christmas transformed even The Great Santini, and for one day of the
year, he masqueraded as a real father. He sang out the name on the first
gift, which always went to the youngest child. "This one's for a little kid
named Tooooom. From Santa Claus." And a loud cheer would come
up from the seven Conroy kids. It was the one day of the year we
seemed to have something—to have everything. All the collected madness of my family took the morning off and let us feel like something
normal and mainstream. I soaked up the glimmer of the disorderly piles
of wrapping paper, glittering bulbs, and strung lights, the streaming
tinsel weaving silver fingers through the ceiling-high fir tree, and the
precious noise of joyous children, happy among their gaudy pile of
gifts. It seemed so healthy and ordinary, so unlike us, addicts of chaos
and angst.

When my parents opened my presents to them, I held my breath. As
always, I had little money to spend for their gifts, but this year I thought
I had lucked out. At the Tampa Invitational, the tournament committee
had given each player a standing pen set and a white electric radio with
plaques proclaiming that he had been a participant in the tournament. I
coveted both gifts. Because I wanted to be a writer, the seriousness of
that pen set, so erect and reputable, seemed almost mystical in importance to me. Because I did not own a radio, the tournament committee
had brought the gift of music to my life.

But I thought the pen set would look good on my father's desk in
Quantico, and that he would call other Marines into his office to display
proudly what his son had given him for Christmas. Since Dad had
played college basketball and I had followed in his footsteps, I thought
the gift would link both us and our destinies as athletes and serve as
some laurel of connection. "See what my boy got me, General. Yeh, he
was in a holiday tournament down in Tampa. Yeh, the Tar Heels, the
Seminoles, and some Ivy League school. Kid got twenty-four in two
games. Wanted me to have this." I could visualize my father having
those talks with his colleagues in the corps.

Likewise, I thought my mother could put the radio in the kitchen and listen to the classical music station while she did her housework. I thought she would think of me every time she read the plaque or heard the music with her hands in dishwater. It seemed like an act of generosity to surrender something I coveted so deeply. I was trying to turn myself into a young man who knew how to make the most correct and faultless gesture. I would link my mother and father to the disturbances of my love for them by giving up the two gifts that meant the most to me.

My mother first opened the portrait I had paid two dollars for in New Orleans. I saw her study it, then frown slightly as she said, "Who is it, Pat?"

"It's supposed to be me," I said.

My mother held it into the air and my brothers and sisters cracked up all around me. I could see even more clearly now than I did in New Orleans that the drawing was a buffoonish caricature of my face.

"It's lovely," she said, but could not help laughing. "How much did you pay for it?"

"Two bucks."

"Son, you got taken for a ride."

"So did Barney." Thirty years later I would learn that Dave Bornhorst had enough sense not to give his mother his own ridiculous portrait.

My father finished opening the pen set and I saw him inspecting it. At the same time, my mother removed the white radio from its box. She seemed very pleased.

"They gave us that radio and that pen set for participating in the tournament."

"It's lovely," my mother said.

Dad said, "So it didn't cost you one centavo, pal. El Cheapo rides again."

"Your father means thank you, Pat," Mom said. "He really likes it."

"What time does your plane leave for Charleston, jocko?" Dad asked.

"Eleven hundred hours, Dad."

My brother Jim said, "Dad, can we go to the airport with Pat?"

"Negative," my father answered.

"Please, Dad," Kathy pleaded.

"That's negative," he repeated.

"Everybody help me clean up this mess," my mother said, inspecting the paper carnage of slain, opened gifts.

"That's affirmative. Let's police this area."

An hour before we left for the plane, I took a huge box loaded with torn gift wrapping and broken ribbons to the front curb. My mother leaned out the front door and shouted, "Check through that stuff, Pat. Make sure none of the kids lost one of their presents in that mess." Then she turned and went back inside.

I sifted through the torn, balled-up paper, but hit something solid at the bottom of the box. It was the pen set I had given my father for Christmas. Wrapping it in paper, I sneaked it into the house and placed it in the bag I had already packed for the trip to Charleston. I never summoned up the courage in my father's lifetime to ask him if he threw that pen set away on purpose or lost it due to negligence. I would never see the white radio again. But I kept that wonderful pen set for years and wrote my second short story with the pen as well as all the poems published my senior year and the senior essay I turned in that May. I took my father's castaway gift and turned it into language and stories as I would one day do against him.

After I said goodbye to Mom and the kids, Dad drove me to the airport in silence. When we pulled in front of the Delta terminal, he said, "We're here. Get out."

I reached behind me and brought my bag out of the backseat. He offered me his hand and said, "I bet Hooper beats you out."

"He's good, Dad."

"No one ever beat your old man out. No one," he said, squeezing my hand harder. "You know what you ain't got?"

"What's that, Dad?"

"The killer instinct."

"Bye, Dad. Merry Christmas," I said, moving quickly into the terminal. My father was wrong about me. I had the killer instinct, but I called it something else. I called it my first novel. I called it *The Great Santini*. It would put a cruise missile into his cockpit that would change my father's life forever. At the end of the novel, I killed the father. I had the killer instinct but it would take different forms with me than it had with Don Conroy.

·  ·  ·

PRACTICE BEGAN PROMPTLY AT 1600 HOURS and it was a killer. Coach Thompson kept yelling that he was going to sweat the Christmas turkey out of us, but none of us had been able to eat Christmas dinner with our families. There was a strange new vanity to his raving. What my team needed was coaching and teaching and praise; what my team received once more was contemptuousness, rage, and abuse. The Christmas practices were a nightmare, a plebe system, one more boot camp run by one more sadist who drove us like dogs until we dropped from exhaustion and the dry heaves. Since the campus was closed down, there were no time constraints on Mel, and the sessions could be as long as he wanted them to be. The Christmas Day practice lasted three and a half hours. One of us had to puke before he would stop. In the first days back, we joked about selecting a designated puker. After that, we quit joking about anything. Those were dark, terrible days made worse by our utter isolation from the world. But that first practice was the worst, the most driven by shock and despair. I still dread Christmas with every cell in my body. Mel Thompson killed it for me.

I had a great surprise waiting for me that first practice. For the first time in my varsity career, I was made a permanent member of the Blue Team. I felt like an absolute traitor to my Green Weenies when I turned my jersey inside out and wore the color I had come to despise as an agent of my humiliation as a basketball player. I was so completely committed to the idea of the Green Weenies that it shook me up to wear the enemy colors. The first Blue Team scrimmage brought me together with DeBrosse, Mohr, Zinsky, and Bridges. For reasons unknown to me, Tee Hooper's demotion and humiliation would continue indefinitely. Hooper's face could not mask his terrible pain. Long and thin and graceful, Tee would look like a single exposed nerve in all that December darkness. I had left my team, the Green Weenies, to join an unteam. When I put on the blue jersey, I did not realize that I was a marked man. It put me between the crosshairs of my coach, the one who seemed to envy the players who composed his starting five.

Mel began the Christmas practice in a black mood made fouler by a phone call he received from Greg Connor. Greg's mother had driven him to O'Hare from the Illinois farm country where Greg's father was a veterinarian who spent his life among midwestern herds of cattle, hogs, and horses. A combination of bad weather and unforeseeable traffic delays made them late for Greg's flight to Charleston. Greg had called Coach Thompson and explained his predicament and was surprised when he realized that Mel thought he was lying, that Greg had conjured up the story so he could spend an extra day with his family. Mel talked about Connor's absence as though Greg had strangled a show dog.

The following day we started what Mel called "the two-a-day." We would be on the court at nine in the morning, practice for three and a half hours, then go back to the visiting team room to sleep, be awakened by the managers at 1515, be on the court by 1600 hours, then released at 1930.

"Conroy," Mohr said to me recently, "we were on the basketball court for seven hours a day. We didn't get breakfast. We got these shitty box lunches for lunch and supper. An apple. Two baloney sandwiches. A Coke. A bag of potato chips. A Snickers bar. Zip. That's it. Sometimes we lucked out and got ham and cheese."

"I remember you and Bridges running all the time."

"We'd get into fights under the board. Mel would scream and scream at us to get tougher, push harder, fight to get the ball. Tempers flared. Doug and I would punch at each other in frustration. Then Thompson would scream, 'Start running.' It was the worst time of my life as a ballplayer. For all of us, I bet. There was no reason for it, Conroy. No reason in the world. He wanted to break us and he did. On Christmas Day, he ran you and me for two hours before practice. Because we didn't own a sport coat."

In those Christmas practices, Mel screamed at me every time I took an outside shot or drove the lane, which pretty much took care of the full arsenal in my offensive game.

"Pass the damn ball, Conroy. Quit shooting it. Get the ball to the big men inside or set something up for DeBrosse. You contribute nothing to this team when you shoot."

The phrase "Don't shoot, Conroy" I carry as both tattoo and motto from that dispiriting time. My teammates and I grew quieter and less playful and tolerant of one another as each day passed with agonizing slowness. We ached and hurt and fought each other in scrimmages that sometimes ran over two hours long. Our heads hung in exhaustion in the shower room, and I once saw Mohr, Bridges, and Zinsky taking showers, all of them leaning on the wall for support. They looked like boys who had nothing left to give, as though someone had let the air out of their hearts.

But the next day awaited them and the next day and the next. At the end of every practice, the team would emerge to pure December darkness. At night, the Citadel campus can exert a field of disturbance and eeriness that can unsettle even the most fiercely loyal alumnus, but The Citadel during Christmastime, emptied out of cadets and purpose, was as surreal and barren as a moonscape. The barracks were dark, the library dark, Bond Hall dark, darkness everywhere. Starlight, moonlight lit the sidewalk that led to the squalid dormitory room that poor visiting teams used.

One memory stands out from the Christmas ordeal. Every night at three in the morning a freight train would pass ten feet away from the visiting team room. Its lights would illuminate the room and its whistle would blast in the night. Our cots would shake and jiggle until the caboose would pass the second-story window and the lion would roar in the zoo in Hampton Park.

On the first night back, it took us by surprise and woke us all in confusion and terror. The room filled up with the profanity of exhausted boys, but laughter followed quickly when Kroboth's mocking, New Jersey–accented voice cried out, "Merry Christmas, guys, and to all a good night."

Finally, on New Year's Day, our ordeal was over. Jacksonville was coming in the next night. Mel believed he had made us tougher. I knew different. He had cut my team's throat.

# CHAPTER 17

# JACKSONVILLE TO RICHMOND

In the *News and Courier* on January 2, 1967, the sportswriter Evan Bussey wrote, "The Citadel basketball team will try to pick up where it left off before the Christmas holidays when it plays Jacksonville University in the Armory.

"Game time is 8:15.

"The Bulldogs have four men in double figures as they have averaged 79 points a game. The leading scorer is senior center Danny Mohr with a 14.5 mark, followed closely by John DeBrosse with a 14.1 average. A pair of sophomores, Al Kroboth and Bill Zinsky, are the other two in double figures with 11.1 and 12.7 averages respectively.

"The Bulldogs got a boost in the last few games before the holidays from Pat Conroy, a 5-11 senior guard. It was Conroy who iced the victory over Columbia by dropping in two free throws in the closing minutes of an overtime period. Conroy is averaging 8.1 points per game."

THE JACKSONVILLE AND GEORGIA SOUTHERN games were the worst two I played in college. I could smell the stench of my own game as I disconnected from the game-possessed boy who loved basketball as he loved nothing else. My legs had lost all spring and freshness and dash, and I played point guard as though I were in a coma. Every time I crossed midcourt with the ball I would hear Mel yell at me, "Don't shoot, Conroy." And despite my strange epiphany in New Orleans, I had begun listening to my coach again. In each contest, I scored only a single free throw. For much of both games, I rode the bench with the

Green Weenies as Tee Hooper replaced me and played brilliantly. His slashing, passionate style brought my team to life.

Against Jacksonville, Tee led the Green Weenies to a dazzling rally with Zipper and Brian "Bean" Kennedy and Connor all over the boards and flying down the lanes on every fast break. But Jacksonville pulled away in the final two minutes, defeating us 87–80.

But let the sportswriter tell the tale: "Finally in an effort to shake some life into the lethargic Bulldogs, Coach Thompson went to the bench with about 10 minutes to play.

"The starters, all except DeBrosse, found themselves watching from the sidelines as Brian Kennedy, Greg Connor, Tee Hooper, and Bob Cauthen scratched and clawed their way back into the game. It wasn't pretty, but it was effective as the huge Dolphin lead slowly melted."

The translation of this is our Green Weenies were kicking the hell out of their Green Weenies, and I felt like a deserter for being on the bench when my real team was on the floor. The malaise of the Blue Team had infected me like some insupportable virus. I felt humpbacked and aghast at my play. Hurt of spirit, I found myself consumed with self-loathing and haunted by the words of my father that Tee Hooper would sense that I was a loser and find taking my place on the first team an easy task.

When I guarded the six-foot-four Wayne Kruer, I had never felt quite so overmatched by an opponent and he was the first guard ever to post me up under the basket. My defense stunk, my offense stunk, and I could barely get my muscles to respond to commands I sent them in the urgency I felt to keep Kruer away from the baskets.

I was even worse when we played against Georgia Southern in Statesboro a couple of nights later. In fact, I think I lost my team that game with my inexcusable, cowardly play. Some paralysis gripped me, and I went through the motions without inspiration or flair or any sense of mission. Hoping to make something happen for myself—myself, not my team—in desperation I drove past the ethereally gifted Jim Rose, a two-time little All-American, and I saw the center Jim Seeley move off Dan Mohr to intercept me leaving Mohr wide open in the lane. But so frantic was I to join the game in any way that I broke every rule of every point guard in the history of the game and did not get it to the open man. Dan would have had a layup but I elected, in an act of pure distress, to try to take it to the hoop myself. Because there is such justice in sport, Mr. Seeley rammed the ball down my throat and sent it sailing into the stands. For thirty-two years, I have felt lousy about not getting Dan the ball, but I was in the dead center of the two worst games I would ever have as a basketball player and I did not feel like myself. In those first two matchups of January, I was a disgrace to my college, my coaches, my teammates, and myself. I let all of them down and we lost those two games because of my incompetence. I had died as a basketball player and no one had bothered to show me the results of the autopsy. In my death, Tee Hooper had found something in himself, and I got to witness his own resurrection as the bold, hellbent nature of his game made its reappearance. He was all over the court against Georgia Southern, flamelike, intense, relentless. We were twenty-one points down at one time, but my team—not me—my team fought back and we lost by one in overtime, 79–78.

Dan Mohr played a magnificent game against Georgia Southern and displayed his immense gifts under the boards all night. His shot was so soft that night that the action looked like a transfer of pillows. He pulled down thirteen rebounds against bigger players from Georgia Southern. It was a joy to watch him and to know him and to have him as a teammate. That game demonstrated how good Dan Mohr was against terrific competition and how amazing his whole senior year could have been if Mel had not crushed his spirit. Mohr had the best game of his season, scoring twenty-five points. Jim Rose ate me alive and his game had a strange sweet grace to it and his jump shot was picture-perfect.

On the bus back to Charleston, I sat on the back seat trying to beat down a sense of hopelessness I had not been able to shake since the Christmas Day practice. Later experience would teach me that I had entered one of those black depressions that would long plague my adult life and bring me to my knees with alarming frequency. I could summon no fire or energy or passion, and my body felt more fatigued and lifeless than at any other time. That Tee had beaten me out for my position I could accept, but that he had done so without the fight of his life made me writhe with shame. In darkness, I let Georgia pass into South Carolina and I thought about quitting the team, telling Coach Thompson that I did not deserve a scholarship and did not deserve to be on the floor with these much finer players. I could no longer bear to hear Mel's words, "Conroy, don't shoot."

Then I heard the voice again, the one that had sprung alive in New Orleans, the one I would come to call my writer's voice, the one that would come to me when I sat down to write my books. "Hey, pal," it said, "I thought I told you not to listen to a single thing Mel Thompson says to you. Let's go over it again. He's bad for you. He gets under your skin. He lowers your morale. Got it? Do I make myself clear? One more time. Tune Mel out. Play the game because you love it. You're thinking too much. Don't think. Play. Get into the rhythm of the game and let it flow through you. Be natural. Be loose. Get yourself back. You've lost yourself."

Again what surprised me most about the return of this interior voice was that it sounded much like that of my father. It was a voice that would come and go for years until I realized what it was, the truest part of me, the most valiant flowering of my character, a source of pure light and water streaming out of unexplored caverns deep within me. Unlike me, this voice knew nothing of shyness or reserve or shame or despair. This voice rang with authority and spoke with a blazing, resonant accuracy, with the clearness and certainty of church bells heard on bright Sundays. It riveted me with its absoluteness of vision, its breathtaking assurance. It left me as quickly as it had come, and as I sat in darkness, the strangeness of the encounter and its eerie nature of intervention and miraculous visitation gave me great pause. Because I was taking a course in abnormal psychology and because my family produced psychotics the way some families pass down freckles, I wondered if that unbidden voice was a sign of paranoid schizophrenia. But the voice offered advice too good to have any connection with mental illness. The voice knew what was good for me.

In the days before the Richmond game the following Saturday night, I again practiced with the Green Weenies and Tee practiced with the Blue Team. But since the return of the voice on that bus ride home, I was on the mend and ready to do battle again. With the University of Richmond coming to Charleston, the guards knew that the great Johnny Moates was coming to town. He was the guard at Camp Wahoo the previous summer who reacted with fury when I was the only camp counselor to take defense in the summer games seriously. At twenty-five points a game, Moates was one of the leading scorers in the nation.

As a Green Weenie again, I very comfortably helped the Weenies dismantle the poor Blue Team once more. Now I took a greater interest in how Mel would turn his scorn on one individual player, pick a victim out of the crowd and humiliate him before teammates. Mel had singled me out over Christmas because I had played three solid games in a row for my Citadel team, and Mel had noticed me for the first time in his life. As a Green Weenie, I was invisible. But as a starter, something in Mel's subconscious (a place I am sure my coach never traveled to or even booked a ticket to) stirred into life and the athlete that still lived within him became competitive with the young athletes on his team. Dan Mohr had made an inexcusable error of judgment—he had dared score twenty-five points against Georgia Southern and played a magnificent game. Because of that, Mel brought up the heavy guns to rain artillery fire at him during practice. Basketball players do not always notice these things, but novelists do. Mel would stop practice, then go after Mohr as though he hated him personally. "Mohr, you just don't give a damn. You don't care about getting the job done. You stand there in the middle like your feet were rooted to the floor. If you don't want to rebound, Mohr, I'll get someone in there who does."

"Can't you see I'm giving it everything I got, Coach?" Dan said, but it came out pleading and whining, which infuriated Mel even further. "You want me to feel sorry for you, Mohr? Is that what you want? If that's what you want, you've come to the wrong place and the wrong guy. I want you to move your ass out of one spot and get to the boards. Kroboth's eating your jock. Every damn time. You're nothing but a can of corn."

Mel's harsh words cut through Dan every practice, and all of his teammates carry with us the image of Dan's great hurt eyes staring down at his coach with disbelief and humiliation. But as the season wore on, the look in Root's eyes began to turn a darker shade of hatred.

On that Saturday night, I dressed for the first time since playing Loyola with the feeling that I had a small chance of starting. I had decided to put the Jacksonville and Georgia Southern games out of my mind and concentrate on playing well the next time I got a chance. As a senior I tried to say something to every player on the team before the game, upbeat words of praise or encouragement. I teased the sophomores and already felt a brotherly solidarity with the juniors. It would never be a happy locker room because locker rooms reflect more the personalities of the coaches than the players.

When Mel entered the locker room with his ritualistic walk before the Richmond game, he surprised the team again by adding my name to the starting lineup. It was a shock to me and a blow to Tee Hooper, who had worked his tail off in practice to get ready for Moates. Tee looked sucker-punched and when I caught his eye, I shrugged my shoulders then lifted my palms up, letting him know that I knew an injustice had been done.

After warmups, I joined the refs at midcourt as captain. Always feeling like an impostor, I stood with the two refs waiting for the Richmond captain Johnny Moates to get out of his warmup pants. As we waited, I said to the two men who had spent the last four years reffing in my games, "Gentlemen, I heard Johnny Moates calling both of you rotten bastards in the visiting team locker room."

They grinned, then one of them asked, "Pat, what did you do about it?"

"Beat the living shit out of the rotten son-of-a-bitch," I said, deadpan.

Johnny never knew why the two men were laughing when he and I shook hands. It was an honor to be on the same court as Johnny Moates that year. But what began as an honor Mr. Moates turned into a challenge.

Yet it was a night when my fate turned bright as a basketball player of marginal skills and limited prospects. Poor Tee's fate as a sophomore would turn to dust on the same night, and his boyish, handsome face would quiver with anguish and incomprehension for the rest of this trying season. I would become the unwilling agent of the destruction of Tee's year. I would be the starting point guard for the rest of the season for reasons both unclear and unfair.

As we broke from the huddle around Mel and took to the court with the roar of the cadets greeting us, DeBrosse said to me, "You've got Moates. I'll take McCann. If Ukrop comes in, I'll take him."

"Thanks tons, DeBrosse," I said. "I get the All-American. You get the midgets."

IN GATHERING THE FRAGMENTS and raw materials to pull this strange-feeling book together, I was fascinated to learn about the gauzy indistinctness of memory itself. I have lost so much from that long-ago season, but I wish I could forget that I played that year against Johnny

Moates. I wish I could forget I ever heard of Johnny Moates. That night he taught me invaluable lessons in the humility that games grant to the lesser order of athletes when they test their skills against those of higher order. Moates had a game of high-arching sublimity. He was unstoppable that night, although I battled him every time he brought the ball down-court and fought him with every ounce of strength I possessed. He taught me that I had not learned how to play defense that previous summer at Camp Wahoo when I held him scoreless during one of those free-for-all counselors games. No, that summer I had learned the importance of playing defense, of putting as much heart into stopping your own man from scoring as on being an offensive threat yourself. From Wahoo, I had gone to Duke and listened to Vic Bubas and Chuck Daley and Tom Carmody talk of the great courage it took to play tough defense all the time. At a basketball camp at Dartmouth College, I heard a young Rollie Massimino teach the intricacies of full-court pressing zones, a slim-as-a-blade high school coach mesmerizing a gymful of young boys by using me as an example to teach the kids. "Get in your defensive stance, Conroy," and I did. "Get your ass touching the ground, Conroy. Get low, son. Like a dog with worms." Later I would watch his career progress with pleasure and enjoyed telling my game-loving friends that I knew him long before he ripened into Dick Vitale. All the coaches preached about the virtues of defense that summer and I thought I had taken those lessons to heart. I had not reckoned on the salient fact that the whole Richmond team would work to get Johnny Moates open.

Johnny Moates glided toward me on Richmond's first possession, his surefooted nerve a component of his high-flying game. Tee Hooper was a perfect choice to guard Moates because Tee's height and athleticism and the brimming desire he brought to the defensive end of the court were perfect foils to Moates's own superlative gifts. As Moates approached me in the dead center of his finest season on earth, I slapped the palms of my hands on the polished floor, got into my defensive stance, and moved out to meet one of the highest scoring guards in the nation.

I would hear warnings from Bridges and Zinsky called out to me every time Mr. Moates came down the court. Tom Greene, a forward built whippet-thin, set the best pick of anyone I ever played against. He rattled me several times when Moates would come off the screen fast and be up in the air as I struggled to break through by straightening my body and beating Moates to the spot. On the other side of the court, Harvey Roberts was setting the screen and Richmond even brought its center, the wide-bodied Buster Batts, to the top of the key to get their boy open. I never played harder defense than I did that night and I never had such limited success doing it.

As Moates came toward me again and again, the one thing I knew for sure was that I would not have the help of my teammates. They had their men to guard and I had Johnny Moates. What they did not have was every other player on the Richmond team trying to free their man for a jump shot. I knew that Johnny, a shooter of immense gifts, would never take me to the hoop. His was a long-range game. He possessed the oddest jump shot I have ever seen but it was deadly. Moates would go off a double pick set on my right, and I would fall a step behind him. In that brief moment, Moates would take to the air in a mongoose-quick movement and bring the ball over his head and then launch it toward the basket with an unconventional high arching shot. I had my hand in Moates's face the whole night, which made almost no difference to him. His shot would soar toward the rafters, go higher than any jump shot I had ever seen, backspinning beautifully, until the laws of gravity brought the ball rippling through the net with that sweetness of sound—the swish, like a flower inhaling grass.

He earned each point he scored that night and I was up in the air with him for every shot. I felt overpowered but not humiliated. I could hear the Corps murmuring its approval of my hustle and gritty pride in trying to stop a much better basketball player. Moates was acting as both point and shooting guard, and before he knew it, he was acting like a one-man team. He was shooting it almost every time he came down-court and we true point guards know in our hearts that this kind of roguish behavior is bad for your team. I also noticed that my team appeared to be winning.

Dan Mohr got his third foul with thirteen minutes to play in the first half and was replaced in the middle by Kroboth. This was a serious blow, which made my team a much smaller team than Richmond on the boards. But we had some things working for us. One, I was playing like the point guard I was meant to be, running the fast break with alacrity and skill, and distributing the ball to my better shooting teammates. Because I had played against Moates for two straight summers at Wahoo, I knew that he could not play defense in the cafeteria of the Pentagon. He could not guard a savings-and-loan company at midnight, and to my great joy, I found at the opening tip-off that Moates was guarding me. I could give Moates a workout on the offensive end and both of us knew that I could go around him, either to the left or the right, any time the desire came over me. Moates watched my back for much of the night. But he did not see me counting the number of shots my teammates were putting up, did not notice me distributing the ball to the guys who were hot, and, on this night, my shooters were all lighting it up. Mohr had six quick points before he took to the bench to sit out the rest of the first half. I started driving the lane against Moates and as soon as Billy McCann dropped off DeBrosse to pick me up, John would move to a spot outside the key and I would flip the ball out to him. I had learned to hit DeBrosse when he was on the move and to give him at least one dribble because his shot was twice as effective when it came off the dribble. All game long, DeBrosse was on fire and Bridges had that engaged look in his eyes that signaled that Doug had shown up with his game face on and was ready to stick it in Richmond's face. Toward the end of the first half, Bridges backed the lithe and talented Tom Greene into the basket and hit a spinning fadeaway jumper that barely eluded Greene's lunging hand. It was the shot of a great and acrobatic athlete, a thing of beauty in itself. My shooters kept The Citadel in the game against their lone shooter. We were leading 39–37 at the half.

Though I was clearly overmatched by Moates, my teammates were encouraging. Rat put a towel around my neck and said, "Keep fighting him, Pat. You're fighting your ass off. It's great." I could feel my team rising up around me. It came rarely during this terrible season, but it was there at halftime during the Richmond game. There is no feeling on earth quite so jubilant and satisfying as to have your team solidifying around you like a pearl in the tissues of an oyster. I went out for the second-half jump ball desperate to win.

Shaking hands with Moates, I said, "Hey, Johnny, how about not humiliating me in front of everybody I know in the world?" He smirked and did not answer. Richmond won the tip, and I found Moates coming up the court again and I met him at half-court and roared at him as I resumed my defensive stance with the sounds of my teammates warning of picks being set behind me. Moates was built like the long blade in a pocket knife and his face looked as though it had been put together with a drawerful of cutlery—a darkly handsome, angular young man who carried the knowledge in his dark blazing eyes that he was much better than I was. Whenever he made a shot, I would work him out in the offensive end of the court, changing direction with my dribble, then flashing past him into the lane. At halftime, Richmond had adjusted to my passing back to DeBrosse near the key and now when I drove the huge, lunging presence of Buster Batts would come menacingly out to me. This left Mohr wide open for a bounce pass and a layup.

Moates would answer with one of his looping jump shots, but Dan Mohr had returned to the game to play the half of his lifetime. His huge hands were everywhere, on the boards, hanging around loose balls, receiving passes as easily as though I were throwing him biscuits at the mess table. What Moates had done to me in the first half, Dan did to Batts in the second. The lead kept changing hands and at one point in the half, Richmond led us by twelve.

In the middle of the second half, the Corps of Cadets began to see my personal battle with Moates for the titanic struggle it was. Before that half was over, I had been transformed in the eyes of the Corps. Later, cadets would tell me that I looked possessed and deranged that night. I grabbed at Moates and cussed at him and screamed at him all night. He beat me time and again, but I came back at him. In the middle of the half Moates began to sag. His legs giving out on him, a look of fatigue spreading on his face. When Moates finally started to pass the ball to his teammates, I knew I had him where I wanted him. Then Tom Greene started to get the ball for the first time all game. Greg Connor had handled Greene all night and held him far below Greene's twenty-two points-per-game scoring average.

Mohr was rolling under the boards, unstoppable, valiant and graceful.

But let the *News and Courier* sportswriter John Hendrix, a spectator and witness to this long-ago game, tell the tale: "Mohr, the 6´7˝ Citadel senior, scored 19 points in the second half to total 25 for the game.

"But even Mohr's outstanding individual effort was overshadowed by that of Moates, Richmond's 6–1 senior guard and Captain. Moates, who scored 34 points during the game, kept the Spiders in the game all by himself. Doug Bridges and John DeBrosse got back-to-back buckets in a space of 32 seconds to put The Citadel ahead 78–75 with 2:08 remaining. Moates hit 16 seconds later to get Richmond within one, but Mohr put in the clincher with 1:32."

By the end of the game, when I brought the ball downcourt Moates was so exhausted he could not even assume his defensive stance. When I blew by him, I got the ball to Dan, who scored on a short, perfect jump shot. "Will you guard your fucking man, Moates?" I heard the frustrated Batts scream at his teammate.

"Fuck you, Batts," Johnny screamed back.

Hendrix reported, "With four seconds remaining, Harvey Roberts shot from the left of the circle and the ball bounded over the backboard. On the throw-in, Conroy was fouled again and he made it. With three seconds left on the clock, Richmond called time and got the ball to Moates just past center court."

I and everyone else in the gym knew the ball was going to Moates, so when the action resumed, I overplayed him and forced him away from the basket. Billy McCann threw a pass that Moates had to bring down over his shoulder like a wide receiver running an out pattern. I forced Moates to throw up a desperation hook shot from past the halfway line. I almost blocked it, but did not want to take a chance on fouling him. The horn sounded and Moates and I collapsed in each other's arms, holding each other up. I did not think I could take another step. The Citadel had prevailed, 81–79.

"You're so good, Johnny," I told him. "You're so goddamn good."

Johnny Moates had scored thirty-four points and that included twelve field goals all shot from long range. If he had been playing in the three-point era, Moates would have scored forty-six points on me that night. Moates said nothing to me in return, but scowled at me then rose and walked in silence to his locker room, lord of that night. I, the young man he had just outplayed in front of 2,345 people, got up and jogged to my own locker room. Some of the fans called out, "Good game, Pat," and I waved to them. It was only when I got into the noisy locker room that I noticed Tee Hooper getting out of his warmups. Mel had not played him for a single moment.

Tee Hooper would have stopped Moates if he had been allowed to play in the Richmond game. I was sure of it that night as I am sure of it now. Something had happened in the mind of our unreadable coach about his assessment of Tee Hooper's character.

•  •  •

THE NEXT DAY I WALKED INTO Colonel John Doyle's modern poetry class to the applause of my fellow English majors. Colonel Doyle was standing leading the ovation. I had to fight back tears as I opened my book and took my seat.

"An epic struggle, Mr. Conroy," the elegant and precise Colonel Doyle said, his eyes twinkling. "You were Hector riding out of beleaguered Troy to do battle with the wrathful Achilles. Mr. Moates played the vile Achilles, of course."

"He scored thirty-four points, Colonel," I said.

"But he wanted to score sixty, Mr. Conroy. You wouldn't let him. You fought him on every shot. It was epic and heroic."

"Colonel Doyle, didn't Achilles kill Hector?" I asked.

"Yes, but Mr. Conroy, you're missing the point. You beat Achilles. We won the game. The Citadel won. Today, gentlemen, we do battle with *The Waste Land* by Mr. T. S. Eliot, a delicious task, if I do say so myself."

On occasion, The Citadel would rise up and ambush me with such perfect and completely unexpected moments. After I graduated I would try to go see Colonel Doyle every year when he was still teaching and cohosted his retirement party with my classmate Jeff Benton. Whenever I called him at his home in Virginia, he would gently chide me. "Ah, my Hector. Why is he sallying forth from the walls of Troy this time? What new battle brings him out to test his foes?"

"Do you know how much I love your ass, Colonel Doyle?" I would ask. The question would always fluster him.

"You've always been very gracious, Mr. Conroy. And profane."

"No. That's not good enough, Colonel," I would say. "Do you know how much I love your ass?"

"Yes, yes, of course," he would sputter. "I know how much you regard me."

"Thanks for finding me when I was a boy," I'd say.

"No, no, no, Mr. Conroy. You always get that part wrong. We found each other, Mr. Conroy. We found each other."

# CHAPTER 18

# DAVIDSON

O N JANUARY 11, THE DAVIDSON WILDCATS CAME TO PLAY THE Citadel in Charleston. Though neither I nor any of my other teammates knew it, The Citadel was ranked number one in the Southern Conference when we took the court against Coach Lefty Driesell's classy Davidson team. I learned of this notable fact thirty years later when I read an article by Tom Higgins, a *Charlotte Observer* sportswriter. My limping, damaged team could have received a great boost by knowing that something was going right for us during that dismal season. But if Mel knew that we had taken over the top spot in the conference with our victory over Richmond, he kept it to himself. On the previous Saturday night, Davidson had beaten West Virginia in double overtime while we were beating Richmond and Johnny Moates in Charleston.

In the period of basketball history of which I write, Davidson represented the big time in the Southern Conference because the wily, fast-talking Lefty Driesell had transformed the small Protestant college into a national power. I never took to the court against them without thinking the eye of sports-loving America had turned its curious gaze on me. When Mel delivered his pregame speech as the crowd began to hum in the field house, he tried to instill fear in us, implying always that he doubted whether we possessed either the talent or the will to be on the same court with the Wildcats. He could give us a thousand reasons why we could not beat Davidson and never came up with a single one that suggested we could.

Davidson was in the middle of a rebuilding year after losing Fred Hetzel and Dick Snyder to the pros in consecutive years. Mel said nothing about this Davidson team's vulnerability and that this team was still recovering from "a disastrous 25 day stretch from Dec. 10 to Jan. 4 during which they had lost six of nine games." This Davidson team did not resemble the juggernaut teams of the past that beat up on their Southern Conference opponents and were frequently listed in the top ten in the nation. This bunch could be taken, could be beaten, but our coach neglected to share this fact with his players. Mel talked of Davidson as though the Boston Celtics were dressing for the game.

When I went out as The Citadel's captain, I shook hands with Rodney Knowles, Davidson's six-ten center. But the real physical shock for me came when DeBrosse pointed to the six-three shoot guard Wayne Huckel and said, "You get Hercules, bubba."

Huckel tried to break my hand when we shook hands before the jump ball. He looked like the side of a mountain or a linebacker who was obsessive about the weight room. Our whole team looked little as we lined up for the jump ball.

The Corps was there in force that night and no team on earth wanted to face the furious wrath of my cadets. I let the full-throated roar of the Corps carry me as Zinsky rebounded their first missed shot and hit me with a pass on the wing. I took the ball down the middle of the court as my fast-breaking team filled the lanes around me. I drove toward Dave Moser and Huckel and decided to show the sophomores what a senior guard could do. I faked a pass to DeBrosse on the left and drove past both the Davidson guards and put in the layup myself. Huckel drilled me and put me on the floor to let me know that he had received my message. The Corps rewarded me with its astonishing power of love that it gave to its athletes when their performance was well-done. Quick learners, Huckel and Moser did not let me do the same trick the rest of the half. Until that move to the hoop, they did not know I was fast. Now they did, and they adjusted brilliantly as the good ones always do.

The sportswriter Louis Chestnut described it this way in the *News and Courier* the next day: "Pat Conroy, the bouncy senior guard, converted a driving lay up into three points as he was fouled in the opening offensive maneuver by the Bulldogs. The lead then changed hands eight times up to the five-minute mark in the first half. At that point, with Davidson up by one point 25–24, The Citadel had its first cold spell."

Let me translate. At that point, Mel Thompson stood up and told DeBrosse and me to slow the ball down. Nothing made Mel more nervous than fast-break, helter-skelter, up-and-down-the-court, on-the-fly, running and gunning basketball. He hated the pace of the game I played the best, the only one I could excel at during the last year in my life I could ever call myself an athlete.

With my team on the move, I thought we could wear Davidson down and bring them to their knees as I saw them begin to wilt before the Corps' derision. I drank in the Corps' burning affirmation of us as we carried their name into the furious night. Knowles and Youngdale, the five-foot-ten guys, loathed the breathtaking pace almost as much as my coach. Davidson hit five straight baskets and held us scoreless after Mel called a time-out. I had eleven points in thirteen minutes and got the pleasure of seeing Wayne Huckel backing up farther and farther every time I brought the ball upcourt. Those of us who live by driving the lane feel a rush of pure pleasure when we see our defensive men backing away from us. It is like the young wolf exposing his jugular to the alpha male in the stern language of arctic packs. When Huckel backed off me, I immediately turned and set a pick for DeBrosse, who held a hot hand from the opening whistle. Huckel was never in position to help Moser when DeBrosse came off one of my picks. This was the game when DeBrosse and I merged our disparate talents as our back-court play lost its randomness and began to cohere into all the disciplines and mysteries of the dance. Suddenly, in the first half of the Davidson game, I would know everything that DeBrosse was even thinking about doing. Our intuitions as athletes locked into place. We began to see the court with the same set of eyes.

We started running again, and the team began to make a spirited go at Davidson. In movement, my team fired into life. In stillness, we lapsed into mediocrity. But we had righted ourselves when Zinsky pulled a rebound away from Youngdale, fired a pass to DeBrosse on the right flank, who hit me with a perfect pass to center court as my team was off to the races for the last shot of the half. Huckel and Moser had dropped back quickly to defend against the fast break and I could hear my teammates filling in the lanes around me. Zinsky called out that he was filling the lane to my right and I heard Kroboth stake out the left lane while DeBrosse was shadowing me as a trailer on the play. In the dead center of our lives as Citadel athletes, my team was assembling around me in a classical, textbook fast break and we were looking good doing it. The Corps was on its feet, and I dribbled toward the Davidson guards borne along by the noise in the throats of the Corps. I came low and fast, and I kept my eyes on Huckel who was deep and Moser who moved out to the key to stop me. I went by Dave in a blur then turned my head toward Zinsky who was making his move to the basket on my right.

As I looked toward Zinsky, Huckel moved out to intercept my pass, forgetting about Kroboth filling the lane to the left. I put the ball in my right hand to shovel it softly to Zinsky, but hurled it behind my back in a perfect bounce pass that landed in the hands of Al Kroboth. The pass took Zinsky and Huckel by surprise, took Moser and DeBrosse by surprise, took Kroboth and Driesell by surprise, and took the Corps and Mel Thompson by surprise.

Al Kroboth was completely alone and I watched as he went up to dunk the ball with two hands. In the middle of preparing for the dunk, I saw the moment of recognition when poor Al remembered that the silly-assed rules committee of the NCAA had just outlawed the dunk because they thought it gave seven-foot Lew Alcindor of UCLA an unfair advantage over earthlings like me. It certainly did. I was part of this misbegotten rule change when it became illegal for the big men of the game to shoot the most emphatic and fabulous shot my sweet game possessed. The dunk to basketball is like the thunderbolt to the gods of storm. Kroboth went up for the slam dunk, remembered the rules committee of the NCAA, tried to alter the course of his shot in midair, and ended up throwing the ball awkwardly up by his wrists, the ball missing both the rim and the backboard to the vocal disappointment of the Corps. The buzzer sounded before Davidson could get off another shot.

"Goddam, Conroy," I heard Mel scream. "You know I hate your nigger basketball."

Big Al came up to me in the locker room and squeezed my shoulders. "Good pass, Pat. I was going to dunk it. Forgot. Couldn't recover."

"We'll get 'em in the second half, Al," I said. "Don't worry about it."

"Little Mel" Thompson put his hand on my shoulder and whispered to me, "We'll have no more of that, Pat. Coach is still upset."

"Coach, it was a perfect pass," I whispered. "I faked out the whole Davidson team."

"But we didn't score," Ed said. "You've got to admit that."

"Al missed the layup, Coach," I said. "But I got him the ball. I delivered it perfectly."

"We don't go behind the back on this team. You've done it three times tonight. Once on the pass. Twice off the dribble. We don't need fancy, just good sharp passes. Okay?"

"Yes, sir," I said.

When Coach Thompson came in, I could tell he was pleased with our first-half effort. He offered us no praise, but he implied it by toning down the volume of his usual harangue. Rat crept up behind me, squeezed my shoulders, and whispered, "Pat, you scored eleven points the first half." The news gave me exquisite pleasure since I had never scored in double figures in the first half during my entire college career. Whatever joy Rat's announcement brought me vanished when Mel substituted Tee Hooper's name for mine for the second-half starting lineup.

My cheeks burned in a fury I could barely contain as I considered the clear injustice of the move. I had played as well as I ever played in my life in the first half, and I could blow by Huckel any time I chose to. Mel's benching me was to his mind a fitting punishment for my temerity at throwing a pass I had learned while playing with black kids. I thought the banishment would be "temporary removal," and that once I had realized the seriousness of my indiscretion, I would be back in the game. But this was not to be. In the bewildering architecture of whatever chaos theory Mel Thompson brought to coaching, I had crossed an invisible line. I would not be forgiven this night. At the end of the bench, enraged and hurt, I watched my team sleepwalking through the opening minutes of the second half. Though DeBrosse and Zinsky played with brilliance, scoring twenty-one of the team's last thirty points, and Greg Connor had a stellar performance under the boards, we still lost by four points.

In his postgame interview with Louis Chestnut the next morning, Mel was positively giddy in his assessment of the game: "After the exciting DeBrosse-Zinsky windup, generated off the pressing defense, Thompson had nothing but praise."

(This marks the first time in my career I saw the pairing of the words "Mel Thompson" and "praise.")

" 'If the kids give that kind of effort from here on out,' Mel said, 'We will do all right in the conference. We had a lull in our offense on occasion and I guess that cost us the game because we were forced to play catch up basketball. But the most pleasing thing was the way we stayed in there and battled. We'll be a problem for some people.'

"DeBrosse, who apparently has decided that he is the man

Thompson has been looking for as a floor leader, again led the cadets in scoring with 21 points. The little scatback made 9 of 17 floor and was 3 of 4 from the free throw line."

In a red-faced snit, I showered and dressed quickly and walked in darkness behind the barracks toward Fourth Battalion cussing with every step I took. Then the voice made its third appearance of the year, again surprising me because it was my father's voice, a voice I had loathed since childhood. Yet this voice came to me like some kind of attendant angel. "Relax, pal. Let's go back to the game plan. You keep forgetting. You're never going to listen to Mel Thompson again. Got it? Nothing he does is going to affect your game. See? He got under your skin again. You play well when you go by instinct. Don't think. Especially don't think about him. Next game's Furman, pal. Think about that game. Got it?"

I calmed myself.

I walked toward my barracks.

I got it.

# CHAPTER 19

# FURMAN PALADINS

No team in America hated the Citadel Bulldogs more than the Furman Paladins. When the Furman players took the court against us, they did everything but foam at the mouth. Fights erupted regularly between the two teams and Furman started all of them. To Furman athletes, it was a matter of high honor to loathe and do harm to a Citadel athlete. As a Citadel athlete I could hardly blame them.

The same year I arrived at The Citadel, a small band of cadets stole the Furman mascot, a high-strung and beautiful horse that cantered up and down the field during football games with a helmeted knight astride his lovely back. Though the cadets were successful in their abduction, their knowledge of horses proved haphazard and unlucky. The legend of this infamous encounter took on a life of its own. When I was a sophomore and on a bus heading to Greenville, my team captain Dick Martini explained to me why a Furman center had tried to decapitate me when I drove the lane: "We killed their horse, midget."

"How horrible, caveman," I said, in shock. "Why did we do that?"

"An accident, leprechaun. It was a bunch of Yankee boys, like me. They had big balls to plan and carry out the mission. But none of them had any experience with livestock. The cadets brought a car to Furman, but no horse trailer. They tried to put the Paladin in the trunk of the car. The horse thrashed around and blinded itself, dumb bastard. The cadets had to shoot the horse. That's why Furman hates our asses."

Martini's version is a perfect illumination of how a story blossoms out of control at The Citadel and grows jungly with wild orchids and pitcher plants that feed on rhinoceros beetles and canaries. I believed every syllable Martini told me and did not question its veracity.

When I wrote *Beach Music*, I took Martini's memory of the death of the Paladin and added it to the history of a Citadel raid to paint the Furman campus a couple of years before the capture of the Paladin. A state trooper pulled up behind some carloads of cadets going 110 mph on I-26 and realized that he had stumbled onto a prank against his alma mater. Instead of pulling over the speeding cars tattooed with Citadel markings and stickers, the trooper simply radioed north, alerting the entire Furman campus to the danger of the approaching cadets.

When the cadets climbed a fence and made their way with paint buckets and brushes toward the center of the vast campus, they did not know of their betrayal until they noted the presence of a thousand Furman boys approaching them from the front and a thousand more approaching their flank. The beatings those Furman boys gave to those luckless cadets were still being talked about with awe in the barracks when I arrived there in 1963. I can attest that Furman teams still hated our guts long after the student body had intercepted this ill-fated raid, and it got worse after we abducted their horse. Jim Stewart, writing for Furman's alumni magazine, went deeply into the Furman archives to reveal the truth behind my fictional account of those fractious events between the two schools.

"In the fall of 1963," writes Mr. Stewart, "Citadel cadets did kidnap the Furman mascot, affectionately known to the Furman students as 'Waldo,' from the stables near the campus the week of the Furman-Citadel football game. Their plan was to return Waldo to Furman officials during the game in Charleston that Saturday. However, after the horse was accidently blinded during the course of the prank, those responsible decided to limit further damage and return the horse early. . . . As for the Furman men successfully outflanking the Citadel's paint-bucket brigade, a similar event happened in 1961. According to the Hornet (which became the Paladin the following year), the 'entire male population of the student body' turned out to meet a convoy of cadets. As in the book, the Furman students were tipped off and the convoy was monitored all the way up the interstate and captured once it came inside the gates. The Furman rout of The Citadel was so complete, the Hornet reported, that Dean Francis Bonner allowed free cuts for Saturday classes.

"Conroy even told the *Greenville News* that he has heard a zillion variations of the Furman-Citadel tales—and he isn't sure what the truth is. But we suspect, that deep down inside, Conroy may believe his version to be true."

THE FURMAN BASKETBALL PROGRAM still carried the aura of a big-time program since the era of Frank Selvy and Darrell Floyd had culminated in glory ten years before. Selvy and Floyd were two of the most prolific scorers in the history of college basketball. The hundred points that Selvy scored against Newberry College on February 13, 1954, still stands as the record for points scored in an NCAA game. When I was a boy living in North Carolina, my father took me to see Selvy play, and his smoothness on the court seemed ethereal. When he shot a basketball, it was like he was folding silk scarves to put in a drawer.

Road trips always provided the best chance to catch up with the sleep lost in the barracks. After sleeping on the four-hour bus trip to Greenville, we went straight to the Greenville Memorial Auditorium, a cavernous yet intimate gym with a seating capacity of 5,344. DeBrosse walked the entire court bouncing the ball hard as though he were expecting the floor to answer him back. He was checking the floor for dead spots he would avoid during the game.

Mel put us through a rigorous four-hour practice that Mohr, years later, remembers as brutal and exhausting and unnecessary. I remembered nothing particularly annoying about the practice, but I do recall that the dinner the team ate afterward was one of the bright spots of that capricious season. Tee Hooper was a Greenville native and favorite son and one of the best all-around athletes to come out of that green and leafy city that prefigured the coming of the Blue Ridge Mountains. His parents had invited the whole team over to their house at 5 Marshall Court to eat a steak dinner with all the fixings.

The team bus deposited us at the bottom of a hill and his uniformed teammates whistled in awe as we walked toward the lovely, suburban home where Tee had spent his simple but privileged childhood.

On the patio of his well-landscaped and spacious backyard, Mr. Hooper entertained the coaching staff while Frances Hooper conducted the team on a tour of the house. Later, Mrs. Hooper served the meal on her finest china and set the table with her family's silver place settings and napkins of the softest linen. That the Hoopers made such a fuss over their son's team continues to move me so many years later. They went out of their way to make each of us feel welcome in their home, and told us we could come back to their house on Marshall Court whenever we felt like it.

My team relaxed and began talking to each other as though the possibility of friendship actually existed for us, beyond the spell and thumb and tyranny of our powerful coach. That night I watched Cauthen and Bridges engage in a civil conversation, outside of all competition and misunderstanding that drove them apart. The sophomores became playful and loose among themselves even though we upperclassmen could observe and pass judgment on their every move. Goofy and raw, with a touch of earthiness, they seemed sophomoric for the first time all season. They seemed like young boys instead of prematurely old men.

The coaches ate apart from us on picnic tables in the backyard while their team took over the Hooper dining room on the only night anyone ever did anything that reflected decency or kindness to the Citadel basketball team of 1966–67. We never saw the inside of the house of any coach or general or colonel or anyone else who belonged to the Citadel family in a year we fought and scrambled and shed our sweat and blood in the name of the Bulldogs.

The Furman game in Greenville is emblematic of everything that went wrong in my last year as a basketball player. It also marks a turning point for me as a Citadel athlete, a game I can point to and say, There. That game. That's when it changed for me. Against Furman, I felt like I belonged for the first time. A Blue Teamer at last. A starter for my college team.

It also marked a culmination in Greg Connor's long fight for recognition as a rebounder and scorer and player to be reckoned with. Zinsky was beginning to fade, to soften and dissolve during his ordeal by Mel Thompson, as the season wobbled through January. Bridges played as though he was unaware that he was one of the best shooters in the country when his game was on. Mohr, exhausted from the four-hour practice the day before, could not get his "legs" even though the Furman gym's floor was famous for its bounce and beloved by the great rebounders and leapers of our time. Our big men outrebounded Furman in the first half 30–18, but fell apart in the opening minutes of the second half.

Our team was a sorry defensive team overall, but we bordered on the pathetic when we jumped into our wobbly 2–3 zone. I had never heard of Furman's sophomore guard, Dick Esleeck, when the game began but after he made three straight shots over our zone, I knew he was for real.

When we changed back to man-to-man defense, DeBrosse said, "You get Esleeck, Conroy."

So I spent the entire game shadowing this elusive guard who seemed huge to me. He sprang out at me suddenly as I was guarding him, put moves on me I had never seen on a court, and got open so quickly that he seemed schooled in the mysteries of snakes and all the quick-striking species. I muttered through the whole game that this kid was a hell of a player, but Dick was having some difficulty keeping up with me. So we fought each other for forty minutes—not evenly—he was a much better basketball player, but he knew he was in a game. He knew that much.

Greg Connor, built more like a football lineman than a basketball player, stormed the backboard that night, played with complete abandon. After missing the Christmas practice and drawing Mel's wrath, Greg figured he had nothing left to lose and tried to win back our coach's approval. Though only six feet four inches tall, Greg was built like they tried to build all their athletes in Illinois, solid and silo-shaped, and that night he played like a freeman, one who has torn away the shackles that bound him. Like me, he played as though Mel Thompson was not his coach. He played to prove his worth to himself and his teammates.

Greg's performance held our team together during the first half with his stellar brave work under the boards. With ten minutes to play, Connor committed his fifth foul, and Mohr followed him to the bench twenty seconds later, the buzzer indicating that he, too, had fouled out of the game.

All discipline vanished, all fire dissolved as Mel ran player after player into the game, looking for some combination that would click. The humiliation of Tee Hooper continued at an accelerated rate; Mel barely let Tee into the game for a token appearance before his hometown crowd of 2,400 fans. In agony, Tee sat on the bench, his face looking up to the stands to see his disappointed high school friends, his parents, and his sweet-faced sister, Jill. Once I looked over and Tee had covered his head with a towel. That is what public shame can do to a boy.

We tied the game five times in the second half, but Furman kept coming back on us, then started pulling away. Soon our game turned nasty and brutish, and our big men showed signs of exhaustion under the hoop.

In the *Greenville News*, reporter Jim Anderson quoted Mel Thompson as saying, "Greg Connor went out early and then Dan Mohr and we were definitely hurt. Doug Bridges was not having a good night. We had to use three sophomores on the front line. We might have lost our poise. I'm inclined to think we did."

In the same article, Frank Selvy said that "he told his team at half-time to do what they were supposed to do. 'Do it better, not differently.' " They followed his advice.

They certainly did. With Dick Esleeck, I was making my own small contribution to a star being born. This kid was a quick study and he gained confidence playing against me as the game went on in its furious pace. With 12:43 left he came toward me at the top of the key, went to his left with a quick change of pace. But I cut him off and he did a quick crossover to his right that I lunged to anticipate, but crossed back over to his left, faked a jump shot that I went up to block, then twisted beneath me and shot a perfect, gliding jumper at the foul line that swished cleanly through the net. I was open mouthed with astonishment.

"That's one of the nicest moves I've ever seen," I said to him as he turned to go back upcourt. Naturally, Esleeck would not talk to or acknowledge me because he, like all Furman players, was still ticked off that The Citadel had killed their horse. But the move, in memory, remains otherworldly just as it was when Esleeck pulled it on me that night so long ago.

In the last ten minutes of the game we made every mistake it was possible to make while pressuring another team. I tried to rally the troops, but even my exhortations began to seem hoarse and rattled. "The Citadel Stare," Mel Thompson's most despised manifestation of our school's influence on his game plan, appeared on every face of every teammate. It was a game in which the slippery, breakneck Tee Hooper would score two points, as would the silky Doug Bridges. Zinsky managed to score only four points. Dan Mohr would put up only seven points, and DeBrosse would break into double figures with ten. Our vaunted and talented Blue Team, our original starting lineup, managed to put a total of only twenty-five points against the Furman Paladins. Our performance during the second half was an embarrassment to our college. We lost, 85–68.

In the locker room, I was undressing, exhausted to the tips of my fingers, when Rat came up behind me and whispered in my ear, "You were a high scorer tonight, Pat. You had sixteen. Connor was next with fifteen. Go Green Weenies!"

Greg Connor and I were exactly the same kind of basketball player, guys who hustled, who went for every ball on the floor, who gave it all we got, and who both had second-string written all over us. We knew it then and we know it better now that we are middle-aged men. But I carry a clear memory from that night at Furman. After I shook Dick Esleeck's hand, someone slapped me on the behind and said, "Good game, Pat."

When I turned to see who it was, it was a startling encounter for me. I am the first novelist in the world who has ever been slapped on the fanny by the incomparable Frank Selvy, the only basketball player to score a hundred points in a college basketball game.

THAT TUESDAY WE TRAVELED TO Greenville, North Carolina, to play the Pirates of East Carolina before we took a ten-day break for our midyear exams. Mel refused to let us do our usual warmup drills before the game and required us to run our offense over and over instead. We looked odd and bush-league, and the East Carolina crowd began to heckle us from the sidelines. Hecklers alone could not alter the stern demeanor of our sphinxlike coach, and he gave no outward sign that he even heard the taunts. Mel later would let us know in an aside that he had played ACC basketball where the crowds were truly massive and rowdy and hatred was just another art form that fanaticism could take.

Up in the visitors' stands, I watched my mother and father sit near Doug Bridges's and Dan Mohr's parents. It would be the second college game my mother had seen me play and the first for my father. My father's eyes fell on me like soot left over from Ash Wednesday. We stared at each other and he gave no sign of recognition at all. I waved and he turned away, embarrassed. My mother spotted me and blew me a kiss, and I blew her one back. At that moment, I wished I could have chucked a hand grenade under my father's bleacher. His presence made me as nervous as if someone had placed a cobra in my locker. He could change the weather of any room he entered. I feared playing a game in front of him.

But I saw my mother's surprise when I went out to meet the East Carolina captain. I held the position in the most tenuous and unofficial manner possible, but it pleased me that I was acting as the captain of my team in the first college game my father had ever seen me play. I made a silent prayer that I would not humiliate myself or my teammates before my father's sullen gaze. I could take my father's fury and had proven that over and over during the long, forced march of my debased childhood; it was his laughter and mocking contempt that unmanned me completely, that I would do almost anything to avoid. Again, I prayed for a decent game; a decent one was enough, Lord.

But we were in trouble from the opening tip-off until the game's final horn. No one on the floor came to play against East Carolina and I found myself in my usual role of head cheerleader, going from player to player, exhorting them to greater effort, applauding every rebound, and trying to be aggressive on the fast breaks. Mohr remembers me dragging my pivot foot near the Citadel bench then Mel leaping to his feet to scream at me as the referee called me for traveling. I remember none of this; this night I had a man I truly feared in attendance.

At East Carolina John DeBrosse seemed like he was floating in a disembodied fugue state, his eyes vacant and lost to the action on the court. He went through the motions, but he never registered his presence on the court with his usual bright authority, and he never got into the flow of the game at all.

Our big men rebounded well and would pull in thirty-one rebounds to the Pirates' twenty-one, but they were as blurry and intangible on the offensive end of the court as DeBrosse. Both Bridges and Mohr shot dreadfully. Mel screamed his way through the first half concentrating his rancor, as always, on the big guys in the middle.

"Do something, Zinsky," he yelled at Zeke, who also could not buy a basket, even though he hauled down a game-high ten rebounds. "Do anything. Get off your ass!"

When I scored on a drive, I looked toward my parents. My mother cheered loudly, but my father was blank. It was a religious belief of my father's not to show any sign of joy or pleasure when his oldest son made a basket during a game. Eventually, I quit looking at my father and concentrated on trying to rouse my sleepwalking team from its trance. I went from player to player when we lined up at the foul line and slapped their fannies hard, yet I could not touch their buried spirits.

Point guards carry the responsibility for their teams showing up with their best games in their eyes. My team never got near Greenville, North Carolina, on January 13, 1967, and the fault lies with me. Tee came in off the bench and played his fiery, up-tempo game and scored twelve quick points in the second half. Mel became unhinged by the game because East Carolina was in a rebuilding year, and Mel expected us to beat the Pirates badly. But East Carolina hit 52 percent of their shots and beat us 80–72. Their victory seemed more lopsided than that. It felt like they had beaten us by thirty points. As I ran from the court, I carried a lingering feeling of shame that my father had witnessed my team receive such a thorough trouncing.

The savage diatribe delivered by Mel Thompson in the locker room after that game marks for many of the players the low point of a season chock-full of them. Mel launched into a deranged, near psychotic rage that seemed half seizure and half cuckoo's nest. I thought he would have a stroke before our eyes. My teammates sat with their heads in their hands and their eyes on the floor. We knew better than to make eye contact with Mel when all his demons were loose and our coach went crackers. He screamed about our lack of balls, courage, will, pride, or any of the other signs that imply honor among athletes. I heard none of it because he had begun the most raving, incoherent harangue against any team I would ever play on with the strangest words I had ever heard come from his mouth. "What I have to say to this team isn't gonna be pretty, and it applies to everybody in this room . . . except Pat Conroy."

Thunderstruck by this unprecedented dispensation, I sat through his savage evisceration of my teammates with a combination of shame and wonderment. In my four years with Mel, I had never once heard him excuse any player from one of his rambling indictments. We had almost hit rock bottom, the place where all the darkness of Mel's coaching was leading us, like it had led all the teams of Mel's I had played on at The Citadel. "I don't even want to see you guys for the rest of the night. It makes me sick to my stomach that I got guys on this club who are just going through the motions. You're nothing. All of you. Except you, Pat," he said, again an extraordinary singling out unheard of in Mel's fiery career, which stunned me.

"You guys are shit. You don't have it. You never had it. And tonight, you played like you didn't care one way or the other. You make me sick to my stomach."

For several minutes after Mel's departure no one moved or spoke. Finally, Zinsky began to peel his jersey off and Root took his head out of his hands. DeBrosse looked perplexed and Tee would not smile for the rest of the year. Even the Green Weenies were shocked by the fierceness of the onslaught.

I sat staring at the locker room when Rat came up behind me and squeezed my shoulders.

"Why did Mel excuse me from his ass-kicking?" I asked.

"Because you were terrific," Rat whispered. "You scored twenty-five points. You made nine out of thirteen shots. Hit all seven of your free throws. You were good, son."

Rat moved down the line to soothe the frayed sensibilities of my teammates as I sat there in complete surprise considering the news he had brought to me. Long before, I had given up all hope of ever scoring twenty points in a college basketball game. I remembered the television interview when Mel had put his arm around me and told all of South Carolina that I was fully capable of scoring one or two points a game. A twenty-point game is a benchmark for every basketball player who ever played the game. It is like scoring a touchdown in football or hitting a home run in baseball. In the calculus of sport, it lets the world know in the thoughtless beauty of box scores that you have played one hell of a game. Rat's news took my breath away because I had felt no sense of elation or heightened powers, nor was I even aware I was scoring a career high. I felt only the keen frustration of a point guard unable to rally his team around him.

The head manager, Al Beiner, came up to me and said, "Great game, Pat. You were high scorer on both teams. Your old man's outside. Wants to see you."

I got up and walked toward my father with my spirits rising. My father had often told me I was not good enough to be a college basketball player, so I felt lighter than air as I skipped across the cement floor to encounter him after I had lit up the scoreboard with my first twenty-point game in my college career. When I saw my father's face, I could tell he was not in an ebullient mood. He looked at me as he always did, as though the mere sight of me filled him with revulsion.

"You were shit tonight," he said. "Your team was shit. Your coach can't coach worth a shit."

"We had an off night, Dad," I said.

"You're shit. You didn't have an off night. Shit don't have off nights. Your full-court press is the worst I've ever seen."

"We agree on that, Dad."

Dad put his hand on my chest, pushed me up against a cinderblock wall, and said, "You couldn't hold my jock as a ballplayer. I used to eat guys alive on the court. I saw you help a guy get up tonight. Stuck out your hand to help him off the ground. I'd've laid his ass out."

My father was six foot four and I was five ten. He towered over me as he whispered these pleasantries in my ear. "What a southern pussy on the basketball court you turned out to be."

"We'll get East Carolina when they come to our place, Dad."

"They'll kick the shit out of you down there."

"Can I see Mom?" I said.

"Negative. We got a long ride back to D.C. We wasted our fucking time coming to see this shit. You couldn't hold my jock. Never forget it."

"Yes, sir," I said, and my father walked out into the cold night.

That night I spent at Danny Mohr's house in Atlantic Beach, North Carolina. The sweetness of Danny's parents offered a vivid contrast to my father's blitzkrieg against me outside the locker room. Both sensed that this basketball season was taking a tremendous toll on their hurt and sensitive son. I had no idea of the extent until I listened to Dan enumerate his list of grievances against Mel to his parents and the endless humiliations he had endured at the hands of our coach. Somewhere, on that long ride to Atlantic Beach, I realized that Danny's disaffection with Mel Thompson was fast taking on all the aspects of sheer abomination. For over an hour, Danny emptied the frustrations of that year onto the laps of his soft-spoken parents. Their love of their son was tangible in that car. His father's gentleness flowed like some rare form of honey over his son's dark mood.

When I prepared for bed, I brushed my teeth in their one tiny bathroom and saw that the shower floor was a wooden slat and that the water drained onto the ground beneath the house. I had never known that Dan Mohr's family was as poor and struggling as it was. It explained why he never had a sports coat over the Christmas break. Before we went to bed, Mrs. Mohr kissed me and said it was a great honor to have another Citadel basketball player sleep in their house. She told me to wake her in the middle of the night if I needed anything. Mr. Mohr then hugged me and thanked me for watching out for his son for four years. It moved me powerfully when Mr. Mohr embraced me, but it was much later that I realized that I had rarely been hugged by a father before, and never by my own.

IN OUR REMATCH WITH FURMAN ON February 19 in Charleston, Frank Selvy made a brilliant coaching adjustment and put the sophomore guard Dick Esleeck on me, and I got to measure how improved the young Esleeck was from our first game together. I was listless and leaden during the whole game. I had liked playing against Furman a lot more when Dick was guarding DeBrosse.

I did a better job on Esleeck in this game on defense, but he got sixteen points, eight of them on foul shots. Esleeck improved as the game went along and no one guarded me better than he did since the magisterial point guard Bobby Buisson of Auburn, in the first game of the season, a hundred years ago. I scored six points and lost the game for my college. Kroboth had sixteen, Mohr fourteen, and DeBrosse eleven, but the team was exhausted. We should have beaten Furman on our home court and beaten them badly. But Esleeck was wallpapered to my back the whole night, and he shut me down with great effectiveness.

Years later, I looked Dick Esleeck up in the Furman media guide and discovered that he was the first-team Helms Foundation All-American his senior year, was in the Furman Athletic Hall of Fame, was twice on the Southern Conference first team, and had been named South Carolina Player of the Year in 1969. I would like to say, Dick Esleeck, wherever you are, it was an honor to take the court against you.

After the game was over, Tee Hooper went to the visiting team locker room and asked for an audience with Coach Frank Selvy. Again, Tee had hardly played and his sense of despair was deepening. "Coach Selvy, if I quit The Citadel, could I come play for Furman? Would you let me play for Furman?" Tee Hooper, who many believe was the greatest athlete in Citadel history, was begging for a chance to play for Furman.

"Tee, you could play for anyone," Frank Selvy said. Frank Selvy knew a little bit about the game.

# ANNIE KATE

THE CITADEL IN WINTER WAS A REFUGE OF COLD, MONASTIC BEAUTY to me. As I made my way across the parade ground at night, the front-lit buildings looked as though they were sculptured palaces of ice and the mist was coming off the river. The cold burned my cheeks and the barracks fell silent as the cadets prepared themselves for exams with great resolution. Most of the time, the barracks were boisterous, noisy places, but always turned monastery-like when our trial by examinations began in earnest. Each night during exam week, I returned to the same desk in the library along the back wall on the first floor. I used it as getaway and pied-à-terre. For four years, it was at this desk where I tried to make myself smart during my Citadel years. The library spilled over with more books than I would ever be able to read in three lifetimes. My soul found ease and rest in the companionship of books. The library staff knew me on a first-name basis; I felt as comfortable entering the Citadel library as a whelk entering its shell.

On a Sunday evening after mess, I spread my papers in that corner of the world and began to memorize the notebooks that I had used to copy down every word my professors uttered in class. I was not happy about the academic progress I had made thus far, and I wanted to prove that I could excel in my coursework the last year I would attend college. In class, I had found myself distracted and unable to train my full attention on the voice of a boring professor. My faculty advisor, Colonel Doyle, had taken note of this and had designed my senior year with six of the most gifted teachers on campus. All were brilliant, self-dramatizing men, and I could not wait to get to class each morning to hear what they had to say about English drama, adolescent psychology, literary criticism, the history of England, the modern novel, and the writing of poetry. It still makes me happy to read that distinguished list of courses and think about the shapes of those textbooks and their varying smells as I marked them up on every page where the professor had placed greatest emphasis. That was the semester I encountered Bernard Shaw and Oscar Wilde, fell in love with Isabel Archer in *The Portrait of a Lady*, followed Anna Karenina to her death in the trainyards of Moscow, and listened to the gregarious Charles Martin lecture about England with such passion and eloquence that I grew enamored of the country and its people long before I stood on Hadrian's Wall and wrote thank-you notes to Colonel Martin for handing me the country of England as a gift. In a manila folder, I studied the ten poems I would hand over to Colonel Doyle in the morning. Though I was still a bad poet, I could see that there was something in my writing that had not been there before, and I felt euphoric as I read words I had written.

In his office the next day, I writhed in discomfort as Colonel Doyle read them aloud. The great gift that John Doyle gave me at The Citadel was treating every word I wrote for him as though it was literature itself. He read my stuff to me in the same reverent voice that he read Pound or Spenser to his English classes. There was no letdown or bemusement or even gentle irony to betray that he knew he was reciting harmless drivel. When I left his office, he handed me a sheet of paper that said, "A for your work in poetry, Mr. Conroy. You've made a fine start. A for your superior performance against the Spiders of Richmond. As always, it's been a pleasure teaching you. John Doyle."

On Monday afternoon, I took the exam for literary criticism and spent the afternoon writing an essay on the theories of William Hazlitt, something I have not thought about since. I had to sprint to the field house when that exam was over and was almost late to practice which began precisely at 1600 hours. The practices never let up in intensity during exams, and it never failed to surprise the team that Mel granted us no quarter during this period. The Citadel basketball team, as always, practiced hard then studied hard.

On Tuesday, I took my exam in English drama and the one on the modern novel the following day. I chose to write an essay on the theme of betrayal in *Portrait of a Lady* because I wanted to spend another two hours in the presence of Isabel Archer, even though I felt unfaithful to Anna Karenina in doing so. I filled up two blue books, then ran across the parade ground to practice, the air delicious and winey and clear. I loved the whole shut-down feel of the South in the cold.

There was a sameness to exam week I found comforting and solid. The whole campus turned inward and serious, as the results of the tests were published on the doors of our professors' offices. No names were given, but we found our grades listed beside our cadet serial number. Cries of "Fuck!" or "Jesus Christ!" echoed through the halls as disappointed cadets filled the air all over campus with their grievances. The Citadel felt more like a college during exam week than any other time of year. I had made four A's and a B in my ROTC studies when the roof fell in on me, and I was faced with a decision I thought could get me kicked out of school.

I was walking up the R Company steps when an orderly of the guard called out, "Emergency phone call for Pat Conroy." Rushing to the guardroom, I picked up the phone and could not understand a single word a drunken, hysterical woman was saying to me.

"Please slow down," I said. "I don't know who this is."

"It's Isabel, Pat," she said. "Just Isabel."

It was the voice of the mother of the only young woman I had ever been completely in love with, the one whose break-up with me still left me shivering with hurt. During my junior year, I had lost myself as a ballplayer. I learned that unrequited love could cripple an athlete as effectively as a broken bone or a torn ligament. I did not know how to bear a life that Isabel's daughter had walked out of.

"Calm down, Isabel. Tell me what's wrong."

"My ex-husband's in town. I got a letter from him today. The bastard says he's going to slit my throat. He'll do it, too, Pat—he was a Marine like your old man. You've got to help me! You're all I've got."

"I've got to go see the Boo, Isabel," I said. "But I'm coming. Hold tight." Then her line went dead.

I raced over to Lieutenant Colonel Nugent Courvoisie's quarters on the Citadel campus and banged on the door. His wife, Elizabeth, let me in and told me the colonel was upstairs in his bed. I took the stairs two at a time and found myself facing the assistant commandant of cadets in his pajamas. The sight startled me, and the Boo said, "Sorry I'm in my pj's, bubba, but a man gets tired running after reprobates like you. You got a half hour before taps, bubba. Sound off." During my freshman year, every upperclassman passed down one law of the land: if you ever get into real trouble, go see the Boo.

I told him about Isabel's phone call and he took down her address and phone number.

"Can I go out there and stay with Mrs. Gervais, Colonel?" I asked after filling in the details.

"Have you noticed this is a military college, Conroy?" he said.

"I did, sir. Yes, sir. Just once, though."

"I'll cover for you, bubba," the Boo said. "But just this once. I'll nail you for something later. Now get out there fast. That woman needs you."

When I got to her house, Isabel was passed out in her chair with her door wide open. I picked her up and took her to her bedroom and covered her up. I checked to see if there were any signs that her ex-husband had already showed up and made sure the house was locked tight. Beside her chair I found the letter her ex had sent her, as nasty a letter as I have ever read. It seethed with hatred and at the end of it, he swore that he would slit her throat and take his time doing it.

I lowered the blinds and turned out all the lights and did a slow surveillance of all the windows of the house. The phone rang and I jumped. When I picked it up, I heard the Boo's unmistakable voice. He said, "You okay, bubba? I worry about my little lost lambs when they wander off the pasture."

"I'm fine, Colonel. If this guy's coming, he's not here yet."

"I called the cops on Sullivan's Island. They'll send a patrol car to circle your block every hour. They know the situation, bubba. Call if there's trouble. I can be there in fifteen minutes."

"Thanks, Colonel. I can never thank you enough for this."

"Caring for my lambs. Part of the job."

Ten minutes later I saw a patrol car cruise in front of Isabel's house for the first time. It made the circuit every hour of that long night. I sat in absolute darkness surrounded by butcher knives, a baseball bat, and a jarful of nails. On the electric stove, I kept four pans of water boiling all night. If her ex-husband made it through the front door, the boiling water would be his first sign that he had erred in assaulting Isabel's South Carolina home.

When morning came, I let Isabel sleep as I made myself a cup of coffee. In the trash can in the kitchen, I found the envelope the letter had arrived in. Though it had a Charleston return address, I noticed a postmark from St. Louis, Missouri. Strange, I thought, and I dialed for directory assistance in St. Louis and asked for a phone listing in the name of Isabel's ex-husband, getting one under the name of a retired master sergeant in the Marine Corps.

For an hour, I waited and plotted until I came up with a usable plan. Then I dialed the man's number in St. Louis. "This is Colonel Donald Conroy, USMC, Sergeant. I'm here between assignments at the Pentagon, and your name came across my desk yesterday. I got a call from a Charleston, South Carolina, police chief with a warrant for your arrest. Do you know one Isabel Gervais?"

"I was once married to the bitch," he said.

"The police chief wanted the Marine Corps' help in tracking you down, Wilson. He said you threatened to slit this woman's throat. That couldn't be true. You're a semper fi guy, Wilson. I know you're retired, but Marines don't turn to shit that fast, do we?"

"Sir, how do I know who I'm talking to?" he said, growing suspicious.

"Surprise, Wilson. You don't. But look me up, pal. I'm a fighter pilot, jocko, but because someone fucked up my orders, I'm lucky enough to find myself privileged to call losers like you who get their rocks off threatening their old girlfriends. Write it down. Colonel Donald N. Conroy. N stands for nothing. No middle name. Call my number at the Pentagon, and you'll get ole yours truly on the horn. Want my fucking ID?"

"No, sir. Sorry, sir. Just checking, sir."

"Let me run an idea past you," I said in my father's voice. "The Marine Corps is a little sensitive about its image these days and tell the truth, Wilson, an ex-Marine who slits his ex-wife's throat does not make the PR guys happy. Get my drift?"

"Yes, sir. I do, sir."

"So let's come up with a plan. Say I call this chief of police guy. I get folksy with the son-of-a-bitch. Then I tell the shitbag that I chewed you a new asshole. Get my drift, Wilson? You got drunk. You wrote the bitch a letter. You couldn't remember a thing in it. You with me, Wilson?"

"Sir, I see where you're going," Wilson said.

"Okay. I tell the police chief that I talked straight to you. Marine to Marine. I said to you, 'Wilson, can you leave that broad alone? You give me your word as a Marine?' We semper fi the shit out of each other. You swear to me on the honor of the corps that you'll leave that broad alone? You gotta mean it. Make me happy, Wilson. Leave the broad alone."

"I will, sir. That's a promise."

"Promise me as a Marine, Sergeant."

"You have my promise as a Marine, Colonel," Wilson said.

"Then that arrest warrant will be ripped up today, Wilson. Semper fi, Sergeant."

"Semper fi, Colonel Conroy."

I hung up the phone and found Isabel on her couch, bent double laughing. She had listened to my entire performance.

She fixed me breakfast that morning before I went back to take an afternoon exam. I left to go back to The Citadel as soon as she brought her daughter's name up. The mention of that name still carried the power to hurt me.


In my entire four years at The Citadel, there was one young woman I truly loved and one woman only. In the novel *The Lords of Discipline*, I wrote a fictionalized version of this young woman and called her Annie Kate Gervais. She will remain Annie Kate Gervais in this book. Annie Kate ended up marrying a fine man, and I know her three children rather well. When I lived in San Francisco, Annie Kate and I lunched fairly frequently although neither of us ever alluded to the events that altered both of our lives forever. We did not discuss the thing that burned most brightly between us. I never once mentioned the ecstasy of my love for her and Annie Kate never once mentioned the baby. I still do not know if she ever read *The Lords of Discipline* or not, and she knows I will never ask that question. Our lost love is a secret that lies mysteriously between us. Our friendship is shallow, brittle, and lacks intimacy, yet remains important to both of us. When I look at Annie Kate I remind myself that I was once a boy who thought this woman was a goddess and her body a field of fire. When she looks at me, her eyes find the boy I once was, the lost, lost boy who woke up in the middle of his life a stranger to himself and heard a hurt and pretty girl call out his name. The boy did not know then he could only love hurt women, nor did he know that all the women in his life who would call his name would come from the cold country of hurt. The sons of beaten women do not often make the best selections among the women in their lives. In my own life, the women I did not choose remain the lucky ones.

I met Annie Kate by accident. At the end of my trying plebe year at The Citadel, one of the seniors I was assigned to in the alcove room next door to me in R Company told me he needed me to date a girl who had been stood up by another cadet. Since the recognition of the knobs had taken place several days before, I could double-date with him without any fear of his being accused of fraternizing. I now belonged to the brotherhood.

D. G. Keyser picked up his girlfriend first, then drove to a more unlucky neighborhood to pick up Annie Kate Gervais.

"You'll just love her," the girl dating D.G. said. "She doesn't know how pretty she is." When we came to her house, she bounded down the steps as soon as we pulled up and was in the car before I could hold the door for her. She held out her hand to me and said, "Very pleased to meet you, Pat. I'm Annie Kate Gervais."

Her voice was country and high-pitched, but her perfect oval face and comely figure were rare enough to leave me speechless. Her smile broke like a thunderclap in that car. Riding to James Island High School that night, I let D.G. do all the talking and I sat in paralyzed silence trying to conjure sentences that would delight Annie Kate and make her happy to be in my part of the world. Wordless, I arrived at James Island High School for the Mr. James Island contest among the senior boys.

I took my seat on the aisle of the auditorium still trying to think of something to say to Annie Kate when there was a tap on my shoulder. A pleasant-faced woman said, "It's traditional to have a Citadel cadet help with the judging. Citadel men know what to look for in a young man."

That might have been true, but I wanted to spend the evening next to Annie Kate and I pointed to D. G. Keyser down the row. D.G. would have none of it and solved the problem by saying, "Hey, smackhead. You do it. That's an order."

As I got up to follow the woman to the front row, Annie Kate grabbed my hand from behind and pressed up against me to whisper a boy's name in my ear. "He's the cutest boy in school. By far," she said. I took that boy's name into my consciousness and went to join the group of judges. I had liked the touch of Annie Kate's hand and the whisper of her breath in my ear. I had liked it very much.

The judges retired to a room backstage where we winnowed the senior boys down to five finalists. With my single vote, I made sure that Annie Kate's favorite made the cut, although the other four adults in the panel met my vote with some discomfiture. The boy who won the Mr. James Island contest was a short, stocky boy who radiated goodwill and the theater exploded in applause when his name was announced. We judges sent the whole high school home happy that night, and Annie Kate was delighted that I had fought for the boy she liked. It was the mother of Mr. James Island who stopped me on King Street the following year and said, "You're the cadet who judged the Mr. James Island contest, aren't you?"

"Yes, ma'am," I said.

"You've got great taste," she said. "That was my son who won the contest. Do you remember the girl you dated that night?"

"Annie Kate Gervais. I tried to get in touch with her."

"Her family situation is somewhat unfortunate," the woman said, and briefly filled in the course of events that had befallen Annie Kate during the summer. She concluded her story by telling me that a group of mothers and teachers were searching for Annie Kate and wanted to help her. "She's a very nice girl, considering the circumstances. She had people in Blacksburg, Virginia, and a neighbor thinks she might have gone there with her mother."

"I'm going to Blacksburg next week," I said. "The basketball team's playing Virginia Tech."

"Let me write you down her mother's family name."

The name was Caldwell. When I arrived in Blacksburg and checked into the hotel room with my team I turned to the Blacksburg phone book and began calling every Caldwell in the book. On the third call, I reached Annie Kate's uncle and he gave me an address on Sullivan's Island, South Carolina, just north of Charleston. I wrote her a letter telling her I had heard about her circumstances and it sounded like she could use a friend. I began writing her letters every day.

When I returned from the long road trip, there was a letter in my post office box 587 from Annie Kate and it was a cry of pure despair. "I have ruined my life," it said, "and the life of my mother. And the life of this poor child I am carrying. Please be my friend Pat Conroy. We have no one. We see no one. We listen to Citadel basketball games on the radio. We cheer every time you get in to play."

On the following Tuesday, I drove after practice over to their small apartment on the north end of Sullivan's Island. Annie Kate was dressed in a raincoat, a prop that she would wear until the birth of her child. She pulled it tightly around her when she opened the door and she burst into tears at the sight of me. Though she hugged me, I did not return the hug, worried that her mother might misinterpret the gesture. The mother's fiery eyes were already aglitter with the easy malice one finds in women whose lives have gone sour in the middle years.

Annie Kate said, "Mama, this is Pat. The one who writes the letters—the basketball player."

Isabel Gervais answered in a gravelly voice out of the poor-born and hardscrabble South of my mother. "Let me get this straight. You're a Citadel cadet in the prime of your life. You play on the basketball team, ain't too hard to look at, and you get to spend your Friday nights with an old woman and her knocked-up daughter."

"Oh, please, Mama," Annie Kate wailed.

"Mrs. Gervais," I said, "my social life needs a little work. I admit that. But a boy's got to start somewhere."

Mrs. Gervais laughed out loud, then eyed me, her pupils yellow like a lioness. "I like a smart-mouthed boy. The letters you write my daughter, Cadet," Isabel said. "Are they love letters?"

"Mama," Annie Kate screamed and I blushed hard.

"No, ma'am," I said. "This is only the second time I've ever seen your daughter."

Then turning to me again, she said, "You write beautifully, Cadet. I wait for your letters as much as Annie Kate does. But I'm curious. Why do you write my daughter now? What are your motives? Is it sex?"

"Mama. Please stop, Mama. Please don't do this to me. To us. To all of us."

"She's ruined herself for a boy like you. A boy from a decent home. A boy with prospects. It's got to be the sex. You know she's easy, don't you, Cadet? Because she went and got herself knocked up?"

"Yes, ma'am," I said in the astonished air of that sad house. "I'm in it for the sex."

Later, Annie Kate asked me if I wanted to go for a walk on the beach. We crossed the street and walked through the backyard of an old Victorian that looked out on Fort Sumter and the shipping lanes of Charleston Harbor. On that first night, I mostly listened to Annie Kate tell the details of her life since I last had seen her. I learned all about the boy she had been in love with since her ninth-grade year, their courtship, and her first missed menstrual cycle. The boy wanted her to get an abortion, but offered no money nor the name of any illegal abortionist. He began to slap her around every time he saw her. Eventually he quit calling and refused to return her phone calls. Then his mother called to let her know that her son had moved to Atlanta and had left no forwarding address. Annie Kate would not hear from this boy for the rest of her life.

"When is the baby due?" I remember asking.

"Sometime in late February," she said on a clear December night.

"Have you thought about names?"

"No. I haven't even let myself think about being pregnant," she said. "I've hated this baby with all my heart the whole time I've been pregnant. It shames me to admit it, but it's true, Pat."

"My mother used to complain sometimes during her pregnancies," I said. "But she was always happy once the babies arrived."

"How many children were in your family?"

"Seven."

"My God."

"There were also six miscarriages," I said. "My sister Carol called them 'the Lucky Ones.' It was her theory that those little embryonic Conroys heard what was going on between my mom and dad and just decided, no way."

"What do you mean? What's wrong with your family?"

"My father's tough. Very tough," I said, uncomfortable with the conversation.

"You ought to meet my stepfather. A real bastard. He makes my mother look like Grace Kelly. She threw him out a year ago. I couldn't have been happier."

"I wish my mother would throw my father out, but that'll never happen," I said.

"Why not?"

"He'd kill her," I said. The three words shocked me as I said them that night on the beach at Sullivan's Island. I had spoken those words to a girl I barely knew, already I was revealing family secrets that I had hidden even from myself.

"I've got to get back to the barracks," I said.

"Why? Please stay longer."

"I'm a cadet. I turn into a pumpkin at midnight," I said using the old Citadel joke.

"Will you do me a favor, Pat?" she asked. "Will you keep writing me every day? It's the only thing Mama and I have to look forward to. They're the things that make me laugh."

"If I've got time. I have six or seven other girlfriends that I've got to write first."

"You're playing George Washington tomorrow night," Annie Kate said.

"Want to go? I'll get you tickets," I said.

"I can't go out. Not like this," she said, patting her stomach. "We'll listen to George Norwig on the radio. The Voice of the Citadel Bulldogs."

"Can I come and see you on Sunday?" I asked.

"I would love it, Pat. I would love it."

So it began. Looking back at the baffled, virginal young man that I was at that time, I can forgive myself for everything that happened with Annie Kate. I had spent a lifetime watching my mother being backhanded by my Marine father. My mother worshiped me because I would rush to her defense and try to pull my father off her. He would turn and slap me to the floor, then my mother would fight to pull him off me. I would rise and try to get between them again. He would hit me and I would go down again and my mother would be on his back pulling him away from me. This was the long dance of my childhood. Love and agony became intermingled for me in profane ways. Rescue would become my theme and my downfall. Whenever I hear a woman weeping, I come back to the dance of my childhood. Long ago, the theme of rescue quit being my tragedy and took up residence as my fate. It can be factored into every great event of my life from the teaching of black children on Daufuskie Island to my recent divorce. My high school friend Bruce Harper summed it up best several years ago when I called to tell him I had fallen in love. "What's her sad story?" Bruce wisely asked.

Each day before practice I would call Annie Kate and we would talk for an hour. I do not remember a day where she did not weep, sobbing miserably that she had ruined her life and had no idea what would happen to her when the baby was born. I became Annie Kate's head cheerleader, confessor, shrink, and mentor during those afternoon phone calls. Daily I wrote letters that I hoped both Annie Kate and her mother would find charming and witty. Subconsciously, I was trying to get both women to fall in love with me, and I think that is exactly what happened.

On a freezing night in December before the team began its Christmas road trip that would end with the University of Toledo, Annie Kate drove me back to the barracks. No, she never once came onto the Citadel campus during our time together, but we would meet at the parking lot beside the Hampton Park Zoo outside Lesesne Gate. It was in this darkened lot a half hour before midnight that Annie Kate first took my hand into hers. I had never tried to hold her hand or kiss her during our long walks on the beach of Sullivan's Island. I was so prudish as a young man, so Catholic-shaped and South-haunted and goody-two-shoes, that my roommates used to tease me that I never looked at the pictures of girls in *Playboy* magazine. Because she was pregnant, I had never thought of Annie Kate in a sexual way. After she held my hand, I constantly and religiously thought of her only in a sexual way. My hand felt like it had gone to heaven.

"Would you like to feel the baby kick, Pat?" Annie Kate said.

"Love to," I said, and she led my hand to her stomach where I felt her child move inside her. With my hand on her stomach, Annie Kate then kissed me for the first time, in the cold darkness of Charleston. When her tongue hit my tongue, all the fire and ice and mystery of what happens between men and women became suddenly clear to me. In her womb, I felt her baby stir inside her and, surprising myself, I promised that unborn child not to worry about a thing—that I was going to take care of it forever.

"I never thought a boy would love me again," she whispered.

"Come over to the barracks, I'll introduce you to two thousand boys who'd be happy to fall in love with you."

Annie Kate laughed, then kissed me again, and I thought that life itself was the most wonderful thing in the world. I made it to Fourth Battalion right at midnight and walked to the middle of the quadrangle and let out a whoop of pure pleasure at being in love beneath the stars of Charleston.

Because of Annie Kate's humiliation over her pregnancy, I told very few people in my life about her existence. No one on my team knew I was in love with anyone and no Citadel cadet ever laid eyes on her from the time I first visited her house until her child was born. My relationship with Annie Kate remained chaste and innocent the whole time we were involved with each other. I started talking about getting married the next summer. I would give up my basketball scholarship and quit The Citadel and go to work to support Annie Kate and the child.

"Have you told your mother and father about me, Pat?" she asked as we walked on the beach one night.

"No," I admitted.

"Are you ashamed of me, Pat?" she asked.

"No, I'm ashamed of what my mother and father are going to say when they find out about you. I'm the first person on Mom's side of the family who's been to college. My getting a diploma means a lot to her."

"What about your father?"

"He'll just beat me up," I said.

"Would you do me a favor, Pat?"

"Anything."

"Don't talk about getting married again," she asked. "I have enough pressure on me already. Let's let the baby get here. Then we'll talk."

So I kissed her like I thought I knew what tomorrow forever felt like—Annie Kate could always stop me from talking by asking me to kiss her. It was a tactical command for silence that I enjoyed.

My game improved while I was in love. Like a madman, I dove for every loose ball, knowing that George Norwig, the voice of the Bulldogs, would send my name cruising along the airwaves into Annie Kate's radio. My love of Annie Kate transported me through the cold months that year. Because I was a Citadel cadet I could not visit her during the week and only could see her on Friday nights and Sunday afternoons. Saturday was always game night and there was not enough time to drive out to Sullivan's Island and get back to the barracks by midnight curfew. But we talked on the phone every day and my letters poured into her house in a ceaseless flood of adolescent emotion. I loved writing letters to a girl who said she loved me every time I spoke with her. I felt handsome for the first time in my life. We beaten boys have trouble liking the faces our fathers tore apart with their fists. I grew to like my face when Annie Kate could not seem to look at it enough.

I did not see the terrible isolation of Annie Kate and her mother until it was too late. Their solitude was so complete that I became their sole link to the outside world. When I would call, the phone would ring once and Annie Kate would answer it with great immediacy and ardor. Always, she would put Isabel on the phone to talk with me for several minutes and Isabel would laugh at everything I said to her. At that time in my life I saw myself as the carrier of a great tragedy—the fact of my father's great violence to his family—and I did not place myself as the jokester who offered comic relief in the drama of my own life. But Isabel howled the whole time I was in her house or on the phone and sometimes would bend double when I was telling some stories of barracks life.

On February 16, 1965, I received a phone call at the hotel where the team was staying. In sheer terror the whole team had gathered in Bob Kiggans and Dick Martini's room to watch an episode of *Alfred Hitchcock Presents*. We had originally been watching this program separately, but by the end of the production, all of us clustered terrified in our co-captains' room. In the pandemonium of that moment, the phone rang by Dick Martini's bed. Thinking it was Mel telling us to keep it down, he answered it. He looked puzzled then looked up to me. "Hey, midget," he said to me, "it's for you."

I answered the phone and heard Isabel on the other end of the line. "Annie Kate went into labor last night. My kid had a tough time. The baby didn't make it. The umbilical cord wrapped around its throat. Strangled it."

"Boy or girl?" I asked, stunning the room still in pandemonium around me.

"What difference does it make? Dead's dead," she said. And then she hung up.

I wept that night for the lost child. I had felt it kick in Annie Kate's womb so many times and had promised that child that I would father and protect and champion it. For a week I called Annie Kate at her house and no one answered. Her letters, which had arrived on a daily basis, stopped arriving at all. We went on another road trip the following weekend and I still had not heard from her. Davidson handled us easily, but my mind was scattered and desperate, and I do not remember if I got in the game or not. The next Sunday I drove out to Sullivan's Island to see what was going on with Annie Kate.

She was expecting my visit. Annie Kate rose to greet me and met me at the door with a sisterly kiss. In my dress grays I looked around the tiny room and saw that someone had removed every clipping and photograph of me with a basketball.

"I'm sorry about the baby," I said to Annie Kate.

"There is no baby, Pat," she said. "It worked out for the best. For all of us. You won't have to drop out of The Citadel. You won't have to break your mother's heart. I get to pretend that none of it happened."

"What do you mean, none of it happened, Annie Kate?" I said, bewildered. "It changed everything. It changed me . . . forever."

"Pat, listen to me. I knew you were going to be difficult."

"Difficult. I'm in love with you. I want to marry you," I said. "What's difficult about that?"

"Please sit down," she said. "Pat, listen to me. You've got to understand me. I've just lived through the worst year of my life. I can't describe the humiliation I've felt. The shame of not being able to leave the house except at night. What I've felt was despair. I thought of killing myself a hundred times, Pat. Then you came into our lives. What a sweet, nice boy you've been to us. You saved my life, Pat. You really did. But you made the mistake of loving me during the worst time of my life. You loved me when I hated myself. You loved me when I hated the world. Don't you see, Pat, I can never forgive you for *when* you loved me. I've tried, I promise. But both of you, you and Mama, are the only two people who saw me during that whole horrible time. I'm going to start over, Pat. I'm making a fresh start. I'm looking for a normal life. That's it. Nothing else. A nice guy. Sells insurance. Goes to the Methodist church. He'll never know a thing about what happened to me. Neither will my kids."

"Were you pretending to love me, Annie Kate?" I said.

"I wasn't pretending at all. But I see your face and I see the worst December I ever spent on earth. I see your face and there's the worst January. I see your face and there's February. It shouldn't be that way, but it is."

Annie Kate and I cried hard and soon I got up and made my departure. I drove back to The Citadel dazed and hurt. It had never occurred to me that I could love someone with my body and soul and simply have that love returned to me as cheap merchandise. That night as I brushed my hair for retreat formation, I looked up and saw my face and my own repulsion as I looked at it for the first time as the face of a boy that Annie Kate Gervais could not bring herself to love. And now, three years later, Isabel said as she walked me to my car, "You found yourself a girlfriend yet?"

"Not yet, Isabel," I said. "Still looking."

"No, you're not, Pat. You still love my girl," she said. "It's written all over your face."

"Then I've got to change my face."

"Timing's everything. Yours was off."

"I didn't know I was being timed, Isabel. I didn't know anything."

CHAPTER 21

# STARVING IN UTOPIA

WHEN THE CITADEL TEAM PULLED UP TO THE SHODDY MOTEL near the interstate that cut straight through the city of Jacksonville, Mel made the mistake of letting his team lounge about the seedy waiting room as he checked in with a sad-eyed, unshaven man at the main desk. Some of the team heard the man ask Mel, "You want these rooms for one hour or for two? Also got half-hour rates." Our laughter embarrassed Mel and he silenced us with a scowl like a lion baring his fangs at the antics of bothersome cubs. Still, we giggled and I looked the place over with renewed interest. The run-down whorehouse seemed emblematic of the depths to which our promising team had sunk.

Later Cauthen poked his head out of his room and said, "You got your room for one hour, Conroy."

"I always need two, Zipper," I said.

"Bullshit, you've never even had a date," Bob said as I opened up the room next to his and threw my bag onto the bed nearest the window. Greg Connor followed me inside and surveyed the room. Both of us got into our underwear to take a nap before the game. Before we went to sleep, Greg said, "Conroy, could I ask you a favor?"

"I'm a senior and it is my job to take care of helpless little sophomores," I said.

"Listen to me, Conroy. This is important. Someone from A Company set me up with a date with a sorority girl after the game tonight."

"Congratulations. I'm supposed to have a date, too," I said.

"You?" Greg said, surprised.

"Rumors of my prowess are beginning to spread among the coeds of the Southeast. Entire sororities surround Fourth Battalion on big week-ends chanting my name."

"Cauthen told me he was positive you were a virgin, Conroy," Greg said. "Have you ever had sex with a girl?"

"I've thought about it," I said. "In fact, I don't think I've thought of anything else for more than four or five seconds since I turned thirteen."

"I haven't had a date since I've been to The Citadel. Not one. It's driving me crazy. This is supposed to be a really nice girl. And pretty. She's supposed to be real pretty. I've got to go out with this girl . . . I've just got to. Will you talk to Coach about it?"

"I'll be glad to. But Mel's never taken a great interest in his team's love life. He doesn't want some strange girl taking over his job of re-moving all bodily fluids from us."

"Conroy, it kills me when I see the cheerleaders on the other teams. They're so damn beautiful. The Auburn girls . . . the East Carolina girls . . . my God, the Florida State girls! I've been so horny the whole time I've been here, I just want to go out on a date. That's not a crime, is it? I've been playing pretty good ball lately."

"You've been playing great ball."

"Who's your date?" Greg asked.

"A girl I met last homecoming. A cadet had stood her up, so some Florida cadets searched the barracks and found me studying. I put on my salt-and-pepper uniform and became her date for homecoming. Her name is Karen, and she apologized when she met me for wearing such thick eyeglasses. They were thick, but I couldn't help noticing that the girl who wore them was lovely. I got a letter from her this week, and she wants to show me Jacksonville. But I don't think we'll be going any-where, Greg. Mel's a little weird about sex."

"I'm not talking about sex," Greg said. "I want to go on a date. I want to talk to a girl."

"I'll ask Coach after the game," I promised.

"You think he'll say no, don't you?"

"I know he will."

"If he doesn't let me go on this date, I may quit the team," Greg said, his voice despairing.

"We'll miss you."

"How many dates—real dates—have you been on after basketball games, Conroy? I want to know."

"Two," I said. "Cauthen set me up with two girls from Winthrop after we lost tournament games in Charlotte."

"Two dates in four years," he moaned.

"It's the price of being part of a big-time college basketball program," I said.

"Conroy, do you have any idea how many times we'd be getting laid if we'd gone to civilian colleges?"

"But we wouldn't be whole men. Citadel men. We wouldn't be able to wear one of these," I said, flashing my Citadel ring in the air.

"We wouldn't be horny. Don't you think it'd be great not to be horny?"

"I wouldn't know what it's like not to be horny," I said, turning away from Greg, trying to sleep. "I'll do my best with Mel. Try to have a good game. We've got a lot better chance if we beat Jacksonville."

"I'll play my ass off," Greg said. And he was as good as he promised.

When I walked into the Jacksonville Coliseum that night for the game, Karen was waiting for me by the door. I was last off the bus and she surprised me by kissing me squarely on the lips, becoming the first and last girl ever to kiss me in a college gymnasium. I was both delighted that she had done so and grateful that Mel had not witnessed this singular event.

"I told the girls in my dorm that I'm dating a college basketball star," Karen said.

"Player. You're dating a college basketball player, not star. And Karen, my coach may not let me go out with you," I explained.

"That would be terrible," she said.

"It certainly would," I agreed, then saw a cadet from Jacksonville that I knew.

"This is my friend, Karen," I said to the cadet. "If I can't go out with her after the game, would you set her up with one of the cadets who came down for the game?"

"Be glad to," the cadet said.

"I'm sorry I wear thick glasses," she said quietly to me. "My mama promised me contacts for my birthday."

"I have two sisters who wear thick glasses, Karen," I said. "They're both beautiful girls, just like you."

"My father used to call me beautiful," she said, her eyes filling with tears. On our homecoming date, Karen had wept for twenty minutes when she told me of the recent death of her father, whose parachute had failed to open in a skydiving accident. I do not think it ever had occurred to me how much a daughter could adore a father until Karen's grief proved it to me.

"Your dad was right," I said, then saw Rat running toward me in his manager's uniform.

"Pat, have you gone nuts? Mel's looking for you," Rat yelled.

"See you after the game," I said to Karen as I broke out into a jog for the dressing room.

As the team was shooting jump shots before the game began, DeBrosse approached me with the strangest look on his face.

"Conroy," John said, "what's that I'm hearing?"

I listened for a moment, then said, "Down South, we call them elephants. I don't know what they're called in Ohio."

"Fuck you," DeBrosse said. "How many elephants have you ever heard at a basketball game?"

"This is a coliseum, DeBrosse. They got all kinds of things going on here. I saw a poster saying that the circus was in town for tomorrow." And then I heard the answering call of a pair of lions.

"Elephants and basketball. Jesus Christ, Conroy," John said.

Before the opening tip-off, Greg Connor pointed out his date who was sitting among the small cluster of Citadel fans. Despite the time span of over thirty years, that young woman's fresh good looks still have not lost the capacity to move me. Without knowing it, she carried all the incalculable and breathless power of a woman's loveliness with her. As she waved down at us, she changed the way Greg and I thought about the world. Three rows above her, my Aunt Evelyn sat with my Uncle Joe and my four cousins Carolyn, Evelyn, Joey, and Johnny. I blew them a kiss. I had left tickets for the whole Gillespie family, and it always made me feel like a big shot that I could do it. My Uncle Joe, who was not a shy man, bellowed out to the crowd, "That's my nephew, Pat Conroy, and you'd better watch out, Jacksonville. He's going to teach you some tricks."

I thought I would collapse from embarrassment, but one of the refs came looking for me, and I went over to shake hands with the Jacksonville captains as Uncle Joe kept screaming out my name and telling the city that I was his nephew. Uncle Joe gave new meaning to the word "irrepressible."

Ed "Little Mel" Thompson came up to me in the pregame huddle. "Hey, Pat, who's that guy calling out your name?"

"That's my Uncle Joe."

"Could you make him stop?" Ed said. "He's getting on Mel's nerves."

"You don't do anything to stimulate my Uncle Joe," I said. "It's best to ignore him."

When Kroboth went up for the opening tip against the very game Dick Pruet, I heard a muffled "Pat Conroy's my nephew," then my Aunt Evelyn regained a measure of control over her husband. Dan Mohr was not starting at center, and his dejection was so obvious that it stood out like a simple sentence etched across his face. The ruination of Dan Mohr's senior year had hit its full stride.

My Citadel team had come to play that night, and we gave the Dolphins the game of their lives. I had never seen my team move with such swiftness, vivacity, or dash. We got after them from the opening tip and I felt like a point guard who belonged on that court as I directed my team.

But the night belonged to the bullish, well-muscled Greg Connor who threw his body at every rebound for the glory and well-being of the Citadel Bulldogs. It was a joy to watch him. He astonished the big men of Jacksonville as he attacked the boards with a relentlessness that bordered on masochism. He scored from everywhere, and I got him the ball as many times as I could. Greg's play made me look brilliant that night. My whole team was cooking, and the fast break was taking care of itself. I could see in the Jacksonville players' eyes that they knew they were playing a different team than the one they had beaten earlier at The Citadel's field house. Connor had not been a major factor that game, but he was as hard to move away from the boards as a freight car on this night. I was the only one in the gym who knew that the brilliance of Greg's performance emanated from the glow of a pure sexual intoxication. He was playing for that pretty Jacksonville girl and no one else. When he was shooting one of his seven free throws that night, I made a mental note that we could win a bunch of games if I could get Connor laid after every game. We pulled away to a 38–31 lead at halftime. We played as good a half as we had all season.

That year Jacksonville's Coach Joe Williams was turning his school into a big-time program that would soon showcase the likes of the great

Artis Gilmore, teams that would take Jacksonville deep into the NCAA tournaments in the early seventies. Already he had two players, Wayne Kruer and Dick Pruet, who could play on the best teams in the country. Kruer was a six-foot-five guard who DeBrosse graciously told me I would be guarding.

Kruer was a new kind of guard in the world that was fast proliferating in college basketball. He would have easily been the second or third tallest man on my team, but he had learned to handle the ball well enough to play outside the lane. His jump shot was wonderful to watch and hard to block. When Wayne saw that I was going to guard him, he looked as though someone had given him a free lunch. He taught me that night what it meant for a larger man to post up a smaller man. During the entire game, he would take me under the basket, establish his position just outside the paint, and call for the ball. Because he was six five, he had played forward and center in high school, and he knew what to do when his teammates got him the ball. All night, I tried to front him, but his teammates would lob it over my head for a score. The guy could play the game and once again, I found myself in over my head. Only one guard on my team could stop a scorer like Kruer. His name was Tee Hooper, and he watched the game from the bench, his year in shambles. He watched helplessly as Kruer ate my jock throughout the first and second half. Though he does not know it, I have had nightmares about Wayne Kruer.

But I fought him, and my team played heroically against the much better Jacksonville Dolphins. Greg Connor led our team in scoring with twenty-one points, final proof of the great potency of sex in the life of an athlete: it hurt our team when Greg fouled out with 1:40 to play. Greg ran to the bench exhausted, a spent, depleted warrior. He had enjoyed the finest game of his Citadel career with his first date sitting in the stands.

Though we led Jacksonville 38–31 at halftime, Jacksonville fought back to a 44–44 tie in the opening minutes of the second half. Though we led most of the second half, once by six points at 65–59, Jacksonville rallies kept us from putting the game away. The game was tied nineteen times before the final buzzer.

Everywhere I looked that night I ran into the courage of my beaten-down teammates. Zinsky played like the magnificent athlete he was born to be. When Kroboth got into foul trouble, Mohr came in and scored fourteen points in the second half alone. DeBrosse was a thoroughbred guard and I was lucky to play in the same backcourt with him that night. Steady as the internal workings of a clock, DeBrosse hit jumpers at vital times when his team had to call on his outside shooting.

A sophomore guard for Jacksonville named Alan Treece hit two free throws with a minute left and put Jacksonville up by two. We ran down and missed a shot, Jacksonville controlled the ball, but not the clock. Instead of freezing the ball, Kruer took me deep to the right side of the court and did not let enough of the clock run off and missed a jumper that was rebounded fiercely by Zinsky. He shot me the ball with less than fifteen seconds left, and I did what point guards were trained to do.

I brought the ball up the court at full speed, made eye contact with Dan Mohr, and Dan read my look with matchless precision. Root made a move against Pruet, and I slipped a pass under Kruer. With sweet efficiency, Root faked left, then pivoted to the right. His beautiful jump shot swished through the net, sending the game into overtime.

In the roar of the crowd I heard a faint cry of "Pat Conroy's my nephew" coming from my indefatigable Uncle Joe, but Aunt Evelyn put the clamps on him once again, to my great relief. Mel was animated in the huddle. The game had excited him, and he screamed at us as though he liked us again. We led three times in overtime, but each time Jacksonville came back with a bucket to even the game. With less than a minute left, Kroboth committed an offensive foul. Jacksonville ran out the clock, then called time with four seconds remaining.

I knew what that play was going to be and so did everyone else who was present in the Jacksonville Coliseum. Fronting Wayne Kruer, I tried to prevent him from receiving the inbound pass from Alan Treece. Treece had to lob it over me and Kruer received the pass deep in his backcourt. Forcing him to his left, he took an off-balance jump shot, and it careened off the rim and went high on the backboard. In the drama of the last shot, one of my teammates forgot about the elusive Mr. Treece who was waiting under the boards by himself, and he tipped the ball in as the final buzzer sounded.

Treece's shot felt like a knife in the abdomen. I fell to my knees, exhausted and beaten and disillusioned in every cell of my body. I had been positive we were going to beat Jacksonville. The Dolphins' team and cheerleaders were mobbing Treece as Barney and Zipper helped me to my feet. Wayne Kruer sought me out to shake my hand, a gesture of sportsmanship I truly appreciated. As I walked toward the locker room, weaving through the jubilant crowd of Dolphin fans, Karen found me and planted a French kiss on me at center court. To say this act took me by surprise is understating my complete astonishment at finding this young woman's tongue in my mouth. My first thought was that Aunt Evelyn and my cousins had witnessed this and would report it in all of its salacious detail to my mother.

Karen then said, "You lied to me, Pat. You are a basketball star."

"I'm not, Karen," I said.

"You looked like one to me," she said. "Can you go out?"

"I'll have to talk to my coach."

"A girlfriend lent me her apartment at Jacksonville Beach," she said.

When I reached the locker room, my team had begun the rituals of undressing. Some of the Green Weenies, notoriously fast dressers after a game, were in the showers already, but Connor was standing beside my locker.

"Conroy, when're you gonna ask Mel if we can go out on a date?"

"Let's give him some time, Greg," I said, looking over at Mel and Little Mel as they spoke in disconsolate whispers to each other on a bench across the locker room. Mel looked more gaunt and haggard than he usually did. It was clear the game had taken its toll on him. I decided to shower and put on my uniform before I approached Mel about Connor's and my sex lives. Then disaster struck. My eyes were suddenly engulfed in an aura of cheap light, and I looked up in horror to see my Uncle Joe filming me and my naked and half-naked teammates in living color. Uncle Joe was well known in my family for filming the entire waking lives of his children. I cannot ever remember him when he was not sticking a camera into my face.

"I told you that you shouldn't mess with my Jacksonville Dolphins. The ol' Dolphins sure came through for the city by the St. Johns River tonight. Hey, Coach," Uncle Joe said, turning the light from my astonished head to my coach's enraged one. "Hey, if you're going to cry about it, Coach, you're in the wrong profession, pal. Crybabies don't make good coaches, I can tell you that. . . ."

I went for the plug in the wall that Uncle Joe had found before he began his impromptu postgame shoot. I saw a look pass on Mel's face, and I thought he was rising up to kill my uncle, so I grabbed my uncle and my cousin Joey and ran them both out of the locker room. Outside,

I kissed my aunt and hugged my cousins while trying to move them deeper and deeper into the coliseum. Before I went back to the shower room, my Uncle Joe said, "I saw your father play ball for the Navy Olympic team, Pat. He was never as good as you, and that's a promise."

It was not true, but it's what my Uncle Joe said that night so long ago in Jacksonville. I am still grateful for his saying it. I went back to the locker room and heard the elephants again, and that alien sound so deep in the bowels of the coliseum did not augur well for the love life of Greg Connor.

After dressing I approached Mel who was smoking a cigarette outside the locker room. I was direct, and simply said, "Coach, a couple of the guys have dates tonight and wanted me to ask you if they could go out."

"Good," Mel said. "You asked me. Now go tell them no way in hell."

"One of them's Greg Connor, Coach," I said. "He hasn't had a date since he got to The Citadel."

"Conroy, you deaf?" Mel said, his voice rising. "How can you even think about women after losing a close game like this? You guys need rest."

"I think Greg's close to cracking, Coach," I said. "The Citadel's getting to him."

"You think I'm going to make any exceptions to the rules, Conroy?" Mel asked. "A rule's a rule for a reason."

I walked across the gym to where Karen was waiting with the other cadets and their dates. Apologizing to Karen, I told her that there was a party over at a Citadel cadet's parents' house, and that it would be easy for her to find a date for the night. A year later, I heard that Karen had met another cadet that night and that he had gotten her pregnant and abandoned her.

When I went outside in the cold, I found Greg Connor pleading his case with Mel Thompson. Coach was shaking his head and Greg was looking more and more desperate. His voice sounded whiny and reed-thin as he fought for his right to spend some time with his pretty date. It was not until the team pulled into our unspeakable motel that I learned that Greg had actually brokered a deal with Mel. Our coach allowed Greg to sit with his date, out by the drained swimming pool on broken-down pool furniture, for one hour and one hour only.

Greg and I still remember this girl's beauty. Greg remembered her kindliness for even agreeing to the ridiculous stipulations of that under-mined date. I looked out my window and saw Greg talking with great animation as this pretty young woman listened to him on a cold January night after he had just played the best basketball game of his life. At fifteen-minute intervals, Coach Ed "Little Mel" Thompson would come out to check on the two lovebirds, making sure they weren't having too much fun. The hour passed swiftly, and the pretty young woman walked out of Greg's life forever.

CHAPTER 22

# WILLIAM AND MARY

IN SECRET, I USED TO STUDY MEL THOMPSON TO SEE IF I COULD FIGURE out what made him so deeply feared and grudgingly respected by his team. From the beginning, I noted how easily Mel got along with other men, especially the sportswriters and sports information directors he met as we traveled around the league. He laughed easily and was garrulous without being coarse; his laughter rang through hallways after games when he had gathered reporters, coaches, and friends into his hotel room. Sometimes, I would eavesdrop beside a half-open door while Mel told side-splittingly funny tales of his brilliant career with the Wolfpack of North Carolina State. Relaxed among other males, Mel was a masterful host who seemed to have a real affinity for friendship. In those far-flung hotel rooms, made pungent by cigar smoke and good liquor, Mel Thompson was a different man when he was not with us.

We had a hard two-hour practice on Friday after the Jacksonville loss when William and Mary was coming into town the next day. "Hey, Mel. Give us a break. We've got to get up at reveille and march to breakfast with the Corps. How about a shoot-around on Friday?" I said to Root as we dressed for practice.

That Friday, Mel took off his whistle and took to the court among the Green Weenies. The Weenies were unbeatable by themselves, but they transformed themselves into a splendid basketball team when Mel Thompson of the Wolfpack took his formidable place at center. When I played for the Green Weenies and Coach played for my team, I looked like an All-American guard by getting him the ball every single time we came down the court.

"Catch, Coach," I would say and put a pass into his waiting hands.

He played the game like a bird of prey flying over a henhouse and he went for rebounds like it was a blood sport. When he played against the Blue Team that day, we did our best to raise our competitive fires against him. Whenever the ball went to Mel, five of us dropped off on him and DeBrosse and I hectored him like wrens tormenting a crow whenever he put the ball on the floor. Our big men fought him heroically for every rebound. Once when he went to the floor, all five of us jumped into the pileup beneath the basket. Although we played much harder when our coach scrimmaged against us, I still do not see the wisdom of having such a practice the night after we lost in Jacksonville, two hundred miles to the south.

The William and Mary Indians looked descended from a race of giants when our small lineup stood beside them with Al Kroboth jumping at center, Hooper, Bridges, and Mohr, three of the leading scorers in Citadel basketball history, with their butts planted on the bench. DeBrosse and I were accustomed to being the smallest men on the floor so it was only noteworthy when one of us was actually taller than the guy we were guarding. As usual, DeBrosse pointed to the taller guard for me to chase around and he took the smaller one for himself.

I would remember this night long and well because the pattern of the season would finally emerge for me, and my long apprenticeship as a point guard would be over at last. From the William and Mary game to my final game of the season, I had figured it out at last and, by God, I knew what I was doing and woe to the man who got in my way while I was doing it. For the first time in my career, I walked out to the basketball court brimming with confidence and a euphoria about the game. I had never dared utter these words to myself in my life, my enclosed and cutoff and malignantly apprehensive life had never once allowed me to take pleasure in whatever skills I brought to the sport of basketball. But as I stood waiting for the ref to toss the ball, the writer's voice screamed at me, "Hey, pal. Anybody noticed that you can play this fucking game? Have you noticed?"

The ball went into the air, the gifted Ron Panneton controlled the tip, and William and Mary jumped out to a 5–1 lead. Tee Hooper replaced Bill Zinsky early in the first half and our team suddenly caught fire because when Kroboth got me the ball on the wing and I took it to the other end of the court, I had DeBrosse on the left wing and the deer-like Hooper filling it on my right. It was the first time the three of us had been on the court together, and we soon discovered that we were the fastest backcourt in the Southern Conference. I played that game like there was a wind at my back. I played it reckless and proud and I drove their guards nuts trying to keep me out of the lane. They couldn't, they simply couldn't, and a great joy came upon me as I kept going by them, the flashy, cocksure, in-your-face point guard I had long dreamed of being.

Our big guys seemed lethargic on this night, but they fought hard under the boards and got the ball into my hands every time they pulled down a rebound. I would take off on the fly with the shouts of my team-mates filling the air around me, and the roar of the Corps of Cadets lift-ing beneath me like a wall of pure noise. Lord, I could feel myself that night, every cell of my body ablaze, I could feel myself borne aloft with the high-geared, game-hardened energy of my bright and powerful youth. I felt charged up and well built and unstoppable. Were the boys from William and Mary better basketball players than I was? Yes, all of them, I could have said before the start of this intensely engaged game.

But now, on this night of January 29, 1967, I wanted and demanded for those William and Mary sons-of-bitches to prove it to me. If they were better, they'd stop me. If they stopped me, I'd get the ball to one of my teammates. But not many people stopped me, and no one stopped DeBrosse or Hooper either.

That night Tee Hooper played like he was delivering fire to man-kind and his eyes revealed a kind of possession, almost an unleashed lu-nacy. It is a condition that is known in basketball circles as "being hot," point guards being the court physicians who are supposed to diagnose this febrile yet volatile condition. In our amazing sport, wild in his lean beauty, Tee slashed through the William and Mary team and hit seven straight shots. His hands were hot, and I stoked his fire by feeding him the ball.

At one point Mel left his seat as I was bringing the ball across half-court and I heard him scream at me out of pure habit, "Don't shoot, Conroy." I dribbled one more time then launched the longest jump shot of my humble-pie career as a jump shooter for The Citadel. Mel howled with frustration as the shot left my hand, but I had transformed myself into a confident young man that night, had infused my spirit with the balms that unquestioning, unhesitating assurance can bring to the heart of a player. The echo of his shouted "Don't shoot, Conroy" rang through the Armory as that shot popped through the basket thirty feet away with a sound like the net clearing its throat. The home crowd roared and the Corps rocked to their feet. Mel Thompson never told me not to shoot again. David Walker, Jack Downing, and Jim Rama were chasing me all over the court, but they were behind me much of that first half as I drove the lane again and again and led my team on fast breaks that fanned out in perfect order like they do on diagrams drawn on blackboards by famous coaches.

It was a night that John DeBrosse and I played like we had been born in the same crib together. I set picks the whole game that peeled his defender from John like a dog coming to the end of his rope. Slipping Johnny the ball, I gave him room for the one dribble I knew he had to have before he took his sweet and architecturally perfect jump shot. Unknown to either of us, John DeBrosse and I, lost in the wordless alchemy of our game's fearless chivalry, its coiled undaunted valiance, its resolute beauty, found that we trusted each other. From this game on, DeBrosse could not make a move without me knowing exactly what he was doing and why he was doing it. We had achieved congruence and we became gallant and courtly as our knowledge of each other deepened with every game. We made each other fearless, and teams began to have trouble with us, starting with William and Mary on this wondrous night that rises out of my past like a starship of hallelujahs and white light. The Bulldogs led by five at the half, and Tee and I had lit it up with fourteen points each. There had been wizardry to our guard play.

In the second half Dan Mohr finally got in the game, hit the first shot of the second half, and gave us some needed size on the inside. DeBrosse cooled off in the second half until the Bulldogs required a hero.

Back and forth we played hard against each other, and there was no question that this William and Mary team was wonderful. The teams were tied eight times, and the lead changed hands on seven occasions in the sprinting, fast-moving delight of that game. Then DeBrosse lit it up with six quick points and put in two calm free throws after he stole the ball and was hammered as he tried to lay the ball in our basket. Then the clock, which had been our enemy all year, became our friend as William and Mary tried to catch up to us in the desperate last minutes of play. DeBrosse had scored twenty-three, I had put up twenty-two, and Hooper eighteen. Forty-five points from their backcourt would put a smile on any coach's face. My Citadel team had beaten a better team than we were, and we did it going away.

I felt like a Roman candle when that buzzer went off and we had won the game, pulling away 85–77. I went into a state of exhilaration that felt like ecstasy. Before I knew what I was doing or why, I ran up into the stands where the Boo was helping his wife, Elizabeth, walk down to the floor.

"Colonel Courvoisie," I said, "could I please have an overnight leave, sir?"

The colonel looked at me then said, "Sure. You were a star tonight. You earned it, bubba."

I had rarely been called a star in my entire college basketball career, and I rewarded Colonel Nugent Courvoisie for making that statement by writing my first book about him and dedicating it to his wife.

After showering and putting on my dress grays, I walked out of Lesesne Gate and straight down to Rutledge Avenue where I turned south and walked toward the heart of the historic center on the coldest night of the year. I had no idea where I was walking or where I would spend the night. All I knew was that I could not bear the thought of returning to the barracks while feeling this elation, this sense of daring and swashbuckling bravado. I skipped and danced along the sidewalks. I sang Citadel fight songs out loud and must have appeared drunk to passersby and strangers. And it felt like intoxication—as though my heart had lit up with secret fires and my soul had fed on manna and sacred honey. I sparkled like a jewel on the ring finger of Charleston as I danced through its streets. I walked beneath the indrawn canopies of water oaks and mimosas in a city where I had not one person to visit or a home to walk into or a place to lay my head. But I could not let go of this bone-rattling optimism that had come over me since that buzzer sounded. I wanted to luxuriate in the waters of pure and free-floating human joy.

In the hushed streets near the College of Charleston I said in a whisper, "I'm going to write about you, Charleston. Listen to me. I'm going to write about you and you're going to like what I say. You are so beautiful. You're so beautiful. Thank you, Charleston. Thank you so much for being so beautiful."

I found myself at the ticket counter asking the clerk when the next bus to Beaufort was. He told me it left in a couple of minutes. I bought a ticket and discovered it was near midnight. In a reverie, I rode that bus through darkness toward the town of Beaufort, the town that found me when I was fifteen years old and graciously let itself become my home. I wanted to tell my hometown that I was a college basketball star, at last.

At two in the morning, I walked down Boundary Street to Carteret. It was close to freezing as I watched the moon fingerpaint the Beaufort River with a long ribbon of silver. I was freezing and could not have cared less. I made the sign of the cross when passing by St. Peter's Catholic Church and picked up the pace as I crossed Bay Street and skipped on to the Lady's Island Bridge. I passed no cars and encountered no pedestrians. I was singing a Citadel fight song as loudly as I could when a voice rang out above me.

"Are you drunk, son?" the bridge tender demanded.

I laughed and said, "No, sir. I'm happy. I scored twenty-two points against William and Mary tonight. I was terrific. I was just terrific."

I had never said anything like that in my entire life, and the words surprised me. Then I said something to the poor man that embarrassed me then and embarrasses me now. I said, "Sir, I'm going to put you into a book one day."

He looked at me as though I had lost my mind. "You better get on home, boy."

"I'm going to put you in a book," I repeated. In 1995, I made good on that pledge when I placed a bridge tender in a scene in *Beach Music*.

I was walking toward the house of W. B. "King Tut" and Sarah Ellen Harper on Sunset Bluff. I did not want the evening to end just yet. I needed time to memorize what happiness felt like because I had experienced so little of it. Looking up into the night sky, I saw the Milky Way. I instantly thought of God and how I was afraid I was losing my faith in Him and the immensity of the fear and cowardice I felt when I thought of facing the world without Him. I was receiving the Eucharist every day of my life and fighting this war with faithlessness with every cell of my body, but I could feel the withdrawal taking place without my consent.

On the causeway to Lady's Island I prayed out loud, "O Lord. Please hear me. I thank you for this year. I thank you from my heart. I needed to be a decent basketball player in college, Lord. I don't know why. But I needed it. We both know I'm no good, but we sure are fooling some people. Aren't we, Lord? I'm sorry about Tee Hooper and I'm sorry about the Green Weenies. They're great guys and they deserve more playing time, Lord. Thank you for tonight. Thank you for giving me the William and Mary game, Lord. Thank you for the river and the stars and every house in Beaufort. . . ."

I prayed my way to the Harper house on Sunset Bluff and found the key they hid on the porch in case I came in unexpectedly. King Tut and Sarah Ellen Harper, parents of my best friend in high school in Beaufort, loved me fiercely as a son in the years I needed it most. When I awoke the next morning, I could smell coffee and bacon cooking in the kitchen downstairs. I went down to the kitchen and shouted, "Good morning, Maw. Good morning, Paw," my nicknames for each of them.

Sarah Ellen ran to me squealing and hugged me hard. "It's not every day we get to have a college basketball star stay in our house."

Paw Harper looked up from his morning paper. "You showed William and Mary a thing or two last night."

I glowed from their love of me and their great, unstriking generosity to my boyhood. That May they presented me with a graduation present Sarah Ellen had bought at the bookshop on Bay Street. It was a Roget's thesaurus, and it sits by my left elbow as I write these words. Here is the inscription written in Sarah Ellen's distinct script: "For Patrick, Our budding young author, with best wishes for great success, and much love. Maw, Paw, and Bruce Harper."

Each morning, before I work, I read those sweet words. They give me courage.


LESS THAN A MONTH LATER William and Mary would dismantle my team when we met them at their diminutive and claustrophobic home court in Blow Gym. It was the worst place to play basketball in America and I felt like someone had put me in a straitjacket every time I went there. Because my father had once played at Blow Gym for the Marines at Quantico, he and the family were coming down for the game. Against a fierce zone I put in two of the longest jump shots I had ever taken as a college guard to open the game. Then I saw my family enter the gymnasium late just after that second shot went in. Something bruised my spirit when I realized I had taken those shots because I wanted my family to see the kind of player I had become and they had missed the display's initial fanfare. The headline in the *News and Courier* said, "William and Mary Bombs Cadets 91–57." I have never played on a team anywhere that got beaten worse than we did. I hate writing a single thing about it or remembering that chickenhearted game at all. It made me sick to my stomach to watch my father's snide face as my team got taken apart. Kroboth had fourteen, I had eleven, and no one else even came close to scoring in double figures.

Again, my father called me out of a cringing, silent locker room. Again he put his hand on my chest and pushed me back against the wall. No handshake or "How you doing, son, it's great to see you," from the Colonel.

My father looked at me with pure, undistilled hatred which I do not understand to this day. "I just wanted to tell you that you were shit. You were pure shit."

"I agree with you a hundred percent, sir." Despite agreeing with him, I did not know I was angry until I heard my voice.

"Your team is shit," my father said.

"They sure were tonight, sir."

"Your coach is shit," Dad said.

"He didn't get much help tonight from his players, sir," I said. "Can I go say hey to Mom and the kids, sir?"

"Negative. We got to get back to D.C.," he said, then turned his back and walked away from me.

Then the voice, the one I had been hearing at times during the year, the writer's voice, the one born during this season, this year—it spoke aloud for the first time and for the first time I knew it was my voice and mine to keep and to use and to wield in any way I so chose.

It said—I said, "Hey, Dad?"

My father turned and looked back at me.

"When I get home for Easter, let's go to the gym at Quantico."

"Why?"

"I want to play one-on-one with you."

"Why? Think you could take me?"

"No, Dad. You don't understand. I'm not only going to take you, I'm not going to let you score. Every time you put the ball on the floor I'm going to take it away from you, every single time."

My father stared at me and I stared back. I think I was born into the world again and given back to myself at that very moment.

Easter came and went that glorious year and never once did my father mention the gym at Quantico.

# V M I

B EFORE THE ROAD TRIP TO PLAY VMI IN LEXINGTON, VIRGINIA, RAT
came up to me in the mess hall at the noon meal and whispered,
"Mel wants to see you at 1500 hours in his office, Pat."

This was never good news. I avoided even accidental encounters
with my coach with the instincts of a cat burglar. Not once in my four-
year basketball career had I walked through the front door of the
Armory which led me directly past Mel's office. In my sophomore and
junior years, I received not a single summons for an audience with my
coach, but in the midst of this season, Mel would periodically require my
thoughts on the gradual dissolution of what we both thought had the
makings of a good basketball team. I feared setting off his hair-trigger
temper, and I also dreaded making some unforeseen mistake of judgment that would bring him out of his chair, screaming in anger.

"Hey, Mrs. Johnson," I said to his pretty secretary, "I hear Attila the
Hun wants to see me."

"Hush," she said, putting her finger to her lips. "He'll hear you."

I opened his door and came upon the familiar scene of Mel discussing basketball with Ed "Little Mel" Thompson. Motioning me to sit
down on the couch, Mel finished his story, and I could not help but notice how much Ed hero-worshiped the head coach. Again I could study
what a good guy Mel could be if you were lucky enough not to play on
his team.

Finally, he turned his attention to me, his unnamed captain. He
fixed me with his Ahab-like gaze for a moment before surprising me by
asking, "You think you're a pretty smart guy, don't you, Conroy?"

I did not answer at first, but thought he was still boiling over the fact that more than half his team had been on the dean's list and that a couple of us had made Gold Stars.

"About average, Coach," I answered.

Mel looked over at Ed and snickered. "He thinks he's fooling us. We're your coaches. We know a lot more about this team than you'd expect. As a ballplayer one of your faults is that you think too much out on the court. An athlete reacts. They don't think. All instinct. Get it?"

"Yes, sir," I said.

"He said he gets it, Ed," Mel said to his assistant. "Do you think he gets it?"

"I'm not sure he gets it," Ed said sadly.

"Do you remember the short story you wrote about me in *The Shako*, Conroy? Remember how mad I was? I called you into this office and ripped you a new asshole. Right?"

"Coach, I told you then and I tell you now. That wasn't you. I made that guy up."

In the previous issue of *The Shako*, I had published my third short story written during my time as a cadet. The previous summer I had come under the touchstone influence of a young novelist named John Updike when my mother handed me a copy of *Rabbit, Run*. Until I read about Rabbit Angstrom, I did not know that basketball could make a guest appearance into the palace of fiction. Nor did I know that my sport could also take a shy bow among the backlit colonnades of poetry until I tracked down Mr. Updike's wonderful poem "Ex Basketball Player."

Under Updike's powerful sway, I wrote the best poem and the best story of my Citadel career. The poem was called "Ted Lucas," and I can detect in that splintery stack of words a hint of the melody that would later come. In the short story "The Legend," I actually see the starting point of my life as a fiction writer. A great high school basketball player, Jimmy Amansky, plays his last high school basketball game and performs heroically in the championship game, then finds, to his horror, the long and ruthless stretch of time laid out before him when he has done not a thing to prepare himself for a job or a career. Both my short story and poem are unartful homages to the hold that Mr. Updike's poem "Ex Basketball Player" had on my imagination. But it had unhinged Mel when he read the short story and he screamed at me for several minutes for holding him up to such ridicule on campus. My writing career has proven to be riddled with such encounters with people wounded by the malice of my portraiture. I had conjured up Mel Thompson when I sat down to imagine the story of young Jimmy Amansky. Mel seemed to have lost part of himself when he lost the game of basketball as a player. I could tell that he thought coaching was a second-string way of staying close to the game.

"Slim Coach Jim. A three-hundred-pounder. Laughed at by his players. Your way of letting me know I'd put on a few pounds," Mel said.

"Coach, listen to me. That coach wasn't you. I based him on a guy who coached me in youth league."

"Bullshit, Conroy. You think you're the only smart guy who puts his pants on in this Armory? That was me. You just don't have the guts to admit it."

"Coach, I didn't think of you once when I wrote about the coach in that story," I said.

"That's crap, but it's okay. I want to make a point with you. Have I held that story against you?"

"There was no reason for you to," I said.

"Follow me on this one. Just a little way, Pat."

"Okay. No, sir, you've not held it against me."

"Do you know why?" he said.

"No, sir."

"Do you know who William James is?" Mel asked.

"He's the brother of Henry James," I said.

"Who the fuck's Henry James?" Mel asked angrily.

"He's a writer, Coach."

"Who gives a shit?"

"Yes, sir. I know who William James is," I said.

"See?" Mel looked over at Ed. "I told you he was a smart guy. You find a player's interest, Ed, and you work those angles. William James is the father of pragmatism." Mel stared at me again. "I'm a pragmatist, Conroy. Do you understand? I have recently become a pragmatist by reading William James." He said this in the same tone of voice he would've used while informing me that he had become a Presbyterian or a chiropractor. "Do you know what a pragmatist is?"

"I think so, Coach. Isn't it a guy that figures out the easiest, most ba-sic way to solve problems, something like that."

"Bingo." Mel nodded happily. "You get to know your kids, Ed. Get to know what makes them tick. Then you do your own problem solving."

I felt like a lab rat but then Mel turned to me and said, "Even though you fucked me with that short story, Conroy, I chose to ignore it. If I let that bother me, it would only hurt the team. But I'm a pragmatist, Pat. I'm reading a book on pragmatism right now. What do you think of that?"

"That's nice, Coach," I said.

"Go get dressed for practice," he said. "And Conroy? You ever write about me again, I'll kick your ass."

Odd encounters with Mel were the stuff of legend in the locker room. Our beleaguered and tormented center, Dan Mohr, carried with him a memory of his most harrowing collision with Mel in his dreaded office. Mel's incessant belittling of Root remains an agonizing memory for all his teammates, occurring with such frequency that it is simply part of the team memory of that year. It is most especially remembered by the aggrieved Dan Mohr himself whose memory about this year proved both encyclopedic and precise.

Dan believes he received a summons to report to Mel's office on the exact same afternoon as I learned that Mel Thompson had embraced the philosophy of pragmatism, and he has some convincing proof of this. With some frequency, Mel would require an explanation from our returning leading scorer about the disintegration of our season. When Dan entered the room, Mel immediately went after him with the curious Ed Thompson getting a much harsher lesson in the shaping of a college basketball player than he had with me earlier.

"Mohr, I want you to explain to me why we can't seem to get any senior leadership out of you and Conroy," Mel said, catching Danny off guard and ill-prepared so that Danny made his first mistake.

"I think the leadership on any team has to come from the guards. At least that's how it's been on every team I've ever played on."

"That's where you're wrong, Mohr. What a dumbo thought! Leadership always comes from the big men on a team. At NC State, I provided the leadership on the floor and the locker room. You earn the respect on the court. You fight for every rebound, you dive for every loose ball. People look up to you because you lay it on the line every single play. Big men rule this game. Understand that, Mohr? Tell me if you consider yourself a leader."

Then Root made a real tactical error when he said, "Well, Coach, when you didn't name Conroy or me captains this year, it was a slap in the face in front of our teammates. It's hard to be a leader when your own coach doesn't believe in you."

I think my childhood prepared me to deal with the complexities of Mel Thompson's mood swings a bit more adequately than Dan's achingly sweet set of parents up in Carolina Beach. As Root recalled the moment in his den years later, he said, "Mel went apeshit, Conroy. Out of his mind apeshit. I'd seen him mad before, but nothing like this. He came around his desk and bent his face down where I was sitting on that cheap couch of his, his face an inch from mine. You know how he loved to intimidate people. He was screaming at the top of his lungs, then he started hissing at me. He said, 'Mohr, none of your teammates have an ounce of respect for you. None of your coaches do. The cadets don't respect you. The fans don't. Doesn't that bother you, Mohr? You know why it doesn't bother you, Mohr? You're soft all over. You don't have the guts your team is looking for. You don't got the fighting spirit where you leave it all out there on the court—your blood—your guts—your heart. No, Mohr. You're a pussy and a weakling on the boards. You let smaller guys eat your jock every day at practice. They eat your lunch. They steal your candy because they know you're gutless, Mohr. You ain't got it where it counts. In the gut. In the heart. They know you'll back off when the going gets rough.' "

Dan told me this in his Greensboro home, mimicking Mel's voice. When he paused I said, "Yep, that's the Dan Mohr I knew."

"Kiss my ass, Conroy," Dan laughed. "It gets worse. Mel pulls me off the couch and backs me into a corner near his desk. Then Muleface sticks out his chin at me with Little Mel looking on, and he says, 'Punch me in the face, Mohr. Hit my goddamn jaw, Mohr. I want to see if you're a man or the pussy I believe you are. I'm giving you the chance to break my jaw. A free sucker punch to see if you've got any fight in you at all. To see if there's anything left to your manhood, your balls, your pride. You got anything left, Mohr? I'm challenging your fucking manhood right here in my office and you're not taking a swing. Do something, Mohr. Do anything. Show me you got something, anything, between your legs.' "

"Why didn't you punch his lights out, Root?" I asked, incredulous at the story.

"I thought about it, Conroy. But all I could see were headlines: Dan Mohr Kills His Coach in Office Brawl. Dan Mohr Arrested for Murder in First Battalion. Dan Mohr Named Captain of Prison Basketball Team. Mohr Named to Convict All-Stars. Prosecutor Asks for Mohr's Death. They kept going through my head, Conroy. I also thought if I hit him I'd lose my scholarship for sure. Finally I said, 'I'm not going to hit you, Coach.' Of course, that drove him nuts and he cussed me out for another minute. Same stuff. Pussy. No leadership. Didn't have the guts of a hamster. Mel-odrama. Pure Mel-odrama. The whole year was a nightmare."

OF ALL THE SCHOOLS IN THE Southern Conference, a conference in which I take a fierce and partisan pride, there was no team I would rather play against than the Keydets of Virginia Military Institute. The campus itself formed an austere grotto of spartan military life in the pretty town of Lexington, Virginia. It was a sadist who placed the handsome, many-columned Washington and Lee, low-crawling with pampered frat boys, adjacent to VMI itself. I found the architecture at VMI to be so melancholic and bleak that it made The Citadel's Moor-inspired buildings appear positively sunny in comparison. While I was walking with a VMI senior one Sunday morning in my sophomore year, a still-drunken SAE frat man from Washington and Lee waved a pair of girls' panties at us from a second-story window as we passed below in our uniforms.

"This is torture," I said to the senior.

"It makes us stronger," the senior stoically replied.

In fact VMI always struck me as a far weirder, eerier military college than The Citadel ever could be. I attributed this to its cutoff sense of displacement and isolation. The jocks of VMI had to endure the great scorn of their corps the same as we did. Jocks are second-class citizens in every military college in this country and in a secret, wordless accordance we acknowledged our aggrieved station in the chain of command by playing our best games against each other for the honor of our schools. Their Rat Line met our Fourth Class system head-on, and we paid homage to each other by raising the level of our games to the highest pitch. The VMI team we had come to play on February 4, 1967, was a team with some shortcomings and insufficiencies, but VMI's fighting spirit could even the playing field.

On the flight to Richmond, my sulky, looming fate received an invisible shiver when Jessica Lynn Jones was born in a military hospital in Kingsville, Texas, to J. W. Jones and his wife, Barbara, neither of whom had the slightest knowledge that our lives had inextricably intertwined with Jessica's birth. Since I was dating no one at the time, it would have surprised me to learn that my first adopted child was nursing at her mother's breast in Texas while I was airborne over Virginia. My flight was uneventful, but Captain J. W. Jones III would take a more meaningful one the following year when he was shot down while providing close air support for a group of beleaguered Marines in the Republic of Vietnam. The year after that, I would marry his widow and adopt the two children he left behind in his short, courageous life. Fate hides in veils and approaches from behind with cards marked and chess pieces disfigured. You never know when a door you left unlocked will usher in a lost exterminator, a deposed queen, or the love of your life. As I write these words my thirty-four-year-old daughter, Jessica, is swimming on the beach of my island home with my seven-year-old granddaughter, Elise, all of us bound when my fate, a work in torturous process, received an imperceptible notch, a marking of inevitability and mystery that makes me believe in both magic and the hand of God.

The Citadel and VMI teams shared more in common than bad military haircuts. All twenty-four players were enrolled in ROTC programs, all could execute an about-face, clean a rifle, perform the manual of arms with precision, spit-shine a shoe to perfection, have an intimate relationship with Brasso—we shared the arcane language of cross webbings, shakos, cartridge boxes, and waist belts. We could speak fluently about four-inch intervals, thirty-inch paces, and a $\frac{9}{16}$ arm swing, all the numerals of regimentation and the divine, obsessional symmetry so cherished by the military. In many ways both deep and surprising, we stood as mirror images to each other.

As I stood at the entrance of the Pit's (VMI field house) seedy visiting-team locker room, I looked back at my teammates lined up behind me and screamed, "Let's show these guys how a real military school plays basketball." With the roars of my teammates behind me, I led the Citadel Bulldogs into a firestorm of boos. While we were playing VMI, the venom of their corps was so toxic it felt like a form of praise. They rained down a steady flood of catcalls as Mohr dunked it home. We knew VMI had entered the arena when the cheering became deafening. Steve Powers led the Keydets out on the court and dunked the ball with authority.

Secretly, I waved to Ralph Wright, Johnny Guyton, and John Mitchell, who had all been fellow counselors at Camp Wahoo the summer before. I had liked all three immensely. Mitchell possessed a pretty, textbook jump shot, and Wright was built like a weight lifter and was a man to be reckoned with under the boards, even among the visiting pros who used to drop in at Camp Wahoo. Coming back from a layup, I actually broke off from my team and ran over to shake hands with Gary McPherson, the coach who had worked with me at Camp Wahoo on my jump shot.

"Hey, Coach, how you doing?" I said. "It's wonderful to see you."

"Hey, Pat," Coach McPherson said. Then Coach Gary stunned me by hugging me before the disapproving gaze of Mel Thompson. "Don't you and Mohr kill me tonight, Pat."

"We're throwing the game for you, Coach. We think that much of you," I answered before rejoining the layup line.

"What was that all about, Conroy?" Mel growled.

"We got close at Wahoo, Coach," I said.

"So what?" he said.

BENEATH THE LIGHTS OF VMI and the stormy velocity of an aroused enemy corps, a fast-talking young referee named Lou Bello threw up the ball. The Citadel basketball team got after the VMI team and by God, they got after us. We gave everyone in that gym a night to remember. The noise in the gym was oceanic. Kroboth had started for Mohr and was battling the powerful and accomplished Steve Powers who was the third leading rebounder in the nation at that time, one notch above the sublime Lew Alcindor of UCLA. He and Wright brought immense intensity to the art of rebounding, but my guys held their own under the boards. This game marked a coming-out for Al Kroboth, the real beginning of his greatness as a Citadel basketball player. Early in the game, he lost Powers after Bridges missed a jump shot and went under the basket to tip it up from behind on the other side of the hoop, a move so beautiful and unexpected that he received a be-grudging cheer from the Keydets. Zinsky and Wright fought over the ball like tigers mauling the carcass of a fallen deer. It was basketball played at its highest level, and we fought each other with all the frantic joy you bring to a rival you respect. I found I loved playing in front of a corps who hated me. I grew flashy as the Keydets grew hostile to me and my team. When they booed me for dribbling behind my back, I dribbled through my legs when I changed direction on Peyton Brown the next time down the court. I blossomed when the jeers and hoots were rained down on me personally. I bathed in the contempt of that bawdy, raucous crowd. I strutted, I roostered all over that court, cocky and in charge, knowing what to do and when to do it, posturing and urging my team-mates to be more than themselves, to turn themselves into heroes for a night, resistance fighters caught in the teeth of the enemy, and cornered champions who wore our college's name on our chest and needed to prove ourselves worthy of that extraordinary honor. I did not want to be beaten by my college's greatest rival on their home court. I did not want to see a smile on a single VMI Keydet's face when that game ended. When the Keydets booed me after I drove the lane and put up a layup while being fouled by Wright, I swaggered toward the heart of their corps, and my eyes said, "Kiss my ass, VMI. Don't fuck with this Citadel point guard. It ain't smart." Then I scooted back to the line and made it a three-point play.

It was in the middle of this fierce and hard-fought game that I again realized that DeBrosse and I were suddenly becoming a big problem for the other teams in our league. Since our polar opposite skills had begun to merge fluidly, we were driving other guards crazy. I heard Peyton Brown, a VMI guard, yelling at John Mitchell after I set a pick for DeBrosse that hurt Peyton and embarrassed him at the same time. Mel taught us how to set a pick right, and we were locked and loaded when the defensive man plowed into us. Brown had not seen the play coming, and he hit a wall when his shoulder crashed into me but it was Peyton who went down. DeBrosse was by himself when he swished a jumper from the top of the key.

"Give me a little help, Johnny," I heard Brown tell the milder-mannered Mitchell.

A telepathy of immense subtlety was still at play between John DeBrosse and myself. I could look at John on the court, just look, and he would know what I wanted him to do. I would dribble toward him to my left and he would swing wide as if to go around me, then suddenly, John would change his angle of attack and bring his defensive man closer to me. In a well-tuned and well-executed maneuver, I would stop suddenly and pivot on my left foot swinging my body completely around—my back both to DeBrosse and his defender Brown. DeBrosse's shoulder and body would pass by mine with millimeters between us, and his defensive man would crash into my back and buttocks. This move in the modern vernacular is called a moving pick or screen and is not legal. Guys like me and DeBrosse made it illegal, and we could run it as well as any two basketball players alive that day. I would hand the ball off to John like a quarterback handing off to a halfback on an off-tackle slant. He would dribble once, then put it up with one of the prettiest jump shots in the American South.

An anonymous VMI sportswriter wrote in their newpaper that "Citadel guards Pat Conroy and John DeBrosse dazzled the Keydets with their fantastic drives and amazing jumpshots." Quite possibly, this is my favorite sentence ever written in the English language.

The Keydets booed us lustily as we left the court at halftime with us leading 38–31. Things were breaking our way; Mel was happy with the way we were playing because his screaming at us at halftime seemed more rote and underfed than usual. Looking around at my teammates, I noticed that Root was still wearing his warmups. Mel had not even put Danny into the game, an oversight so obvious that Wright and Powers came over to Danny right before the start of the second half to ask him if he was hurt.

The game stayed fast-moving, and we ran along the surge of the VMI corps' urgent tidal roar. When VMI scored, the earth would move with their corps' saber-rattling applause. They spoke in one thunderous voice, then quieted when Zinsky put in a jumper and Bridges followed with one of his own.

VMI made two strong runs at us in the second half, pulling about even with us after we built a ten-point lead. We finally worked back to another ten-point lead with 3:58 left when I scored on a drive to make it 68–58.

The VMI team asserted itself and came for our throats. They fought us and hounded us and scrapped us all over that basketball court. Exhausted, Powers and Wright and Denny Clark fought our big men for everything that went up on the boards, and I found myself in a pileup with Mitchell and Brown when a ball skittered across the court and was heading out of bounds. We grunted and snorted and made inhuman sounds as we fought each other because our schools instilled a fighting spirit in our bloodstreams. It was the pledge and anthem and benchmark of all the men who wore the rings of these two singular colleges. The gym was a vessel of tumult and pandemonium. VMI's corps clamored like some terrible new beast set loose on the world, vociferous, jungly, and magnificent. The VMI players lifted their game to be worthy of such praise and they closed it to two when Steve Powers scored to make it 68–66 with 1:16 left in the game.

Then John DeBrosse showed why he is still remembered as one of the best guards to ever suit up for the Citadel Bulldogs. He took over the game for us and in a gymnasium turned to uproar and bedlam, he drove the ball down the length of the court, saw an opening, and made a jump shot from the top of the key. It takes the courage of a special kind of player to shoot a jump shot under those conditions with a corps of Keydets screaming for you to miss. The headline in the next day's *News and Courier* said, "John DeBrosse lifts Bulldogs over VMI."

The reporter wrote, "Denny Clark matched DeBrosse's shot for VMI after Pat Conroy had made a free throw to give The Citadel a 71–68 lead. DeBrosse clinched it with a pair of free throws on a one-and-one situation with six seconds left.

"Al Kroboth and Pat Conroy shared scoring honors for the night with 17 points a piece for The Citadel with DeBrosse collecting 16 and Doug Bridges 11. Top Scorer for the night, however, was Ralph Wright of VMI who had 24."

Before I followed my teammates into the locker room, I took a delicious moment watching the corps of Keydets filing out of the gym to walk back to the barracks. It pleased me that I could not find one of them who was smiling. I ran to find Coach Gary McPherson.

"You call that throwing a game, Pat? What a great game for everyone. But we're going to get you when we come to Charleston."

"We'll be waiting for you, Coach," I said. "Tell your team they were wonderful."

Before I got on the team bus, Rat stopped me and whispered, "Root didn't even get in the game. Can you believe it?"

On the bus, I saw Root sitting in the very back by himself. I took a seat near him and tried to think of something to say. Dan Mohr had been a star to me since I saw him at our first practice during our plebe year. He possessed the prettiest turnaround jumper I had ever seen on a big man and I still have not met the man I thought could keep Dan from scoring during a basketball game. Though not a good leaper, he had long arms and massive hands, and I saw him score at will on Lenny Chappell of the NBA during a counselors game at Camp Wahoo. Root should have averaged twenty points per game his senior year, but something had gone fundamentally and terribly wrong with his season even though he was still averaging a respectable fourteen a game. When the basketball issue of *Dell Sports*, the bible of basketball reporting at that time, issued their annual scouting reports, they listed thirty-three guys as the leading players in the South. These included Clem Haskins of Eastern Kentucky; Louie Dampier and Pat Riley of Kentucky; Bob Lewis and Larry Miller of North Carolina; Jay McMillen of Maryland; and the boy sitting beside me on that bus outside the VMI field house, Danny Mohr. Dan Mohr, who had already received a letter of inquiry from the Denver Nuggets, had finally met the center who could keep him from scoring. His name was Mel Thompson.

# FOUR OVERTIMES

THEN THERE WAS THE GAME OF ALL GAMES ON THE NIGHT OF ALL nights in the waning hours of the longest season in the last year I would ever call myself a cadet. VMI came to Charleston to try to beat us on our home court to pay us back for embarrassing them in Lexington. Because we had beaten them at VMI, I gave them very little chance of handling us with the whole cold-blooded fury of our corps behind us. Our house was tough on visiting teams, but our house was hell on VMI. There was no such thing as a bad game when the only two military schools in the South got together. But on February 13, 1967, I played in one of the most exciting basketball games I'd ever seen. I watched the boys on both teams honor the character and nature of their schools by playing a game that glitters in remembrance.

I have written about the second VMI game in Charleston in what I call the basketball chapter of *The Lords of Discipline*. Yet on a return visit to my twenty-year-old novel, I discovered that I combined two games of my Citadel career to craft the single basketball game I shoehorned into the plot of the novel about my college. As I reread the chapter for the first time since the book came out, I kept stumbling across the half-hidden skeletal remains of the final game of my career when I faced the indomitable Johnny Moates for the last time. In the fictional version, I called my nemesis Jimmy Mance, and I placed him in the position of an All-American shooting guard for VMI. Fact and fiction have been engaged in an abnormal and fanciful dance since I first began my writing career. There are lost geographies in my psyche because I fictionalize events stolen from my actual life. The fictions have caused the actual memories to melt like icebergs that have drifted into the temperate water of the Gulf Stream. My made-up doubles and stand-ins and understudies, from Ben Meecham to Will McLean to Tom Wingo to Jack McCall, have stolen all my stories and taken all my wives and girlfriends and hijacked a trainful of all my friends and tampered with and whittled away at and changed the punch lines of my brightest bumpercrop of stories.

When I tell you about the single greatest game I ever saw played at the Armory, I find the character of Will McLean—the protagonist of *The Lords of Discipline* and a boy that I created with a fountain pen while sitting at a desk—standing at the door of the locker room, dressed for the game, ready to lead his Bulldogs out to the lights and the feral hum of the Corps. I finish tying my Chuck Taylor Converse All Stars, the '57 Chevy of basketball shoes, and I approach my changeling who stood in for me when I wrote about my tortured and deeply lived-in time as a cadet. The kid was fired up and ready to go and there was both resolve and a blaze in his eyes.

"Will," I said. "Will McLean."

He met me with a ready, half-amused gaze, then said, "You Coach's father? How'd you get in the locker room?"

"I'm your father, Will. I created you out of words. I made you up."

He considered this, then said, "If you made me up, then why am I standing here? Why am I talking to you? Listen to the band out there. I saw the bus drop the VMI players off. They're getting dressed over in the visiting team room. Coach Bynum gave us the pep talk. I'm guarding Jimmy Mance, and I've got to think about the game. It's my last game. It's important to me."

"Coach Bynum doesn't exist. I made him up, too. I based him on my coach, Mel Thompson, but he softened as I wrote about him, became much nicer and more sympathetic than Mel."

"My teammates are counting on me," Will says. "I can't let them down. My school is counting on me. I won't let her down."

"I've got to sub for you tonight, Will."

He looked at me with contempt. "You're an old man. You can't play this game. You'd make a mockery of it."

"I'm not going to play it," I say. "I'm too old for that. But I'm going to try to remember it accurately. You'll get in my way, Will."

Will McLean nodded his head slowly and I struck him as mute as Lot's wife. His blood began to ice up and his liver convulsed when the heart began to slow and the eyes filmed over with the inconsequence and irresponsibility of fiction. I began to erase Will McLean from the world, then thought better of it. I restored the boy to his shining, radiant young manhood again. "I've got to rescue this VMI game from you and your teammates, Will," I say.

"Thanks for thinking of my teammates. Do they get benched, too?" he says.

"No, Reuben Clapsaddle is Dan Mohr. Johnny Debruhl is actually Johnny DeBrosse," I answered. "Doug Cummings is Doug Bridges. Dave Dunbar stands in for Dave Bornhorst. But I have to take your team back, Will. I've got to make it my own again."

Will McLean threw the basketball to my suddenly twenty-one-year-old self and looked back into the locker room where my teammates were dressing for the game.

"I'm trying to find out who I was back then," I say. "I was something like you, Will. But not completely. I really like you, Will McLean. I liked you best of all."

"Why didn't you make me happier?" he says. "Why didn't you let me stay with Annie Kate? Why did you kill Pig Pignetti?"

"Annie Kate led a very happy life, Will," I say. "I keep in touch with her. Pig's great, too."

"Did you, Pat? Did you live a very happy life?"

"No. It didn't happen for me."

"I'm sorry," Will says, looking around. "It's odd being fictional."

"No odder than being real," I answer and watch as Will McLean walks out into the Armory and disappears into the light.

I returned to my teammates to finish dressing when Dave Bornhorst, dressed only in his jockstrap and Converse All Stars, rose suddenly by his locker and cried out, "Hey, guys, I forgot to tell you. I got me a date for this Saturday night. And you guys are going to turn green with envy when I tell you what her hobby is."

"I bet she's a hooker," Bob Cauthen said.

"Wrong, Zipper," Barney said.

"Don't rain on Barney's parade," the Bean said. "This is his first college date."

"Close," Barney said. "Any other guesses?"

"General Harris's dog?" Kroboth asked.

"No, my horny teammates. Ole Barney's got himself a date with a Greek belly dancer. Can you imagine it? Can you imagine what it would be like to make love to a real live Greek belly dancer?"

As he spoke these words, Dave Bornhorst, Catholic boy out of Piqua, Ohio, engaged in the lewdest, bawdiest, and most obscene dance I had ever witnessed. As he thrust his pelvis back and forth, looking like a warmup act at a strip show, Dave moved across the cement floor up and down the row of lockers, his head thrown back in ecstasy and moaning like a dog in heat. His teammates began clapping and cheering in time with the orgiastic thrusts of his groin.

Our locker room was a happier place after Dave started dating Maria Kirlis, and we hungered for the stories of this hilarious and sexy girl. Dave and Maria were married on June 14, 1970. They recently celebrated their thirtieth anniversary.

That night it relieved me when I saw Mel write Danny Mohr's name on the blackboard as the starting center. In four straight games, Mohr had ridden the bench, and it had not strengthened our team at all. I still believe the benching had more to do with malice than strategy.

Before I led my team out on the court I did what I always did that year, I lifted the Wilson Special I held in my hands and put it up to my face to inhale its delicious odor. The smell was the sacred fragrance of my boyhood, the distilled essence of the thing that made me most happy when I was growing up.

"Get 'em, Pat," Rat said as he flung the door open. I felt Rat's hand slap me on the ass as he did to begin every game, and I led the Citadel Bulldogs into the thunderous greetings of the Corps of Cadets and the rollicking, rip-roaring performance of "Dixie" by the Citadel band. I took enormous pride in being named the team captain against VMI, being the one boy at The Citadel named to lead his team against the school where Stonewall Jackson once taught and whose Keydets once answered the call of their Confederate nation by putting down their books and marching off to war at the Battle of New Market.

As in every game we played against VMI, the Keydets came at us hard and fast from the opening tip-off. DeBrosse told me to guard Jim Kemper because Kemper was that rarest of guards we faced that season, he was quick as we were and an inch smaller than us at five nine. He had a pretty jump shot and Ralph Wright set bone-jarring picks for him during the whole game. But under the boards, the play was fierce and merciless. Steve Powers was a relentlessly persevering rebounder, but Root was fighting him hard and Kroboth was hanging tough against Wright.

Then a guy I had not paid much attention to in the first VMI game, the forward Denny Clark, started playing like an All-American. Clark was ubiquitous on offense and defense and he hit the boards as hard as his two teammates, Wright and Powers, and would light up the scoreboard with twenty-four points that night. There were very few teams in the country who could outrebound a Mel Thompson–coached team. But on this night, VMI fought our big men for every shot taken. VMI was magnificent but so were we. And the Corps, my God, the Corps.

There were times when the Corps could rise up in one cyclonic voice of such partisanship that it made you feel that you could take on the Bruins of UCLA and throw Lew Alcindor's head into the crowd as a token of your affection. The Corps could reach a fever pitch of perfect hatred in a heartbeat and there was a volcanic immensity to its voice that gave us courage and VMI pause. Its voice passed through us and washed over us and lifted us in the sheer integrity of its standing shoulder to shoulder with us.

Each time Zinsky or Kroboth hauled down a rebound, the Corps would bless them with its bone-chilling roar. Whenever I would break past Mitchell and pass it to Mohr when Powers came out to deck me, the Corps would scream for both the assist and the basket. When I would set a pick for Kemper and slide the ball to DeBrosse who would take his single dribble then go up with his glorious jump shot, the Corps would will the shot in, ride it home on pillars of unimaginable noise and air.

I saw DeBrosse intercept a pass for Kemper and John saw me break downcourt. He threw me a perfect pass that I caught on the full run over my shoulder like the tight end I was in high school. I saw the Green Weenies leap from their seats screaming out my name, and I knew that no one in the world loved me like the Green Weenies did. But it was the Corps that saw me break and rose as one to fly down that court with me. I ran straight at the heart of the Corps, toward the indefectible pride of their affirmation, their violent, bestial love of teams that wear their colors and bear their name. I wore the name The Citadel on my chest, and I blazed with the pride of my school as I put a layup in that brought the Corps to its feet.

We led VMI by five at the half.

But VMI came out ready to hunt for lions in the second half and the

VMI team that the Institute put on the court that night was worthy of everything their college stood for. We would go up by six, then VMI would fight back to take the lead by one. The score changed hands a dozen times. Though we led by six with two minutes left to play, Denny Clark hit a spectacular jump shot and was fouled by Bridges. His three-point play narrowed our lead by three with 1:08 left in the second.

Al Kroboth tied the score at 63 all when he made the first of two free throws with 1:01 remaining. Then both teams missed a shot to send the game into overtime. As I went to the bench, our manager, Al Beiner, gave me a Coke and I drained it and asked for another. Exhausted, I looked down the bench and could see that the big guys had really taken a beating.

Johnny popped me on the fanny as we waited for Root to jump with Powers.

VMI controlled the tip and Jim Kemper put a terrific move on me and hit a jumper during their first possession of the overtime. Kemper put the same move on me his second trip down the court, and I was ready for it this time and blocked the shot, but fouled him with my body. With great poise, Kemper hit the two free throws. You learn about courage during the close games. Kemper had it, and he had it in spades.

My team fought back to within two and had to find a man of courage. It found him in John DeBrosse. I drove the lane with Mitchell in pursuit and saw Kemper drop off DeBrosse to help his teammate. DeBrosse drifted to his favorite spot on the court to shoot and I got him the ball. With fifteen seconds on the dying clock, DeBrosse showed the Corps that he was steadfast as he swished it home. VMI did not get off another shot and as we went to the bench I wanted to French-kiss DeBrosse for the sheer Ohioness of his broad, steely face.

When the buzzer sounded for us to return to center court, two of the Green Weenies, Cauthen and Kennedy, had to help me out of my chair.

As we took to the court, the volume of the Corps seemed to grow louder and it was not until I got back to the barracks that night that I learned why. When news of the overtime reached the four barracks, cadets sprinted out of their rooms. Later, a cadet guard would tell me that it looked like a track meet dashing toward the game in progress. When news of the second overtime reached the cadets who were studying or playing cards or who just didn't like basketball, they poured out of the barracks, running harder than the first group.

Of all the images I carry from my years at The Citadel, the one of cadets leaving the barracks to watch the best basketball game my sad and humiliated team would ever play is one that resonates most thrillingly. Whoever those tardy cadets were, they got their money's worth that night. The Bulldogs and the Keydets were fighting each other with everything they had.

In the second overtime, I drove the lane and was knocked into the stands by both Ralph Wright and Steve Powers. Wright, whom I knew well from Camp Wahoo, leaned down and said, "Don't pull that shit on me, Conroy. Don't come in here again. I own the paint."

I laughed, got up, and sank the two free throws. Wright answered by hitting a jump shot of his own. We missed a shot on our end and were surprised when VMI went into a slow-down offense where the guards held it and waited for the clock to run down. Mel screamed for DeBrosse and me to pressure their guards. So I went out after Kemper and chased him until he threw it to Mitchell, and DeBrosse got to go center stage. I overplayed Kemper trying to block any passing lane to him. With ten seconds left, VMI ran a play with a double pick for Kemper. I got by the picks and tried to keep Kemper from getting a good angle for his layup and knew I could not foul the guy. The angle was bad and that was my only hope. With two seconds left, Jim Kemper's layup bounced off the rim and I loved him for it.

In the third overtime, VMI used the same tactics and stalled the ball, once again putting pressure on the Citadel guards. Johnny and I worked hard to contain Kemper and Mitchell while Zinsky covered a third guard, Peyton Brown, that Coach McPherson had inserted to help with the ball handling. In agony, Johnny and I tried to pressure the VMI guards into a mistake, but they were good at what they did. As time died on the clock, I lived in the rarest of states—full consciousness of the extraordinariness of the moment. I was in the center of myself. Bill Zinsky got called for goaltending with fifty-five seconds left in the third overtime. DeBrosse threw me the ball from out of bounds and I hustled it up the court and threw a pass to Zinsky, who drove hard to his left and was fouled by Wright while shooting, with forty-four seconds left. When Bill was at the foul line, he recalled later that I came up behind him, ordered him to sink the two shots, and slapped him on the butt so hard that he carried a bruise shaped like my handprint for a week.

Zinsky, showing immense heart for a sophomore, sank both free throws. VMI set up another play to get Kemper open. Again, he got around me on the double pick but Kroboth knocked it down his throat when he went for the layup with three seconds left. The buzzers sounded and the howling Corps turned the Armory into a receptacle of exquisite chaos.

Mel never had a new play for us to run, and The Citadel never offered any surprises or new wrinkles to our offense. "Keep doing what you're doing. It's working for us out there," he said. But Mel's eyes blazed with the excitement of the moment. Coach Ed Thompson was pacing behind the bench and checking with the scorekeeper about foul trouble. Rat stroked the sweat from my head and eyes. I was wet enough to qualify as a member of the swim team. When the buzzer sounded for the fourth overtime, Cauthen and Kennedy again pulled me from my seat. I do not believe I could have gotten up without their help.

Johnny and I put our arms around each other's waist as we walked to the center of the court to deafening applause. When I shook hands with Kemper, I put my arm around his waist. Johnny Mitchell came over and we hugged each other. DeBrosse came over and said, "I'm dying, son."

"That's because you didn't have a real plebe system in D Company," I gasped. "We've got to end this one, Johnny."

Before the referee went to center court for the jump ball, I looked at my teammates, the ones on the floor and the ones on the bench. The Green Weenies were standing, screaming and urging us on, their spirits marked by both generosity and the hurt of not playing. My team on the floor was spent and fatigued, but still game, still on our feet, and I lifted a prayer to the dome of the Armory. I said a silent prayer that screamed out of me, "I love my team and my teammates, Lord. I love these boys and thank you for bringing each one of them into my life. They're teaching me how to be brave, Lord."

The fourth overtime again saw VMI stalling and setting up for a last shot. Again Johnny and I chased the VMI guards all over the court as they continued to play keep-away. But I could see that Kemper and Mitchell were so exhausted they could barely control the ball. Mel kept screaming for me and Johnny to pressure the guards, but we were losing our legs fast. I turned around once to see all the big men, theirs and ours, simply staring out toward the guards where all the action was.

When the clock passed the one-minute mark, Mel jumped up and started yelling for me or Johnny to foul someone. When the clock hit thirty-seven seconds, I leaped out and tried to steal the ball from Peyton Brown but slapped him on the wrist instead. We senior guards like to put the sophomores on the line with the outcome of the game in the balance. When Peyton went to the line, the Corps thundered at him in its most untamed, barbaric voice. I went up to Al Kroboth and said, "Get it to me, Big Al. I want it."

"No prob," Kroboth said.

"I'm taking off," I said.

Since VMI had stalled it for three overtimes, it occurred to me that everyone on both sides of the ball had become accustomed to the engines of the game idling down as the maddening pace of VMI's stall frayed the nerves of everyone watching or participating. When Peyton moved toward the line, I had a premonition of what was going to happen, and I let myself be seized by it. I was going to be the one to end this game. The ball was going to come to me, the runningest boy in this part of the world, the basketball-lovingest boy in this Armory was going to get the basketball and take it where it was supposed to go. I watched as Peyton bounced the ball twice on the floor, then looked up toward the rim. I'm going to end it. I'm going to end it. I know how to do this. Peyton shot and the ball rolled off the rim to the left and was taken by Al Kroboth. I took off.

Kroboth hit me with a perfect pass that I caught deep on the wing. I took off as fast as I could with the Corps exploding around me, the Corps breaking as I ran, and the noise held me aloft in its hallucinatory power. I sped along on its amazing wave as the surprised VMI guards scrambled back to get into defensive position.

I came slashing and ready and at full speed and heard DeBrosse filling the lane to my right and Zinsky calling on my left and Kroboth trailing behind me. All around me my teammates were streaking toward the heart of VMI in letter-perfect formation. But the point guard was the key to the success of the fast break, and it was the point guard who made the decisions that would lead his team to either victory or defeat.

John Mitchell stepped to the top of the key to try to stop my headlong charge. From Camp Wahoo the previous summer, I had learned I was quicker than this superlative shooter and that would help me at this moment. Behind him was the sophomore guard, Peyton Brown, who had just missed the free throw. While dribbling hard, I turned my head to the right as though I were telegraphing a pass to DeBrosse. It was a trick that all point guards master. When I saw Peyton drift to the right, I knew he had fallen for the trap. With a crossover dribble, I went to the left hand and went by Mitchell in a flash. Before Brown could recover I was going up for the basket. As he lunged to stop me, I pump-faked, took his hit, and put the basketball high off the backboard with an underhand scoop. I was on the ground when I saw the ball slip through the net. The Armory approached meltdown. The score was 72–70.

Only when Root lifted me off the floor did I realize how tired I was. I looked out to the Corps and I drank in their applause through the pores of my skin as I tried to memorize how I felt at the happiest, most fabulous moment of my life. I sank the free throw. In what seemed like seconds later, the buzzer sounded to end what is still the longest basketball game in Southern Conference history. We won, 73–70.

Then my team and the Corps engulfed me and they lifted me into the air and into the pure exultancy of that triumphal, ecstatic march to the locker room where I looked down at the faces of teammates who looked happier than I had ever seen them. Cadets leapt in the air to touch me, maddened to be part of this one delirious moment in the history of my college. The noise and the madness of joy, and the transcendent elation of a four-overtime basketball game kept me high in the air. My feet never touched the ground as I was borne off the court like a king.

In my novel I gave the final scene of that chapter to Rat, and I'm going to give it to Rat again. My teammates talk about Rat often because it disturbs us greatly that he died without having a clue how much he meant to us. It was Rat who undressed me that night. I could not lift my arms to take off my jersey, so Rat pulled it over my head. Rat untied my shoes and removed both shoes and the nastiest socks in the city. I undid my belt buckle and Rat helped me stand up and my shorts dropped to the floor. My jockstrap followed and I lifted one foot, then another. Rat turned and gently sent me toward the shower room.

"The sixty-minute man," Rat said. "You played all sixty minutes, Pat. You never came out once. You, DeBrosse, and Dan Mohr. All sixty-minute men. That was the greatest game ever played in the history of the world."

"C'mon," I said.

"That's just my opinion. I get to have any opinion I want because this is a free country," Rat said.

And it was a free country, one that Joe "Rat" Eubanks thought enough of that he went to Vietnam as a combat helicopter pilot. An Army unit got itself surrounded by some North Vietnamese regulars and were taking on a murderous fire from a numerically superior force. The patrol was about to be annihilated when Captain Joe Eubanks arrived on the scene in his Huey slick. He went in the first time and was repelled with heavy machine guns, RPGs, and small arms fire. Joe pulled back, circled around, and went back in with the same predictable results. He repeated the maneuver a third time when—in the spirit of the college that shaped him—Joe Eubanks, the assistant manager of my basketball team, was shot down and killed. He was awarded the Silver Star and the Purple Heart for valor. Not a single member of my basketball team attended his funeral, and we can barely forgive ourselves for that indefensible fact. I did not learn of Joe's death until a year after it happened.

"Rat was the best of us, Conroy," Doug Bridges says over and over again. "The very best one of us. Your book won't mean shit unless you tell them about Rat. More than any of us, Rat turned out to be the real Citadel man."

Whenever I approach the Wall in Washington, D.C., I carry a list of all the names I came to see etched in the black marble, and I always come alone. The first name I visit is the father of my two eldest daughters, Captain J. W. Jones III. I bring him news of his pretty daughters and, more recently, of his beautiful granddaughter, Elise. Then I visit my classmates from The Citadel. I am shaken by the names of Bruce Welge, Dick O'Keefe, and Fred Carter because I had admired them when they were boys and knew them well. I trace their names with my fingers the way other visitors do.

The last two names belong to two of the managers of my basketball team. I touch Carl Peterson's name then move to the last on my list. I move my finger to Joe Eubanks's name, the orphan from Concord, North Carolina. I come to the Rat. Last, I always come to the Rat.

It is always here, at this name, that the Vietnam Veterans Memorial unhinges me and I weep as though I will never be able to stop. My weeping is so public and visceral that I always draw the attention of other visitors, and they put their arms around me to try and console me. Veterans ask me if Joe was a member of my unit and I shake my head no. Women ask me if I lost a brother. The sons and daughters of men whose names are on the wall want to know why Joe Eubanks meant so much to me, and all look disappointed, even dismayed, when I blurt out in a tear-strangled voice, "He gave me towels. The Rat gave me towels."

WHEN I BEGAN THIS BOOK I DID NOT realize that I would come to look upon my twenty-one-year-old self as simply another fictional creation. But now that I am dressed in my middle-aged suit that will change and weaken and deteriorate until I can officially refer to myself as an old man, I have felt an eerie tenderness for the lost, vague boy I was at that age. At times, I would sit down to write about myself and see myself as I am today, then have to countervail that image by restoring my vigorous young manhood by an act of will. After the glorious VMI game, I wanted to walk myself out of the gymnasium where I would dance and glide and sing my way home to the barracks. When I went onto the floor of the now-empty gym, I found myself middle-aged and heavy and red-faced and was about to transform myself when I looked up in the stands and saw the figure of Will McLean sitting in the shadows waiting for me. Will was waiting for the novelist, not the young basketball player.

"Hey, Will," I said, "how'd you like the game?"

"Your wife's right," Will said. "You don't write fiction."

"There was no reason to change it," I said. "The game was perfect. I never felt that way before or since. I wanted the reader to know how it felt."

"You let me know how it felt," Will said. "It was great. Just great. I was worried that it was all bullshit. That you never got off the bench and just made the whole thing up."

"John DeBrosse thought he made the winning layup. When his kids told him Will McLean won the game after four overtimes in *The Lords of Discipline*, John told his kids, 'Bullshit. Conroy's making that up. I won that damn game!' That's how confusing memory is, Will. That's how unreliable it is."

"We're not really having this conversation, are we, Mr. Conroy?"

"No, we're not. I'm making it up. You can see how it works for yourself, Will. This really is fiction," I said. "But I'm going now."

"Why do you write these books?" he asked.

"It's the form that praying takes in me," I said, walking out of the gym across the shining floor. Then Will McLean surprised me as fictional characters often do.

"Hey, Mr. Conroy," he said.

"Yeah, Will?"

"Nice game, sir." Will delivered a salute, a sharp one, the way it's done at a good military college. I stopped and bowed deeply, then walked back into my life.

# EAST CAROLINA

THROUGHOUT MY SENIOR YEAR, I HAD TO HIDE FROM MY BASKETBALL coach the number of activities I participated in outside of the Armory. Mel considered basketball as our paramount consideration and had no interest in our becoming well-rounded in the process. Mel knew I was poetry editor of *The Shako* because he teased me about it, saying, "I guarantee you you're the first and last jock ever to hold that position, Conroy." But I went to great lengths to hide the fact that I was an active member of the Fine Arts Committee, the Round Table, the English Club, the honorary cadet member of the Charleston Ballet Board, and had delivered a long paper on Thomas Wolfe to the Calliopean Literary Society, one of the nation's oldest societies. I had delivered this talk on a Thursday night before the William and Mary game; it was important to me that I was a member of the oldest club on the Citadel campus and part of a cadet tradition that stretched back to 1845. The Calliopean Literary Society was older than my game of basketball, and I knew that, too.

By then, I had a strong sense of myself as a cadet and as a member of the Citadel family. Since I refused to participate in the plebe system in any way except by being pleasant and helpful to knobs (at VMI I would be known as a Rat Daddy, but The Citadel had no equivalent term), I had to find other outlets to be a valuable, contributing citizen of my realm. Given the antipathy to jocks at The Citadel, I tried to prove my worth in areas where athletic ability gave me no advantage or currency. I wanted to make a mark on the only college I would ever have, and I wanted that mark to represent the highest standards of achievement. Because I grew up with the United States Marine Corps, I was fed the word "excellence" constantly.

But it was my work in the Honor Court during my senior year that would have brought Mel Thompson to the point of apoplexy and beyond. Mel would not have understood that work, or liked it, or approved of it, and I think it likely that he might have gone to General Harris to get me relieved of my duties, at least during the season. Nothing in my cadet career had shocked or perplexed me as much as the cadets of Fourth Battalion electing me to the position of battalion honor representative. The Honor Court was both the most feared and the most respected organization on campus, but the fear may have been preeminent. I tried to figure out what signals I was giving off to indicate to anyone that I was honorable. In those days I lacked all powers of insight or self-knowledge and saw myself as a kind of cipher, a hollowed-out shape of a boy waiting for personality to be poured into the empty shell of the man I might become. Inside, I thought something was developing in the depths of me the way diamonds formed under pressure in the earth's crust, but I could not give it a name. When I was tagged with the word "honor" by my peers, I spent many hours considering the question of whether I had any or not.

I tried to imagine myself sitting in judgment of one of my classmates and whether I could actually vote to kick him out of school when graduation was only months away. If I could not pass judgment on a classmate's guilt, then I thought I was not worthy to serve on the Honor Court and should resign from it immediately. I studied the honor code which said: "A Cadet shall not lie, steal, or cheat or tolerate anyone who does." It was a stern code, but I thought then and I think now, it is a good one. Since I took my oath as a cadet, I had tried to live by this code and thought, for the most part, I had lived up to its standards. In the barracks, we cadets were forbidden to lock our doors, and I had never lost a stick of gum or an M&M peanut nor had I taken one from another cadet. The honor code seemed like a logical extension of the Ten Commandments as a foundation to my ethical life, so I decided to accept the choice of my battalion and join the court. If the members of my battalion paid me the high compliment of considering me to be a man of honor, I would strive to prove them right. My service on the Citadel's Honor Court changed my life forever.

When I told my roommates Mike Devito and Bo-Pig Marks that if they ever appeared before the Honor Court and the evidence proved them to be guilty I would have no choice but to vote against them, there was some tension in the room until Mike said, "We already know that, asshole. That's why we voted for you."

In the first meeting of the newly selected Honor Court in the spring of my junior year, Steve Grubb's name was put up for the chairman's job, and he was elected by acclamation. This pleased me greatly because Steve and I were friends and I think he was the sharpest, most heads-up cadet in my class. When the court selected me to the position of vice chairman, I stopped breathing and could hear the blood drumming in my ears. I blushed with the incongruity of it all. Because of my election, I was required to attend every session that met in 1966–67 unless one was scheduled when the basketball team was on the road. The Honor Court was a busy place to be that year, and I took my work on that court with great seriousness. I had nights of agony and nights of abiding joy when I cast an innocent vote for a man I thought unjustly accused. There were three nights that I remember with agony, all three of them taking place during the basketball season. All ended well after midnight, and one found me walking across the parade ground at five in the morning with tears streaming down my face.

One of the cases involved a classmate who had been accused of lying after he swore he was in the hospital when witnesses put him squarely in the city of Charleston. Though he had talked a Citadel employee into saying she remembered admitting him to the hospital and produced documentation that proved it, it was clear to me that the woman was lying to protect him. I voted guilty and so did eight other seniors on the court. But one member of the court believed the woman and cast an innocent vote. Since the vote had to be unanimous, my classmate survived his ghastly ordeal. In complete darkness, I crossed the parade ground deeply shaken because I had spent the entire trial staring at my classmate's Citadel ring knowing full well that I might be required to ask for that ring before I put in the phone call to his parents. I still have nightmares about asking one of my classmates to remove his ring and hand it over to me.

But the trial that began on the night before the East Carolina game was so knotty and convoluted and troublesome that the court did not come to a decision until 0500 hours the next morning. It was the first time in Citadel history that a rising member of the Honor Court was accused of an honor violation and found guilty by the sitting court. The humiliation of the young man who stood accused was agonizing to watch and to hear his voice break when he delivered the terrible news to his mother was a killing moment. It was always unbearable to me and experience made me no better at it. But on February 9, 1967, as I rang the bell to wake the sleeping guard in Fourth Battalion, I wondered how in the living hell I was going to play in a game against East Carolina in fifteen hours. The answer was that I was a Citadel cadet and a Citadel athlete and it was my duty to rise at reveille in one hour and fifteen minutes and start at point guard when the whistle blew that night. That's what I did.

My team was still bristling about the lacerating postgame screaming that Mel had launched against us after we had lost to East Carolina at their home court. But on this night our coach seemed subdued and resigned as he marked off the offenses and defenses he thought East Carolina would throw at us. He wore the expression of a coach who had lost faith in his team and was only going through the motions. There was no hint in that beaten-down, nonplussed locker room that gave off a sign that my team was going to play its most complete and accomplished game.

It marked the first game of the season that our spectacular sophomore, Bill Zinsky, played the way I thought he was going to every night of the year. It was the first time Zeke let the Citadel cadets in on the secret of what a blue-chipper his teammates thought he was. An aficionado of the game sitting in the Corps always carried a sign that simply said "Z," pure homage to Zinsky.

From the opening whistle, The Citadel ran its fast break with such efficiency and speed that the floor looked like a cross between a raceway and a stampede. Kroboth and Zinsky controlled the boards all night, and the paint was a dangerous place to go for all players. A total of fifty-five fouls were committed by both teams. But Kroboth would haul in a rebound, pass it to DeBrosse on the wing, who would feed it to me coming to the center of the court. I would take it flying toward our basket, my teammates thundering to fill the lanes around me. My teammates were calling to me as they moved into position and I moved toward our goal looking left, I threw a bounce pass to Zinsky on the right who took it on full fly and laid it in. On the next time down the court, I looked right and threw it to the right when the East Carolina guard guessed that I was going to go to my left and guessed wrong.

All night we ran it and we ran it hard and everything we did worked and worked well. Doug's jump shots were perfect and natural like rainbows or mountain streams and he hit them from long range. When East Carolina tried everything to slow Bridges, Zinsky took over on the other side of the court. As always, DeBrosse was putting together another solid performance and would finish the night with eighteen points.

The sportswriter John Hendrix covered the game for the *News and Courier,* reporting that "the win was the fifth against four defeats in Southern Conference play. It was only the third time in history and marked the first time since 1965 against Erskine that the cadets had gone over 100 points in a game.

"Despite liberal substitutions late in the game after leading by as much as 18 points, the Citadel hit 59.2 percent of the shots from the field, by far the best team effort of the season.

"With Bill Zinsky and Doug Bridges turning in their best performances of the season, the cadets got the lead for the first time at 4–3 with fifty-four seconds gone and never gave it up.

"Zinsky scored 23 points and Bridges 20. Zinsky shared rebounding honors with Al Kroboth who carried three fouls with more than eight minutes in the first half and saw little service in the second half after quickly drawing his fourth foul.

"John DeBrosse who hit the bucket with 19:06 left in the first half that gave The Citadel the lead for keeps, followed with 18 points. Pat Conroy, who at times displayed dribbling and ball-handling tactics that could match Marcus Hanes of old Globetrotter fame, chipped in 15, including the pair of free throws that carried the total to 101."

I could justify the writing of this entire book for the excuse to reprint that last sentence of the more than generous John Hendrix. I carry the memory of that game against East Carolina because it came to represent the randomness and unpredictability of the appearance of perfection in human life. I could not throw a pass that night without it seeming brilliant and improvisational. Bridges could not fire up a shot without it looking predestined to swish through the net with the sound of a sudden inheld breath. All night I would see Kroboth's hands above the rim or DeBrosse maneuvering to choose his spot on the floor for one of his explosive jump shots. Connor brought havoc from the bench and the Green Weenies got to finish the game. I got to watch Hooper slash and burn and rev up the crowd while Cauthen, Kennedy, and Bornhorst came in to rule the boards during the final three minutes of the game.

It was a fine East Carolina team we had manhandled and belittled, but they caught us on one of the only nights of that year where we played like the team I dreamed we could be. That night my team took the court with a swagger and a strut and a gleam in the eye that I had rarely seen before.

Only Dan Mohr did not receive the sudden visitation of bounce and swiftness that infected the rest of us. When Rat handed out the mimeographed stat sheets to all the lockers, I saw Root take his and crumple it with his fist and toss it casually into his locker. I'd not thought it possible that any team in America could hold Dan Mohr to a single point. But once again, Mel Thompson proved to be the best defensive man East Carolina could not put on the floor that glorious night.

That twenty-four-hour period when I was acting as chairman of the Honor Court with a trial that ended at five in the morning, then walked out as captain of the Citadel basketball team that night and helped my team to victory—I mark that day as the finest I spent as a citizen of the South Carolina Corps of Cadets.

# ORLANDO

AT LUNCH IN THE MESS HALL, THE DAY BEFORE WE WERE TO TRAVEL TO Orlando to play the Stetson Hatters, Rat approached my table and said, "Mel wants to see you in his office after lunch. He says it's an emergency."

"What kind of emergency?" I asked.

"I don't know, but he looked worried," Rat said. "Not mad. Just worried."

When I walked into his office ten minutes later, it had a different feel to it, and I didn't sense the usual dread of every encounter with Mel. "Hey, Coach," I said as I entered his domain. "Joe said you wanted to see me."

At first I did not see the tall figure of Bob Carver, the six-five center of the freshman basketball team, sitting on the couch to my right. Bob was a superb athlete, and by far the best of the big men Mel had recruited in this year's class. I thought he had a great chance to be a starter the following year, but it was a shaken, ashen-faced boy who sat before me.

"Hey, Bob, how you doing?" I asked.

"Not so good," he answered.

Mel said, "Pat, don't you have some kind of pull with the Honor Court?"

"I'm on the Honor Court, Coach," I admitted. "I don't know if I have any pull with it or not."

"You've got to help us out of a jam. Someone's accused Carver of an honor violation," Mel said.

"What's the honor violation?" I asked the freshman. He wore that look of pure terror I had come to know so well that year.

"I wrote a report, an ERW, saying that I didn't miss any chemistry classes," Bob said, and I saw his hands trembling.

"Did you miss any chemistry classes?" I asked.

"Not one. I swear to God, Pat. I've been to every class," Bob said.

"Then you've got nothing to worry about. Absolutely nothing. In fact, I'll be happy to defend you when you go up before the Honor Court."

"I knew you'd come through for us, Conroy," Mel said.

"Who reported you for the honor violation?" I asked.

"Colonel Durkee. My chemistry teacher," Bob said.

"He taught me chemistry, too," I said. "I know him. Let me go talk to him right now. But, Bob, this is very important. The Honor Court is strict and it's hard and it's cold. But we swear to live up to it. It's an agreement we make with each other as Citadel men. I can't go to Colonel Durkee if you're lying to me."

"I promise, Pat. I didn't miss one chemistry class. Except when we were on the road trips playing games."

"Those are excused absences," I said. "Nothing to worry about. Stay here, Bob. I'll do this quickly, Coach."

"The team's counting on you, Conroy," Mel said.

I FOUND COLONEL DURKEE SITTING IN the same room where I had taken his class three years earlier. He was a no-nonsense kind of man, but not humorless, and he wore his hair in a nineteenth-century manner, parted almost, but not quite, down the middle.

"Mr. Conroy, what a pleasant surprise," Colonel Durkee said as I walked into his classroom. "Have you been in Bond Hall since you got out of the sciences?"

"I sometimes cut through here when it's raining, sir."

"You struggled mightily with chemistry, but you came out with a gentleman's C," he said, reviewing a book annotated with his fastidious inscriptions.

"I've come here on behalf of Bob Carver. You've accused him of an honor violation."

"Yes, I have. It's a great pity, but I had no other choice," Colonel Durkee said.

"Bob just told me that he attended every class," I said.

"He said that, did he?" Colonel Durkee adjusted his eyeglasses. "I haven't had the pleasure of meeting Mr. Carver. I've never laid eyes on him."

"Sir, that's impossible. I just talked to Bob. He's in Coach Thompson's office waiting for me. You must've made a mistake, Colonel."

"Let me show you something, Mr. Conroy," Colonel Durkee said, and he brought a roll book out from his desk. He opened it up and showed me how he counted the roll; it was the same as when I was in his class.

"Remember you were arranged alphabetically in my class, Mr. Conroy?"

"Yes, sir. I sat in that seat. Four rows above the bottom."

"Very good. Mr. Carver sat in the seat behind you—or would have if he ever came to class. I call the roll alphabetically and I look up and see the cadet whose voice calls out 'present.' That way I get to associate a name and a face. It's how I get to know the cadets I'm teaching. Whenever a cadet is absent, I circle his name with a black marker. Then I send in a report on the absent cadet. Let's look at Cadet Carver's record. Here's the first day of class." There was a black circle around Carver's name and at the second class and the third and the fourth.

"I'm very sorry to have wasted your time, Colonel Durkee," I said.

"It was a pleasure to see you again, Mr. Conroy," he said. "I'm sorry the topic was so disagreeable."

When I walked back into Coach Thompson's office, Bob Carver immediately covered his face with his hands. He could no longer hide his great shame or the mess he had made of his young life.

"Will you need help packing, Bob?" I asked. "I'll be glad to help you."

"What in the hell are you talking about, Conroy?" Mel said, yelling at me, trying to regain some control over the situation that had slipped out of his hands forever. "You're supposed to be on our side."

"Tell him, Bob," I said.

"There's nothing to tell," said Mel. "It's an open-and-shut case. The professor fucked up and the kid's getting a bum rap. You were supposed to clean up the mess, Conroy, not make it worse."

"Tell him, Bob," I said again.

"I lied, Coach. I didn't go to any of those classes," Bob said, his voice breaking. "Not a single one."

"So he walks tours. Give him a punishment order. Conroy, this is my stud for next year. He's going to be one of the great ones," Mel said, his voice now pleading with me.

"Not anymore, Coach. He gave his word when he wrote his ERW. His word isn't much good. You can resign and you won't have to face the Honor Court. Believe me, Bob, you don't want to face the Honor Court with the evidence I just saw. There'll be nothing on your record, Bob. You can learn from this. You can start over."

Mel looked hammered and hangdog as he fell back into his seat.

"Sorry I lied to you, Pat," Bob said, and he shook my hand as he left the room. Mel Thompson and I never saw Bob Carver again.

Then Mel turned on me in fury. "Conroy, I just want you to know you let me down, let the school down, and let your goddamn team down."

I turned to face my coach, and I stood at attention.

"What do you have to say for yourself? What do you have to say in your defense?"

"I just upheld the highest standards of The Citadel, Coach. I'm required to do it every day. They don't give us days off."

"Don't give me that pious bullshit," Mel sneered. "You goddamn cadets are no different than the guys I played with at NC State. I barely went to class, Conroy. They took care of their athletes at NC State. They knew how to be big-time. I'll be frank. I didn't know a ballplayer who didn't cheat to get by. So what? I could cheat at cards as well as anybody. It was all a joke. We were at school to play basketball and the rest was icing on the cake. The only time I remember being in a classroom was when I ducked in to look at a clock to see if I was late for practice. Hell, the school even paid us to play ball. I took a pay cut to go to NC State. You think there's that big a difference between us, Conroy? You going to tell me you've never cheated since you've been here?"

"I've never cheated since I've been here, Coach," I said.

"You're as full of shit as a Christmas turkey. You're just like me,

Conroy, and you know it. There's not an ounce of difference between us. Or do you think there is?"

"Yes, sir. I do. You're a graduate of North Carolina State and I'm going to be a graduate of The Citadel. From what you just told me, there's a huge difference between us, sir."

"Get the fuck out of my office, Conroy, and never come back."

I left Mel Thompson's office, and I never went back.

I WROTE TO PRETTY LAUREL CARUSO of Winter Park, Florida, and asked if she would be my date after The Citadel played Stetson in Orlando on February 21, 1967. It still bothered me that I had not played a basketball game during this entire season and then gone out on a date afterward. Always, clusters of pretty girls would crowd around the entryways to locker rooms of our opponents on road trips. One of the reasons I played basketball was to attract pretty girls to my shy part of the world. It had not worked very well for me at The Citadel nor had it produced great dividends for my teammates. Except for Bill Zinsky, Dave Bornhorst, and Jim Halpin who were already pinned to the women they would marry, no one on the basketball team had a girlfriend of any kind. So, thinking far ahead, I wrote Laurel that I would love to take her out after the Stetson game. Laurel had been and remains the only girlfriend that my sister Carol ever arranged for me to date. We had courted the previous summer and had liked each other very much, I think, but her parents owned the Blue Bird Orange Juice Company, and her mother let me know by her coldness and reserve that I did not rank high on the list of young men she wanted sparking around her daughter. Laurel was lovely and breathtaking and only now, over thirty years later, do I realize that she was a dead ringer for Annie Kate Gervais, the girl who had put my heart on the floor two years before. There was something so disturbing about Annie Kate's rejection of me that I thought no woman would ever love me, that all would see the marks or disfigurements of spirit that caused Annie Kate to take her leave. Laurel answered by return mail that she would love to go out after the Stetson game and couldn't wait to see me play basketball.

Then I had to summon up the courage to ask Mel if he would allow me to have a date after the game. I would rather have asked Mel if I could moon the entire Corps of Cadets when they passed in review the following Friday. He could be courtly and charming when our mothers came to visit, but the subject of sex made him shifty and uneasy. Not once in my cadet career did Mel ask me if I had a girlfriend or if I was interested in meeting one.

Now I believe that Mel was the enemy of all passion and all sense of engagement where one of his players might drift into realms Mel couldn't control, and I include the carnal arena in this appraisal. His fury at my showboating at guard, my behind-the-back passes and dribbling between my legs—these actions would bring him leaping from the bench because the passion I revealed was antithetical to his desire to tamp down, repress, undermine, and usurp anything original in our games. His rule over us was high-handed, despotic, and totalitarian in nature. He sucked the life out of us and turned a good team into a bad one. By the time our plane landed in Orlando, Mel had lost Bill Zinsky, Tee Hooper, and Doug Bridges and ruined the season of Dan Mohr. Greg Connor's season had ended with a pretty girl in Jacksonville. The Green Weenies were buried alive on the bench, their names appearing in no box scores, their heroic play against the starting five unsung and unrecognized. By the end of the long season, we were fully under Mel's control and his iron thumb. I knew this because I fretted about asking him if I could take Laurel Caruso out after the Stetson game.

I thought about asking Mel on the flight to Orlando, but I chickened out. I almost approached him in the baggage claim area, but thought better of it. When I got to the motel room, I lifted the receiver of the phone several times and once even dialed his room before slamming down the phone. On the bus ride to the gym, I walked from the back of the bus, then sat down with Bob Cauthen who sat directly behind Mel and Ed Thompson. Walking behind Mel, I tried to summon the courage to ask him as we drifted through the gym on the way to the locker room. Then I dressed in my uniform and got ready to play Stetson. I would pray for a victory and then ask Mel, in his moment of triumph, if I could take Laurel out after the game.

When I led the Bulldogs out for warmups, I spotted Laurel immediately and winked at her after I made the first layup. She blew me a kiss that I prayed Mel did not see. On the other side of the court, I panicked when I saw my Aunt Helen Harper talking with Mel Thompson. I sprinted toward her and my befuddled coach and took her by the elbow, leading her back to her seat with my Uncle Russ and my four cousins, the Harper boys.

"Hey, Pat," my sweet Aunt Helen said in her musical southern accent. "I just invited your coach and your whole team over to the house after the game for a Bible reading."

"He worships Satan, Aunt Helen," I said. "So do all my teammates."

"That's just terrible! Then they need a Bible reading real bad," she said.

"They sure do," I said, shaking hands with Uncle Russ and hugging my cousin John. "I may bring Laurel Caruso by after the game. Remember her?"

"A sweet girl," Aunt Helen said. "We'll have a Bible reading."

I ran by Mel and apologized to him. He looked at me, then said, "How many more of your fruitcake relatives do I have to deal with, Conroy?"

"That's the last one, Coach," I said, returning to the layup line, loving Aunt Helen even more than I did before.

Naturally, the game was a disaster, and I spent it trying to get my teammates to snap out of the Citadel stare. We didn't score for the first four minutes and my team looked as though we were playing in a rainstorm. This was a good Stetson team, but we should have handled them easily. Even the reliable John DeBrosse played without style and ended the game with only six points. We made only ten of twenty-one free throws while Stetson was making twenty-six of thirty-seven. Mohr led our team with nineteen points and I got eighteen. My team stank up the court, and we were cringing when we staggered off the court after the final buzzer.

No master of timing, I finally asked Mel if I could take Laurel Caruso out on a date after the game. Because of that critical lack of judgment, I still take the blame for everything that happened later.

Mel looked down at me like I was a stool sample. His face grimaced with his utter contempt. My question was met with disbelief.

"How can you even think about sex at a time like this, Conroy? Losing rips my guts out. It makes me want to curl up like a wounded animal and go somewhere to die. Losing makes you think about sex, Conroy? I don't reward losers like you. You aren't going anywhere."

Then Mel turned and headed for the locker room in a rage. I trotted over to where Laurel Caruso was sitting and said, "Laurel, my coach just told me I couldn't go out with you tonight."

"You want to sneak out later?" Laurel said, surprising me.

"With my luck, he'd catch me."

"So what, Pat?" Laurel said. "You're twenty-one years old."

"You know something, Laurel?" I said. "With Mel Thompson, I've never thought of myself like that. Not once."

Pretty Laurel Caruso kissed me on my sweaty cheek and walked out of my life forever.

My depressed team boarded the bus in somber disarray. We looked like soldiers from a beaten nation being sent to a point of extermination. Not a word was spoken as we drove back to the motel. Mel Thompson's fury burned like an ember in the dark. When the bus stopped, the manager, Al Beiner, stood up and said, "Team meeting in the coach's room. Right now."

Dan Mohr looked over at me and said, "We haven't had a team meeting all year, Conroy."

We herded ourselves into Mel's room preparing ourselves for a long harangue about our lack of pride. Little Mel did a head count and went over to whisper something in Mel's ear. Mel looked up furiously as his eyes surveyed the room. "Conroy," he said, causing me to jump. "Where is Tee Hooper?"

"I thought he was here," I said.

"Well, take a look around, Conroy. It seems Mr. Hooper took a little joyride. I seem to have got me a team of quitters and losers and whiners and now joyriders. I got me any other joyriders on this team?"

Mel screamed at us for ten minutes. The specter of Tee Hooper loomed over the entire diatribe. Tee was a great guy and a solid citizen and I was more worried about his safety than his absence. In his commitment to athletics, Tee was in a league of his own.

"Get back to your goddamn rooms and if anyone hears from Hooper, tell him to report his ass to me on the double," Mel said.

I was the roommate of Doug Bridges on this road trip, and Doug said to me, "Wherever Hooper is, I hope he's having a good time, because tomorrow he has to die."

"Do you think he'll kick him off the team?" I asked.

"No," Doug said. "If Mel does what he really wants to do, he'll bury

Tee up to his neck in shit, pour honey over his head, and let the ants eat him."

"Tee's a dead man," I said.

I was reading *As I Lay Dying* because the first draft of my senior essay was due soon and I was behind in my reading, when there was a harsh knock on our door. Doug was in the bathroom so I went to the door in my underwear. I opened it and found my two coaches, Mel and Ed Thompson, standing before me.

Before I could say a word, Mel spoke in his most doomsday, prophetic voice. "We finally know what's wrong with this team, Conroy. We've finally patched it all together and come up with a reason why this season turned to such shit."

"What'd you come up with, Coach?" I asked.

"Pussy," Mel said.

"Pussy?"

"That's right, Conroy. You guys are more interested in pussy than you are in winning basketball games."

"Coach, if you're right and the reason we are losing so many games is pussy, then I assure you, it's the *lack* of it that's causing these losses," I said.

"Get out of our way, Conroy," Mel said.

"What're you doing, Coach?"

"Searching your room for pussy," Mel said.

"What? Coach, there's no girls in my room. You've got my word. I'm on the Honor Court and kick guys out of school for lying. You can take my word to the bank and I give my word of honor there's no girls in this room."

"Get out of my fucking way," Mel said, putting his hand on my chest and shoving me across the room. I was outraged.

"Stand against the wall," Mel ordered. "Look under the bed, Ed."

Little Mel got on his hands and knees and lifted up the spread under both Doug's bed and mine.

"No women here," Little Mel reported.

"You know," I said, "I hope you guys find some girls in this room. Yes sir. I'd like that better than anything in this world."

"Shut up, Conroy," Mel said, and I did. "Look in the closet, Ed."

Ed Thompson approached the closet as though the Rockettes were going to spill out when he opened the door, their hundred legs a-kicking. He threw the door open suddenly and peered into the closet's shadow.

"Nothing here, either, Coach," Little Mel reported.

Mel glowered at me then said, "Where's Bridges, Conroy?"

"He's in the bathroom, Coach."

"What's he doing in there?" Mel asked.

"I think he's taking a shit, Coach."

"Oh, sure, Conroy. Think we're going to fall for that one?" Mel asked. "Knock on the door, Ed."

Little Mel knocked on the door.

"Yeah?" Doug Bridges said.

"Open the door, Bridges," Mel demanded.

The door swung open and I found myself in a direct line, staring at a nude Doug Bridges sitting on the toilet seat. When he saw me, Bridges simply cracked up laughing. He had heard the entire scene and thought he would wait it out on the toilet. The two coaches peered in suspiciously.

"Check behind the shower curtain, Ed."

Little Mel took the shower curtain and pulled it back quickly to reveal the presence of a bathtub. Bridges put his head down and began laughing hysterically. "Hey, Conroy. These guys think I'd be taking a shit with a girl in here!"

When the two coaches left our room, I was shaking with rage, but Bridges came out of the bathroom screaming with laughter. The sheer ludicrousness of that encounter had tickled Doug like nothing else. He fell across the bed and howled, holding his stomach with one hand.

"It isn't that damn funny, Bridges," I said.

"It's hilarious, Conroy."

"Tell me the funny part."

"Conroy, he was searching your room and mine. You and I've never been spotted with a girl on our arms."

I said, "Speak for yourself." But I was surprised to hear Doug admit this about himself. Doug's extraordinary handsomeness was a given on the team, and his physique was legendary in the weight rooms. DeBrosse would say later, "If I'd been born with Bridges's body, I'd still be playing pro."

At three in the morning, I received a phone call and heard the voice of a very distraught Tee Hooper on the other end.

"Pat, I hear Mel caught me."

"He sure did."

"What do you think my chances are?"

"I don't think they're good, Tee," I said.

At breakfast the next morning, the team was on edge, so filled with a vague sense of dread and premonition of disaster. Tee wore his mood swings on his face. He was jumpy and exhausted and afraid that morning. The team ate in silence like teams always do when they stink up a court as we did the night before. The question that was whispered among us was, "Where was Hooper?" In whispers, the story made its way from table to table.

Tee, sensing that his sophomore year lay shattered around him, and that there was nothing he could do to redeem it, was at the point of despair. Since Mel had settled on me and DeBrosse as guards, Tee was often the third forward called upon and found himself coming into games after Kroboth and Bridges. He still found his demotion from starting guard a travesty of justice. Simply stated, Hooper thought he was a far better player and athlete than I was, and it was a crime and an outrage that I was starting in his place. His behavior became bizarre even to Tee.

After playing a small amount of time against Stetson, something snapped in Tee and while I was asking Mel if I could go out with Laurel Caruso, Tee had beelined his way toward the comely Stetson cheerleaders and begged two of them to take him to any kind of party they knew was going on that night.

"I just lost it, Pat," Tee told me years later. "You know I was a solid citizen. That I would never do anything like that to hurt the team. I'd gotten bitter about what happened. I snapped when I went over to those cheerleaders. But they were nice girls and they took me to a nice party. It was wonderful. Just wonderful. That year was so hard. There was never anything to look forward to, Conroy.

"Coach Thompson didn't even look at me the next morning. I just waited for the ax to fall, but it didn't. I felt terrible about what happened, but I didn't know if he was going to kick me off the team or take away my scholarship or what. It was agonizing getting back to school. We had a five-hour layover in the Jacksonville airport. When the bus finally pulled up beside the Armory, Mel and Ed jumped off and Al Beiner made the announcement that Mel wanted to see me in his office right away. Conroy, you did something funny. You jumped up and pretended to play the violin at my funeral. It was funny, not mean. It broke the tension and the team laughed."

Tee then walked into Mel's office as emotionally unbalanced and distraught as he would ever be at The Citadel. He passed the spot where the plaque honoring his induction into the Citadel Athletic Hall of Fame would hang one day. The best athlete in the history of The Citadel would enter Mel Thompson's office to learn both his punishment and his fate.

Though Mel was a wizard of absolute control, I bet Tee's opening volley must have surprised him greatly. Tee looked at Mel and said, "Coach, I'm so sorry about what I did. I'm so sorry about it and I'll do anything to make up for it. But why did you bench me, Coach? Why did you do it? I earned my way back to playing. Everyone knows that. Even Pat knows that. I'd go through the wall for you if you asked me to. You know that. But you bury me alive on the bench. Why, Coach? Please, just tell me why?"

The rawness of unharnessed human emotion was not the arena where Mel Thompson distinguished himself. I imagine Tee's outbreak unnerved him. It took a few moments for Mel to regain control of the situation. When he did, Mel said, "Someone who works in the athletic department told me you were saying some things in the barracks."

"No one in the athletic department's even allowed in the barracks," Tee said.

Mel looked at Tee and then to Ed Thompson and then back to Tee. "I was told that you tell the cadets that you fill out my lineup cards for me. That you decide who'll play and who'll not play on a given night."

With the mystery of a loused-up season finally clear, Tee Hooper burst into tears. Through great, gut-wrenching sobs, he said, "Coach, I never, ever said or thought anything like that at all. Ever. I wouldn't say such a thing. It's not like me, Coach. I'm not that kind of a kid. My whole season screwed up for something stupid like that. Coach, why didn't you come to me and ask if that was true? I didn't play because of a rumor some jerk hears from the barracks? It's not fair, Coach. You should have told me. You should have told me man to man. Man to man."

I first learned of a stranger's participation in Tee Hooper's ill-fated season thirty years later in Tee's elegant office headquarters in Green-ville, South Carolina. None of the pain of that season had diminished for Tee as we talked about what had gone wrong for him. The memo-ries still stung like paper cuts. But he told me something that surprised me. Because of his fiery tears of denial that he had spread the rumors at-tributed to him, Tee Hooper did not run a single lap or receive a single punishment for having skipped off to a party with two Stetson cheer-leaders.

Thirty years later, I was sorry I hadn't gone to the party with him.

CHAPTER 2 7

# LEFTY CALLS MY NAME

S INCE BECOMING A NOVELIST, I HAVE FOUND MYSELF FASCINATED BY the many ways that writers construct theories about how the passage of time affects the tone, structure, and seriousness of their work. I once studied Proust and the theories of time and duration that he had absorbed during his infatuation with the works of Henri-Louis Bergson. Both men seemed to think that time, as it is generally thought about, did not exist or existed on a very different and theoretical plane. I could not help but notice, however, that, according to the biographies of each man, both of them happened to be dead.

In my own lifetime, nothing has been clearer or more unremitting than the inflexible and man-eating current of time. My life is chock-full of madeleines that send me reeling back on tides of pure consciousness to moments in my life lit up with consequence. But no matter how mystical my encounters with my past, I remain fully cognizant that my body is a timepiece that can kill me tomorrow or let me live a hundred years. It is this hard, inexorable passage of time that, I believe, is the one great surprise in every human life.

Because I was a basketball player, time itself has a solid substructure to it. I have felt it passing through me with terrifying insistence with each sunrise, every beat of my heart. In all my books, there is a beginning, a middle, and an ending. My experience with time is based on my cold eye when gazing at reality. At The Citadel, I answered to the gold-tongued voices of bugles that woke me up at reveille then put me to sleep at taps, with hard, busy hours in between. I also had developed an expertise with the measured times of games where a first half contained twenty minutes, a halftime break ten, and a second half another twenty.

I would begin a game with a crisp, sweet-smelling uniform and end with a uniform that looked as though I'd thrown it into a lake. I could begin a game fresh and ready to roll and would end it exhausted to the bone, spent of every ounce of energy. I am time-steeped and time-cured and time-infused and time-beaten. I know how it works in life and in the pages of fiction. It moves, claw-footed and famished, toward the end of my days, as it always has. It moves the way it did before the Davidson game when I was shocked to realize that I was playing my final regular-season game in my Citadel career. Take the word "final," roll it around on your tongue, gum it well, cut your tongue on its edges, taste its metallic finish, spit it to the ground in scorn and distaste. It will still mean the same thing. It shocked me on the day after, where I read it in the *News and Courier,* and it shocks me as I read it again and write about it thirty years later.

WHEN I LED THE BULLDOGS OUT OF the locker room on Davidson's home court, I was overwhelmed that I had come to the end of the season so unprepared for the finality of it all. Dan Mohr, Jim Halpin, and I were ending our lives as basketball players, and I could still remember the first day I met them in the middle of our fear-haunted Hell Week. Why do they not teach you that time is a finger snap and an eye blink, and that you should not allow a moment to pass you by without taking joyous, ecstatic note of it, not wasting a single moment of its swift, breakneck circuit?

The sellout crowd booed us heartily as we took to the court and I drank in their jeers as though they were an intoxicating extract. I loved the taunts of the enemy crowds, and I wanted to show this Davidson crowd some of my new tricks. I wanted to beat Davidson so badly I could taste it, vinegary and sharp in the back of my throat. They had ruled the Southern Conference and been ranked in the top-ten teams in the country since my freshman year. Beating them this night would be my going-away present to myself. This Davidson team was young and in the process of rebuilding. It still rankled me that Mel had benched me for the entire second half of the first Davidson game because of my per-fect—and I repeat—my perfect behind-the-back pass to Kroboth. With the Corps behind us, we should have won that game.

As I dribbled past the Davidson coach, Lefty Driesell, I heard him call out to Mohr. "Hey, Danny, Mel benched you for four games? Has he lost his mind? You'd be my main man this year. My go-to guy."

Dan was muttering to himself when we went to the rebounding line. "You hear that, weasel? I'd be a fucking first-string All-American here, and I'm a can of corn to fucking Muleface."

"We've been through this before, Root," I said. "Before every game with Davidson, Lefty tries to get under your skin. It works every time."

"It'd get under your skin, too, Conroy, if you had pro potential like Hetzel and Synder—the way I do. Hell, if I'd come to play for Lefty, there'd be scouts from the Celtics in the stands tonight. Playing for Muleface's screwed up my whole life."

"But you march so well. And you learned how to clean a rifle and execute a snappy about-face."

Back in the layup line, Lefty made another pass at Danny, Lefty's long, good-humored face shining brightly as he said, "Come on, Danny. You didn't even play at VMI. The whole league was talking about it. Up here, you could write your own ticket, Danny. That's the damn truth."

"You hear that, Conroy?" Dan said to me on the other side of the court. "I could write my own ticket at Davidson. I don't get jackshit at El Cid."

"What about friendship, Root?" I asked. "That must count for something."

"Fuck you, leprechaun," Dan said, without a trace of malice.

I rebounded the ball and hit Brian Kennedy with a bounce pass that he caught on the run and put through the hoop. While waiting for my next layup, Lefty surprised me by saying something to me. "Hey, Pat. Why did Mel bury you alive the last couple of years? Mel even told me you couldn't score for shit. I'd've played you up here, boy. Guarantee that."

I put the next layup in and as I rose to shoot that basketball off the board I rose up as the happiest boy in North Carolina because the great Lefty Driesell had proven to me that he actually knew my name. Long ago, in the Southern Conference, I had conditioned myself to the trauma of anonymity that mediocre athletes have to endure during every waking moment. In my first two years in the league, I don't think Lefty could have fingered me in a police lineup, but now he was teasing me the way he had always done to Mohr, and I basked in the glory of it.

When the managers began to feed us passes for jump shots, I took a ball and dribbled it to the half-court line to study the Davidson team.

They looked massive, but I would beat them. I felt different than I had ever felt, and I could not place a name on what it was. But it lit my blood. I took it all in, the crowd, the noise, the smells of the arena, the nervousness of the referees—this was the last time that I would stand at center court at Davidson College, savoring my days as a basketball player.

Dave Moser saw me staring at his team, motioned to Wayne Huckel, and they moved out to stare me down. They were bold and wonderful sophomore guards and would ripen into great ones. Both were brilliant students who gave honor to the phrase "scholar-athlete." Moser pointed to me and then back to himself, letting me know he would be guarding me tonight. I bowed, accepting his challenge. In the first game, Huckel had guarded me, but I was quicker than Wayne and this was a change in strategy for Lefty. I said to myself, "Hey, Moser, I hope you like going to the hoop, pal."

I returned to my teammates, overflowing with a strange exhilaration. I could not suppress the confidence I felt, or deny it, or hide from it, or lose it, or dig a hole for it to burrow in. I simply had it in aces and spades and I gloried in it and strutted around the court and stuck it down Davidson's throat. If my teammates did not share it, tough shit—because I had earned it the hard way despite the savage eye of Mel Thompson. I had fought my way back from despair and self-loathing, from a coach who screamed "Don't shoot!" every time I touched the ball. Tonight, The Citadel had a point guard who believed he could hang the moon with the stars of Betelgeuse thrown in as a bonus. There wasn't a boy in the country who could stop me from getting to the paint. I could not wait for the game to start.

But Davidson used their crowd, and their early run at us was devastating. Moser had turned into a fine point guard and he and Wayne Huckel were taking rebounds and fast-breaking us right from the start of the game. Wayne Huckel gave DeBrosse and me fits. It was not just his height, six three; he was built so solidly he could chase Spaniards down crowded streets of Pamplona. He was the strongest guard I faced that season, and he posted me up near the basket all night. They were running away from us in the first few minutes. Rodney Knowles scored the first seven points as the Wildcats jumped to a 21–7 lead in the first five minutes. It stretched out to a fourteen-point lead until, with twelve minutes left to play, Mohr and DeBrosse began hitting from the outside. In the next three minutes, the Citadel pulled to within two, and finally when I drove the center lane, flashed past Mohr, and put up a reverse layup against a lunging Knowles, we tied it.

On this night, DeBrosse and I were again seamlessly matched and fine at what we did. Moser paid me the high honor of guarding me tightly. Huckel was overplaying DeBrosse and I caught DeBrosse's eye, knowing exactly what he wanted me to do. I dribbled toward John and we executed a pick-and-roll that peeled Huckel right off DeBrosse and left John open for a jumper which he sank. All night, DeBrosse charged by me and left Huckel planted into me. Other times we faked it and I drove between Huckel and Moser and Knowles towered over me and I flipped it to Mohr for an uncontested layup. But DeBrosse and I had merged our talents, and he could do all the things I could not do as a player, and I could do all those things that John would not even consider doing. He was a cautious player and I was a bold one. John had a beautiful jump shot and mine was a bad rumor, at most. He did not like to drive to the basket and I lived to do it. John loved shooting, not passing; a good pass made me as happy as I could feel on a basketball court. We drove the Davidson guards nuts that night, and I can still see Moser's tough, Indiana face trying to figure out how to keep me out of the middle or stop me from delivering the ball on the fast break.

But Knowles and Youngdale went to work on the boards again, and Knowles had twenty-three points in the first half alone. Davidson had built their lead back to fourteen when we went in for the half. "We can beat these guys. We can beat these guys," I kept exhorting my teammates, but was met with those resolute Citadel stares that could drive Mel into such a fury. I drank a Coke, chewing on the ice, convinced we could win the game.

Only four of the Bulldogs had shown up to play that night. Zinsky and Bridges carried a vagueness and lostness in their eyes that I couldn't wave away. But Kroboth performed heroically while rebounding against the sequoia-like Youngdale and Knowles.

The guard play was quick and fierce and in the trenches. Huckel knocked both me and DeBrosse to the ground during the second half. He hit like a nose guard and loved the sheer physicality of the game. The pick-and-roll worked for me and Johnny; I opened up my boy DeBrosse and his jump shot was picture-perfect all night long. I loved it when DeBrosse got hot and made me look like an All-American handing it off to him. We began to get back into the game, point by point, and with nine minutes to play, Mohr hit a jump shot to bring us within five at 78–73.

Mohr turned around to go back upcourt when he saw Lefty Driesell come off his bench trying to get the attention of one of his players to call time-out. But Mel was on his feet screaming at me to call time-out, and I did so. As Danny ran beside Lefty, the Davidson coach shrugged his shoulders at him and said, "Goddamn, Danny. What the hell did you need a time-out for? You guys have got all the momentum. It's us that's flat."

"Got me, Coach," Danny answered.

After the time-out, my team went stale again, and Davidson began to play more conservatively, picking their shots with great discretion. Once more, we played for a long three minutes without scoring a point as Davidson began to light it up again with an insurmountable lead. We played sloppy, desperate basketball toward the end of the game, and John DeBrosse fouled out of a game for the only time in his college career, and Davidson won the game, pulling away by 97–85.

The *News and Courier* said the next morning: "The Bulldogs had three men with twenty or more points. Conroy had 24, Mohr 22, and DeBrosse 20. Conroy and Mohr were playing their last regular season game for the Bulldogs."

Our bad year had ended badly but I went over to shake hands with Dave Moser and Wayne Huckel. I told Wayne that he and Dave were the best guards I'd ever seen come into the conference, and I wished them luck in the tournament.

On the bus ride back to the hotel, Rat handed out stat sheets to all the players. The coaches had not gotten on the buses yet and a general malaise had settled over the team. Suddenly there was screaming in front of me as Dan Mohr read that he had taken down only a single rebound during the course of the game. He was furious with Joe Eubanks, the statistician. "Fucking Rat. You can't count worth a shit. I can remember at least six rebounds I pulled down and you say I only have one. Goddamn, you got Conroy and DeBrosse with five rebounds each and they're the two littlest shits in the league."

"Watch it, Root," DeBrosse said. "Conroy and I were skying tonight. We had to hit the boards hard, because you were only bringing down one board all night."

"Pipe down, Root," Cauthen said, enjoying the chance to get on Mohr.

"Eat me, Zipper," Dan shot back. "It's fucking Rat's fault. The midget duck-butt can't count. I bet I got at least ten rebounds."

"I don't think you even got one," Cauthen said.

"I'm sorry, Danny," Joe Eubanks said. "I'm sorry. I'm really sorry."

"Fucking Rat," Mohr said, dismissing the manager with a gesture.

Later, at the hotel, I knocked on the managers' door. Joe Eubanks opened the door and I could see that he'd been crying.

"Where's Al?" I asked. "Is he with Coach Thompson?"

Rat nodded his head then walked over to the sink and began washing his face and hands. I walked up behind him and said, "Root didn't mean to hurt your feelings, Joe. This season's been hell on Danny. He thought he had a chance to be an All-American."

"I thought he would be, too."

"He took his frustration out on you."

"He sure did. He embarrassed me, Pat, in front of the guys."

"Don't worry about it—the guys love you. All of them. Even Root," I said.

"Hey, Pat," Joe said as I was leaving the room. "Thanks for not calling me Rat. I hate it."

"Want me to get them to stop?" I said.

"No. They don't mean anything by it."

"All of us think you're the best part of this team."

"They do?" he asked.

"They sure do."

"Why don't you call me Rat?" Joe asked.

"My three nicknames on this team have been 'weasel,' 'midget,' and 'leprechaun.' Which one do you think I like?"

"None of them," he said.

"Right," I said. "Now, because Danny Mohr hurt your feelings, I'm going up to his room, cut off his pecker, and feed it to a coon dog. I'll make him pay for this. Good night, Joe."

That was the last time I talked to Joe Eubanks before I received a phone call in Beaufort informing me that he'd been killed in Vietnam.

# THE TOURNAMENT

W E COME, THEN, TO LAST GAMES.
We come, as we inevitably must, to the tournament game against Richmond which would flush John DeBrosse out of his Dayton suburb to connect his life again with mine, and in the process, give me back the team I had lost through neglect and memories too painful to recollect. We old athletes carry the disfigurements and markings of contests remembered only by us and no one else. Nothing is more lost than a forgotten game. The game that branded DeBrosse with his own earmark of stigma was upon us, the memory John would carry like a small-craft warning in his interior weather for the rest of his life.

But there was optimism and zeal loose in our locker room after the defeat by Davidson, the thought that we had given a great effort against the Wildcats and had actually frightened them on their home court. Before the tournament, our practices were lively and our enthusiasm catching. From four to seven, we practiced hard and put our faith in next Thursday. I was convinced we were part of a down cycle in the Southern Conference and that we had as good a chance of winning the tournament as anyone. The tournament could provide redemption for the whole lost year. If we could only win three games in a row, we could spend the rest of our lives calling ourselves champions.

Louis Chestnut said in the *News and Courier* that "the Bulldogs will be led into the game by seniors Danny Mohr and Pat Conroy, who will be tasting their final competition. Mohr is a top rebounder who sports a 13.3 scoring average and Conroy, who has not been a starter until this year, has shot for an 11.8 average. The top scorer all season has been junior John DeBrosse. The small (5´ 10˝) floor leader has a 14.4 average." Mr. Chestnut agreed that out team was peaking at the right time and could do some unexpected damage in the tournament.

WHEN THE CITADEL WAS WARMING UP in the Charlotte Coliseum, the place which represented the big time for any Southern Conference guy, I noted something in the layup line that had been peculiarly absent for most of the year—Doug Bridges snorting and clapping and dunking with authority, if not fury. The key with Bridges lay in the eyes. When Bridges hustled during warmups, it was a grand sign that he had come to the court ready and willing to play. When Bridges was lit up to play his best game, he could score thirty against any team in the country, and I mean any team. He was the best athlete on our squad. If you could have put my will or DeBrosse's or Hooper's into Bridges's head, his name would still be sung in clear anthems by basketball fans. He had as beautiful a body as I have ever seen, and could look like a combination of Michelangelo's *David* and Baryshnikov when he soared to bring down a rebound. For four days, I had dropped hints that we needed Bridges in the lineup to Little Mel when he was overseeing the one-on-one drills between the guards.

"We need Bridges, Coach," I said. "He's got the firepower to match Moates."

"The big fella thinks he's been erratic," Ed Thompson said, in his quiet, serious way.

"But when he's on, Coach, there's no one like Bridges."

"The big fella makes all the calls. You know that," said Little Mel.

Bridges's eyes looked like the place where madness was born, and I almost screamed aloud when I saw Mel include his name in the starting lineup. I looked around the room and I heard the crowd outside. I felt my team coming together at last, the way teams are supposed to feel, the ones who you would go to the wall for, dive on the floor for, and shed your blood for. Our blood was up, and I was ready to play the game of my life. That morning I had read in the *Charlotte Observer* that "The Citadel's getting the best guard play in the Southern Conference." Coach Gary McPherson of VMI had said that about DeBrosse and me.

When I shook hands with Richmond's captain, Johnny Moates, I was shaking hands with the tenth-leading scorer in the nation with a twenty-five-points-plus per-game average. This had been a dream season, for Moates wore the mantle of greatness with a cockiness that bordered on arrogance. He had the same look in his eye that I had spotted in Bridges's during warmups, and I took that to be a bad omen for myself. Moates had disliked me since the last counselors game at Camp Wahoo, and even more so after our epic battle in January.

As we walked out to start the game, DeBrosse told me to take Moates and he would guard Billy McCann, the son of Bill McCann, the Camp Wahoo coach who used to coach at the University of Virginia. I shook hands with all five of the Richmond players, feeling rested and peppery and charged up. Moates regarded me with the slight contempt one of the best ballplayers in the Southern Conference can afford to express when they are being guarded by one of the worst. Moates could do contemptuousness the way Olivier could deliver high tragedy. He was magnificent in his disdain for me, then spent the next forty minutes proving why I fully merited it. When I was busy diving into the wreckage of this lost season, I kept coming across the fact that I spent the entire season playing defense against a splendid platoon of shooting guards who were stronger, taller, and much better athletes than I was.

I met Moates as he crossed half-court every time he came downcourt, his other four teammates lining up to pick for him in endless combinations all afternoon long. "Pick left," I'd hear Doug cry out behind me. "Pick right, Pat!" John screamed. "Double pick," Danny cried out as Buster Batts came out to set a high post screen. Because I was Mel Thompson trained, I knew that my only job was to stop Johnny Moates by myself. Moates dribbled toward me, six feet one inches, lean and long and flowing, his game princely and dangerous. I went into my defensive crouch and slapped both hands on the shining floor and motioned for Moates to come and get it. Unfortunately for me, Johnny Moates accepted my invitation.

Richmond's coach, Louis Mills, based his game plan on his belief that I was neither athletic enough nor big enough to stop Moates. Like a wide receiver in football, Moates roamed the perimeter as his four teammates set a series of picks that started to look and feel like the Maginot Line to me. Sometimes Moates would dribble right where Tom Greene set a devastating pick on me, again driving one of his bladelike knees into my left thigh. Fighting over the top of that pick, I would lose one step on Moates and in that step, Moates would go into the air, his eccentric-looking shot held high behind his head. He would release it straight up, then it arched high in the air, so high that the crowd would hum with disbelief. Gravity would bring it down, and the hiss of nylon would echo through the gym.

In one agonizing three-minute stretch in the first half, Moates came at me four times in a row, took me over a series of ten well-placed picks, and hit four long-range jumpers and a free throw when I fouled him out of frustration on his last shot. My teammates shouted encouragement: "Get 'em, Pat. Fight him, Pat. Fight your ass off. We'll make these other guys work their asses off. Fight Moates." In the customs and courtesies of my team, the only time they ever called me by my given name was in the dead center of games. Then and only then did I become Pat.

On our first offensive play, I moved the ball down the right-hand side and Doug Bridges called for the ball. Doug did something awkward and strange, something arrhythmic and ungraceful, suddenly shot the ball without his usual stroke and flair, but the ball clanged in for our first two points.

"Get me the ball," Bridges said as he passed by me and I went out to meet Moates again. After Moates made the nine straight points against me, I changed my tactics. Now I realized he was planning to and fully capable of scoring sixty against me. In the first ten minutes of the game, he had shot almost every time down the court and had made a high percentage of them. I started taunting him: "Hey, Moates, don't you have some other guys on this team? Hey, Greene, don't you like to shoot, every now and then? I've seen ball hogs in my life, but this guy thinks he's the only guy out here."

"Shut up, Conroy," Moates said as he passed to Tom Greene for the first time all day.

"Wow, give him an assist," I screamed. "Nice pass, Moates. You're not a virgin anymore."

Though Moates seemed like the only player on the Richmond team in that first half, The Citadel had also brought their A game to the coliseum. In both halves I looked like I knew what I was doing whenever I got the ball to Doug Bridges or Dan Mohr. Bridges played in a special realm, as though he was not subject to laws of physics that bound the rest of us. Every time I threw it to Bridges—every time he called for it— I simply got out of his way. Several times I backed out to the far wing instead of cutting to the corner, simply to give Bridges more room to work against Tom Greene. When Doug was hot, his jump shot was a work of impossible art. He made shots that game, spinning, wheeling jump shots, as he faded backward toward the out-of-bounds lines, off-balance, uncontrolled. He would stroke them in, one after another, each more preposterous than the last, our antidote for their antichrist, Johnny Moates.

Under the boards Mohr was scrapping for rebounds against the taller Buster Batts. In fact, the rebounding was relentless and physical. Our big guys were beating their big guys, keeping us in the game as Moates emphasized the difference between a first-team All–Southern Conference guard and an also-ran like me. Taking me over three picks set to free him, he put up a jump shot that arched at a much steeper angle than a rainbow. When it scorched the net it felt like the sky was falling in on me. Moates was exposing me for the fraud that I knew I was.

Yet my coach was a man famous for the spotless integrity of his fighting spirit, and I heard him scream at me, "Fight him, Pat! Fight him for everything it's worth. Don't quit on me."

Those words ignited like gasoline inside me, and I vowed to put Moates on the floor the next time down the court. Then I had a better idea. We had run the court since the opening whistle, fast-breaking every time we touched the ball, and keeping the lead for most of the first half. I first noticed exhaustion on Moates's face with nine minutes left in the first half, and I saw him gasping for breath as he guarded me. "Hey, Moates," I yelled. "You know what I noticed at Camp Wahoo last summer? You can't play defense worth shit."

"I can sure score, though, can't I, Conroy?" he said back.

"But Johnny, how you gonna keep me out of the paint?" And I blew by Moates and left him flat-footed at the top of the key. I was flying into the lane when six-foot-eight Buster Batts moved out to intercept me with his hands held high. Here is how a point guard thinks on the fly: if Batts is covering me, then Dan Mohr is free. I flicked a bounce pass to Mohr who laid it up under the basket all by his lonesome. Each time we came downcourt I drove past Moates, and if no one came out to contest me, I laid it up. If Tom Greene picked me up, I passed to Bridges at the wing. If McCann or Ukrop dropped off DeBrosse, John would drift to a spot and I would hit Kroboth or Zinsky or anyone else who was open.

To end the half, John retrieved a jump ball and hit Danny Mohr going upcourt before the foul line. Mohr dribbled once, then launched a shot from half-court that flew to the basket in a predestined arc and swished through the net at the buzzer. Richmond led us 47–45. They had shot for an amazing 65.5 percent accuracy from the field. On fire, Johnny Moates had lit me up for twenty-one points. I walked into that locker room feeling like the worst defensive player in America.

Sportswriter Louis Chestnut described the first half in the *News and Courier* the following morning: "The Citadel and Richmond played each other to a standoff in what may turn out to be the best basketball game of the Southern Conference Tournament which opened here Thursday. . . . Doug Bridges, having possibly his best game as a Bulldog, and little Pat Conroy, jumped The Citadel out to an early seven point lead after seven minutes of play. Moates then went on a nine-point spree and the Spiders finally pulled even at 26–26. From that point the lead swayed back and forth until the Spiders took their two point lead into the intermission."

In the locker room, the Green Weenies surrounded me and told me I was making Moates earn every point he got. Adrenaline pumped through us like enzymes of pure energy. Mel was as animated as I had seen him all year. It felt like we were on the edge of something big. I prayed to God that He would let my team win this game and I prayed hard.

The Citadel came out into the second half scratching and burning and clawing for every loose ball and rebound, and at the twelve-minute mark, the score was 61–61. The crowd swooned for both teams that afternoon; they loved us with their applause and their joy at the valor on the floor.

Every time Moates guarded me, I drove the lane as hard as I could push it, flashing by him, dangerously loose in the paint. Richmond knocked me to the floor again and again. I ended up shooting fourteen free throws—a career high—and made eleven of them. Both Roberts and Larry Patterson fouled out taking me to the floor.

Bridges remained ethereal and untouchable throughout the second half. His shots grew longer and more preposterous, but he kept shooting and Mohr kept shooting. I screamed at Moates and dared him to shoot it, he screamed back, went off two picks, put up his odd jump shot, and hit it from what seemed like a quarter of a mile away.

Six times during the game, Greene's knee, which he used as part of his screen, hit my thigh squarely, the pain as bad as anything I'd experienced on the basketball court. It was smart, not dirty, basketball that Greene was playing, and it was having a damaging effect on my game. But I noticed that Moates was slowing down and fighting for breath at the same time I was running out of gas completely.

We went ahead—they went ahead—we responded—they answered. The game was tied at 84. We stormed back and went ahead. Greene scored. Mohr scored. Batts scored. The game went into overtime.

DeBrosse later told me that at the end of the regulation game, I looked like I'd been in a death march. I'd chased down Moates for a full forty minutes, scored a bunch of points for our side; I was one beat motherfucker.

Gasping for air, I wished the time between the game ending and overtime beginning would stretch to an hour. When the horn sounded, Connor and Kennedy lifted me to my feet. Cauthen pushed me out toward the court and I heard the Green Weenies screaming for me. I looked back at them—Cauthen and Kennedy and Bornhorst and Connor and Halpin—and filled with admiration for these unrewarded and invisible, disparaged boys. The heart of our team was there, right there, on our bench. That is where all the spirit and fight was. That is where I had to go when I reached back to them for the awesome tenderness of their sweet praise. I bring your spirit to this court, Green Weenies, I remember thinking. And I promise you and myself that I'll walk the world a Green Weenie forever. My boys, the Weenies, were cheering for me and the Blue Team, and I raised my hand to salute them as they screamed their salutes back at me.

When Mohr controlled the jump ball in overtime, I dribbled up the right side looking again for Bridges. "Get me the ball," Doug had said every time he passed me, and it paid dividends each time I did. This time Doug took it deep in the corner and shot a jump shot that seemed stupid and selfish, but an act of daring and genius when he hit nothing but net.

Buster Batts answered on the far end of the court with a tap-in over Mohr. Bridges, Mohr, DeBrosse, and I had not been out of the game. Zinsky had replaced Kroboth only when Big Al had fouled out. Only six of my twelve-man team played during the whole game. When our big men fell prey to exhaustion at the end of the game and in overtime, I looked to the bench at our fresh and willing guys like Hooper, Connor, and Cauthen—guys that could rebound with anybody—and wondered why Mel was not resting any of us. The overtime period proved just as racehorse and chaotic as the first forty minutes. Our rebounding slowed down and our big guys ran out of gas under the boards. Though we were the third-best rebounding team in the conference, the Richmond big men began to dominate the boards as exhaustion caught my big guys in the open floor. Bridges had given everything he had to give and Mohr had left everything he had on the court. DeBrosse and I held each other up during foul shots and jump balls.

When Moates took me around Tom Greene's pick, the Richmond forward's lethal left knee knifed into my left thigh again and something broke inside the muscle. Mel called time-out and I limped to the bench. Moates staggered back to the Richmond bench gasping for breath, being helped by Ukrop and McCann. My leg hurt so badly I thought I'd be hospitalized that night.

Mel screamed at the big guys to hit the boards, but they had given everything they had to give, and stared at him with oxenlike passivity. When the whistle blew again I reached out for Cauthen and Kennedy and they lifted me off my chair. I almost screamed out loud when I put my full weight on the hurt leg. I grabbed DeBrosse in desperation and said, "John, I can't move my leg. You've got to take Moates for me. I can't guard him now."

"Fuck you, Conroy, I'm not taking that son-of-a-bitch. He's your man. I got my own man."

"Your man's scored two or three all game. Mine's scored a hundred and two. You're fresh, Johnny. He's tired as I am. Take him now and I'll take him back in the next overtime. You gotta do this for me, Johnny," I said, feeling delirium coming on. It embarrassed me to ask Johnny to take my man, but I wanted to win this goddamned game and I wanted to give my team its best chance to do so. Now I realize that I should've stormed over to my bench and ordered Mel to put Hooper in because I had become a liability. The simple fact of my being on the court jeopardized any possibility of a victory for us. That's what a real leader would have done, how a classy floor leader would've played it. But I was a bottom feeder and born second-stringer. And let us face it—I had developed a finely honed loser's instinct. I had years of practice doing the precisely wrong thing. Before the game, I should've approached Mel and said, "Our best chance of beating Richmond is to let Tee Hooper guard Moates. I think Hooper has the size and speed to stop the son-of-a-bitch. I don't think I do, Coach." I had actually rehearsed that speech that previous week, but I lacked all courage when it came to handing out advice to my temperamental coach. I feared that he would consider me a coward, someone who wouldn't rise up to the challenge, someone his teammates couldn't put their trust in—in other words, someone exactly like the fearful, tentative ballplayer I was. My insecurities had lost out again to my best instincts as they would so often in my life. I would always display a small genius for making the improper gesture or following the wrong impulse. Because of my moral cowardice, I hadn't told my coach what I thought in the deepest, most honest realms of my heart: I was not a good enough athlete to guard Johnny Moates. My stellar defense had held Moates to a mere thirty-nine points, and I was lucky as hell he hadn't scored fifty or more.

In nausea and pain, gasping for breath, I watched an exhausted Johnny Moates bringing the ball upcourt. If he had worn me out with his extraordinary offensive performance, it was a dog-tired Moates who came upcourt to face a fired-up DeBrosse. I had driven the lane the whole game and there was nothing Moates could do but chase me. I made him pay for his humiliation of me in front of every coach and player and reporter in the Southern Conference. I put him in the run-ningest, passingest, ass-kickingest horse race of a game Moates had ever seen. I had scored twenty-five points against him, equaling my career high. There were pro scouts in the building that day and I'm sure they noted the unearthly skills that Moates brought to the task of scoring. I hope they also noted that a college guard who could not stop Conroy might have some difficulty with Jerry West or Oscar Robertson.

I had my hands on my knees, literally gasping for air, when I saw DeBrosse make his move. Because of his weariness, Moates was incau-tious as he dribbled. He was bouncing the ball too high when DeBrosse stuck a hand in and swiped it clean. Then DeBrosse broke for our bas-ket and Moates, embarrassed and spent, did not even give pursuit. Instantly, I knew what I was supposed to do. Because I was not a shooter or a scorer, I made my name as a guy who dove for every ball, who fought you belly to belly for everything he was worth, a guy who would shed his last drop of sweat for the good of the team. That was my image of myself. The image proved false and damning to me as a man and as an athlete.

When DeBrosse broke, I broke also as I'd been trained to do. It was my duty to follow John DeBrosse down the court, to spring fast and trail my backcourt partner, to be there to tip in his layup if he missed it. I took one step out of instinct, then stopped out of exhaustion and lack of character as an athlete. Shamefully, I stood on their foul line and watched DeBrosse's glorious, triumphant flight down the court. I can remember being surprised that he was taking it straight in instead of laying it in off the glass as I would have done. When DeBrosse took off his layup there was an exaggerated bounce to his leap as though he had jumped higher than he ever had before. But his form was picture-perfect. I had never seen DeBrosse miss a layup in practice or a game. His game was steady as clockwork. He released the basketball at the height of his jump. The ball nicked the front of the rim, bounced off the backside of the rim, then rolled out, off to the left side. Any guard worth his salt would've been there to lay it back in, to cover his teammate's back, to do for DeBrosse what he had always done for me. John DeBrosse went into a state of shock when he realized he had missed the layup. Moates sprinted to retrieve the ball, and I had to leave Billy McCann to pick Moates up when he came across the center court with DeBrosse hustling to get back in the game. Richmond immediately scored to go up by one. If DeBrosse had scored, we'd have led by three with less than two minutes to play. They scored. We scored. Richmond got four straight offensive rebounds against our bone-tired big men. Greene scored. We got the ball again. Heroically, Doug Bridges scored. Moates made a free throw.

With two seconds left, a jump ball was called. Mohr tried to tap it to Bridges but hit it too high, and the ball was rolling out of bounds when the buzzer sounded. We had lost the game 100–98 in overtime. Our terrible and deflating season had come at last to its sorrowful and fitting end. My modest career as an athlete had crashed and burned on the floor of the Charlotte Coliseum. I stood beneath the lights for the last time, then Bob Cauthen came over to help me limp off the court and into the locker room.

All of my teammates remember what happened next—all of them. I sat by my locker for a brief moment, then fell apart at the far end of my boyhood, at the exact spot where it connected to my hesitant, unconfident young manhood. The first sob caught me by surprise and the second one was so loud that it didn't seem to come from me at all. I wept as I had never wept before in public. I wept out of sheer heartbreak, unable to control myself. I was lost in the overwhelming grief I felt at losing my game, losing basketball as a way to make my way and define myself in a world that was hostile and implacable. How do you say goodbye to a game you love more than anything else? What was I to do with a sunrise when I didn't get up thinking about going to a gym to work on my jump shot? What does a boy do when they take his game away? In front of boys I had suffered with, I sobbed and I couldn't help it. I removed my jersey and put my face into the number 22 and my sweat mingled with my tears in the sacramental moment, when I surrendered my game to the judgments of time. I gave it up, gave basketball up, gave my game up, the one I played so badly and adored so completely. I gave it up in Charlotte, in emptiness, in sorrow, in despair that I played it so badly yet in gratitude for what the game had given me. Each one of my teammates squeezed my shoulder as they passed on the way to the shower room. Basketball had rescued me from the malignant bafflement of my boyhood. It had lifted me up and given me friends that I got to call teammates. The game gave me moments where I brought crowds of strangers to their feet, calling out my name. The game had allowed me to be carried off the court in triumph. The game had allowed me to like myself a little bit, and at times the game had even allowed me to love the beaten, ruined boy I was.

I have always been a closet weeper, a man who cries easily but does it better behind closed doors, hidden away. When my father would take me apart as a child, I could not cry in front of him or the beating became more savage. I learned to disembody myself from the boy who was getting beaten. Later, I would cry for much of the night for that kid whom I abandoned when he was being torn up. I never thought of him as belonging to me.

In the locker room in Charlotte, that boy caught up with me and put his arms around me and swore we would never leave each other again. He understood my tears at saying farewell to my game, and that boy joined me as I gave up the thing that had brought me the purest and most shining and most unconditional happiness I had ever felt in my unhappy life. I gave it up. I left my game forever in Charlotte.

The next morning Mel Thompson, who had never offered me a compliment in my whole life, said in the *News and Courier:* "Pat Conroy gave another great performance. That kid gets more mileage out of his talent than any player I have ever coached."

CHILDREN, HEIRS OF MINE.

You may put those words of Mel Thompson's on my tombstone, and I will smile in joy for all eternity. I take those words to the writing desk every day of my life. When I cannot write or find the words cunning in their refusal to present themselves to me or bend to my will, I read his words again. I say, "Mel Thompson, my Ahab, my demanding and melancholy coach, one of the hardest, most authoritarian men I have ever met. The hardest taskmaster, the demon-driven coach of my college days, the dark icon of madness told the world that I got more mileage out of my talent than any player he has ever coached."

I took Mel's words and applied them to my future life. I used them as talisman and mantra and omen for what I wanted to become. I took those words of praise and applied them to the writing life I had dreamed about since childhood. I took Mel's words as metaphor. I soared upon them, gathered strength from them as I stormed out to my life as a writer who wanted to create winged and roaring sentences, the kind that would set the language free and make people come to my house and sit on my knee and listen to the song I was born to sing.

# CHAPTER 29

# EX–BASKETBALL PLAYERS

For the first time since I was nine years old, I awoke as an ex–basketball player. The most I could hope for now was to ripen into a knowledgeable fan. Because I couldn't sleep well, and my leg throbbed with pain, I finished rereading *Absalom, Absalom!* sometime in the middle of the night, taking careful notes for my senior essay. I still felt humiliated by Moates but William Faulkner tamed and mesmerized me. I loved the way he could pack the whole world into a single sentence. Faulkner could inhabit a line the way God loomed over the universe.

In the next bed over, Root slept happily after playing his last wonderfully accomplished game. Because of the incandescent joy I take in reading, a secret alchemy worked without my knowledge, and I ceased to be the boy who has just given up thirty-nine points to Johnny Moates and felt myself transformed into the word-stung boy who let himself be taken on the floor by the flashy, unapologetic, grandstanding prose style of Faulkner, the agonizing descent into madness of Quentin Compson. From that troubled, long-ago night, I have forgotten neither Compson nor Moates.

In 1995, I spoke at a gathering at the University of Mississippi, delivering the main address for the Annual Conference on the Book. I was three months away from John DeBrosse's dramatic approach at the bookstore outside of Dayton. The afternoon before the speech, Dean Faulkner Wells, the pretty niece of William Faulkner, led me on a hushed tour of Rowan Oak, the legendary home of her famous uncle. My father was with me, and so was my high school English teacher, Eugene Norris, and my editor, Nan Talese. As I roamed through the many-roomed house listening to Dean tell the necessary stories of her uncle, I thought of Root and Moates and the Richmond game, and of reading far into the night.

When we returned to her house, Dean and her husband, the writer Larry Wells, asked me if I would sign their copy of *The Prince of Tides*, pointing me to a desk by a window that looked out onto a gas station.

As I signed their book, Dean said, "Pat, I'd like you to know something. That desk you're writing on is the desk where my uncle, William Faulkner, wrote *Absalom, Absalom!*" To this day, this remains the most thunderstruck moment of my writing career, which has been far too lucky already. I turned to Gene Norris, my teacher, but Gene was walking to the front door at a fast clip. I found him staring off into the traffic, as moved as I was.

"Mr. Norris. Gene," I said, after a moment. "I first read *Absalom, Absalom!* in your class. You assigned it to me."

"I know that, scalawag," Gene said, his voice catching. "Now please go back inside. I need to be alone with this moment. I don't think this has ever happened to a high school English teacher. I need to savor this moment, Pat, for all of us. Every last one of us."

The day following the Richmond game, an article about me appeared in the *News and Courier*, written by Louis Chestnut. Louis had gotten much closer to my team than any other sportswriter who covered us that season. I return to that interview when I need to hear myself speak as a twenty-year-old.

Louis wrote: "Two hours before what was his final basketball game of his college career, Pat Conroy was his usual bouncy, peppy self.

" 'I don't have any real feelings about not playing anymore,' Conroy said. 'I do, however, wonder how I will adjust and what I will do to stay in shape. I don't want to ever allow myself to get out of condition.' [The fifty-four-year-old novelist reads this eighty pounds over his playing weight and writes in the margin, "Shut up, kid."]

"It's difficult to imagine the slender 5′10″ guard out of condition," Chestnut wrote. "He seems to be charged with a certain electricity that will keep him on the move forever. He moves even when he is sitting down. I asked Pat about this tremendous energy: I asked him if he had to drive himself harder on the court in an effort to make up for his lack of size.

" 'Not at all,' Conroy laughed. 'The reason I always try to move toward the basket in a big hurry is because I can't shoot from the outside. I am probably the worst outside shooter in the history of the game. One reason is that my eyes are rotten. I have no depth perception.

" 'All I try to do is get close enough to the basket to see it,' he said. 'And when you drive the basket you sometimes have to go through people, and you sometimes get decked. I think I picked up the driving technique in D.C. where it was considered chicken to shoot from the outside.' "

Louis, often writing of my life as a Marine brat and my love of the town of Beaufort, South Carolina, asked me about my future. " 'My ultimate aim,' Conroy went on, 'is to write. I love to write poetry, and I think eventually I would like to write for a living. I know one thing—I have no desire at all for a military career.' "

On March 5, 1967, I had declared in public my desire to be a writer, having no idea how to go about it. Afterward, I watched every tournament game and tried to remember every move of every player, noted the colors of the uniforms, the faces and hairstyles of the cheerleaders, the hairlines of the coaching staff. A writer, I thought, must notice everything, experience life more deeply and spiritually than anyone else, and let every cell of his or her body quiver with a lust to take in every stimulus that came along. I wanted to develop a curiosity that was oceanic and insatiable as well as a desire to learn and use every word in the English language that didn't sound pretentious or ditzy. As I sat in the Charlotte Coliseum watching Moates's Richmond team lose in the quarterfinals against West Virginia, I knew that I would one day write about my humiliation by Moates. I would write about everything that touched me or hurt or cut or bruised or bedazzled me. I ordered myself to be brave. A writer, like a point guard, was not allowed to show fear. In the Southern Conference program, I began outlining my first novel about the Citadel baseball team I had played on the year before. It was an odd choice to make, but this was long before I learned that I had to turn the writer's eye inward to find the gargoyles and stunted trolls that ate me alive. Then, I didn't know that I would build my house of art on my demonic, yet powerless, hatred of my father and my wrecked, guilty love of my fabulous and treacherous mother. But I promised myself I would be ready when my heart began to tell me its stories and reveal its secrets.

With my teammates, I watched the championship game and saw West Virginia tear the Davidson Wildcats apart. Then I walked out of my life as a basketball player and left my game behind me. I had gone as far as I was going in the game of basketball. My mediocrity in my chosen sport has kindled in me my whole life, and I have suffered for it. Athletics is mercilessly fair.

I had returned to the Armory very few times until my graduation day, but Root had an encounter with Mel that April. Danny had gone there to collect his laundry money when Mel came out of his office suddenly. Mel began shaking his head sadly and approached Danny with a look of derision or possibly contempt on his face.

"What're you doing here, Mohr?" Mel asked.

"Picking up my laundry money, Coach," said Danny.

"You only have to pick it up once more," Mel added, beginning to walk away. Then he turned back to say, "You know something?"

"What is it, Coach?"

"I've always been jealous of people who had more talent than I had. You're one of those people, Mohr."

Mel turned and walked back into his office and never saw Danny Mohr again.


My LAST THREE MONTHS AT The CITADEL were lyrical and elegiac to me. I joined the Corps for the first time, marched with Romeo Company during parades on Friday, drilled on Tuesday, ran PT on Thursday, and put on full dress for Saturday morning inspection. I learned about barracks life as it was lived by the average cadet and not the jock I'd been for four years, and I thought it was all terrific. It surprised me that marching in Friday's parade pleased me and how proud I was of my classmates who called the cadences and shouted the orders and commands that put the two-thousand-man Corps into a dance as intricate as flamenco and as symmetrical as ballet. The easy camaraderie of parade was unknown to me and the congeniality of the seniors making jokes, trying to get the plebes to laugh and draw down the wrath of the juniors and sophomores was all brand new. When R Company finished first in most of the parades that spring, we would wait impatiently for the adjutant to announce the results over the loudspeaker, then explode in a cacophony of joy and machismo when R Company came on top again and again. Romeo Company felt like a team in a way my poor basketball team never did. I have rarely felt as close to a group of men as

I did in that triumphant, crowing moment when we would break into the Romeo song on the way back to the barracks after parade:

> *Oh, we're the men from Romeo,*
> *we just don't give a damn.*
> *We come to school to win parades*
> *the hell with our exams.*
> *The hell, the hell with studying,*
> *the hell, the hell with school.*
> *And if you're not from Romeo—*
> *the hell, the hell with you.*

There was nothing like it in the world, I tell you, there was nothing like it.

Another secret of the regular Corps revealed itself to me as I worked on my senior essay. It had never occurred to me in my career as a cadet that anyone could use the afternoon to study or relax or just talk. After the chaos of that losing season, life in the Corps felt leisurely, uncomplicated and rhythmic. I had large quotients of free time as I finished the five great novels of Faulkner and compared them to the five best novels of Sinclair Lewis. When asking me to compare the works of those two, Colonel Doyle expected me to be severe with and contemptuous of the novels of Mr. Lewis. When I ended up loving both writers, he chided me. "But surely, Mr. Conroy, it had to occur to you that the talent level of Mr. Faulkner makes Lewis look flatfooted and vulgar."

"Colonel Doyle," I argued, "they're different writers completely. Faulkner's magisterial, but Lewis is great in his own way."

"I find him loathsome and untalented," Colonel Doyle said. "There is no poetry in his soul. He wrote some terrible books."

"*Arrowsmith* was wonderful," I said.

"If you say so," he said.

"Colonel Doyle, will you let me write my senior essay the way I want to?"

"I certainly will not," he said. "We have had this discussion many times, Mr. Conroy, and you pilloried me in the last issue of *The Shako* because of it. You made a fool of me in your piece 'The Great Senior Essay Scandal.' My wife, Clarice, was much put out with you."

In the spring issue of *The Shako*, I had written a second short story that I thought was satirical and funny. A senior private named Tim Jackson gets kicked out of school for daring to write a senior essay that is entirely his own original work and does not contain a single footnote. It was a running argument that Colonel Doyle and I carried on all through the year, but because of Doyle's impeccable courtliness, it was conducted at the highest level of discourse. I told the good colonel that I wanted to find out what I would write about *The Sound and the Fury* and *Light in August* much more than I cared what academics and critics I had never heard of thought of those books.

"It is a matter of discipline, Mr. Conroy," Colonel Doyle said. "A quality that you are much dismissive of, both in your life as a cadet and as a student of literature."

"I want to be free to write about Faulkner and Lewis the same way you wrote about Frost in your book, *The Poetry of Robert Frost*. You wrote what you thought about Frost's poetry and didn't rely much on the opinions of others. There's not a single footnote in your book. I know, because I read it."

"It was a work of deep scholarship, a distillation of my lifelong love affair with Mr. Frost's poetry. Every word I wrote was deeply felt and deeply considered."

"I promise that everything I write about Faulkner and Lewis will be deeply felt and deeply considered."

"I trust the depths of your feelings, I truly do," Colonel Doyle said in all his sweet formality, "but I doubt if you've taken the time to deeply consider anything."

I laughed out loud, and Colonel Doyle twinkled with pleasure. "That's a perfect description of my personality," I said.

"You give off much static electricity, Mr. Conroy, and I would like to see you more grounded," he said. "How many pages of your senior essay have you written thus far?"

"About fifty, Colonel."

"Be honest, as I know you will. How many footnotes do you estimate having used?"

"I estimate approximately none."

Colonel Doyle covered his eyes with his hands and sighed. "Mr. Conroy, Mr. Conroy, what am I going to do without you?"

"Where do you think I should go to graduate school, Colonel Doyle?"

"Tell me again where you've gotten in?"

"Virginia, Emory, and Vanderbilt," I said.

"And where were you rejected?"

"Duke and the Iowa Writing School," I said. "The last is the one I really wanted to go to."

"Mr. Conroy," he said, "I've told you before. You do not learn how to write novels in a writing program. You learn how by leading an interesting life. Open yourself up to all experience. Let life pour through you the way light pours through leaves."

"Have you ever seen light pour through a footnote, Colonel?" I asked.

"They will devour you in graduate school, Mr. Conroy," he said sadly. "They will simply devour you."

WHEN I RETURNED TO CAMPUS AFTER the Easter break, I received a note from Mel that summoned me to a mandatory meeting of all the team captains of the athletic squads to vote for the Senior Class Sportsmanship Award. I entered the front door of the Armory for the first time all season because I realized I had nothing to fear from Mel anymore.

In a meeting room, the fifteen captains representing every form of athletics from the rifle team to the golf team arose one by one to deliver a short speech in support of their nominee for the award. When my turn came, I gave a speech far more passionate and emotional than any other speeches given. I nominated Jim Halpin, then told the story of playing freshman basketball as Halpin's backcourt mate, and my sense of awe when I watched his prodigious talent. I described his leading the Philadelphia Catholic League in scoring his senior year in high school and his extraordinary guard play his freshman year at The Citadel when he led our team to the best freshman record in history.

I said, "I could not have played a single minute of a single game if Jim Halpin had remained healthy, gentlemen. He had the quickest, most accurate, most beautiful jump shot I've ever seen. I think he'd be in The Citadel's Hall of Fame if he had not sustained a terrible knee injury. How did Halpin handle it? Like a champion. Without complaint. Without bitterness. Whatever light was in our locker room, Halpin provided it. He represents the very best of what a Citadel athlete can aspire to be. His fate as an athlete was bad. His character and sportsmanship were what we all wish we could be."

The room was deadly quiet when I finished praising Halpin, and when I walked back into the sunshine from that meeting, I thought I had won Jim Halpin the Senior Class Sportsmanship trophy. It was a killing thing to me when I interviewed Jim for this book, and he told me that the injury that ruined his basketball career in the 1960s was easily treatable with modern sports medicine. I cannot walk by the wall of plaques that honor the Citadel Hall of Fame inductees without thinking that Halpin's name would be on that wall if I could take back one ruinous moment during a single scrimmage of our sophomore year. Though Halpin was unlucky, his grace under misfortune was moving and inspirational. If my class wanted sportsmanship, Halpin helped write the book on that particular virtue, found only in athletes who knew how to handle both success and misfortune with wordless, uncomplaining class.

Then The Citadel began to prepare me for my life as a writer. Though my college is well-known for the militancy of its spirit, no college in America has had as powerful an influence in pushing one of its sons or daughters in the direction of the writing life as The Citadel exerted on me in my final month as a cadet. The dean of the college, General James W. Duckett, called me into his office in the beginning of May to tell me The Citadel Development Foundation had selected me as the first recipient of their CDF Fellowship. The foundation would pay for me to receive my master's degree if I would promise to come back and teach for two years in The Citadel's English department. I sprinted across campus to Colonel Doyle's house to tell him the amazing news. Colonel Doyle and Clarice had already received the news and were waiting for me. I picked Colonel Doyle up and danced around as Clarice pleaded with me to put her husband down. Clarice fixed me a cup of English tea, and they toasted me with two dainty glasses of Amontillado sherry.

"I knew you would catch the Poe reference, Mr. Conroy," Colonel Doyle said.

"I'll have a cask of Amontillado when I teach here, Colonel," I promised. "Not just a bottle. A whole cask."

Colonel Doyle raised his glass and said, "I look forward to the day when I can call you colleague."

The following week The Citadel dispatched me to Columbia with six other cadets to represent the college at the annual conference of the South Carolina College Press Association, with representatives of all publications on college campuses throughout the state. I was sent as the official representative of *The Shako*, The Citadel's only literary magazine. It was exhilarating for me to represent my college in something besides an athletic uniform. I sat beside a beautiful young woman named Donna Fuller from Converse College who had been elected co-editor of her yearbook the next year, and she was mysterious and ambitious. She was the first southern girl I'd ever met who talked of New York and Europe and a life far removed from the South and its steely, unbending tyranny over the lives of its girls. She did not utter a single uninteresting word the entire night. She picked me up that night, and there has never lived a young man any riper for the picking. As I sat there falling for this blond flame of a woman, the president of the organization announced the winner of the award for the short story, and I heard my name called. I was numb with surprise as I walked toward the head table to receive my award for the story that had only won me the wrath of Mel Thompson until that moment. When I returned to my table, Donna Fuller squeezed my hand and said, "I didn't know you were a writer."

"I'm not," I said.

"Don't be embarrassed," she said. "It's a wonderful thing to be."

The following weekend, at The Citadel's annual awards day ceremony, General Hugh P. Harris announced that I had won the Shako Award for creative writing in both poetry and the short story. I walked to the stage in full dress and was met by Major William Alexander, the faculty advisor to *The Shako*. The major presented me with two medals, then held my wrist and said, "This is only the beginning for you, Mr. Conroy. The Citadel expects great things from you. Great things. Do not let us down."

JOHN WARLEY AND I HAD BECOME INSEPARABLE during our last months at The Citadel. We saw each other every day and often rode off into the Charleston night on weekends to talk of the lives we were about to begin living in earnest. In those months leading up to our graduation, our souls locked into place and our friendship deepened and held, and

John became one of those friends that I call on when I am most limping and troubled. John turns to me when he needs a friend who will not turn his back on him, either. It is friends like John Warley that make me wish I had a dozen Citadel educations.

Toward the end of the pollen-scented days of that long spring, I walked with John Warley beneath the avenue of live oaks that ran between third and fourth battalions to the mess hall. Final exams were upon us, and John had been accepted into law school at the University of South Carolina. My mother had just written to tell me that I was on my own in graduate school, that my family would not help me with any expenses I incurred while seeking my graduate degree. Suddenly, the future seemed like enemy territory. Because I thought a graduate degree would make me smarter and make me read even more of the greatest books and read them with a mordant eye and an ear for cant and sentimentality that'd serve me well, I looked toward graduate school as some place of deliverance. Though I felt that there were books locked inside me, they needed coaxing or luring out toward the light. I needed a final seasoning, a deepening, before I sat down to play in the fields of language.

John and I entered the mess hall in the great gathering of the jocks and lettermen who were pumped and noisy as they took their seats in a disorderly fashion for the Athletics Award Banquet. The teams were all folded into each other, basketball players towering over golfers, swimmers looking svelte and raffish beside linebackers. Warley and I grabbed seats at a front table near the dais. I waved to Cauthen and Kennedy, who sat at the end of our table. Across the room I spotted Root and blew him a kiss. He rewarded me with his giant middle finger. The trophies glittered on their own special table. I had never won a trophy at The Citadel although I had come to this event nursing the secret hope that I might win the basketball trophy for "Most Improved Player." Even though I was proving my own pettiness by harboring such a wish, I couldn't help it. I had walked away from three previous award banquets with an unquenchable lust for the flashy gold of trophies. I wanted one and wanted it badly. This was my last chance.

The swimmers and the golfers and the soccer players and the other minor sports went first, and friends of mine held their trophies aloft and shook them to loud cheers. The wrestling team drew a standing ovation of several minutes in duration when they were recognized for their un-defeated season and Southern Conference Championship. The Corps knew how to praise and when to praise and whom to praise. The wrestlers stood on their chairs to receive our applause.

Then, the president of the senior class, Ed Cole, rose to present the Senior Class Sportsmanship trophy. I looked over to where Jim Halpin was sitting. I wanted to make sure I was watching Halpin's face when his name was called. I was watching it closely when Ed, after giving a brief history of the award, said, "This year's sportsmanship trophy goes to a great guy, a great cadet, a great basketball player, and a great writer—Pat Conroy."

Through warm applause, I staggered toward the dais to receive the trophy, wondering where I went wrong with my fiery endorsement of Jim Halpin, and how in the hell Ed Cole knew I was a writer. It was a point of pride in the Corps that no one read *The Shako*, yet Ed became the first person to announce to a roomful of people that I was a writer. With a great sense of shame, I brought the large trophy back to the table and set it down beside Warley, who said, "I'll help you carry it back to the barracks. It's going to take two of us."

The basketball trophies were awarded last. I held my breath as Mel Thompson gave a lukewarm speech about our team's dismal year. He tried to be generous and businesslike, but I could feel his disappoint-ment and the bitter aftertaste as his words settled over the crowd. Mel announced that the first trophy was to go to the most improved basket-ball player on the team. I held my breath and lofted a prayer toward the stars. I bit my lip, then bit it harder when I heard Mel say: "The most improved player on the 1966–67 basketball team is . . . Greg Connor." With everyone else, I applauded, though I was crushed that my best chance of winning a basketball trophy had just slipped through my fin-gers. I touched the sportsmanship trophy, tracing my name on the plaque with tenderness.

Then the mess hall grew quiet as Mel lifted the largest trophy to the dais. It was a gleaming gold basketball, regulation-sized, mounted on an oak base. The Coca-Cola Bottling Company gave it out every year to the most valuable player on the basketball team. I had watched Mike West, the splendid point guard, win it in 1964; Dick Martini had walked it to the barracks in 1965; and in 1966, Wig Baumann had accepted it. I looked across the room at John DeBrosse and Danny Mohr. Their faces were both taut and drained of color. I thought DeBrosse had an edge, but Danny had come back strong at the end of the season, so he had a real shot at it, too.

Mel played the moment and took his time. Then, he said in a slow, deliberate voice, "The most valuable player for the 1966–67 Citadel Bulldogs is . . ." And he held this secret for several long moments until he sent one last thunderbolt through the heart of his damaged team when he said these two shocking words: ". . . Pat Conroy."

Blushing deeply, utterly horrified by the injustice, I made my way toward my coach. In my head I heard my own voice silently reel off some facts of my season: "I didn't even play against Wofford. Two points against Old Dominion. One point against Jacksonville. One against Georgia Southern. Three against George Washington." I was grateful that my teammates did not roar with laughter or walk out of the mess hall in protest as I approached my coach. I wanted to say something, argue with Mel and make a case for DeBrosse or Mohr or both, but I was still reeling from the concussion of my name being called, catching me completely unprepared.

Mel handed me the trophy, smiling at me warmly when he said, "Congratulations, Pat. You were a lot better than I ever thought you were. A lot better."

"Thanks, Coach," I said, and turned back toward my table and the applause.

So, I rose and began the slow, miraculous, even triumphant walk back to Fourth Battalion, with John Warley at my side, a friend for the ages. Slowly, we moved beneath a colonnade of oaks, the air spiced with tidal creeks and hidden gardens. John had won the first Frank Murphy Award, honoring the football captain who had been killed in Vietnam. Trophy-laden, Warley and I made our drifting promenade of gold last as long as we could, both of us with full knowledge that we were holding fast to what would certainly be one of the best days of our lives. On the walk, I let myself, at last, be taken by the utter wonder of the moment and how I must let it teach me the urgency of dreaming hard and dreaming big.

When we reached the guardroom, I put in a collect call to my parents' house in Falls Church. When my mother answered, I could not control my excitement and blurted out, "Mom, you're not going to believe the next thing I'm going to tell you! I can't even believe it myself. It's a miracle, Mom. I got the Most Valuable Player award for the basketball team and the Senior Class Sportsmanship Award."

"My Lord, Pat," my mother said. "You must be so proud. You worked hard for those awards."

"I didn't deserve it, Mom." I wanted to talk to her about the enormous guilt I felt about DeBrosse and Mohr, when I heard my father's voice on the extension: "You sure didn't deserve it, pal. What a shitty team to have you as its MVP! The way I rate talent, son, you were the twelfth best basketball player on that team."

"Don, don't you dare ruin Pat's night."

"He knows what I'm saying is right, don't you, son?" my father asked.

"Yes, sir. I do know that," I said.

"What was the other award you got?" he asked.

"The Senior Class Sportsmanship Award, Dad," I said, bracing for what I knew was coming.

"The Senior Class Pussy Award. You won that in high school, too. If there's ever a pussy award for a ballplayer, it always goes to my favorite little girl."

"I've got to go," I said. "Big day tomorrow. I'll see y'all at graduation. Say hi to the kids."

I took my two trophies, one in each arm, and walked out to the quadrangle and slowly made my way across the textured, moonlit landscape of my cadet life and toward the history of the one to come. Then, I heard the cheering begin along the galleries of Romeo Company. Word had come to R Company that I had won the two trophies, and my company poured out of their rooms to greet me. The applause grew louder as I climbed the stairs to my room on fourth division. I walked through the joyous noise of my shouted name, of boys who liked me because I was one of them and had brought honor to our company.

Entering my room, I saw my roommate Mike Devito studying for his English history exam. He was surprised when he noted the size of the trophies I bore in my arms. Wordless, Mike rose and approached, my handsome and powerful roommate, my protector, my wingman, my paisan.

Mike picked me up by the waist and hoisted me into the air. Mike, who had known of my great self-doubt as a basketball player, who had awakened when he heard me crying in the lower bunk after I didn't get in the Wofford game, and who comforted me with soft words from a rough yet tender boy who made the word "roommate" a holy one. Mike walked from the door to the window with both me and my trophies high above him. Then he turned and walked me back to the door. He and I didn't say a word, and I let him do it twice more because I understood the necessities of ritual. I was so moved that I couldn't have spoken if I'd wanted to when I realized that my roommate was honoring me for my struggles and disappointments. He was giving me a one-man parade at the end of my losing season.

Two weeks after my graduation from The Citadel, Mel Thompson was fired as head basketball coach. Louis Chestnut wrote: "The fact that a change was taking place had been known positively by the *Evening Post* for some months but, in deference to the school's recruiting program, and Thompson's own negotiations for other employment, confirmation was withheld."

Chestnut quoted Mel as saying: "I have talked to a number of people, but I have not determined in my own mind if I'll remain in coaching or take a job in private business. When you make a change, you want to make the right one. Anytime you change, you must consider what is best for your family. I do not think anything is open in basketball right now that I would be interested in."

I sat down to write a letter to the *Charleston News and Courier* telling that newspaper exactly what I thought of The Citadel firing Mel Thompson. Though I did not know it then, it began a long and honorable letter-writing exchange between me and that newspaper. Whenever I wrote a letter, I found out that I had a small talent for bombast and petty fulmination. In this letter, I tried to tell Charleston and The Citadel about the overarching difficulty of putting together a winning basketball team at a military college that prided itself in having the world's toughest plebe system. I told of watching six-foot-ten centers walking out of Lesesne Gate, and five-foot-ten guards like me with small hands and no outside shot deciding to stick around for four years. I raged about playing on the best freshman basketball team in history and losing half that team to the plebe system. I told the story of how we'd lost Donnie Biggs to Florida State. How could a coach win under such circumstances, and why didn't anyone in this city understand the impossibility of Mel's situation?

Then I segued into a long disquisition on the traditional hatred of athletes that every military college embraces as one of the secret gospels of the long gray lines. I spoke of scoring twenty-two points against the Furman freshmen and finding a group of cadremen waiting for me back in the barracks to put me through my own personal sweat party so I wouldn't feel that I was superior to my classmates. It happened to DeBrosse and Bridges and Mohr and Zinsky and Kroboth and Hooper—it had happened to every jock I knew at The Citadel. If the Corps hated its jocks, how were the athletes and coaches supposed to win in such an alienated environment?

I wrote far into the night. I postured, I railed, I tongue-lashed and blistered General Harris for firing my coach. That Harris had dared fire the only college coach I'd ever have did not sit well with me. There was something about Mel's dark, unapproachable solitude that touched me as I launched even more deeply into my passionate and out-of-control defense of him. I finished my letter at three in the morning, addressed it to Thomas Waring, the editor of the *News and Courier*, and mailed it the next morning before I left for work. It was my first letter to any editor.

A week later Mr. Waring answered my letter with one of his own. I wish I had saved his letter, but I was so humiliated by its demure arguments that I buried it on the bottom of the garbage can. It said something like this:

Dear Mr. Conroy,

I would have liked very much to publish your letter to the editor. But I'm afraid we're loath to publish thirteen handwritten pages, written on legal sheets, on our editorial pages. You understand, I pray, that we have certain space limitations. I found your letter interesting. Have you ever thought about writing with economy and restraint? Have you ever thought about the power of concision? The elegance of simplicity? Would you consider resubmitting your letter? Could you say in three paragraphs what you said in thirteen pages? Could you drop the anger, the self-righteousness, and that irritating didacticism? I would appreciate your attention on this matter.

Yours very truly,
Thomas Waring

That letter marked my final act as a Citadel basketball player. Mel Thompson simply walked out of our lives forever. As a coach, Mel was lord and master of his environment at the Armory. There was not a player on my team who was not afraid or intimidated by him. His will to win boiled over in his black-eyed fury to push us to our physical limits at practice. Mel wanted with all his heart for us to be warriors on the court the way he was at NC State, and it frustrated him that we sprang from a softer, less driven tribe. My team, that began the season with such wide-eyed wonder and optimism, became Mel Thompson's Achilles' heel, his pass at Thermopylae, his OK Corral. When the shouting was done, Mel left town with his family none of us knew and returned to Richmond, Indiana. Like a storm center, he drifted out of the sea lanes of Charleston and moved all the eerie power of his darkness toward the plains of the Midwest. My misguided, hopeless awe of him had nowhere to go, and my team broke up like an archipelago of volcanic islands formed out of heat and chaos. Not one of my teammates said goodbye to me when I graduated. My team was an accurate and flawless reflection of our coach's theory of coaching: we lacked all unity, camaraderie, and fellowship. Mel was suspicious and paranoid, and he discovered that these rueful gifts were easily transferable to his team's unstable psyche. His paranoia proved reality-based, and his firing loosed him from the moorings of his game. Mel Thompson never coached another basketball team. Mel never got to know us at all, and it seemed against his most basic philosophy to try. Abruptly, he left as a stranger to us, and even worse, left his players as strangers to each other.

The team itself melted into the history of those days without a trace. So alienated was my team that I was not invited to a single one of my teammates' weddings nor were any of them invited to mine. We turned our backs on each other and for the most part, played no part in each other's lives. We did what all bad teams do. We pretended our losing season had never happened, or that losing was good for anything but a cause for the deepest shame. There were no covenants between us, no treaties to be broken, and no promises to honor. Our team was composed of twelve islands, bound by an uneasy alliance, and mindful of the dysfunction of our commonwealth and the vanity of even thinking we could take to the court as a unit forged by unbreakable bonds. We vanished into time, and tried to forget all we could about each other.

# PART 4

# THE POINT GUARD'S WAY OF KNOWLEDGE

CHAPTER 30

# NEW GAME

L URKING AS BOTH TOUCHSTONE AND THE DEFINING MYTH BEHIND this book has stood the evasive, mysterious, and wordless figure of Mel Thompson. As I was taking notes and coaxing out memories from my teammates, I resigned myself to Mel never emerging long enough for me to interview him about a season that he had every reason to forget. In the first year, when Doug Bridges called to tell me he had located Mel on the Internet, I thought it was only a matter of time before I would fly to Indianapolis to strip-mine Mel's memories of that long-ago year. Finding Mel was not difficult, but getting him to answer my inquiries proved almost impossible. He would not even return my phone calls.

In my own mind, Mel assumed the shapes of great, impersonal forces of nature like the Gulf Stream or the Gobi Desert or some remote, snow-dusted Alp—all dominate in their landscapes, yet are impersonal and impossible to know. I moved against Mel's storm front each time I wrote a page of this book and neared the critical point of deciding whether I should just fly to Indianapolis and knock on his front door. I lacked the journalist's instinct and comfort with bad manners, and thought I might catch a break if I remained patient. Mel's sense of privacy protected him like the shell of a tortoise. For his players, his silence became both our obsession and our wound.

Though I wrote Mel as well as leaving messages on his answering machine, I never received a reply. Then one day in deepest winter he answered the phone himself.

"Coach Thompson?" I said.

"If you're calling me 'coach,' we haven't seen each other for a long time," he replied.

"This is Pat Conroy, Coach. I'll be in Indianapolis in a couple of weeks and would like to take you to dinner."

"Okay," said Mel.

The first dinner went without incident, but Mel was withholding and off-putting, giving away very little of himself in conversation. I learned that after being fired, Mel and his family had returned to his hometown of Richmond, Indiana, where he had owned and operated a pizza parlor and a steak house for many years before a horrendous underground explosion destroyed a large portion of the downtown area, killing dozens of people. Though his buildings suffered damage, they were not destroyed, but the fear of other explosions turned downtown Richmond into a no-man's-land, and his clientele vanished overnight. In Indianapolis, Mel took a job as manager of a cement factory, but had recently retired after the death of his second wife.

As we sat in the rooftop restaurant, The Eagle's Nest, I noticed again Mel's thirty-eight-inch-long arms and his huge hands with fingers tapered like a pianist's. When I was in college I used to envy those arms and huge hands. Mel still looked every inch the basketball player. The waitress led us to a window table and as I sat down, I felt slightly seasick and then I realized we were in one of those dreadful restaurants that revolves 360 degrees while you pick at your arugula salad. In my travels, I have discovered there is an inverse ratio in the quality of the food to the number of full circumnavigations of a city's four quadrants that I was forced to endure in a single evening. As my coach and I moved counterclockwise above the city of Indianapolis, I told him about my encounter with John DeBrosse in Dayton in 1995. I told him how I had thought about him and that team often since I walked out of the Armory for the last time. I had interviewed every guy on the team extensively, and I thanked him for letting me interview him.

Mel said, "I'm afraid I'm not going to be much help. I talked to Ed Thompson about this, and neither of us can remember much about that year. It was a real up-and-down year, and I wasn't at all surprised when General Harris fired me. I was Mark Clark's guy. The general and I liked each other. Understood each other. We were both fighters deep down and respected that about each other. Harris was more of a bureaucratic type guy who liked to dot the *i*'s and cross his *t*'s. We never clicked much. The chemistry wasn't there."

"Do you think General Harris knew how hard it was to win in a military college, Coach?" I asked.

"We had to recruit a certain kind of kid, one who didn't make a face when we mentioned The Citadel was a military college. It wasn't for everyone. You know that. But if I could get a boy there, I thought I could keep him. Didn't always work. I remember one kid who showed up at eight in the morning outside the Armory. When I gave him the old pep talk about why it was important to stay at The Citadel, he looked me right in the eye and said, 'If you were in my shoes, Coach Thompson, would you stay here and take the shit that goes on in the barracks?' I didn't have an answer for him. That guy was a real player, too."

"The ones that left were always players," I said. "Did you know what the plebe system did to your athletes?"

Mel looked at me for a moment, then said, "I didn't care what happened in the barracks. I couldn't control that. I worried about what happened in practices. I got guys ready for games. But I will admit that when I was trying to recruit against other coaches, they had one word they used that became my biggest enemy."

"What word?"

He laughed and said, "Clink."

"Clink?" I said, puzzled.

"Yeah, clink. That's the sound of the gates locking at The Citadel every night. That's the 'clink' that takes away your freedom for the next four years. I have to admit it was a pretty good strategy to keep a boy out of The Citadel, but we went for the type of kid that word wouldn't bother," he said as we completed our first circling of the Indianapolis skyline.

The next morning Mel picked me up at nine o'clock sharp and drove me to his condominium. His neighborhood was modest, and inside, the house was clean and comfortable and well-lit, but it seemed strangely unlived-in and underpopulated. His recently deceased wife, Julia, had arranged her basket collection on the upper shelves in the kitchen. There was also a platoon of empty wine bottles arranged as orderly as cadets.

"What are the wine bottles, Coach?"

"Great evenings to remember. Me and Julia," Mel said. "Man, we had some times together. No one could've gotten me to go to all the places she did. Hell, she got me to go to Mexico. Can you imagine me in Mexico?"

"Sounds like she was something."

"Julia," he said. "Julia was the best. The best."

I thought I would learn little things about my coach on my visit, but I learned few. My great surprise was Mel Thompson's haunted tenderness whenever Julia's name came up. My coach had been deeply in love with his second wife, and there was a fierceness and urgency in the way he missed her.

"What about your first wife, Coach?" I asked.

"Didn't work out. Problems."

"The kids?"

"Great. I got the best kids. They really take care of me now. The girls look out for me; the boys worry about me. Did you know my son Mike played basketball at Valparaiso?"

"Barney told me that. Was he any good?"

"Yeah, he was good. But he just didn't have the mean streak athletics requires. He wasn't the killer his old man was, if you know what I mean."

"I know what you mean, Coach."

"I wanted him to go to East Carolina, but he made the choice. I never believed in pushing my kids into doing things I loved. Reliving the past through your kids is a mistake. But Mike, he was too nice. The kid was just too damn nice. All my kids are."

Mel softened when the subject of his children arose, and though I could not tell what kind of father he had been, I knew he loved his children with all the ardor that his fierce heart could muster. I saw pictures of them, and they were attractive and fresh-faced. I realized I had come into Mel's place thinking he fathered like he'd coached. I expected to find terminal malfunction loose in the household he had brought up.

But whenever I turned to the year I was writing about, Mel's ability to remember the slightest detail deserted him. If I mentioned a game, it had slipped from both consciousness and memory. If I mentioned his players, Mel would provide me with the most banal descriptions of them. When I tried to dig deeply, Mel would answer me with vagueness or disinterest until my questions began to sound rude even to me. Mel never got angry, he simply seemed not to have lived through the same year I had. Where I wore scars, contusions, and bruises, it seemed not to have laid a single finger on him. My years at The Citadel were nothing compared to his years with the Wolfpack. So I let him drift back to his playing days, his glory days in the ACC when he was king of all he saw and bright with all the passions that still enlivened him and all the poisons that still defined him.

That night, John DeBrosse drove over from Dayton to join us for dinner in the movable restaurant on top of the Hyatt Regency. Again, Mel seemed in good spirits and happy to be with us as we told some of the stories the team had conjured up when piecing our last year together. Time and again, Mel would turn the conversation back to State or Everett Case or himself.

During one long, animated conversation, Mel told us how Case used to urge his guards to get the ball to the big men underneath the basket, the guys like him who could score. When the guards failed to make the passes, Case would reward them with lifetime seats on the bench. "I wanted the ball all the time. I loved shooting more than anything in the world. What was the point of basketball if you couldn't shoot it at the hole? I'd call for the damn ball every time down the court and the damn guards better get it to me if they knew what was good for them. You know what I've always hated? You know what I've always really hated?"

Mel was in a reverie as he remembered. "No, Coach," DeBrosse said, "what do you really hate?"

Mel looked at me and John and spat out the words. "Guards. I've always hated guards."

Stunned, his two guards from the '67 team stared at him as he resumed eating his steak.

When I said goodbye to Mel, I thanked him for meeting with me, and said, "Coach, I need to tell you something. I loved having you as my coach. I was proud to suit up and take the floor for you. And I wanted to thank you for all the time you spent with me as a boy. You never missed a practice."

"Not me," Mel said. "Not one in my whole career."

"On the team I'm writing about," I said, "nine of us loved you. Three didn't. That's not a bad percentage."

"None of my boys ever quit on me," Mel said. "Every one of them gave me everything they had and everything I asked."

"I'll tell them that," I said.

"Gotta go," Mel said.

"You want to meet me and Johnny for breakfast tomorrow?" I asked.

"No," Mel Thompson said, and walked back out of my life.

ON THE FLIGHT BACK, I flipped through my notes and thought about Mel. He remained untouchable at his core. He had dominated me in every conversation and then I realized something more astonishing. Mel had not asked me a single question about any of my teammates or myself. He never asked me if I had married or had children or if my parents were alive or where I lived or what I had done with my life. Before I interviewed him, I thought he would like a rundown of his team and how the lives of his players had played out. Mel lacked all curiosity about us, and only once during my time with him did I receive any indication that he knew what I did for a living.

"I hear you write books," he said.

"Yes, sir," I replied.

"I've never read one of them."

"That's not a requirement, Coach," I said.

"Don't plan to read any of them," he said. There were no books in his apartment.

I did not say it, but I thought it: I bet you'll read one of them, pal.

I believe Mel asked me nothing because he is still lost in the strangeness of being Mel Thompson. I think that is a full-time job, a bizarre trip to the fun house and a lostness into self that produces confusion and dilemma. I do not believe that Mel Thompson ever thought about his ex-players once in his Indiana life. His mind drifted toward the years of victories and championships when he spent every waking moment with winners shaped and tormented by Everett Case. I spent my senior year exiled among losers shaped and tormented by Mel Thompson. Alone, among my coaches and teammates, the year was painful in the extreme. It also was the finest year of my life. Not once since then have I felt so fully alive, so vital and necessary.

FOR FOUR YEARS I DRIFTED BACK INTO the homes and lives of my lost team, met their wives and grown children, ate dinner with their friends and neighbors, and questioned them about the memories they carried from that year. They helped me resurrect games from uncharted depths that were all but unrecallable to me. When DeBrosse mentioned the sounds of elephants somewhere in the deep bowels of the Jacksonville Coliseum, a whole herd of circus elephants gathered in my head, rescued from oblivion at last, bellowing out into the north Florida night. Bornhorst told of the escape routes from an old hotel in the middle of Richmond, and Connor spoke of the provocative beauty of an East Carolina cheerleader who would be fifty-five years old today. But for Greg and me, that pretty girl will be twenty-one and glowing with radiant youth until the day we die. Some of the guys remembered the restaurants that served the best steaks, and others the hotels with the most comfortable beds; others the unstable, effervescent details of the games themselves. I discovered that no one forgets a star player, but it is very difficult to remember a role player or a set-up man or a sixth man off the bench. Though I thought I was invisible to my teammates, they were watching with uncommon vigilance, remembering things I said that I have not the slightest recollection of saying. In my own mind, I was a slouching, ill-tempered boy trapped in a phlegmatic, baffled personality; my teammates tell me that I was bright and good-natured, trying to spread good cheer among them.

I traveled to Houston to interview Bob Cauthen then flew to Dallas to talk to Brian Kennedy. I spent two days with John DeBrosse in Huber Heights, Ohio, followed by a meeting in the Newark Airport Marriott with Jim Halpin and his wife, Eileen. I could not get Bill Zinsky to answer my letters or phone calls, so I left New Jersey without talking to him. I drove to Charleston to interview Dave Bornhorst, then drove up I-26 to listen to Doug Bridges talk. With Bridges I hit a solid mother lode of information, discovering that he had returned to that year hundreds of times and tried to figure out why it remained so painful and so meaningful. The year had marked him with its scars and had stayed with him.

"I'm not surprised you're here, Conroy," he told me. "I knew this year was going to come back into my life. I always felt that. I just didn't know it would come disguised as you."

One night in 1998, I received a surreptitious phone call from Bridges, who surprised me by saying, "Zinsky's in my living room, Conroy. He just showed up from Glassboro, New Jersey."

"I'll be there in two and a half hours," I said, then grabbed an overnight bag and raced for my car.

When I reached Doug's lakeside home on the outskirts of Columbia, Zinsky and I embraced and he said, "Mel Thompson ruined me as a basketball player, Conroy. He wore me down a little at a time, until there was nothing left. Mel and The Citadel were too much for me. I left that place and never played ball again."


THE NIGHT BEFORE I TOOK A TRAIN TO interview my teammate Al Kroboth, I attended the one hundredth anniversary of my publishing company, Doubleday, and stood on the top floor of the Bertelsmann Building in Times Square chatting with Margaret Atwood, a Canadian novelist I admire immensely. Doubleday had included both of us in the *Doubleday 100th Birthday Reader*, and I had opened it to see my name listed with Bram Stoker, Booker T. Washington, Rudyard Kipling, Aldous Huxley, Anne Frank, and Joseph Conrad. I remembered coming into New York over twenty-five years before, proud as a dragonfly and insecure and fidgety as a baitfish, feeling like a con man for staking any claim as a writer.

I walked to a place commanding a view of south Manhattan where I lifted a glass of champagne and asked my agent of twenty-five years, Julian Bach, to join me in a toast to New York City. To the east, I saluted the glorious Chrysler Building and the UN Building and the silken, turbulent lights of Brooklyn. Julian had taken me to my first opera at Lincoln Center, having no idea that I had neither heard of an opera named *Otello* nor of a place called Lincoln Center. I raised my glass and bowed, then said, "I'm thanking the city of New York for its extraordinary kindness to me. It spits boys and girls like me out by the tens of thousands. It keeps asking me back. I'm grateful beyond words, Julian."

Then I walked to the west windows where I looked out toward the New York Times building and Broadway and the West Side Highway and the great black gash of the Hudson and the glittering stream of lights of New Jersey where Al Kroboth was awaiting my visit. Of all the interviews this was the one I feared most. Looking at my reflection in the massive window and the great spillage of man-made lights in the diamond-braceleted streets below, I knew that tomorrow I would face my hardest encounter with how I conducted myself during the Vietnam War.

AL KROBOTH MET ME AT the train station when I got off the second stop from New York City after Newark. We shook hands and took each other's measure, then Al turned his truck toward home and began quizzing me. "Why are you writing this book, Conroy? No one wants to read about a losing team."

"If that is true, it will have serious consequences in my career."

"Americans love winners. They want to read about people like Michael Jordan."

"I think Michael Jordan might like my book," I said.

"Jordan's the best basketball player that ever lived. By far."

"I agree," I said. "But I saw Michael Jordan play baseball. He understands losing. He understands coming up short physically."

"Oh," Al said. "I see."

"Eventually, all of us play on a losing team. I'm trying to figure out if you learn more by losing than by winning."

"You always were a little weird, Conroy," Al said, smiling as he turned into his driveway.

On a clear fall day in Linville, New Jersey, Al Kroboth, one of the best big men to line up at center for the Citadel Bulldogs, gave me everything he had taken out of the Vietnam War. He asked that his wife, Patty, be present, and she was. The interview took a long time because I would have to wait for Big Al or Patty to stop weeping. Finally, all three of us were weeping at the power of the emotions unloosed upon us by Al's heart-stopping narrative. The story I tell now is the one Big Al told me in New Jersey as my face streamed with tears, the one told where we could not look at each other.

"Al," I said, with Patty sitting beside him. "Tell me what happened to you in Vietnam. Not just the facts; I'd like you to tell me how it all felt. I want you to make me feel it. America needs to hear this story."

"Just one thing," Al said with severity. "I am not a hero, Conroy. Don't you try to turn me into one."

"Do you believe that?" I asked Patty.

"No, I don't," Patty replied.

"Tell me your story, Al," I said. "I'll let it speak for itself."

"I'm *not* a hero, Conroy," he said again and again. "I met guys who were, but I'm not one of them."

"Just tell me," I said, and here is the story he told:

On his seventh mission as Captain Leonard Robertson's navigator in an A-6, Al was getting ready to deliver their payload as Robertson began to make his dive for the target area. Somewhere in that dive, the A-6 took on enemy fire and though Al has no memory of this, he punched out somewhere in the middle of this ill-fated dive and lost consciousness. Al does not know if he was unconscious for six hours or six days. As for Captain Leonard Robertson, his name is on the Wall in Washington, and Al wears a POW bracelet with Captain Robertson's name engraved on it.

When Al awoke, a Vietcong soldier held an AK-47 to his head. Al had broken his neck and back as well as shattered his left scapula bone. When he was well enough to get to his feet, two armed Vietcong led Al from the jungles of South Vietnam to a prison in Hanoi. For three months Al Kroboth walked barefooted through the most impassable terrain in Vietnam, and he did it in the dead of night. He bathed when it rained and he slept in bomb craters with his two Vietcong captors. Infections began to explode on his body as they moved north, his legs alive with leeches picked up in rice paddies.

At the very time of Al's walk, I had a small role in organizing the only antiwar demonstration ever held in Beaufort, South Carolina, the home of Parris Island and the Marine Corps Air Station. In a Marine Corps town at that time it was difficult to come up with a quorum of people who had even minor disagreements about the Vietnam War. But my small group managed to attract a crowd of about a hundred and fifty to Beaufort's waterfront. With my mother and my wife on either side of me, we listened to the featured speaker, Dr. Howard Levy, suggest to the very few young enlisted Marines present that if they got to Vietnam, here's how they could help end this war: roll a grenade under their officer's bunk when he was asleep in his tent. Called fragging, he explained, it was becoming more and more popular with the ground troops who knew this war was bullshit. I was enraged by the suggestion. At that very moment my father was asleep in Vietnam. But in 1972, at the age of twenty-seven, I thought I was serving America's interests by pointing out what massive flaws and miscalculations and corruptions had led her to conduct a ground war in Southeast Asia.

In the meantime, Al and his captors had finally arrived in the North, and the Vietcong traded him to the North Vietnamese soldiers for the final leg of the trip to Hanoi. Many times when they stopped to rest for the night, the local villagers tried to kill him. His captors wired his hands behind his back at night, so he learned to sleep in the center of huts when the villagers began sticking knives and bayonets into the thin walls. After air raids, old women would come into huts to excrete on him and yank out hunks of his hair. Al Kroboth's walk north was nightmarish, Dantesque, and courageous. It was a relief when his guards finally delivered him to the POW camp where they kept the prisoners captured in South Vietnam.

It was at the camp that Al began to die. He threw up every meal he ate. An American doctor thought Al was the oldest soldier in the prison because his appearance was so gaunt and skeletal. But the extraordinary camaraderie that sprang up in all the POW camps caught fire in Al in time to save his life.

When I was demonstrating against Nixon and the Christmas bombings, Al and his fellow prisoners were holding hands during the full fury of those bombings, singing "God Bless America." It was those bombings that convinced Hanoi they would do well to release the American POWs and my college teammate. When he told me about the C-141 landing in Hanoi to pick up the prisoners, Al Kroboth said he felt no emotion, none at all, until he saw a giant American flag painted on the plane's tail.

"The flag," Al said, choking. "It had the biggest American flag on it I ever saw. To this day, I cry when I think of it. Seeing that flag, I started crying. I couldn't see the plane, I just saw that flag. All the guys started cheering. But that flag . . . that flag."

It took a full five minutes before I could see the page I was writing on again. Al and Patty held on to each other, weeping. It took another minute before Al could find his voice again.

"Candy-man, our Vietcong guard on the bus to the airport, said to me, 'Come with your family and visit us after the war is over.' I said, 'I'd love to come back to your country. In an A-6. To drop a nuke on this whole place.' There was no shaking hands, Conroy. No farewells. No teary eyes. When my name was called I walked in military fashion toward an Air Force colonel at the foot of the plane. I saluted him and said, 'Lieutenant Alan Kroboth, reporting for duty, sir.' He returned the salute and said, 'Welcome home, son.' I walked up the ramp and was met by the most beautiful Air Force nurses I had ever seen. They sat me down. Everyone was quiet, the POWs just sitting. When all our guys were on board, the doors closed. The ramp went up. The engines started. Still no sound from the POWs. The plane taxied. The pilot's voice came on and he said, 'Everyone sit down. We got low cloud cover but we're getting out of here.' Then we're lifting off. That quiet continued. No emotion. No sighs of relief. It was eerie. Then the pilot's voice comes on again. 'Feet wet'—which means we are now flying over water. 'Feet wet. We are out of North Vietnamese air space.'

"That's when the cheering started, Conroy. The tears. The screaming. The yelling. That's when I knew it was over. Finally over. The whole thing. Over."

It took a minute or two for Al to be able to speak again. Then he told me that the POWs had no idea how America would react to their homecoming. Since their prison guards constantly told them that all Americans considered them to be war criminals, and it was well-known that the war was widely unpopular, Al and the other POWs were uncertain what awaited them at Clark Field in the Philippines. They were stunned to be met by an adoring crowd of ten thousand who gave them a hero's welcome. Al was the last off the plane, and he saluted the commanding general of Clark Field, then marched between the surging crowd on a red carpet as people handed him flowers and reached out to touch him. A small girl leaned down from her father's shoulders to hand Al a piece of paper, telling him she had made it for him. Al took it, but did not read it until his bus started moving toward the hospital. In a childish scrawl, the little girl had printed out these words: "Greater love than this hath no man."

Five minutes passed before Al, Patty, or I could say a word. Then Al continued, "I still have that piece of paper. Got to the hospital. Marine guys separated from the Army and Air Force guys. Psychologists and psychiatrists were there for the guys with family problems. From the moment we got there they took care of us. Really were there for us. In every way possible. Took us to the mess hall. Every table and every tray and every plate was piled high with food. Lobster, steak, hams, turkeys, salads. For thirty guys. All of us piled it on our plates as high as we could, then sat down and ate two or three spoonfuls.

"People on the base kept bringing us pies and cakes and cookies. Night and day they came. On the second day they fitted us out in uniforms and I got a pair of glasses. Basic psych evaluations. Debriefing. Then an enlisted man said to me, 'Someone on the first floor wants to see you.' We were on the eighth floor and no one got up there. So I had to have an escort to go with me. When I got down there I see John Vaughan. You remember him, Conroy? Class of '68?"

"Sure I do, Al. He was a cheerleader. He was one of the guys who lead the Corps in cheering us, on the team I'm writing about."

It had become common knowledge among the Citadel alumni stationed at Clark Field that the Vietcong had stolen Al's Citadel ring, evidently when he was unconscious after being shot down. When Al came off the elevator on the first floor, Johnny Vaughan, an Air Force pilot, was waiting for him in the lobby. The two men shook hands, then embraced. Johnny began to remove his Citadel ring from his right hand. "Al, I'm not letting you go back to our country without wearing a Citadel ring. I'm not going to let you do that."

"No, Johnny," Al protested, "I can't. I lost too much weight. I'm too skinny. I'll lose it."

"You didn't hear me," said Johnny Vaughan. "You're not going back to our country without wearing the Citadel ring." He then put his own ring on Al Kroboth's finger.

As Al wept again, I thought about Johnny Vaughan, a young man I had not seen in thirty-two years, a man who, like me, was no longer young. I thought about the remarkable generosity of his grand gesture and I know of no other story that reveals the powerful forces that bind the entire Citadel family to the wearing of the ring. The ring was sacramental to us, the great enfolding circle of gold that was the coded, mysterious symbol of our singularity, which carries all the wonder and oneness of our fire-tested tribe. By removing his Citadel ring and placing it on the POW Al Kroboth's finger, I believe Johnny Vaughan wrote his name into the history of my college.

The Vietnam War was never just theoretical with me. It is deeply personal. My father served two tours of duty there, and almost every Marine I knew growing up spent time doing battle against North Vietnam and the Vietcong insurgents. A number of those men returned to this country in body bags. Practically my entire class of 1967 left the graduation stage as a first step that would take them almost directly to the war in Vietnam. It was not until I started losing classmates that I began to grieve for boys that I knew well.

News of my classmates' deaths began to reach me as I taught psychology and government at Beaufort High School the year after my graduation. Bruce Welge, who defended more boys accused of honor violations than any of my classmates, was killed while leading his own Army platoon. Dick O'Keefe, who stopped me in the gutter in front of the Citadel chapel our plebe year to tell me that President Kennedy had been shot in Dallas, died in a plane crash on his final mission before returning to the States. With Fred Carter I had played outfield on the freshman baseball team and was sick when I heard his plane disappeared from the radar screen while on an attack mission. There were many others, and I hold the memories of these boys sacred. I feel the brief flame of each of them when I finger the letterings of their names as I move along the black marble on the majestic and terrible wall in Washington that bears witness to their sacrifice. Their names scream out this question to me: "Did you do right by your country, Conroy? Did you do right by it?"

There is one Vietnam veteran's grave I will continue to visit until my death: Captain Joseph Wester Jones III, whose two daughters, Jessica and Melissa, I adopted when I married his widow, Barbara, in 1969. Throughout their childhood, I took the girls to visit their father's grave in Beaufort and would explain what all the inscriptions on his tombstone meant.

"What's the PH, Daddy?" Jessica would ask me.

"That means your father won the Purple Heart. Our country gives that to soldiers who get wounded defending their country."

"What's KIA, Daddy?" Melissa would ask.

"That's the greatest honor that can be on the grave of any soldier, Melissa and Jessica. That means your father was killed in action while fighting for his country."

On Memorial Day and Veterans Day, I make sure a rose is placed on West's grave. Frequently, I talk with him and let him know how his daughters are doing and where they are living and that Melissa's married the sweetest boy in the world and that his pretty granddaughter, Jessica's daughter, Elise, is doing well in school. I let him know that his girls are beautiful women now and that he would be proud as hell of them.

I met West's parents almost a year after Barbara and I married, and had no idea what to expect. Colonel Joe Jones was an Air Force pilot and his wife, Jean, was an exemplary military wife. Barbara's mother and father, also Air Force people, had hated me on sight, neither of them ever forgiving me for my antiwar sympathies. If the Joneses had spit in my face and said I was unworthy to raise their son's children, I would have understood perfectly. But the Joneses had a great surprise for me. With amazing generosity, they embraced me and folded me into their family. "Mom" and "Pap" Jones have been two of the most surprising and necessary friends of my adult life, and I admire them beyond all reckoning.

A few years ago, Mom and Pap spent a weekend with me at my home on Fripp Island. They insisted I take them on one of my "famous" tours of Beaufort. Showing off the incomparable beauty of Beaufort is one of the great joys of my life, and I do it with passion, quite well. But I got a surprise as I was ending my tour and took them to visit my mother's grave in the Beaufort National Cemetery. I had noticed the Joneses becoming uncharacteristically tense walking back to my car and did not speak as I drove over to their son's grave. Showing everyone where my girls' daddy is buried is always the last stop of my tour.

I did not realize my mistake until I got out of the car and approached West's grave. It never occurred to me that the death of their only son would be so unimaginably painful to the Joneses that they could never bring themselves to visit his gravesite. I had to catch Jean Jones as she leaned against my car, sobbing. Finally she said, "Thank you for knowing where our son's grave is, Pat. We haven't been back here since his burial."

I turned and watched Joe Jones kneel by his son's grave and clean some debris from the grass. Then Colonel Jones stood at rigid attention and brought his hand up to salute. Colonel Jones, the man I call Pap, completed that lovely salute and said in a clear, commanding voice: "Well done, son. Well done."

In the darkness of the sleeping Kroboth household, I began to assess my role as citizen when my country called my name and I shot her the bird. Unlike the stupid boys who wrapped themselves in Vietcong flags and burned the American one, I knew how to demonstrate against the war without flirting with treason or astonishingly bad taste, having come directly from the warrior culture of this country. But in the twenty-five years that have passed since South Vietnam fell, I have immersed myself in the study of totalitarianism in the unspeakable twentieth century. From *The Gulag Archipelago* to the works of Simone Weil to accounts of the unimaginable goose-stepping of the Third Reich across the borders of Germany, I have read the histories and commentaries and eyewitness accounts of those soul-killing events. Curious by nature, I have questioned survivors of Auschwitz and Bergen-Belsen and talked to Italians who told me tales of the Nazi occupation, to a Croat whose father had entertained Goering on his honeymoon, to partisans who had counted German tanks in the forests of Normandy, and to officers who had survived the disgraceful Bataan Death March. I read the newspaper reports during Pol Pot's shameless assault against his own people in Cambodia, and the rise of Saddam Hussein and Gadhafi of Libya. I have watched the fall of communism in Russia and have a picture of my father pushing against the Berlin Wall during the time it was being torn down. Many times I have quizzed journalists who reported on wars in Bosnia, the Sudan, the Congo, Rwanda, Angola, Indonesia, Guatemala, El Salvador, Chile, Northern Ireland, Algeria—I have come to revere words like "democracy" and "freedom," the right to vote, the incomprehensibly beautiful origins of my country, and the grandeur of the extraordinary vision of the founding fathers. Do I not see America's flaws? Of course I do. But I now can honor her basic, incorruptible virtues, the ones that let me walk the streets screaming my ass off that my country had no idea what it was doing in South Vietnam. My country let me scream to my heart's content, the same country that produced both me and Al Kroboth.

Now, at this moment in New Jersey, I come to a conclusion about my actions as a young man when Vietnam was a dirty word to me. I wish that I had entered into the Marine Corps and led a platoon of Marines in Vietnam. I would like to think I would have trained my Marines well and that the Vietcong would have had their hands full if they entered a firefight with my men. From the day of my birth, I was programmed to enter the Marine Corps as a fighting man, but then my eyes locked onto the headlights of the sixties and took me far afield of the man I was supposed to be. Now I understand I should have protested the war after my return from Vietnam, after I had done my duty. I have come to a conclusion about my country that I knew then in my bones, but lacked the courage to act on: America is a good enough country to die for even when she is wrong.

So I looked for some conclusion, a summation of this trip to my teammate's house. I wanted to come to the single right thing, a true thing that I may not like, but that I could live with as a man. After hearing Al Kroboth's story of his walk across Vietnam and his brutal imprisonment in the North, I found myself passing harrowing, remorseless judgment on myself. I had not turned out to be the man I had once envisioned myself to be. I thought I would be the kind of man that America could point to and say, "There. That's the guy. That's the one that got it right. The whole package. The one I can depend on." It had never once occurred to me that I would find myself in the position I did on that night in Al Kroboth's house in Roselle, New Jersey: an American coward spending the night with an American hero.

AT MY THIRTIETH HOMECOMING AT THE CITADEL, my team reassembled itself in Charleston for our own personal reunion. Eleven of us met in the field house, toured our old locker room, looked around the recently restored Armory, then walked out and viewed the Friday-afternoon parade. As we were watching, Caldwell Warley, a recent graduate and my friend John Warley's eldest son, came up to me and said, "Conroy, I thought it was illegal for you to come on this campus. Didn't the legislature pass a law or something?"

That same Friday night, my team and I went to root for the opening basketball game of the Citadel Bulldogs. To further complicate the emotions of the gathering of my team, The Citadel was playing its first game against Francis Marion University, which had just hired my young cousin, Ed Conroy, as its head basketball coach. It was easy for the Conroy family to root against Francis Marion, but it was impossible for us not to want the very best for young Ed.

My father had driven down from Atlanta for both the team reunion and Cousin Ed's first game against his alma mater, where he had been a brilliant point guard twenty years after my Citadel career had ended. My aunt and uncle, Carol and Ed Sr., had flown in from Iowa with the same set of dual loyalties aflame in their psyches as the other members of the family. Even when I lived in Europe, it was a matter of honor for me to look up the scores of Citadel games before I read another entry in the *International Herald Tribune*.

My team sat in the stands beside the locker room where we had dressed for four years. We stood and cheered when the Bulldogs burst out to the court led by a seven-foot Russian kid whom the cadets called BRK, for Big Russian Kid. He was the first legitimate seven-footer the Citadel basketball team had ever recruited. There were not many cadets in the stands, which stood in stark contrast to our era when we could count on five hundred cadets to attend all of our games. We were told that the status of athletes had deteriorated badly since our time, and that the Corps resented the athletes with a bitterness that seemed almost incurable.

"How do they expect The Citadel to attract athletes if the Corps hates them and tries to run them out?" Bridges asked.

"They have to be rocks like we were," Mohr said.

"They just don't make men the way they used to," Barney said.

The wives groaned in a collective chorus. They had heard most of the stories of this star-crossed team, and now they would be able to put faces and stories together. My teammates had married beautiful, accomplished women, and the children they had helped raise would make America a better country.

"Where were you women when we really needed you? In 1967?" I asked the wives.

"We were out looking for *you* boys," Kennedy's wife, Cynthia, said.

Francis Marion came out to the floor, and I stood to cheer my cousin Ed's entrance into the world as a head basketball coach. Ed walked over, and I went down to the court to embrace him. "This feels funny, Ed," I said. "How's your team?"

"We'll give The Citadel a game," he said. "I like some of my players a lot."

"These guys are my team, Ed," I yelled up into the stands to my teammates. "This is my cousin Ed, guys. This is the team from the history books—the one they all talk about. The Citadel powerhouse from the mid-sixties."

"Conroy was full of shit even back then," Cauthen said.

I was never happier to see a basketball game begin, but it was a bad omen when Francis Marion controlled the opening tip from our big center. Instantly my teammates smelled trouble for the Bulldogs as we whispered among ourselves that the Citadel team seemed listless and uninspired. The Citadel's coach, Pat Dennis, considered one of the young hotshots when he had taken on the job, was encountering the same difficulties as had the twenty-five head coaches who preceded him, with the notable exception of Norman Sloan. Though young and dedicated and gifted, Pat was trying to balance the exigencies of putting a winning team together with the expectations and pressures his players felt being part of a military college. Coaching at a military college is the hardest coaching job in America, and my team watched the effects of years of stress settle into the lines around Pat Dennis's eyes.

The game became a metaphor of Citadel basketball itself. We watched five Citadel men who were fighters, who would go to the wall for their college, and who would never quit or throw in the towel. They were kids just like we had been; they were cadets just like we had been. They were exhausted and in a kind of unnameable despair, and they looked like they did not think they were supposed to win, just like us.

My cousin Ed proved that night that he was a coach to be reckoned with. The Citadel was favored to win against Francis Marion, but Ed's team was playing as though they had not received that news bulletin. My cousin had infused his team with his own easy confidence. The exhaustion and the malaise that had plagued our team hit this Citadel team in the middle of the second half. They made a late run, but Francis Marion got the win. Pat Dennis and his players looked stricken as they made their way off the court, and in the stands, my teammates and I hurt for them, having once walked in their shoes.

On Saturday evening, we gathered in the dining room of the Lodge Alley Inn, well dressed, successful, and middle-aged. It was the first time we had come together as a team since our final meal in Charlotte when we lost to Richmond in overtime. Thirty years had passed through us all with bewildering, merciless swiftness. We had come together because John DeBrosse had found me to seek forgiveness for a layup he had missed dozens of years ago. DeBrosse had no idea that I had thought about that team and that season almost every day of my life. We toasted each other all night, lifting our glasses time and again, dining on veal and grouper, then more toasts.

On both Friday and Saturday, we met in a large suite I had rented in the Lodge Alley Inn. We talked, and the stories began to flow. We made Bridges perform his dead-ringer imitation of Mel entering the locker room at halftime, and he could still do that hunched, loping walk of Mel's while smoking a cigarette with a perfection of detail. When Bridges, without breaking character, walked between all the players and the wives, carrying a towel folded on his left wrist, we were laughing as hard as we had in the locker room during the Old Dominion disaster, only this laughter was high-spirited and unsuppressed.

I watched as my father sat and talked with Al and Patty Kroboth. It was important for me to get to know my father after the surprising mellowing that took place after the publication of *The Great Santini*. My father had dedicated the rest of his life to proving that I was wrong about him as a father and that my fictional portrayal of him in that novel had been both libelous and wrongheaded. The transformation of Don Conroy into a reasonable facsimile of a father was the great miracle of my adult life, and I wanted my teammates to share my joy in the metamorphosis.

"Hey, Conroy, did you invite Mel to this?" Tee Hooper asked.

"I wrote him a letter," I said. "He never answered it."

My father said, "After hanging around you and your teammates, Pat, my heart goes out to Mel. This isn't a group I'd pay money to see again."

"The door's over there, Pop," I said. "Use it any time you like."

"My son is a little bit on the sensitive side, if you haven't noticed," Dad said.

"Noticed, Colonel?" Barney said. "We lived with the boy. He obviously had no direction in his youth. No discipline."

"I was too soft on all my children," Dad said, playing to the crowd. "I was too tenderhearted for my own good. I should've cracked the whip a time or two."

"Nothing would've worked with Pat, Colonel," Barney said.

From across the room, DeBrosse yelled, "Hey, Conroy, I want this book to be fair to everyone, okay? I don't want you to go after Mel or anyone else."

"Conroy fair?" Cauthen said. "You guys see what he did to his old man?"

"Old man?" Halpin laughed. "How 'bout what he did to our college, El Cid?"

"Let's go back to what he did to his poor old man," said Dad. "It's tough on a fella when his son turns out to be a Judas."

"Boys, what's he going to do to us?" Barney asked.

Connor said, "It makes me sick to think of it."

I went to the middle of the room and handed out a present to each of my teammates, putting a cassette in the VCR. We sat with the women in our lives to watch the only piece of film I had discovered of my team in action during that dismal year. When I first began the project, I thought I would retrieve the film of all our games and simply study them for salient details. The Citadel had thrown our game films away years ago, and so had every other college team we played. A researcher from Loyola of New Orleans managed to come up with a five-minute segment of our game with Loyola, and because it was the game that my voice revealed itself, the film held great significance for me.

In the grainy film of a handheld camera, the year suddenly materialized as my team, so beautiful in their prime, were seen running up and down the court. Tee and Debrosse were having trouble containing two terrific Loyola guards; the Blue Team was on the court again in a 1–2–2 press both tentative and weakly conceived. Zinsky made two lovely jump shots, and we rewarded him with a round of applause. DeBrosse threw it out of bounds and we booed him soundly. Our team's tragedy was unfolding for all of us to study in agonizing detail. Dan Mohr threw up a textbook hook shot, and Bridges ripped a rebound from the boards. The referees called fouls right and left, mostly on us. DeBrosse hit a jumper and so did Hooper, but Loyola seemed to be scoring at will.

Suddenly Kroboth was in the game, and so was I, and there was Greg Connor.

"Green Weenies to the rescue," Barney cried.

"The hell with the Green Weenies," Dan Mohr said.

His wife, Cindy, said, "I've never heard you use language like that, Dan!"

"Then you don't know the guy, Cindy," Cauthen said.

"Eat me, Zipper," said Dan.

I hit Tee with a pass on a fast break and he was fouled driving to the basket. Then after Loyola missed a shot, Connor rebounded it and I took it down the court and drove the lane. I was looking for someone to pass it to, found no one, twisted my body away from their center, and sent a silly, hopeless shot over my head, without looking.

DeBrosse shouted, "The play summed up Conroy's whole career."

Luckily, the center fouled me, and I watched the young stranger disguised as me use his father's archaic underhand free throw and swish it through the net. We watched the rest of the film mesmerized by the strange magic of image and lost time. Even in this film, we could see the proof of our team's downfall and evidence of its fate. In its last seconds,

I was dribbling full speed on a fast break when Kroboth filled the left-hand lane, and I laid a sweet pass behind my back which Al bobbled. The ball went out of bounds forever. The Zapruder film of our lost youth went black, and we turned back to our middle-aged selves again.

With me that evening was Cassandra King, a lovely blond novelist I had met in Birmingham, Alabama, at a Hoover Library writers' conference. I had liked her instantly and had praised her first novel, *Making Waves in Zion*, when it was published. We were both locked in loveless marriages at the time, and it would be years before our paths crossed again. When they did, I never wanted to be with anyone else. I had met the woman I wanted with me when I died. Since none of my teammates had known my first two wives, I wanted and needed their approval of Sandra. I had been delighted by all the women they had married, without exception. When I began this book, I was the only divorcé on the team. All night, I watched Sandra talking to the wives and the boys I had once played basketball with when I had not yet been born to myself and had no clue who I was or how I was going to find my place in the world.

Teena Bridges came up first and said, "Sandra is a doll, Pat. I'd keep this one."

Sandra Cauthen said, "A keeper. Don't let this one get away." Cindy Mohr and Barbara Connor both said, "Sandra's precious. Just precious." In the old-speak of southern talk, the word "precious" is like money you can take to the bank. Sandra King and I were married the following May.

Toward the end of the evening, I was standing in the kitchen with my arms around Tee Hooper and Dave Bornhorst, listening to my team. The talk of teammates seemed at that moment like all the wonder I ever needed to know. I felt a great calming come over me. Dave squeezed me and bent down to kiss me on the cheek. "You look so happy, Pat. You look like you're in heaven."

Tee Hooper hugged me, then said, "Do you feel it, Pat? I feel it for the first time. We actually are like a team. Like a real team."

BEFORE THIS REUNION, THE CITADEL authorities had decided it was still too dangerous for me to be on campus. My whole team was greatly disturbed by my thirty-year war with our college, and so was I, though I entertained few illusions about it ever getting better. My first book, *The Boo*, which I self-published in 1970, was a boyish defense of

Lieutenant Colonel T. N. Courvoisie, the assistant commandant of cadets in charge of discipline. A year after I graduated, General Hugh Harris fired Colonel Courvoisie, and the word went out among the alumni that "Courvoisie was bad for discipline." It is a bad, poorly executed, and greatly flawed book, but *The Boo* was a setting forth, a point of departure, a timid announcement that I was a boy to be reckoned with, and that I'd be heard from again. The book's message was limpid and simple; its statement flat out and not marked by ambiguity. It declared in an adolescent voice that The Citadel had treated Lieutenant Colonel Thomas Nugent Courvoisie abominably and I demanded that something be done about it. The book was banned on campus for six years, and all I succeeded in doing to Colonel Courvoisie was to turn him into a pariah. When I reprised his role in my life as The Bear in *The Lords of Discipline*, I deepened the Boo's estrangement with the college he loved with all his heart. For thirty years the Boo and I were unwelcome at The Citadel.

When Shannon Faulkner came roaring out of her South Carolina life by becoming the first woman to challenge The Citadel's all-male admission policy, I was living in San Francisco and had no desire to test The Citadel's ire after the explosiveness of my college's reaction to the publication of *The Lords of Discipline*. The administration hated my novel and everything in it. Though I had managed to write myself out of any relationship with my college, it caught me by surprise when I made it worse than it ever had been.

In a lecture tour of colleges in the early nineties, I spoke one night at the Rhode Island School of Design and was surprised that I was speaking at the Coast Guard Academy the following evening. Since *The Lords of Discipline*, my name was anathema at all military schools. The poor English professor who had invited me was distraught when he met me at the airport.

"I had no idea you were so controversial," he said. "The commandant of the Coast Guard is flying up from Washington. He's going to be sitting in the first row. He swears he'll fire me if you say anything that irritates him."

"Relax, professor. I've never talked to a whole corps. We'll have a blast."

And so we did. I addressed the freshmen in the morning, and before I began speaking, I looked out into the exhausted sea of plebes and said,

"What in the hell are all you girls doing here?" Fully a quarter of the class was female.

The female cadet who was one of my escorts stepped up and said, "Congress passed a law in 1974 admitting females to all the academies."

"I had no idea," I said. "This is amazing."

That night I told stories of my life as a cadet at The Citadel, and those midshipmen became the most animated, rollicking audience I have ever spoken to. The commandant rushed up to the podium after the speech and asked me to fly down with him to the Pentagon to meet his staff. He invited me to address the Coast Guard Academy every year. The night was so successful it made me mourn for the loss of The Citadel in my life.

Four women of the Coast Guard Academy drove me to the airport the next day. All of them were sharp, radiant, lovely. I asked the woman driving what she wanted to do in the Coast Guard.

"Fly an attack helicopter, sir," she answered.

"No kidding? What are the rest of you going to do?"

All three wanted to captain their own ships. When I was about to board the plane, one of the women said, "How did you like your stay at our school, Mr. Conroy?"

"Loved every minute of it," I said. "I had the time of my life."

"How did you like us, sir? The women of the Coast Guard Academy?"

"You're fabulous. I want my daughters to grow up to be just like you women."

"Sir, we'd like to ask you a favor," another one said.

"Anything," I replied.

The fourth woman said, "When the first woman applies to The Citadel, will you support her? She's going to need some help and she won't have much."

Her suggestion shocked me, and I said, "Young women of the Coast Guard Academy, you don't know my college. It won't happen. No way. Not in my lifetime. You don't know The Citadel."

The first woman, an Asian from San Francisco who had introduced me the night before, said, "Mr. Conroy, you don't know women."

I looked at the four women and said, "You've got my word of honor. If a woman applies to The Citadel, I'll support her one hundred percent."

Several years later after I read about Shannon Faulkner's entry into The Citadel, I received a letter from one of those women and I tore it up as soon as I read it. She reminded me of my promise, and said what had moved her the most in my speech was my talk about serving on The Citadel's Honor Court. She said because of that, she knew I could be counted on to keep my word.

As I threw the letter into the garbage I said out loud, "Those goddamn women are going to get me killed."

But I thought about the invoking of the honor code of The Citadel. In those words, I heard a subtle, secret taunt that The Citadel's honor code didn't quite measure up to the standards of their code at the Coast Guard Academy. I thought about who I was as a man and what was important to me and what I believed in and the things that mattered. Later that afternoon I placed a phone call to South Carolina, and when Shannon Faulkner answered I said, "My name is Pat Conroy and I'm about to become your best friend."

When I got to Shannon it was already too late. Her sources of guidance sprang out of the febrile cultures of the American Civil Liberties Union and the National Organization for Women, and she was already savvy enough to call a press conference. When I was on my tour for *Beach Music* in the summer of 1995, I attended a going-away party Shannon's parents were giving her the night before she became the first woman to matriculate at The Citadel. It was a bleak, somber-mooded party, for the entire nation would be watching Shannon's entrance through Lesesne Gate. I had never seen more pressure put on a single woman. I heard her tell her friends, "I'm not afraid of the plebe system. If those upperclassmen try to get me to submit to them, I'll tell them where to get off. I don't submit to anyone."

I listened to those words and knew that Shannon Faulkner did not have a chance of surviving the plebe system of The Citadel. She did not make it through plebe week, and her leaving set off a spontaneous, ecstatic dance of both cadremen and plebes screaming out their joy on national television as the women of our nation cast their withering, gimlet-eyed glances toward my college. *60 Minutes* came to town and broadcast two devastating critiques of The Citadel's culture. I called a friend who worked for the college and said, "Who's your public relations officer—Heinrich Himmler?"

The Shannon Faulkner years marked the nadir of my parlous relationship with my college, and I thought nothing could ever repair the damage. There were alumni and classmates who thought I meant to destroy the college and were eloquent and passionate in their hatred of me. When the brotherhood turned mean against this lone South Carolina girl, I used my own infinite capacity for meanness in return. I thought the entire affair could be conducted with gentlemanly restraint, disgusted when the bumper stickers began sprouting throughout the state—"The Citadel, 2000 cadets and one bitch." There was a sweatshirt sold at football games that had a picture of Shannon's face imposed on a Citadel bulldog. Around her all the other Bulldogs were crying, and the words printed below said, "You'd cry too if the only female on campus looked like this."

When The Citadel responded to my criticisms by telling the press that I did not represent the average Citadel graduate's thoughts on the subject, a reporter asked me to explain the difference between myself and the average Citadel man. "Easy," I replied. "I'm richer, smarter, more famous, and nicer." My gift for advocacy was not tempered with the subtler tones of diplomacy, and I believe that my championing of Shannon Faulkner made her path all the more difficult.

Naturally, it was worse in the city of Charleston than anywhere else. It got so bad that I could not enter a store or restaurant without being screamed at by an enraged grad. On King Street, a man slammed on his brakes in the middle of the street, leapt out of his car, and shouted, "Fuck you, Conroy!" I waved, and he jumped back into his car, then climbed back out and shouted, "Class of '59!" In a restaurant, a woman whose father graduated from The Citadel asked me why I wanted to destroy my college. A woman from an adjacent table joined in the fray, and finally my waitress entered the shouting match that had risen up around my Chilean sea bass. There was nothing pretty about the Shannon Faulkner affair as it played itself out in South Carolina. I was in the middle of a firestorm and had no clue how to get myself to an exit. A huge ex–football player threatened to beat me up in a Hardee's in Ravenel, South Carolina, until his frantic wife managed to pull him back into their van. Hate mail and death threats began to roll in again. But I knew that all of it stemmed from the great passion Citadel men feel about their college. I have shared that passion since I survived my plebe year.

After Shannon's departure, The Citadel found, to its dismay, that it was surrounded on all four sides by the United States of America, and its name became synonymous with woman-hating all over the world. Enrollment tumbled and applications were dwindling. American mothers did not seem interested in their boys joining the mob who taunted a young woman they had just run out of the Corps of Cadets. Meanwhile, the girls still came and their march through the gates of Lesesne was resolute and unstoppable.

My father asked me to call The Citadel. "The Citadel needs you now, son. It's in a free fall." I called the school and thus took the first shy steps back. For two years in a row, they offered me honorary degrees, but offered them late when I had already made other commitments. I also had a nonnegotiable stipulation—the Boo had to be part of my reconciliation. The Boo had remained a fierce loyalist to me when it would have earned him great favor to renounce our friendship.

Near the Boo's eighty-fourth birthday, The Citadel honored the two of us with a full-dress parade and threw in honorary doctorates. Before the parade began, Brigadier General John Grinalds, who guided the rapprochement every step of the way, told us what was required when the Corps passed in review: "Colonel Courvoisie, Mr. Conroy, because you are graduates of The Citadel, you are required to take one step forward and sharply salute the company you were in when you were cadets."

The Boo and I stood at attention as the bagpipes and drummers led the Corps out onto the parade ground before a thousand onlookers. I was emotional that my long war with my school was over, and because of my history, I am moved by all things military. As a boy I was awestruck and dazzled by the marching of uniformed men. Now I stood watching a parade of Citadel men and forty women marching out to a field where I once marched. Beside me stood the man who was the subject of my first book; my family stood behind me. I felt all the nostalgia and anxiety of homecoming when I said to the Boo, "Hey, Colonel. Did you ever think this day would happen?"

"Hell no, bubba," he answered. "But you're on guard duty. You watch Mark Clark Hall for snipers. I'll cover the chapel and the library."

Near the end of the parade, I waited for Romeo Company to pass in review before me. Since I was a cadet I knew how to salute and knew how to do it right, but I'd been practicing in front of a mirror for a week. When the R Company guidon snapped down in salute, I raised my right hand to my eyebrow. It took me by complete surprise when I saluted Cadet Captain Rosie Gonzalez, the first woman ever to rise to company commander of the Corps of Cadets. She further delighted me by giving me a wink of complicity as she passed. I was back in the brotherhood—and brand spanking new to the sisterhood.

My books are all disfigured by the sullen presence of my child-beating father, Don Conroy, and this one is no exception. I can remember hating him when I was a two-year-old boy and first came to consciousness when my mother tried to stab him with a butcher knife and he backhanded her to the floor, laughing, a scene I observed from my high chair. My hatred of him lit up my eyes, causing him to hate my eyes from the time I was a little boy. Playing basketball was my pathetic attempt to build some common ground between us, and it never worked, not once. When I wrote the chapter about the first East Carolina game for this book, I remembered only that my father put his hand on my chest after the game, pushed me against a wall, and hissed at me, "You're shit." While doing research for this book, I was flabbergasted to discover I had scored twenty-five points in that game, my career high, and as the smallest player on the court had led both teams scoring. It is a strange and hollowed-out American father who cannot be proud of a son who scores twenty-five points in a college basketball game. But that was my father. I served twenty-one years under him trying to learn how to become a son he could learn to love. When I decided to major in English I was a "homo," when I published my first poem I became his "favorite faggot," and when I wrote my first short story for *The Shako*, I was "Mama's most precious little girl." His taunts and his fists turned my boyhood into a long nightmare.

When I was growing up, I thought that not a single one of my father's seven children would attend his funeral, if the improbable happened, and this vital, seemingly immortal aviator actually had to die like everyone else. I used to dream of spitting on his body in the mortuary, spitting into the center of his dead, embalmed face again and again, until my mouth was dry. Those were the happy daydreams that sustained me in the flyblown classrooms of my impossible childhood. I think I would have skipped his funeral completely if I had not accidentally built the bridge that would lead us back toward each other. When I began to write the first sections of *The Great Santini*, I had been preparing my entire life for that public unveiling of the ruthless bastard who raised me. My rage was the molten lava of my art.

I did not tell the whole truth in *The Great Santini* by any means. At that time, I lacked the courage and I did not think anyone would believe me. It was my belief that if I told the truth about Donald Conroy I would lack all credibility and no one would want to read a book that contained so much unprovoked humiliation and violence. It was not just that my father was mean, his meanness seemed grotesque and overblown to me.

My father put me on my knees throughout my childhood, until that magic year when I turned seventeen and it became dangerous for him to do so. To be honest, I do not think I was a physical match for my powerful father until I was five years out of college. But he thought so. The reason I know this is he did not touch me after my seventeenth birthday. He was not a sentimental man, but he was street-smart. Also, he did not need me for a punching bag any longer; I had four more brothers still serving as prisoners of war in his shameful household. I can barely look back on my sorrowful youth, yet it haunts my every waking moment and makes me a terrible husband, father, and friend.

The character of Bull Meecham in *The Great Santini* is a toned-down version of Don Conroy. I added touches of humor and generosity to Colonel Meecham that my father had never displayed in his military life. I humanized him and sanctified my mother by making Lillian Meecham an emporium of human virtue with a saintliness that would become even Carmelite nuns. My portrait of my mother rings sappy and shallow, but I survived the dependencies of those times because I idolized Peg Conroy, and I needed a flawless icon.

In my life as a writer, each day I bring the ruined, terrorized boy I was as a child and set him trembling on my desk, so I can study the wreckage of myself at leisure. If necessary, I can slap his youthful face, set in the rigid immobile defiance of bravado that he believes, quite falsely, will impress his Marine father. But the Marine sees right through the boy's most elaborate defenses, sees straight to the yellow core of him, the place where cowardice goes to pucker and hide. Cruelly, I can watch the boy's eyes fill up with tears, then watch the great internal war convulse his body as he fights with every cell of his imperiled boyhood, not to let one tear breach the spillage of an inflamed lid. I have purposefully shrunken the boy to the size of a barn owl, so I can move him around and turn him easily. As a desk ornament, he is easier for me to study by pretending he has nothing to do with me. As I watch him, the boy hiding his desperate urge to cry, I realize that all my books inch their way out of my flesh because of the million things this boy wanted to say for twenty-one years, but could not. I am simply writing down the screams that stopped in this boy's chest during the voiceless solitude he felt in his trial by father. I am not an artist, I think. I am a recording secretary. The boy screams my books at me. It is not the violence of his childhood that repels me; rather, it is the violence of his sensibility now, after all these years. The rage does not offend me, but its incurability does. Its acid eats away at the boy's face, but nothing fades out or drifts into memory or smokes up into time. The acid leaves neither scar or patina; it just makes the boy's eyes glisten more fiercely with unliberated tears. Then it strikes me that the boy is a vessel of tears and nothing else. My father did not allow his sons to cry after he backhanded us. If we did, well, then the beating turned serious and then my mother had to pull him off us and, then, my father would turn to her. That was always the most killing moment . . . because we wept, because we did not take our punishment like men, we drew our mother into the bloody, fiery zone of our boyhoods where she would receive her beatings for our cowardice. Those are the steps and the tune and the words of the song that framed the savage dance of my long-ago southern childhood.

In 1996, my father was diagnosed with an advanced case of colon cancer. For two years he fought with courage and resilience, but on St. Patrick's Day in 1998, Don Conroy began to die in earnest.

In the last three weeks of Dad's life, I would go every day to my sister Kathy's house in Beaufort and interview my father about his life. He had become a savvy protector of his own legacy and he knew what I was doing when I first set up my tape recorder beside him.

"I've always been your best subject, son," he said from the bed he would never leave.

"No doubt about it, Dad," I said.

"What'll you call this book about me?"

"*The Death of Santini,*" I said.

"Hey, great title. You know how to make a guy feel swell. You sold it yet?"

"Yeh. Nan Talese and Doubleday want it badly," I lied. "Julian Bach wants to have a bidding war."

"You need to get another subject, pal. I've been a cash cow for you for way too long. Any movie interest?"

"Warner Brothers. Paramount. Twentieth Century. The usual suspects."

"The money any good? This should be the hottest thing these Hollywood fruitcakes've seen in years. This is Academy Award shit we're talking about here. Oscar time guaranteed. Huh, jocko?"

"That's the talk, Dad," I said, extending my lie.

"The money, pal. Talk figures here. We're talking big bucks, aren't we? Seems to me, we'd be talking millions."

"Millions," I said.

"Any actors interested yet? Talk about a role. The guy ought to be polishing his Oscar night speech. Getting his tux cleaned. Lining up a new agent. Getting his ducks in a row. Any names in the hat?"

"Redford, Newman, Hoffman," I said.

"Too small. I'm tired of being played by midgets."

"That's a line I can promise won't make the final cut."

"I guess this will be one of your old love-hate numbers. At first I'll be the biggest bastard who ever lived, then slowly you'll reveal the true humanity hidden beneath my rough exterior."

"Bull's-eye, Colonel."

"Does it bother you, son, that you're a mediocre novelist? That's what all the critics say."

I looked at my father's face and saw the look of the trickster, the playful wisecracking imp with the touch of pure malice in his mean Irish eyes. "They say you're not as good as Updike or Roth or Styron or even that broad from Mississippi—what's her name? Dora Delta."

"Eudora Welty," I said. "They're all better writers than I am, Dad."

He looked at me with hard eyes. "Never admit that again. That's an order, pal. You're my son and you get it in your goddamn noggin that you're the best writer that ever lived. You got it, pal? There's no such thing as second best. I raised you to be the best, so you bear down and kick Updike and Roth's asses. You got me, jocko?"

He had risen to a full-pitched fury and was his old self again. It was one of his bravura performances. Red-faced and enraged, he had raised up on his right arm and was pointing at me with his left forefinger.

"Hey, Dad," I said. "Name me one book John Updike ever wrote."

My father roared with laughter, laughed until he hurt. He motioned for me to hand him the tape recorder, fumbled with it inexpertly, and said, "Time to get going, pal. Hollywood's waiting for this stuff. They don't make guys like me anymore. Guess they broke the mold."

"It's your modesty that's so unusual, Dad."

"Let me tell you about Chicago. Now there's a city to grow up in," my father said.

After the publication of *The Great Santini*, a book my mother and father and most of my family saw as a ruthless and unforgivable act of treachery and betrayal, my father grieved at my betrayal of his life as a family man and Marine Corps officer. Then he remade himself and walked into his new life that I had willed and made possible for him. He returned to his children in the disguise of The Great Santini, the fictional one, not the real one. He became the Santini who gave his son Ben a flight jacket on his eighteenth birthday, the one who sent his daughter Mary Anne flowers at her first prom, who left his duty as officer of the guard when his son got in trouble. I believe my father used my novel as a blueprint to reinvent himself and make a liar out of me.

My father may be the only person in the history of the world who changed himself because he despised a character in literature who struck chords of horror in himself that he could not face. He had the best second act in the history of fathering. He was the worst father I have ever heard of, and I will go to my own grave believing that. But this most immovable of men found it within himself to change. I could not believe how much I had come to love my father when he died on May 11, 1998, and his children buried him in the National Cemetery in Beaufort, not far from our mother's grave.

He died a richly beloved man, even an adored one. His children were prostrate and bereft at his funeral and remain so to this day. When his funeral procession wound through the old town of Beaufort, the police stopped traffic in every street leading to the National Cemetery. Gene Norris said at the gravesite, "They've never done that in Beaufort. Of course, today they're burying The Great Santini."

# EPILOGUE

IN WRITING THIS BOOK, I HAVE FORCED MYSELF TO CONSIDER THE PER-
ilous and shifting nature of memory itself. There was a time in my life
when I could replay these games in my head and remember, with astonishing precision, each move I made in a game and most of the ones my
teammates made. For years, I held on to the capacity to relive the games
of this dispiriting year in all their livid and living detail, rolling out in my
consciousness like a game tape. As I aged, those details have faded almost completely and the games still float within the constellations that
make up memory, but with a ghostly pallor and the stick-figure movements of disembodied teammates lost in the streams of time. I should
have written this book when I was twenty-five, but I needed John
DeBrosse to startle me back to the awareness that this season of badly
played basketball had been seminal and easily one of the most conse-
quential of my life. John's sense of timing was perfect because I had
begun to turn away from the boy I was—the one who wrote those
wounded books where I cried out against the injustice and violence of
my youth. I was beginning to turn a cold eye toward the misery I had
brought into the lives of my own wives and children. It had never occurred to me that I would carry my childhood in a backpack to spread
its coarse havoc and discord far into my adult life. In Ohio, John caught
me at the exact moment I was becoming aware of the terrible brevity of
life, its eggshell fragility, its unutterable sanctity. He caught me at the
precise moment I was considering my own diminishment. And because
of Dickie Jones's death and my own breakdown, DeBrosse caught me
mortal and afraid in Dayton.

Yet, as I intercepted my long-neglected teammates in the middle of living out their lives, it troubled me that I did not know what to call the book I had begun to write in my head. It was not a memoir, I hoped, as I wrote in a nation awash and aflutter with memoirs. I could not remember enough about this last season to call it anything. As I began to write, it felt shockingly akin to fiction, yet I was trying to tell the truth about how that time felt in the dead center of living it. Throughout the ordeal of writing this book, I have worried that my teammates would read it with total disbelief and that the book would represent some betrayal of our time together, just one more hurt to add to a season that still causes much suffering for several of them. Their wives have been understandably concerned about how I would portray their husbands, their families, and themselves.

THIS BOOK HAS BEEN AN act of recovery. When DeBrosse found me in Dayton, it was the first indication I had that the 1966–67 basketball season could cause perpetual hurt to any other person besides myself. I wore the memories of that season like stigmata or a crown of thorns. I had watched my optimism bloom at Camp Wahoo then turn to despair at the tournament game in Charlotte. I had been chief witness, then major participant, in the collapse of my team. When I turned in my uniform for the last time, I told myself I would never think of that pockmarked, quicksilver year. At the end, the team felt like a wing of a lunatic asylum, malfunctioning at every level, unable to right ourselves or save ourselves or even know that we were in need of deliverance.

Some of my teammates thought all of us needed to be on Prozac and others thought that we suffered a collective nervous breakdown because we were not strong enough in spirit to endure the gale-force winds of Mel Thompson's personality. Here is how badly fortune grimaced at my poor team: when I interviewed my teammates and had them rate all of us by our talent as players, I ranked eleventh on a team of twelve players, yet I walked the world as the team's most valuable player. That is how skewed and heartsick that year was for us. In every home I entered as I reconstituted my team, I found instead of memory scar tissue and nerve damage. Great teams look back at their college days through banners of streaming light. Bad teams glance over their shoulders with great reluctance at streets that will always be paved with their own hangdog shame. There is no downside to winning. It feels forever fabulous. But there is no teacher more discriminating or transforming than loss. The great secret of athletics is that you can learn more from losing than winning. No coach can afford to preach such a doctrine, but our losing season served as both model and template of how a life can go wrong and fall apart in even the most inconceivable places.

Losing prepares you for the heartbreak, setback, and tragedy that you will encounter in the world more than winning ever can. By licking your wounds you learn how to avoid getting wounded the next time. The American military learned more by its defeat in South Vietnam than it did in all the victories ever fought under the Stars and Stripes. Loss invites reflection and reformulating and a change of strategies. Loss hurts and bleeds and aches. Loss is always ready to call out your name in the night. Loss follows you home and taunts you at the breakfast table, follows you to work in the morning. You have to make accommodations and broker deals to soften the rabbit punches that loss brings to your daily life. You have to take the word "loser" and add it to your résumé and walk around with it on your name tag as it hand-feeds you your own shit in dosages too large for even great beasts to swallow. The word "loser" follows you, bird-dogs you, sniffs you out of whatever fields you hide in because you have to face things clearly and you cannot turn away from what is true. My team won eight games and lost seventeen . . . losers by any measure.

Then we went out and led our lives, and our losing season inspired every one of us to strive for complete and successful lives. All twelve of us graduated from college and many of us with honors. Bill Zinsky would leave The Citadel after his sophomore year and return to his hometown to finish his college years at Glassboro State University in New Jersey. He has had a distinguished career in city and county management, and he married his high school sweetheart, Peggy, who is a school principal. Many of us thought Bill was the best of us on the court, the complete package, but he never played basketball again after he left The Citadel. He deeply regrets not receiving his Citadel ring, and he was moved to find out how often his teammates spoke about him and in what high regard we held his talent.

In Houston I found Bob Cauthen, who had turned himself into a legendary insurance salesman and had become president of a big insurance company. Tee Hooper and a partner had founded MOM, an acronym for Modern Office Machines, and turned it into a multimillion-dollar chain which they sold for an enormous profit in the late nineties. Bob and Tee are the millionaires on the team, turning their enormous competitiveness on the court to their advantage in corporate America. Both men were handsomer than they were in college and both looked like they could suit up today and take to the courts at the sound of a whistle. Of all the players, Bob loved Mel Thompson the most. I believe that there was something congruent with their fighting spirits and the fierce nature of both men. Tee will never forgive Mel for starting me in his place. Tee feels strongly that a great injustice was done to him, and, as I have stated many times, I could not agree with him more. I have never taken to the court with a more competitive athlete than Tee Hooper. Bad knees have taken Tee from the tennis courts so he has taken up the game of golf at the age of fifty. My Citadel friends in Greenville are astonished at how good a golfer Tee has become. I expected him to be terrific and would expect the same thing if he took up archery, hurling, lacrosse, or badminton.

Dave Bornhorst was a full colonel in the Judge Advocate General's Corps in the Army, and Jim Halpin was the national account and export manager of the Irish multinational corporation Jefferson Smurfit. Dan Mohr is the CEO and owner of four real estate schools in North Carolina that bear his name while DeBrosse is an assistant principal at Studebaker Middle School in Huber Heights, Ohio, a job he took after a successful stint of teaching and coaching basketball both on the college and high school levels. In Dallas I visited Brian Kennedy in his office where he was vice president for American Greeting Cards, and he told me, "You know Hallmark cards, Conroy? We're the other guys." Doug Bridges is one of the most successful real estate agents in Columbia, South Carolina, and Greg Connor is a beloved radiologist in the college town of Hartsville, South Carolina.

But it's Al Kroboth that represents the soul of this lost team that I gathered out of time and the great distances that had come between us. In his heroic walk, we saw the stuff our team was made of—that we might have been hurt, humiliated, exhausted, and defeated, but we never would quit on our school or our coach or each other. The exemplary courage that Big Al exhibited on his forced march through the jungles of South Vietnam was the same valor he took to the boards every game at The Citadel. Al's heart was my team's heart. Yes, our team lost, but an American hero was shoulder to shoulder with us as we stood at attention for the national anthem during a year our country was at war and our alumni were dying in Asia.

All of my teammates agreed that they took the lessons they learned during that long fatiguing season and applied them to their jobs. They had learned the value of praise because they had suffered from the lack of it by their coach. Yet they could see the strength of what Mel had accomplished also—because he lacked all capacity for praise, they had learned to live without it. Because they had endured their test by Mel Thompson, no bad manager or hostile employer could shake the confidence of my teammates so that they could not do their jobs under great adversity. My teammates thought they could walk to hell and back, and they praised Mel because under him, they had proven it. When speaking of our coach, our voices are lit with mythmaking and awe. His name still inspires dread and foreboding in us. His boot is still on our throats and there is honor in how we bent to his will and danced to the tune of his whistle. He was the dark father of our college years, but worthy and manly and volcanic. My team is Mel Thompson shaped and Mel Thompson broken. He has driven us all to turn our lives around and to be worthy of him, at last. The flame that was Mel Thompson burned in us all and will brightly burn in our inner fires for the rest of our lives.

So I wandered in search of my team and I found them all. I rejoiced in their success and their contentment. They all lived in large, two-storied houses, with green sloping lawns and acres of land. The wives of my teammates welcomed me into their houses and lives, and these beautiful and accomplished women did much to enrich the days and nights when I stole their husbands for hours at a time, made them return to a year that was painful to all of them. Often, the women and children would ease into a room to hear the man of the house tell about games they had never heard a word about, practices that would end in fistfights, or running endless laps around an empty gym. Those wives became friends, and some of them as close as sisters to me as I asked them questions about their husbands' memories.

The children of my basketball team are all bright and dazzling and tall. They brim with confidence and radiate joy easily. The children were numb with father-love and these guys, for the most part, had made excellent fathers and husbands. My own two divorces and my incautious, squirrelly home life blighted the portrait of my whole team. Our nation's health is sustained by families like my teammates made. From New

Jersey to Texas, my teammates and their families showered me with hospitality. I walked into their homes after a desertion of thirty years, and they opened their arms and announced that I was a member of the family. They told the stories that they could tell and slowly we foraged for memories in both the thickets and the clearings of that year, then moved them out toward the light. Hour by hour, we tried to put that year back together and to describe how it felt to be part of that unlucky team.

I left The Citadel as a point guard and walked straight into my life as a writer. I thought I was the luckiest man on earth. I carried The Citadel inside me, and I knew it was not just a college I had gone to, and I have never pretended it was. It's a civilization and a way of knowledge, a paradox, a bright circus of life, a mirror and a bindery of souls, a hive of sweat and hard work, a preparation for the journey, a trailblazer and a road map, a purgatory, an awakening, and an insider's guide to the dilemma of being alive and ready for anything that the world might throw your way.

My experience as a point guard at The Citadel still remains miraculous to me. I began the season with my coach putting his arm around me and confiding to a television audience that he thought I could score a point or two to help his team. But I found myself in the locker room at Loyola of New Orleans, found the self who sprang alive in that game, and I turned myself into the best point guard I was capable of being. That I averaged twelve points a game, and scored over twenty points in four college games that season, dazzles my imagination even now and reinforces the fact that belief in oneself—authentic, inviolable, and unshakable belief, not the undercutting kind—is necessary to all human achievement. Once I began believing in myself and not listening to the people who did not believe in me, I turned myself into a point guard who you needed to watch. I could bring it upcourt, I could stick it in your face, I could take care of the ball, I could get it to my big men, I could work the break, and pal, whoever you are, wherever you are, I hope you like going to the hoop. At the end of the season, I came at the whole world like a point guard. Point guard. It's the most beautiful phrase in sports to me, and for a year, for a glorious year, I walked through the world as one with a team that was dying at the same time I was finding myself.

I came to the writing life as a point guard, and it became the metaphor of my transition. The novelist needs a strong ego, a sense of arrogance, complete knowledge of tempo, and control of the court. As a novelist, you tell people where to go and bark at them when they are out of position. It's up to you to fill the seats by your style and flashiness and complete mastery of tempo. You thumb your nose at critics and academics and keep your eye on the flow of the game. You stand in the center of things and you create the world around you. You must retain your poise and confidence, and you dare them to box you in or trap you in the corners. The point guard knows that the world is fraught with pitfalls and dangers, and so does the novelist.

The metaphors of basketball have carried over into my world of fiction, the novels that are the great joys of my life. When I receive a bad review, I smile my enigmatic point guard smile and I shoot a bird to the press box as I mutter to myself, "Mel Thompson. They're all Mel Thompsons." I have seen bad reviews stop writing careers dead in their tracks, but I learned how to handle Mel Thompson early in my life, and I learned how not to listen to the malignant sounds of negativity—but to listen to the black sounds of my own heart instead. When I get a sneering review, I ask myself, "Could this writer bring it upcourt against Florida State? Would I rather have this bad review in my hands or would I rather report to my first sergeant's room after mess tonight? This review or running the suicide drill for Mel Thompson after practice?" The answer is always the same: No critic can bring it upcourt against Florida State. All of them whine in the press box while you prance and posture and direct the flow of the game at center court with everyone in the field house watching.

Does the point guard help me with other writers and their books? When I read an overreaching, fully oxygenated, lightning-struck novel by a novelist like John Updike or William Styron or A. S. Byatt or Terry Kay or John Irving or Anne Rivers Siddons or Jonathan Carroll or a hundred other novels that are works of art in the rich golden age of fiction in which I have been lucky to be alive—I say when I finish these life-altering books, "Ah! A Johnny Moates. A masterpiece. They wrote me a Johnny Moates."

My surprise is that my losing season still haunts me and resides within me, a time of shadows now, but a time still endowed with a mysterious power to both hurt and enlarge me. I did not know I could carry the year with me always, a dromedary hump of pain and recognition. The frustration of being mediocre at what I loved best in the world lingers through the years, not as a wound but as an acknowledgment of a truth I would rather not know. Though I possessed a great and driving will, I could not overcome the twin handicaps of my smallness and lack of talent when it came to those games of impartial judgment on the basketball courts of my youth. I wanted to be one of the great point guards of my time, and I could not even make myself into a memorable one.

So I found my team again, and they were in bad shape. I brought them together and I apologized to all of them. Not one of them knew how much I had loved and respected them when I was a young man disguised as the would-be captain of their team. They did not know how highly I held their skills and how I marveled at their talent. They did not believe me when I said I consider it a great honor to have taken to the court with them. Few accept my declaration that I filled up with pride whenever I dressed out with them and led them into the blazing lights of strange arenas with the name of our college blazoned on our jerseys.

Many of my teammates wish that year had never happened. I consider it one of the great years of my life, if not the greatest. If I could change history, if I could change everything that happened that year, if I could bring us a national championship, I would not do it. I would choose again the same teammates I had in 1966–67. I would take to the court with them forever, these same guys. It was the year I learned to accept loss as part of natural law. My team taught me there could be courage and dignity and humanity in loss. They taught me how to pull myself up, to hold my head high, and to soldier on. I got dizzy from loving that team, and I never told them.

But my team taught me most importantly to accept my fate with valor and resoluteness, and I say this to all of you and believe it with every fiber of my humanity: I came to the right college, to play ball with the right players, and I was born to be coached by Mel Thompson and to learn everything about loss and life and everything in between as we struggled and limped and staggered toward March, brothers of loss and, so much more, bound forever by our losing season.

# ACKNOWLEDGMENTS

The essential, life-sharing family and friends: Anne Rivers and Heyward Siddons; Doug, Melinda, and Jackson Marlette; Greg and Mary Wilson Smith; Cliff, Cynthia, Norman, and Rachel Graubart; Terry and Tommye Kay; Jane, Stan, Leah, and Michael Lefco; Zoe and Alex Sanders; Suzanne, Peter, Pete, Christopher, Charles, and Caroline Pollack; John and Barbara Warley; Scott and Susan Graber; Dr. Marion O'Neill; J. Eugene Norris; Bill Dufford; Harriet and Richard Anderson; T. Nugent Courvoisier; Tim Belk; Sylvia Peto; Irene, Ryan, and Patrick Jurzyk; Colonel Joe and Jean Jones; Morgan and Julia Randel; Bert, Julie, Randy, and Julia Legrone; Skip Wharton; Nan and Gay Talese; Julian Bach; Carolyn and Babe Krupp; Anne Torrago; Jeff and Kathleen Kellogg; Marly Rusoff and Mihai Radulescu; Linda Andrews and Michael Melton; Bill and Loretta Cobb; Tom and Carol Harris; Kerry Payne and the SSGs; The Citadel tailgaters; the Fish House Gang; the staff of the Surrey Hotel; the women of T. T. Bones, my hangout on Fripp Island: Kathy Wise, Sylvia DeCost, Jackie Chrisman, Carolyn Summerall, Kazue Cottle, Beverly Edwards, Mary DeRosa, Georgeanna Mills, Ashley Schwartz; Barbara Conroy and Tom Pearce; Kathy, Bobby, and Willie Harvey; Mike and Jean Conroy; Mrs. Jean Shealey; Tim and Terrye Conroy; Jim, Janice, Rachel, and Michael Conroy; and Carol Conroy, poet extraordinaire; and to all of my mother's and father's far-flung families.

The girls and their families: Jessica and Elise; Melissa, Jay, and baby Joseph Wester Jones or Lila Blaine; Megan, Terry, Molly Jean, and Jack; Susannah, Gregory, and Emily.

My first cousin, Ed Conroy, a Citadel point guard in the eighties, now assistant coach at the University of Tennessee, and one of the hottest young basketball coaches in the country.

My college coaches who gave me their time and devotion when I was a young man: Mel Thompson, Ed Thompson, Paul Brandenberg, Bob Gilmore, and Chal Port.

My new Alabama family, though I will not say "Roll Tide!": Tony King; Beckie, Reggie, Eric, Kyle, Matt, and Elliott Schuler; Jim, Nancy Jane, and Will Hare; Tyler and Michael Ray; and the you-know-what stepsons, Jim, Jason, and Jake Ray.

To Alex and Zoe Sanders; Zoe Caroline and Bill Nettles.

Lastly, Peter Olson of Random House who asked me if I would ever write a book specifically about sports.

## A NOTE ABOUT THE AUTHOR

PAT CONROY is the bestselling author of *The Water Is Wide*, *The Great Santini*, *The Lords of Discipline*, *The Prince of Tides*, and *Beach Music*. He lives on Fripp Island, South Carolina, with his wife and two dogs.

## A NOTE ABOUT THE TYPE

This book was set in Janson, a typeface designed in the late seventeenth century by Nicolas Kis, a Hungarian living in Amsterdam. The type is a wonderful example of the influential and sturdy Dutch types that prevailed in England at that time. It is an old-style book face of excellent clarity and sharpness.